The
Business Side
of
Creativity

Fourth Updated Edition

The
Business Side
of
Creativity

Fourth Updated Edition

The comprehensive guide
to starting and running
a small graphic design
or communications
business

 **Cameron S. Foote**
Illustrated by Mark Bellerose

W. W. Norton & Company, Inc.
New York • London

This book is dedicated to all those unselfish individuals who willingly share their business experiences, tips, and techniques so that others can shorten their learning curve.

The author wishes to acknowledge all the contributions of the Creative Business staff and particularly David Lizotte. Without their support this book would not have been possible.

The sample forms at the back of this book can be downloaded for your own use from www.creativebusiness.com/bizbook.html

For information about permission to reproduce selections from this book, write to Permissions, W. W. Norton & Company, Inc., 500 Fifth Avenue, New York, NY 10110

For information about special discounts for bulk purchases, please contact W. W. Norton Special Sales at specialsales@wwnorton.com or 800-233-4830

Book design by Charlotte Staub
Composition by Ken Gross
Manufacturing by Edwards Brothers Malloy, Lillington
Production manager: Leeann Graham

Library of Congress Cataloging-in-Publication Data

Foote, Cameron S., author.
The business side of creativity : the comprehensive guide to starting and running a small graphic design or communications business / Cameron S. Foote ; illustrations by Mark Bellerose. — Fourth Updated Edition.
pages cm
Includes bibliographical references and index.
ISBN 978-0-393-73400-3 (pbk.)
1. Commercial art—United States—Marketing. 2. Self-employed—Professional ethics—United States. I. Bellerose, Mark, illustrator. II. Title.
NC998.5.A1F66 2014
741.6068—dc23
2014005824

ISBN: 978-0-393-73400-3 (pbk.)

W. W. Norton & Company, Inc., 500 Fifth Avenue, New York, N.Y. 10110
www.wwnorton.com

W. W. Norton & Company Ltd., Castle House, 75/76 Wells Street, London W1T 3QT

1 3 5 7 9 0 8 6 4 2

CONTENTS

PREFACE

Creative talent is a unique and wonderful gift. It not only gives us an opportunity to earn a living by doing what we like to do, but it allows us, if we're so inclined, to establish a business inexpensively and easily. Furthermore, we can expand our business both profitably and rewardingly with a relatively small investment in capital and management skills. Very few other careers offer this much practical flexibility.

But how do you start? What's the most effective way to market your services? How should you charge and bill? When does it make sense to expand? What's the best way to structure a multiperson firm? How do you protect your future? What business performance standards should you aspire to?

This book is written to answer these questions. If you are wondering whether to establish your own business, or how to go about it, or how to better manage and grow the one you've already established, this book will tell you.

It is the most comprehensive source available on what it takes to become a prosperous self-employed graphic designer, interactive designer, illustrator, or copywriter. It is written and designed to be easy to read today, and to be used as a business guide for many years to come.

In its focus on founding and growing a creative business, this book complements *The Creative Business Guide to Running a Graphic Design Business* (2009, W. W. Norton), and *The Creative Business Guide to Marketing* (2011, W. W. Norton). These volumes provide more detailed information on managing creative organizations. They pick up where this book leaves off.

Much of the information comes from the contributions of thousands of freelances and owners of creative firms across North America. It was gathered over a period of several years at Creative Business roundtables and workshops, and from *Creative Business* newsletter subscribers. It has also been given the tests of relevance and accuracy through extensive peer review.

Much of the material appearing here has been previously published in the *Creative Business* newsletter (www.creativebusiness.com).

ESTABLISHING A FREELANCE BUSINESS

"The greatest thing in the world is to know how to be self-sufficient."

MICHEL DE MONTAIGNE

Wouldn't it be great if your pay was directly related to how hard you work? Or if you could pick the jobs you wanted to work on? Or if you could be in control of your own future?

This is only part of the lure of freelancing. But many creative individuals—graphic designers, interactive designers, illustrators, and copywriters—question whether they have the experience, talent, and business sense required.

Others are already freelancing and know that the lure and the reality are very much different. The lure is newfound freedom. The reality is learning to structure your activities as a viable business, so that freelancing becomes successful enough to support you.

This section is about those subjects, whether you are the right person to freelance for a living and, if so, how to go about it in a way that gives you a reasonable shot at personal satisfaction and financial success. To make the opportunities and risks of freelancing as clear as possible, the section is written to answer the questions of one who is considering it as a career change option. If, however, you are presently working for yourself, don't fail to at least skim it. It also contains many useful tips and techniques for the experienced pro.

1. Why the Opportunity Has Never Been Better

For many of us, starting our own business has always been a dream. Although entrepreneurial trends wax and wane, there has never been a better time to be one's own boss than now. Because small businesses are generally perceived as having a better record of productivity and innovation than larger companies, governments continue to develop entrepreneurial incentives. These initiatives, united with recent sociological trends emphasizing individual freedom and values, have created the healthiest climate for the entrepreneur in the last one hundred years.

Is all this just temporary? Surely it is to some extent, for economic trends will always be cyclical. Nonetheless, there is also considerable evidence of deep, structural change. In many areas of business, particularly creative services, the trend of "smaller is better" will continue, even strengthen. This is why it is a great time to have a freelance business.

Skills for a postindustrial economy

Economies worldwide are undergoing a transition from an industrial base to one based on services and information. It's a changeover as potentially sweeping as the industrial revolution or the mechanization of agriculture. In this new society, communication skills are increasingly important and the number of jobs available for creatively skilled individuals will continue to increase. More important, however, is where much of that increase will take place.

In the past, because most markets were relatively stable, manufacturing industries relied largely upon vertical integration for the control necessary for profit-making efficiency. Now, the value added to a product increasingly comes from marketing, sales, and distribution, not manufacturing. In this time of market volatility brought about by the speed of information transmittal and the globalization of markets, economic efficiency often comes from reliance upon a flexible network of suppliers. By instituting such a network, companies can move more quickly, concentrating on what they can do best and leaving the rest to outside specialists like you.

The changes brought on by information technology are also having a profound effect on service businesses, such as marketing communications. Organizations of today and tomorrow are electronic workplaces in which traditional references of time, space, and geography are blurred. It is possible (albeit not always practical) to have writers in New York working with designers in Los Angeles, production people in Chicago working on projects for clients in London, or an interactive firm in Sydney handling the web design and hosting for a client in Auckland.

Technology makes it possible for creative individuals to work easily outside the traditional work environment. Word-processed copy can be transmitted between continents in minutes. Digital design allows everything from concepts to proofs to finished art be created and modified anyplace. Graphics can be transmitted and rendered in realistic color anywhere a desktop printer is available. Fax machines and overnight delivery services remove all limitations on where illustration is created. A client looking at a website makeover on his or her office computer doesn't care where the creator is located. Moreover, even with the tremendous advances in the last decade or so, communication technologies are still in their nascent stages. (A caution is in order, too. See "Can you do it anywhere?" in Chapter 3.)

Marketing communication, as we know it, went through two major phases in the last half-century. The first phase was largely concerned with analysis: what should be communicated using what techniques. The second phase was largely concerned with creativity: how to attract attention and ensure memorability. Now we are well into the third phase: how to do things more productively. In an era of high and escalating communications costs, productivity plays an increasingly large role in determining communications efficiency.

As a freelancer you will be in an excellent position to take advantage of this trend; you will be in the right place at the right time in history. Like other à la carte business suppliers, a freelance can bring to the communications efforts of an organization excellent work without the inflexibility and expense of a large staff and overhead.

In other words, a freelance supplier offers an organization the opportunity to reduce communications expenses without reducing communications quality.

The ripple effect of corporate change

Your success as a freelance will also be directly related to the revolutionary changes in corporate structure that have taken place. That's not because you will necessarily be working directly for corporations, but because of the positive impact corporate changes have on the market and pay for freelance services.

Agencies, small companies without staff, public service organizations, and institutions have always generated a certain amount of freelance work. Many individuals have made a very respectable living from these sources in the past. Nonetheless, most freelances recognize that the larger and more sophisticated an organization is, the bigger the job, paycheck, and satisfaction that usually result.

Unfortunately, it has also been largely true that the larger the organization, the more likely it was that substantially all its creative needs would be handled internally, or provided by a large creative organization, such as an advertising agency or design firm. Because of their training, most managers felt most comfortable dealing with people who had line responsibility within their company, or within a similar hierarchical organization. They did not feel comfortable working with outside, entrepreneurial suppliers.

This in-house method of operation has been increasingly called into question. It has been demonstrated that many of the most efficient organizations, and perhaps the only ones that can do very well against certain types of international competition, are those that efficiently purchase specialized services à la carte as required. Supporting large inhouse staffs is no longer cost-effective. This is especially true in areas such as creative services, which are by nature antithetical to the traditional corporate structure.

The result is a management system often referred to as interactive decentralization. Its thesis is that voluntary, mutually beneficial customer/vendor relationships are inherently more efficient in producing quality work than the hierarchical internal structure of bosses and subordinates. The reasoning is that in the traditional structure efficiency is lost as power is passed down through the organization. In an interactive, decentralized structure, on the other hand, efficiency is increased as each external supplier competes to bring the highest possible level of expertise to the solving of a specific problem.

Corporations subscribing to this thesis subcontract much of their work. In some cases they subcontract virtually all of it. (The latter is the so-called virtual corporation.) Their management skills are developed around coordination rather than control. As would be expected, these corporations

tend to be concentrated in newer, emerging industries without large capital investment, strong manufacturing traditions, or well-defined labor/management practices. Nonetheless, as competition becomes keener in every industry, it is increasingly accepted that internal flexibility, coupled with external expertise, is now more critical to success than vertical integration.

In fact, in some areas—particularly in trend-setting, technology-intensive regions—these beliefs already dominate the producing sector of the economy. In such areas there has been created what economists like to label a "niche economy"—a place where many small units perform in individual niches, meshing with other units in other niches to create a strong, diversified economic base. Creative services make up just one of those niches.

Independent of the change in management thinking and the growth of niche economies is the growth of the "soft sector" of the communications industry (i.e., services, as opposed to equipment and hardware). The explosion of electronic media has created countless new opportunities. The advertising industry, which as recently as twenty years ago only created identities for existing products, now increasingly determines what products are produced based upon how well their features can be communicated. This growth in the communications industry paints a bright picture. There is no part of the industry that is not affected by, and more likely dependent upon, our talents. More important, because much of the growth in the industry is generated by small, flexible economic units with limited resources, the opportunities for independent creatives are even brighter.

In summary, changing management trends and the growth of communications make freelancing a growth business.

Today, security is what you make it

Creative individuals have never been particularly security conscious. After all, we have always lived in a world that rewards talent more than seniority, and working for agencies has meant frequent job changes. Nonetheless, many of us appreciated what little security agencies offered, and some of us looked enviously at the stability that seemed to be a part of working for large manufacturing or service organizations. If the opportunity presented itself, some of us even opted to join organizations with more job security, although it often meant personal and creative trade-offs. Well, today security should be of much, much less importance in evaluating the relative merits of working for yourself versus working for an agency or corporation.

Many of the benefits employees assume they have turn out to be overvalued or nonexistent. Large corporate pension plans are often discovered to be underfunded. The long-term effects of inflation have reduced the value of many retirement benefits to only a fraction of what would actually be required to live comfortably. Some employees discover comprehensive medical plans are much less than that when longterm illness strikes. And so forth.

In short, events have shown, often rather dramatically, that the security blanket that comes from working for someone else is a myth. While it remains true that companies can provide medical, disability, life insurance, and retirement benefits for employees more cheaply than individuals can for themselves, it is also true that the only way an individual can obtain true security is to provide it for him or herself.

Everything you dream of, and perhaps more

When you first decided to become a designer, illustrator, or writer, you probably had visions of communicating with your creative muse, producing art that would inspire generations to come. At some point, however, reality intruded and you realized that the purer the art you produced, the more difficult it became to make a living. If you're like most of us, the pressures of food, clothing, material desires, and families propelled your career in a far different, far more commercial direction than you had imagined.

That this happened is probably not all bad. Working in a commercial environment with noncreative people forces one to think through ideas, to defend them, to accept criticism, and to learn the art of compromise. This discipline is not only helpful for you as an artist, but also helpful to you as an individual. Even so, however, it is hard to escape the fact that your creative muse is now most likely supported by people who need a purchase order to write a memo.

As long as you deal in the arena of producing art or copy for commercial purposes your creativity will continue to be muzzled. That much is for sure. So when you consider freelancing, what you are really considering is how much less creative muzzling takes place and how much greater are the rewards for the creative compromises you make.

At some time, too, most of us come to a point in our careers where we feel stymied. In our present job we feel blocked from the creative challenges and career-advancing moves that lead to new challenges and greater rewards. We feel in limbo, our career languishing in some type of creative halfway house. The thrill is gone, and we want to recapture it.

Or perhaps our motivations for considering freelancing are a combination of circumstances and dreams: we want to be our own boss, make our own opportunities, have more job variety, make more money, keep more of what we make, be treated with more respect, escape from office politics, have more time for personal work. All these reasons and more are why you should consider freelancing.

Most of all, however, you should consider freelancing because not to do so is to ignore an option that people in most other occupations would consider a God-given opportunity. Few other occupational categories offer their practitioners such an easily available way to create their own working conditions. Of course, this is not to say that you should become a freelance immediately, or ever, for that matter. Being successfully independent takes motivation, and there are many drawbacks, as we will discuss later. But you should at least consider working for yourself for all the reasons that follow.

You'll be your own boss. We all work best for someone who shares our values, someone whom we can respect. Who could possibly share more of our values than the person we grew up with, who knows all our abilities and limitations, who is sympathetic to our every ambition? No one but ourselves. That is why we respect ourselves most of all.

Indeed, it is the absence of shared values and the lack of respect that comes from it that most of us are referring to when we speak of a "lack of chemistry" between ourselves and another individual. When that other individual is our boss, we chafe under the necessary employer/employee discipline. Even when we are happily working for a good boss, we never know how long it will last. The only way we can be assured of a continuing pleasant arrangement is to choose our boss, an impossibility unless we work for ourselves.

If you search your conscience, you'll probably find that you were happiest and doing your best work when you were working independently. That's because you were able to proceed at your own pace, in your own way, without the intervention of someone else's arbitrary procedures and rules. As a freelance you'll continue to work under arbitrary rules and procedures, but you'll be the arbiter.

You'll make your own opportunities. Even if you work for a great boss in a good, stable organization (a seldom-attainable ideal), you are still selling your skills for someone else's profit, so you'll never rise higher in the organization than it perceives the value of your skills to be. Moreover, you will never be given more than a perfunctory say in the future direction of the organization. Everything you do will necessarily be directed to attaining the organization's goals, not your own.

But what if you get a piece of the action, a share in the organization you now work for? Doesn't this provide a way to help determine your future? It is certainly a step in the right direction, but it still doesn't provide the complete control over future opportunities that freelancing offers. Only 100 percent ownership of any organization gives you all the responsibility and all the rewards. With anything less, other people will continue to make decisions that will directly affect your future. Only when you become totally independent can you finally, permanently be assured of addressing opportunities that fit your needs, do away with age or sex discrimination, end interference with your creative output, and establish a working style and habits that are truly your own.

There'll be more variety. For most creative people, variety is a crucial and motivating component of life. Nonetheless, most job opportunities involve working in organizations that do one highly specialized type of work like designing and writing ads. Or the jobs involve working in organizations that are primarily concerned with one market or product, like retail clothing or Perfecto-brand garden tools.

It is difficult to continue to enjoy your work when you do the same thing day after day, year after year. It is even more difficult to remain creatively fresh. Yet, as we all know, creative occupations put a high premium on youth and freshness. So when we allow ourselves to grow stale, we contribute directly to our own future problems. In addition, you may think in your heart of hearts that you could be good at, say, package design, or writing speeches. But because of the limited types of work and the rigid job descriptions of most organizations, you never get the opportunity to try. The only way to try something different is to take the sizable risk of quitting and getting a new job.

Compared to nearly all companies and organizations, and to most agencies and design firms, freelancing provides tremendous variety. There's a constant change of projects and clients, very little that's routine, and ample low-risk opportunity to try new things. Mostly this will come out of the economic necessity of not being too dependent upon one client or market. Also, the broader your experience becomes, the more attractive you become to a broader client base.

You'll get paid what you're worth. In most organizations, size and structure make it impossible to reward individuals according to their true worth. Unproductive individuals are overpaid; productive individuals are underpaid. If you are among the talented and productive, chances are high that you are being discriminated against. For you, working for yourself is the best—maybe the only—legitimate way to get paid what you are worth.

All organizations must mark up what they pay for talent to make a profit. In fact, the going employment rate for talent is usually about one-third the going market rate. (See "How much to pay creative staff" in Chapter 17.) By owning your own business, you do away with the middleman and sell your talent directly for its true market value.

Finally, your small business will have much lower overhead than a large organization. So when you do charge market rates, your company (you) actually gets to keep more of what comes in than would a large organization.

In dollars and cents, all the above means that if you work for yourself you can easily double the salary you are being paid to work for someone else. And, of course, you'll have the satisfaction of knowing that you earned every single cent.

You'll get to keep more of what you make. More important than what you make, however, is what you get to keep. As a freelance, it will be a much larger percentage. The reason is simply that lots of things you now pay for out of your own pocket will henceforth be business expenses. This means they will become pretax company expenditures rather than after-tax personal expenditures.

Depending on your company's structure, it is possible that many automobile, health care, household, retirement, travel, entertainment, recreation, meal, and miscellaneous expenses can be legitimately charged to your company. (For more on this subject, see Section Two.) Because a significant portion of your gross income will be used to pay for these expenses, your net income (salary) can be less without lowering your standard of living. This means that you can maintain your present lifestyle in a lower income tax bracket. So not only do you pay for some expenses with pretax dollars, you end up paying proportionately less tax on the income you do declare.

You'll be treated with more respect. Outside experts, especially highly paid outside experts, are afforded a degree of respect seldom given to persons with the same credentials who work within an organization. A proposal rejected when it comes from within an organization will often be enthusiastically endorsed when it comes from outside. This respect for outside ideas and work is due partly to the need to rationalize expenditures, partly to the notion that independence equals objectivity, and partly to the fact that a variety of past experiences gives an outsider a better perspective from which to analyze problems and present valid solutions. Whatever the reason, however, you benefit. If you position yourself and your services right, you'll become a respected and sought-after expert in your field. Not only will your work be seen by more people than ever before; it will be looked at more appreciatively than ever before, too.

You'll also gain the immediate envy of all your peers, every one of whom will suddenly see you through different eyes. Most will wonder what you did right and they are doing wrong, what gives you the bravura they lack.

You'll escape office politics. Every organization has its politics, the alliances and manipulations that inevitably spring up whenever a group of individuals is put together in a competitive situation. As much as they are decried and as many attempts as may be made to discourage them, we must face facts—politics will continue to be universal to organizational behavior. Moreover, the higher the stakes and the less defined an organization's jobs are, the more pervasive politics become.

The only jobs that are guaranteed free from politics are those in an organization of two or fewer people. Anything more than three people provides the potential. That is why a freelance, working by himself or herself, is one of the few professionals who can completely escape the stress and creative drain that politics in the workplace always produces.

There is, of course, the potential to get drawn into the internal politics of your clients, but you have the advantage of distance, most assignments are short-lived, and you can always resign an assignment if necessary.

How important escaping politics is depends on your personal constitution and on the structure and people of the organization where you presently work. Whatever your present or future situation, however, just remember that the only place you'll ever find that is 100 percent free of politics is your own, single-person office.

You'll have more time for personal work. When you work alone you can work very productively. You control your work environment, the phone rings less often, no colleagues stop by to chat, and there are fewer last-minute meetings. The result is the ability to get a lot accomplished in a short time. In fact, it will probably amaze you to discover that you can produce up to half again as much work as before, with quality that is similar or higher.

Also, you may pick up several hours a day that you formerly spent commuting. Your new commute can be as short as a walk from bedroom to office/den. Or you can locate your office in a building five minutes away. Or you can continue to commute to a city, but much faster, at non-rush hours.

Being more productive and saving time will give you two options you never had before: you can accept more work knowing that it will result in more income, or you can take more time for personal creative work and recreation. If you opt for the latter, you will probably find that for the first time you have adequate energy to develop your own personal creative outlets. This not only makes life a little more worth living, but also has the side benefit of improving your commercial creativity.

You'll be better for it. From time to time we all need to try something different, if for no other reasons than to test our capabilities and expand our thinking. How can we ever know if we live in the best possible world if we've never lived anywhere else? And isn't to try something, even unsuccessfully, better than not to try at all?

Fortunately, unlike other professions where to experiment often means risking everything, creative individuals can try freelancing without burning any bridges behind them. Deciding to freelance is seldom an irrevocable decision. There is no stigma attached to leaving a regular job in favor of freelancing, and none in deciding later to return to the everyday working world. Indeed, to have worked independently will give you valuable business experience, sharpen your appreciation of client needs, and increase the depth and variety of your portfolio. In short, it makes you a more valuable commodity in the marketplace.

So, what are you waiting for?

If you are not already working for yourself, what you are probably waiting for is reassurance. Despite motivations like those outlined in this chapter, the reason more creatives do not try freelancing is that as bad as a present job may be, at least it is a known quantity. Freelancing is an unknown quantity.

Do I have the right temperament? What, exactly will I give up, and will what I give up be more important than what I gain? Will the business burdens outweigh the creative benefits?

Right now, these questions and more are probably going through your head. That you are smart enough to consider them already shows that you have enough business sense to understand that there will be trade-offs. So next we consider the trade-offs in detail. The following chapter will help you determine whether you are the type of person who can successfully work for yourself, and exactly what you will have to give up to become successful at it.

2. But, Is It Really For You?

Becoming successfully independent takes talent. There's no doubt about it. But there is a tendency to overestimate the amount of talent necessary. If you have more than a couple years' experience in a reputable agency, corporation, or institution, chances are you have already proven you have the talent required to strike out on your own.

This means that right now you're probably good enough to charge the $90 and up per hour you'll probably need to build a successful business. This is true even if $90 per hour is over twice your present salary. Your present wages have nothing at all to do with the going market rates for freelance talent.

The reason is the value a client will receive, his or her return on investment. For most clients, paying $90 per hour or more for outside creative talent has a very, very good return. By not having creative talent on staff, overhead is substantially reduced, not to mention the inestimable value of access to fresh creativity and ideas. In a world where mechanics and carpenters charge $75 per hour, no client worth considering should balk at paying $90 per hour for freelance creativity. In fact, most are willing to pay far more.

What to charge, however, is not the subject here. (It is covered in detail in Section Two.) For now it is enough not to hang back from considering freelancing because of a concern about your ability to charge adequate rates and not to be overly concerned about financial risks. The risk-to-reward ratio is actually quite low.

What this chapter is about is something far more elementary and important than either talent or risks. It is about motivation.

The fact is, most individuals overestimate the need for talent and the potential risks of working for themselves and most underestimate the personal motivation required. To paraphrase the French poet Paul Valéry, motivation without talent isn't much, but talent without motivation is nothing. Thus, the way to begin considering whether freelancing is the right long-term career decision for you is to first carefully examine your motivations.

The wrong motivations

Working alone will be fun. It's not; it's damn hard and often lonely work. At least, the type of freelancing that will allow you to make a good living is hard work. If you have dreams of writing or drawing away in your garret—reveling in doing your own thing, your own way, to your own schedule—don't make any decisions until you wake up. Freelancing can be an enjoyable way to make a living, but you must approach it as a business that requires concentration and hard work. If you end up having fun in the process, fine. But don't make the common mistake of getting your priorities mixed up.

I want more security. If so, forget freelancing. It will probably result in even less financial security than you have now. You'll never know where your next job will come from. And paydays will be very irregular. It is true, however, that you'll control your own destiny to a greater extent than ever before. You'll also enjoy far greater financial potential. But neither necessarily provides security. If security—a steady paycheck, a predictable future—is really your goal, your best bet is a large, bureaucratic organization.

I'm fed up. Whatever your reason, it's probably justified. However, it's probably not a good foundation upon which to build a stable business. Successful creative businesses are based on a positive, long-term approach to opportunities, not on a short-term reaction to negative circumstances. Unhappiness is always a valid reason to consider change. But don't think working independently is going to be a bed of roses. For every problem you leave behind, you'll pick up a new one. Without enthusiasm and positive reasons for making the switch, chances are you'll end up just trading disappointments.

It's time to take life easy. Every day you get a day older. And creative activity does carry with it a high risk of burnout. Wouldn't it be nice if you could take life a little easier now—start work later in the morning, leave earlier in the evening, take more days off? Well, unless you are extraordinarily lucky, exactly the opposite will actually happen when you start working for yourself. You'll work more intensely than ever. You'll put in more hours. Your hours will be less regular.

The right motivations

It's time for a change. We all grow professionally and intellectually in direct proportion to the variety of our experiences. For creative people, variety is more than the spice of life; it is usually essential to the very enjoyment of life. Nonetheless, many organizations can't provide creatives with a variety of challenges. So both professional growth and personal enjoyment eventually suffer. Freelancing for many organizations, doing a variety of assignments, could be the answer. Most of us will find even a limited diet with variety preferable to a glut of monotony. Fortunately, too, the accumulation of experience that eventually leads to fewer new challenges in an organization actually makes us more valuable as freelances. It is both fortunate and ironic that our potential as freelances increases proportionally to the decrease in the challenges we find as employees.

It's time to cash in on my experience. Maybe your background includes working for large organizations who have sent you to professional seminars, educational courses, and training classes. Maybe you've spent years honing your talents in small organizations serving specialized markets. Either way, you've accumulated specific skills and general wisdom others don't have. You've paid your dues. Perhaps now its time to see just how much your experience is worth to others on an à la carte basis. You may be pleasantly surprised. Small organizations often can't provide the training, opportunities, and salaries necessary to attract persons of your caliber to full-time employment, and it is seldom cost-effective for large organizations to staff up for an occasional special need. In both cases your experience can be invaluable.

I have a very specialized talent. For any organization to stay solvent it must be run efficiently. This means that every employee must contribute more than he or she costs in salary and expenses. If you have a very specialized talent, that can be very difficult, unless you're willing to work for relatively low wages. Also, the only way to move up the salary ladder in many organizations is to accept increasingly broad or general management assignments. To earn more, you may end up doing less of what you do best and like most. Under such circumstances, the best way to have both fun and money may be to start working for yourself.

I want the opportunity to make big money. There's an old saying that you'll never get rich working for someone else. It has the force of truth. There is no organization that can afford to pay you what you have the potential to make as a principal in your own company. That's not to say that you will make more, only that the opportunity is greater. To stay viable, every organization, your own included, must make a return on invested capital—in this case, your talent. In a profit-making company the return will be paid out to shareholders. In a not-for-profit institution it will be paid out as more extensive or less expensive services. Only in an organization that you own 100 percent is it possible for all profit after salary and overhead to flow directly to your pocketbook. Of course, when you own the organization, you are the one who determines salary and overhead.

My circumstances make freelancing the best employment alternative. Maybe you have young children at home, or have a physical handicap, or are forced to live just far enough away from a city to make regular commuting impractical, but regular service practical, or would personally benefit from specific tax deductions available only to businesses. All these and more are valid reasons to consider working for yourself, provided you make a serious commitment and put your circumstances in the proper perspective. By and large, the clients you will serve won't be interested in, or particularly tolerant of, the causes which led you to independence. Indeed, the larger the client—and large clients usually pay best—the less comfortable they will be with any unconventional arrangement that is designed around your personal needs. When dealing with clients, always remember to focus on what benefits your freelance status provides, not on your personal reasons for adopting the independent work style.

The maybe right/maybe wrong motivations

I've just been laid off (or fired). Losing your job, usually suddenly, has always been something of a fact of employment life for creative individuals. Since the beginning of recorded time, agencies and studios have hired and fired based on workload. Moreover, the security of corporate employment has mostly disappeared, too. Anyway, it couldn't happen to a nicer person. You really are better off for the experience. What do they know about talent anyhow? Someone with your gifts certainly deserves better. The question is, is freelancing it? Perhaps yes. Perhaps no. The fact that you've been let go doesn't change anything; you are either well suited to work alone, or you aren't. All being laid off or fired does is force you to make a decision now. As you're about to discover, necessity is not only the mother of invention; it is also the slayer of procrastination.

I want more time to do my own thing. This is a good reason to be a freelance, provided you are willing to pay the price. Unlike working for someone else, you can set your own hours and work as little or as much as you like. This means you can sometimes work on rainy weekends and play on sunny weekdays, or take afternoons off to work on a screenplay or indulge your passion for engraving. But recognize that, unlike working for someone else, when you don't work, you don't get paid. Free time stops being free and starts being very expensive. Further, the rest of the world, including your clients, will continue to work regular hours. They may not be available when you are, or they may be available only when you aren't.

I'm sick of wasting time commuting. You should be. After all, who wants to spend hours each day fighting traffic jams or riding trains? It is years out of your already-too-short life. Think of how much more productive you could be if your commute were a flight of stairs or at most a short walk or drive to a nearby office building. Unfortunately, this is not as straight-forward an issue as it seems. A home office may be convenient, but it is also a very lonely place. When you work by yourself, even an office in a downtown building often isn't much better. You may find yourself simply trading the stress of commuting for the stresses of cash flow, and working alone. Moreover, since you'll have to make a lot of client calls, you may find that you will actually be driving and traveling more.

The need for capital

One of the major advantages of freelancing over other types of busi-nesses is the small amount of start-up and working capital required. But small is a relative term, and if you focus on it too closely you may find out too late that what's small in business terms can actually be quite large in personal terms. Focus instead on the fact that you will need capital in order to become a successful freelance. If you can't raise adequate capi-tal, your chances of financial success—indeed, of continuing to work as a freelance—will be seriously jeopardized.

There are four basic reasons why a freelance needs adequate capital: 1) to cover start-up costs; 2) to provide income while getting established; 3) to smooth out income variability; 4) to cover unexpected expenses.

Covering start-up costs. This is the most variable capital need, depend-ing upon whether you are a copywriter, designer/art director, or illustrator, and upon your type of talent and individual circumstances. For example, do you have a home office already well furnished, or do you plan to move into unfurnished space in an office building? Have you accumulated pro-fessional equipment over the years, or will you need to go out and buy everything? You'll need a myriad of items, potentially everything from desks to computers to software to office supplies, to start your business. Estimate how much start-up money you'll need. Then add 25 percent more as a safety factor.

Providing getting-established income. Authorities claim it normally takes a minimum of two years before any business reaches its full potential.

Chances are it will take you at least this long to make the contacts and build the reputation that will assure you of a stable, long-term business. Fortunately, during this time your income should continue to grow and within about a year will probably equal your present salary. To cover the beginning months when you have little or no income, and later when income still has not reached its pre-freelance level, you should have three months of pre-freelance take-home pay available to draw upon. (A few words of warning: Since this need is tied to your lifestyle, you may be tempted to try cutting back on personal expenses to reduce the capital necessary. Although at first this sounds attractive, it is not wise. Most of us become accustomed to a certain income level, and it takes a long time to change spending habits. If you think you can cut back on expenses and thus reduce your need for capital, do it before you start to freelance. Don't wait until after you start freelancing to find out how difficult it really is.)

Smoothing out income variability. The day you start working for yourself is the day the checks stop coming regularly. Henceforth, money comes occasionally, in batches. Bills, however, continue to arrive with the same distressing regularity as before. The fact that you are now freelancing and your income is irregular is solely your concern. Your creditors still expect to get paid on time. And, of course, you will wish to continue to live life as usual. To guard against those times when there is a long stretch between checks, you should have capital equal to two months' salary set aside. Keep it in an easily accessible, interest-bearing account, drawing upon it when necessary and replenishing it as new funds become available.

Covering unexpected costs. Failure to anticipate the unexpected can strongly affect the profitability of your business, and can even destroy it. No matter how hard you plan, the unexpected will occur— probably at the most financially disadvantageous time, too. For example, what would happen if you were suddenly laid up for two weeks? Or your car needed extensive repairs? Or you had to enter into expensive litigation? For these and other eventualities, you must have adequate capital readily available. Just what adequate means is best defined by your own comfort level (when capital is well invested you can't have too much), but at very minimum you should have a month's salary available to meet unexpected costs.

Totaling all your capital needs shows that a minimum of six months of your present salary will probably be needed to assure your success. Only about half of this need be in cold hard cash; the rest can be in the form of lines of credit, but availability is critical to assure success. Because it often takes months to get paid, and because many of the advantages of freelancing, such as tax breaks, come later, it is possible to be quite busy and still end up belly up. Adequate capitalization is the only way to keep this from happening.

Things you'll have to give up

Now that you can estimate how much financial risk you'll take, it is time to consider the psychological risk. Here are some things you'll probably miss. Although most are obvious, their ramifications usually aren't.

Security. You may think your present job doesn't have much security, but it is very secure compared to freelancing. Other jobs may have low security; freelancing has absolutely none. Period.

Paid vacations. If you bill your time at, say, $800 per day, every week you take off costs you $4,000 in lost revenue. That's $8,000 for a two weeks vacation, not including how much you spend. Thinking too much about it could turn you into a terminal workaholic.

Sick time. Feel bad today? Tough. If you take the day off, your pay will be docked. Break a leg? Learn to work on crutches. Perhaps now you see why adequate capital is so important.

Benefits. In many companies perks and benefits—health, medical, and disability insurance; subsidized lunches; expense accounts; retirement programs—can easily add a nontaxable 40 percent to the purchasing power of your paycheck. Henceforth, they will all be subtractions from your paycheck.

Regular paychecks. Try as you will to make your income regular, you'll find it impossible. For a month the mailman will only drop bills in your mailbox. Then one day he will deposit four fat checks. Can you accept this variability? Have you set aside enough capital to carry you through the lean periods?

Social contacts. For most of us, the workplace accounts for much, sometimes most, of our social interaction and contact. Also, freelancing will probably cut more deeply into free time, so chances are your social life will suffer unless you work actively at developing it. You'll have fewer casual friends and get invited to fewer parties.

Things you'll have to do

Perhaps "have to do" is too strong a phrase. Certainly you can get by without following all the advice listed here. But make no mistake, every one of the items below is important to building a viable, independent creative business.

Become a businessperson. In a creative sense, being a freelance will allow you to do more of the things you like, to be less commercial. But at the same time, you'll also take on a whole new set of small-business responsibilities. You'll become an account representative, clerk, manager, worker, bookkeeper, and, yes, janitor. When stripped of all creative pretensions, freelancing is simply a small business requiring all the diverse skills of a businessperson.

Look and act professional. A professional is someone who consistently performs in an efficient, businesslike manner, someone who puts reliability and customer satisfaction at the top of the list of priorities. Once you start freelancing there will be no other person to review or clean up your work, and no one to present or make excuses for it. Also, when you create and someone else presents your work, you can dress in the way that makes you most comfortable, that reflects your personal tastes and sense of style. But when you also do the calling on clients, like it or not, the way they perceive your work will be affected by the way you look. So dress for success (conservatively) and don't try to make a creative statement with your clothes. With most clients it will only backfire. (There's more on professionalism in Section Three.)

Be assertive. Introspective, shy people are often very creative, but they don't make successful freelances. This business requires cold-calling, bugging clients, making hard choices, dealing firmly with others. You must generate your own opportunities by going after them. When clients employ you on an assignment, they believe they are hiring a highly skilled (and paid) expert. They want you to take charge, to do what has to be done to assure that the job gets produced on time and on budget.

Market yourself. It would be nice if the world would beat a path to your door. It may, initially. But sooner or later you'll need to market yourself, either to generate enough business or to generate better business. Some ways to go about it are covered in Section Three. For now, though, just understand that marketing will be a necessary time- and money-consuming expense.

Things you'll have to accept

It takes a while to get established. Chances are you will have a flurry of initial business, then gradually business will taper off before it starts to build. This tapering off can be a time of psychological and financial hardship unless you are prepared. It will be a good two years before you're well known enough to have developed a stable business.

Many calls go unanswered. When you telephone from your present position you probably get right through, or your call is promptly returned. No more. As a freelance you lose the recognizability, prestige, and clout that comes with a job title in a recognized organization. You've given up your power base and all that goes with it. You'll find this not only damaging to your ego, but to your ability to get things done.

Sooner or later you'll get stuck. Despite your best efforts, not everyone you deal with will be professional, solvent, and honest. Then, too, there will be occasional valid disagreements about the quality and price of your work. The result is that every so often you'll have a client who makes unreasonable demands, goes bankrupt or just plain refuses to pay. These eventualities are a cost of doing business and you must learn to deal with them. (For information on how to handle this situation, see Section Two.)

Your future may be less flexible. Once you decide to be a freelance your future will be even more closely linked to your creativity than it is now. This is not the path to take if you aspire to greater management responsibilities, or value the occupational flexibility offered by many large organizations. At best, freelancing can be a holding pattern; at worst, a setback. So if you have any upwardly mobile pretensions other than growing your business, or want the flexibility of being able to change occupations, think again about the advisability of freelancing.

You'll work more intensely than ever. Freelancing is very intensive work. With few or no distractions, disruptions, coffee breaks, phone calls, conversations, and meetings, you'll get more accomplished than ever before. But you'll also feel more fatigued than ever before. You'll be more prone to burnout. And you may fall victim to the freelancer's maladies: loneliness and depression.

A test of your freelance potential

Rate yourself from one to ten on each of the ten following questions. Give yourself a rating of ten if the question perfectly describes you; a one if it describes someone totally different than you. A rating of five should be considered a normal, average response.

1. **Are you disciplined?** With no one to direct you, can you set priorities and do what has to be done, even when it is unpleasant?

    Rating:_____

2. **Do you fully understand the value of time?** As soon as you go into business for yourself, every coffee break starts to cost you money. If you are laid back and relaxed about how you utilize the time available to you, you'll have difficulty being a success.

    Rating:_____

3. **Do you have enough capital?** You'll have to live until the checks come in. You should have a bank account large enough for six months' salary and expenses.

    Rating:_____

4. **Can you live with variable income?** Can you hoard during good months so you'll have adequate resources for not-so-good ones?

    Rating:_____

5. **Can you give up the office life?** Don't laugh. Working by yourself can be very lonely. There will no longer be office politics to gossip about, workers of the opposite sex to flirt with, or constant interaction with professional peers.

    Rating:_____

6. **Can you give up the perks of your present job?** The free lunches end the day you declare your independence. From then on you pick up the tab.

    Rating:_____

7. **Do you like selling and presenting?** The more you do, the more successful you'll be. As your own account executive, you'll need to look for business, make calls, be articulate, develop good people skills, and deal on a friendly basis with people to whom you wouldn't otherwise speak.

    Rating:_____

8. **Can you be a one-person band?** The more multitalented you are, the better. Employing outside services often takes too much time or cuts too deeply into profits, especially when you are getting started. The more functions you can handle yourself, the more options you'll have.

Rating:_____

9. **Can you take direct criticism?** There will be no creative review of your work before it is presented to the client. There will also be no one to filter the client's reaction to your work. No matter how stupid a client's comments are, you'll have to handle them diplomatically.

Rating:_____

10. **Do you have broad interests?** Chances are you'll need to deal with a greater variety of clients than you've ever had before. The broader your experience and the wider your interests, the better your chances of relating to and solving their problems.

Rating:_____

Total:_____

The results: If you scored below 60, if is probably best to forget freelancing for now; if your score was 60–70, you can make it, but with some difficulty; if your score was 70–80, you have a good shot at success; if your score was 80–90, you are a natural for the freelance business; if your score was 90–100, chances are you weren't completely honest on this test.

Use your individual question scores to indicate those areas in which you are weakest and which you must address to maximize your success.

3. Planning Your Future

O kay. You've seen the opportunities. You've carefully weighed the risks. And you've decided that freelancing is for you. Now it's time to actually start planning your break from the organizational world, to begin laying the groundwork that will ensure your successful future as an independent creative.

It's tough knowing where to start, what to do. As soon as you begin making serious plans, the reality of the change you'll be making hits you—hard. Chances are that the very process will start you second-guessing your decision, which, in turn, makes planning even harder. The result is to discourage you from planning—to encourage you either to charge ahead on impulse, or to chicken out. But you know that both are cop-outs. You've got too much riding on this decision to start playing Russian roulette with your career.

As uncreative and discouraging as you may personally find planning to be, it is essential if you want to ensure your success. The more you can do to take the variability out of what will always be, at best, a very unpredictable business, the more stability your freelancing will have. And the more you can accomplish now, the more financial security you will end up with, too.

The purpose of this chapter is to help you overcome the planning hurdle, to help you structure a stable and financially secure business. It identifies those things you'll need to know and do before you actually hang out your shingle.

Should you first consider freelancing part-time?

Yes. And no. It all depends.

This book is written for the person who wants to leave the organizational world and earn a comfortable, secure living by freelancing and/or growing a creative services business. To do this, in addition to following the tips contained here, making the grade will take time and motivation—more of both than can be reasonably expected with anything less than a concerted, full-time effort.

Even if you are willing to settle for considerably less than $60,000 to $120,000 annually, freelancing ten or twenty hours a week won't make you a quarter or half that successful. The reason is that the effort and energy you devote to freelancing accumulate geometrically. In short, you need to reach takeoff speed before you start to fly.

Nor will it be possible to extrapolate most of the experiences you'll have as a part-time freelance to when you start full-time freelancing. The financial and business pressures will be considerably less. Your working and calling hours will be different. Your client list won't be the same because many large clients will only deal with full-time professionals. And you won't have the economies of scale that are important to establishing efficient procedures.

So if you are thinking of part-time freelancing as a way of first testing the waters, don't. If you are thinking of part-time freelancing as a way of starting small and growing larger, do it cautiously and with this knowledge: it is quite possible to be a success at part-time freelancing and a failure at full-time freelancing, and vice versa.

Now, with that understanding, if you wish to freelance part-time to accumulate capital, or to build long-term client relationships, or expand your portfolio, or just plain have fun—please do. You'll find much of what is written here to be applicable. Use it selectively as appropriate.

Freelancing part-time is the next best thing to doing it full-time.

Can you do it anywhere?

Where's your personal Shangri-la? Ever wonder whether you could actually live and work there? Intriguing thought, isn't it? Or maybe you're not interested in some vaguely idyllic lifestyle; you just want to be able to use your talent to support yourself where you now live. Unfortunately, you happen to live in East Backwater. Is it possible?

It would be nice if there were a simple answer to such questions, even nicer if the simple answer were "yes." But this being the real world and all, there are only complex answers, and most of them are unfortunately more negative than positive. The business of commercial creativity is one that is focused primarily in metropolitan areas. Like any other industry, it needs raw materials to operate, and metropolitan areas are where raw materials (clients) are mostly located. The bigger the area, the more raw materials there are, the more we can prosper. This may change in the future, but it is the situation right now.

But, you may say, my small business won't need much raw material. With only a few clients I can do very well, thank you. Certainly, there are a few potential clients everywhere. Yes, true, there are. But maybe not clients with the sophistication or needs that will allow you to do work that is creatively satisfying. And maybe not clients with the budgets that will allow you to charge what's necessary to keep your business financially viable, even acknowledging that your costs probably will be a little lower in Shangri-la or East Backwater.

Wherever you decide to live and work, to be successful and happy you must be proud of what you do, and have it provide at least financial stability, if not outright prosperity.

But isn't it possible today to live in Shangri-la or East Backwater and serve metropolitan-area clients through electronic connections? After all, today a telephone call from virtually anywhere will sound as though it came from next door. An electronic file or message can go halfway around the world in seconds. Express delivery services can have hard copies delivered the very next day. Again, yes, but because we provide a very subjectively evaluated product, creativity, most good assignments require a client to be personally comfortable with us. This usually means establishing a face-to-face personal relationship.

Unfortunately, the ability to operate in an electronic home office far removed from clients has been oversold, mostly by people who have never tried it. It is possible. It is also usually not practical if one wishes to work on stimulating assignments for sophisticated clients who pay well.

These clients demand today what they've always demanded—personal attention and service.

What about the possibility of a writer making a living in the country freelancing magazine articles or books, or an illustrator doing the same by selling art to consumers? Is this a realistic opportunity or an unattainable dream? My experience is that he or she will have to be very talented, very prolific, and very lucky. These types of creativity command a fraction of what is paid for commercial writing or illustration taking the same time and effort. It is seldom enough to live on. (Is it possible to eke out a living when a painting or magazine article you worked on for a whole week sells for only $500?)

If all this sounds terribly negative, it is intended to. It is intended to inject a dose of reality into the myth that today it is at last possible both to make a good living and do exciting work practically anywhere. Ah, that it were true. If so, *Creative Business*'s publishing office would be on a favorite small island in Maine, and most of its readers would probably be working from a beach somewhere in the tropics. But it is not true. Perhaps someday. For now, though, most of us who want to have a financially viable business have to be within easy visiting distance of clients, and most of them are in metropolitan areas.

What if there's no choice? The only honest answer is that it will be difficult. I believe that any individual of average talent who is willing to work hard can be successfully independent in a metropolitan area. Yet when it comes to working in a rural area, success is a toss up. Many discussions over the years with those who have made it in rural areas indicate that, on average, they had to work harder for less money. They also had to be more flexible (and sometimes less professional) than their big city counterparts. Unfortunately, I know many who have tried, and not been successful. It used to be said if you could make it in the Big City, you could make it anywhere. Now it apparently is just the opposite: today, if you can be successful in East Backwater, chances are you can be successful in Megalopolis, too. So the first necessity of working successfully in a rural area is to recognize up front that it will be more difficult, and to be prepared. That said, let's consider how it can be done.

Adapt to the local environment. The ability to be flexible and adapt to the needs of the local market is the single most important ingredient in rural success. Because clients are fewer and less sophisticated, local character, traditions, and style have much more of an influence on business than do any national standards. Nationally recognized working procedures and pricing turn out to be only as appropriate as a given creative person's ability to convince a client of his or her suitability. Further, unlike metropolitan areas where the answer to unsophisticated clients is often to ignore them and go after better educated and mannered ones, out in the country giving up any client may mean giving up an irreplaceable opportunity.

Emphasize marketing skills. Success in rural areas often demands more of an emphasis to clients on business-building than on creative talent. Being able to solve a broad range of communications challenges is usually more important to them than creative excellence. This often requires an ability to stop thinking parochially as a designer or writer, and to start thinking catholically as a businessperson providing a range of marketing services. Although these services may be focused around your particular talent or specialty, many clients have to be offered a full menu. Rural America is more the land of the blue plate special than of à la carte specialties.

Be a generalist. The more communications/creative tasks you can undertake, the better off you'll be; the more specialized your talent, the worse off. Ideal is a one-person, full-service marketing communications operation. Not only is other creative talent difficult to find, but it is too expensive for most assignments. So the bad news is that to succeed you'll probably have to be someone who can do a passable job at everything—strategy, writing, print and web design, and photography, as well as such occasional tasks as placing ads and programming. The good news is that with a couple of good computer programs to help, you probably can get by with just mediocre skill and talent.

Know your market. The normal market area for most creative individuals is within a 50-mile radius of where they work. In very remote locations it may be possible to stretch this to 75 or even 100 miles for a really good client, but the farther one has to go for business, the less profitable it becomes. Given the paucity of local clients, it is important to leave no stone unturned. Look at your market, identify each potential client, and set your sights on calling each and every one at least once a year. Although perseverance in making sales calls is a beneficial attribute even in metropolitan markets, in rural markets it is often the difference between success and failure.

Educate your clients. The nature of many rural clients is that they are unfamiliar with the need or value of the services we provide. In addition, most are unfamiliar with the process of how things get done and how long it takes. Smart individuals recognize this and use it to their advantage. They focus their promotions on client education, not on creativity ("How to get results from your advertising"), they provide information sheets on what clients can expect ("Our process of creating a new identity for your company"), and they take nothing for granted, explaining every step of the job as it progresses. They may also bend the rules for honest-appearing clients and do spec work (a no-no in metropolitan areas) to demonstrate the effect of good creativity.

Know your competition. Most commonly, local competition comes from midsize printers who offer creative services as an added service, local and franchise copy shops that advertise "full service," newspapers that also provide job printing, layout, and writing, and internet service providers (ISPs). What these competitors have in common is that their primary business is something else. Therefore, another secret to success is positioning your company as the local communications expert, a firm offering a level of professionalism otherwise unattainable.

In those cases where there is local creative competition, or competition from distant agencies who come in to service local accounts, your positioning should be as the "big-league" talent who just happens to be conveniently located nearby. As in any other business in any other place, prosperity depends upon identifying your uniqueness, then telling customers why it is important to them.

Picking a good name

Every boy named Sue and girl named Charlie can readily attest that names very much shape the world's perceptions of individuals. Everyone in business who has ever thought about it also recognizes that company names often provide clients with their very first impression of a company, and of its sophistication. In short, your company name will be among your most valued possessions. Knowing how to choose, register, and protect it is an important component of long-term business viability.

Unlike the naming of individuals, which is mostly ruled by emotion, business naming should be more logical and rational. Setting aside personal likes and dislikes for a moment, there are three criteria that every business name should be able to meet.

Is it appropriate? This is the subjective criterion, and by far the most difficult one. Good business names quickly and memorably identify the company (or product), match its personality (or attributes), and position it properly in its market. The better a name does all this, the more positively memorable it will be, and the less money need be spent on promotion and marketing.

Is it distinctive? The more unusual a name is, the more memorable the services offered will be, the less chance clients will confuse it with competitors, and the more easily it can be protected.

Is it registerable? Although not usually an issue for sole proprietorships or partnerships using only the individuals' names, name registration can be a concern otherwise. In most cases, the name must be checked and registered with state or local authorities to ensure that it does not violate the rights of others.

In addition, there are several considerations specific to a freelance business.

Avoid "freelance." This advice may sound incongruous. After all, isn't freelancing what it's all about? Nonetheless, unless you are unusually well connected and do business mostly with agencies or publications, it is better to stay away from the word. You may be proud of the independence it conveys, but to many individuals in the organizational world, "freelance" connotes instability. To them, it is synonymous with unemployed and unreliable. There are always lots of untalented, inexpensive creative individuals between jobs and looking for work who call themselves freelances, so why take the chance of getting lumped together with them? There are alternatives which carry much the same meaning but don't carry the same pejorative connotation. For example, "Sally Smith Illustration" looks better than "Sally Smith Freelance Illustrator," and "John Smith Business Writing Services" looks more professional than "John Smith Freelance Copywriter."

Create an impression of size and stability. For most self-employed individuals—whether working alone, with other freelances, or with permanent employees—the best positioning is usually as a company providing communications services with an expertise in design, interactive, advertising, PR, marketing communications, etc. In other words, as a small business serving other businesses with creative communications services. Keep in mind that most medium and large organizations (the ones that pay best) are most comfortable doing business with other companies, not individuals. If you do work alone under your own name, consider adding "Company" or "Associates" to it. Doing so will make your business look larger and more stable, and it will also provide you with a structure to keep your business affairs (checkbook, etc.) separate from personal ones. (This may also require additional filing, as described below.) Do not attempt to mislead clients; rely on the impression created and adopt the "if they don't ask, don't tell" posture about others in your company. If a client wants to know who else comprises your organization, the answer is simple: "Mostly I work alone, but I do occasionally bring in others to help me out when necessary."

Be wary of personal indulgences. There's no need to coin a company name totally different from your own. Few other names are, after all, as appropriate, distinctive, and registerable. There is a long tradition of service businesses operating under the name(s) of their principal(s). Some have even outlived their founders and have survived transfers of ownership. If you would rather not have your own name on the business, be careful not to get carried away and select a fanciful or cutesy one. Names such as "The Mac Man," or "The Write Connection" may sound nifty to you, but may also convey a lack of sophistication to some clients. Likewise, names such as "Midnight Graphics," or "Mi Casa Creative" may indicate working procedures better left unstated. Business names adopted to satisfy a personal whim without regard to outside impressions can be a serious liability, requiring substantial effort to overcome. The larger and more buttoned-up potential clients are, the more this holds true. In the same vein, when names are chosen primarily for personal, rather than business, reasons, they can be easily outgrown. Although there is nothing wrong with changing a name, it is best avoided if possible. Every name change reduces the company's marketplace recognition and the valuable equity that goes along with it.

Go with your gut. Keeping in mind the above guidelines, there is no right or wrong name for a creative services business. "Joe Jones & Associates" is as good as "Jones & Smith," which is as good as "Corporate Words" or "The Communications Design Group." It's your call. Just make sure that whatever your decision, it's well thought out.

Checking it out. Once you've decided upon a name, the next step is to see whether anyone else has pre-empted it. Although federal, state, and local laws vary, by and large a name cannot be used if it, or one confusingly similar, is already in use in the same locale in the same type of business.

Look through the appropriate Yellow Pages sections in the metropolitan area directories where you plan to do business, and do a web search. If you operate as a sole proprietor or partnership, you should next check with the county clerk's office of each county in which you do business, or your state's Secretary of State if your business is statewide. If you plan on incorporating, the name must be searched in the records of the Secretary of State in the state where you will incorporate. Searching records for name conflicts is something you should be able to do yourself in several hours, for free or a minimal access fee, often over the internet. Most authorities will allow a name to be reserved for up to thirty days.

If you are ever involved in naming a company or product with national aspirations, or considering registering any trade name or symbol (logo), a national search should be undertaken. Trademark application fees are hefty and nonrefundable if the application is denied because of a name conflict. The best source I know for conducting national name searches is Thomson CompuMark (www.trademarks.thomsonreuters.com), a firm specializing in it, and the one used by many lawyers. Their fees run several hundred dollars and up, depending upon the level and detail of search. You should also be aware that even if a thorough search comes up clean, it is possible someone else has a prior claim to the name you have chosen. If the claim is valid, and the owner complains, you may have to change it.

Registration. Unlike years past, today almost every creative business, including freelance ones, is required to be registered with one or sometimes several city, county, or state agencies. This ensures that the business is in compliance with local ordinances (e.g., zoning), helps the government collect its taxes, and protects the public and other companies by maintaining a registry of business names and their principals.

Also, every state has laws requiring a sole proprietorship or partnership that operates under a name different from those of its owners to file a "fictitious business name statement." A business name is generally considered fictitious unless it contains the surname(s) of the owner(s) and doesn't suggest the existence of additional owners ("Company," "Associates," etc.). Requirements usually involve some type of public notification (such as a newspaper legal notice), local filing, and issuance of a DBA (Doing Business As) or Fictitious Name Certificate.

For information on what is required in your area, contact your county clerk's office or your state's Secretary of State. Registration and annual license fees for small creative businesses in most areas of the country usually run around $50. (You may also want to contact your accountant first, especially if you have never registered your business. In some areas registration requirements can be ignored with minimal risk, especially if taxes are not involved.)

For incorporated businesses, incorporation includes registration. The only additional requirement is that businesses incorporated out of state ("foreign corporations") must also be registered and pay taxes in other states in which they do business. Again, seek the advice of your accountant.

Selecting an accountant

Now it's time to consider any business owner's most valuable outside asset—the accountant. The tax obligations of even the simplest enterprise are much too complex today for even interested and knowledgeable individuals to handle without good professional help. Rules change quickly, often without public notice, and the price for not following them to the letter can be steep. In addition, all businesses occasionally need an outside, objective analyst to help them set up and follow standard financial operating procedures, or make important decisions.

In short, henceforth you shouldn't even consider doing your own taxes.

Okay, so we all need a good accountant. But how do you go about getting one? How do you know when you've found him or her? How do you make the most of what your accountant has to offer?

A creative occupation. Several times in the past, *Money* magazine has given a hypothetical and rather complex tax-preparation problem to some fifty randomly selected accountants across the United States. The question: how much is due in taxes? The right answer? Well, it depends upon whom you ask.

What *Money* got back is up to fifty different answers. Even more incredible, the differences are up to 100 percent—that is, some accountants would tell a client that he or she owed twice as much in taxes (several thousand dollars more) than would other accountants with the same information. A demonstration of accountant incompetence? Not at all. It simply shows that accountancy and tax determination are complex fields that involve at least as much creative interpretation as a formulaic "running the numbers." It also demonstrates the importance of picking the right individual to be part of your business team.

Who's who in the world of numbers. Not everyone in the world of financial numbers crunching is an accountant, and not every accountant is the same. Here is the hierarchy, and the distinctions that will be important to your business:

Certified Public Accountant (CPA). This is a state-granted designation available only to accountants who have taken a comprehensive series of financial courses and passed a rigorous exam. CPAs are licensed to perform audits and are required to subscribe to a high set of ethical standards. They also must take and pass continuing education courses throughout their careers. In addition, a CPA is required to undergo a business practices audit by another CPA every three years. Having passed these numerous and rigorous professional tests, any CPA is theoretically capable of handling all your financial affairs. This includes everything from obvious and pressing business needs (tax returns, audits, and financial statements) to personal investment and estate planning. Your accountant should be a CPA.

Certified Management Accountant (CMA). This is a hybrid specialty. The requirements are not as rigid as for a CPA, and CMAs cannot perform audits. For some larger businesses, a CMA functions as a numbers cruncher, helping to set prices or determine purchases. Because of the need for the functions only a CPA can perform, CMAs are inappropriate for most creative businesses.

Enrolled agent. An enrolled agent is anyone who has been qualified to represent taxpayers at an IRS audit. Because of the danger of "putting your foot in your mouth," your accountant should represent you at an IRS (or state) audit unless you are specifically requested to attend. All CPAs are enrolled agents, but not all enrolled agents are CPAs.

Tax preparer. This can be anyone who has experience preparing taxes—from H & R Block personnel to moonlighting bookkeepers. These individuals serve a useful purpose, but it does not include business tax advice and preparation. You need more than a tax preparer.

Whom and how to interview. Think of the way most clients choose a freelance, design firm, or ad agency: they ask around, consider reputations and experience, interview several, then select one. Most clients figure that everyone on their short list can do competent work, so they usually go with the creative firm they like the best. This is how you should go about choosing an accountant.

Start by asking your creative colleagues about their accountant. If this route comes up dry, call local creative clubs for possible recommendations and look for ads in local creative publications. If you have a relationship with a local bank, ask them for several names.

The best accountant for you will probably be either a self-employed individual, or a small, 2–4 person (plus support staff) practice. Either way, look for an individual or firm specializing in small businesses. Unless you like to live dangerously, stay away from the moonlighter who works for a large corporation, or the "friend of a friend" who works for a prestigious partnership. They may be experts in dealing with the problems of larger businesses, but chances are they have inadequate experience with small-business issues. Likewise, it is unlikely that you will require the specialized services of one of the "big" accounting firms.

Try to interview at least three candidates to find the one best suited for you. You should not expect to pay for a first, let's-see-if-we-get-along meeting. When interviewing, look for a reputation for, or capability of, understanding your unique business. Most accountants specialize to some degree. Ideally, you'd like someone who has worked with creative businesses of a size and focus similar to yours. Don't cut a good candidate out of the running just because of a lack of this experience. Trust the accountant to tell you if your business is not within his or her purview, just as you might turn away a direct-mail client if the bulk of your work (and interest) was devoted to web work. Just as a creative individual can create effective communications for a wide range of clients, so can a good accountant work with a diverse mix of clients. Finally, don't be negatively influenced by lack of creativity in his or her interests. Remember, you are looking for someone who is fundamentally different from you, someone who is much more detail- and process-oriented.

Personal chemistry. Although complementary differences are important, even more so is basic compatibility. You need personal rapport, someone you can respect and trust, someone you can talk to on a first-name, peer basis. After all, your accountant is going to know everything there is to know about one of the most intimate aspects of your life—your money.

To establish long-term rapport it is crucially important that you understand your accountant's advice and reasoning. Just as you occasionally have to explain to an unsophisticated client why you do what you do, your accountant must be able to give the rationale for his or her recommendations in understandable, jargon-free English. This is important because other than in cases of gross negligence, the government will hold you—not your accountant—responsible for tax and accounting mistakes. You need an accountant you can feel free to question until you are comfortable, one who is also cognizant of your aspirations, risk tolerances, and financial limitations.

The more your accountant knows about you and your business, the more he or she will be able to contribute to your future success. Expect this getting-up-to-speed process to take six months to a year. If after this time you have made a good effort to communicate and are still constantly baffled by what your accountant does, it is probably time to seek a new one. Before you do so, however, make sure first that the problem is really not your own unrealistic expectations.

The more knowledgeable your accountant is about your day-to-day operations, the more specific and helpful advice he or she can provide. Figuring and preparing tax returns is only one reason to have an accountant, and it is seldom the most important one. Unfortunately, some freelances feel that they can't afford an accountant except at tax time. It's an understandable mistake. As you will learn below, an accountant's time is not cheap. But when used wisely it is always worth far more than it costs. This is where taking the time to look for compatibility really pays off. During the interviewing process you should have obtained a good feel for what the accountant can do beyond tax preparation, and how much it is likely to cost.

Once a working relationship has been established, you should probably see your accountant at least twice a year—once at tax preparation time, once in midyear for a business review update. (If your business grows, you may require a meeting monthly, or even more often.) At these business reviews you should go over any changes that might affect taxes and financial planning. In addition, ask what else he or she sees that could be helpful to your business, and what any trade-offs might be.

In working with your accountant, it is important to note that he or she can't be expected to make strategy decisions for you. In nearly all cases you must provide the information or the germ of an idea; then the accountant will point out the feasibility and the financial ramifications. In other words, you have to provide a "what if" scenario. Also note that you can't expect your accountant to advise you on anything illegal or dishonest, such as cheating on your taxes. It is, however, perfectly fair to ask "what if" questions regarding legal risk and penalties. What you should expect, indeed demand, is an aggressive pursuit of all legal avenues to minimize taxes. You should also expect your accountant to be current on appropriate tax rulings and to give you—not the IRS—the benefit of the doubt in key areas.

Finally, you should expect your accountant's approach not to be so aggressive as to risk repeated audits, or the later disallowance of deductions that will result in the payment of additional penalty and interest fees. A good accountant is not one who pushes hard, betting you won't get audited. An audit is not only very expensive (at very least, the cost of the accountant's time to defend you); it may also mark you for special attention in the future.

Services worth asking about. You should feel free to ask your accountant to assist you in any business or personal financial matter. Here are some of the most common services—other than tax preparation—performed by accountants for creative individuals and businesses: *Recordkeeping.* Good records are crucially important to business analysis, paying your taxes, and keeping out of trouble. Start things off right by asking your accountant for his or her advice on what type of records you should keep. Then make sure you continue to keep them the way he or she recommends.

Retirement planning and funding. This is not only a way to set aside money for future years, but also a way to reduce your current tax obligation. But which of the several choices is right for you?

Business structure. Sole proprietorship, limited liability company, partnership, "C" corporation, or "S" corporation? Only an accountant, viewing both your current tax status and future business plans, can properly advise you.

Tax reduction strategies. Ways to reduce your tax bill are too many and too varied to list, ranging from employing family members to accelerating or decelerating certain payments.

Negotiating a loan. The best way to increase your chances, or to get the best rate, is to involve your accountant early. Nothing provides more credibility to a banker than a financial statement prepared by a CPA.

Bookkeeping. In addition to setting up, reviewing, or modifying book-keeping procedures, your accountant can help you find a competent bookkeeper. (Some accountants also provide this service, but it is probably better to have your books kept independently, subject to his or her overview.) For freelances and firms too small for a bookkeeper, he or she can also prepare required year-end forms—1099s, W-2s, etc. (See "Hiring a bookkeeper" in Chapter 17.)

Employee considerations. Sometimes employees cost more than they are worth. There are tax risks involved with hiring other freelancers, too. So don't hire anyone without first checking with your accountant. (See Chapter 17 also.)

Tax advice. Because the types of work we do and how our work is defined are constantly changing, you'll probably need a sales tax interpretation sooner or later. If you do get in a fight with local tax authorities, you will also want an "expert witness" in your corner. And your accountant can help you obtain sales tax account numbers and employer tax numbers.

Professional counsel. When you need a competent insurance person, sympathetic banker, or aggressive lawyer, call your accountant for a recommendation.

"Succession" planning. Do you have a partner in your business, or a "significant other" in your life? Do you want to build marketable equity in your company? Ask your accountant for structuring advice before it's too late.

How much should all this cost? Accountants working for small businesses typically charge from $125 to $325 per hour. Total fees vary, naturally, depending on how much work they do. Even the smallest freelance business should expect to pay a total of $1,000 to $1,500 yearly. A multi-person shop should expect to pay from $2,000 to $10,000 or more. These fees include tax preparation, a midyear planning session, and answering a reasonable number of information-only or "what if" calls. You should also expect your accountant to contact you when tax laws affecting you change, or when new options for deferring income or taxes become available. Finally, don't look for a bargain; personal compatibility and interest in your business are far more important than price.

Selecting an insurance agent

If you haven't thought much about insurance in the past, it's probably because one of the major benefits of working for most companies is their inexpensive or free group insurance coverage. Up to now your insurance dealings have probably been limited to the family auto, home owner's policy, and life insurance. That's about to change. For a self-employed person, insurance is a complicated, necessary, and significant expense. And the organizations that provide it are important to your future well-being.

Given the complexity of casualty, medical, and business insurance today, and the personal and financial idiosyncrasies we all have, selecting the most effective insurance package requires objective and ongoing professional help. In other words, probably not your local Metropolitan, John Hancock, or State Farm agent. The reason is simply that single-company agents can offer only what their company provides, which may not fit your needs. What you need is an *independent* insurance agent specializing in small businesses. Because independent agents represent many different companies and types of coverage, you can get a custom-tailored package from them that fits your needs exactly. (In industry parlance, independent agents are often referred to as "brokers;" persons working for a single company are called "captive agents.")

Moreover, by buying most of your insurance—both personal and business—in one place, you'll probably also become a large enough client to get the personal attention and constant reviews you'll need in the future. Equally important, an independent agent can help you get proper coverage, which is sometimes difficult for small, home-based businesses. Also, when you do have a claim, you'll want to have an independent working for you.

To get the names of local independent agents, simply look under "Insurance" in the Yellow Pages. In any city there are dozens; in some cities they may even be listed as members of the Association of Independent Insurance Agents. Even better, ask for recommendations from other freelances, shop principals, or your accountant.

Before actually selecting an independent agent, call and ask for an interview. Mention what type of business you're in and say you're in the process of selecting someone to review and consolidate your present personal insurance coverage and make recommendations regarding business coverage. Bring to the interview information on all your present policies—types, coverage, premiums, etc. Be prepared to describe what additional coverage you think you may need (see "Buying insurance" in

Chapter 4), where you believe your business is headed, and exactly what it is you do. (If you do not describe what you do, chances are strong that "design" will translate into interior decoration, "illustration" into fine art, and "writing" into literary activities.)

Ask whether the person you are talking with will be your primary contact. Indicate that you will expect an initial, written recommendation and yearly written reviews of your account. Also ask what, if any, costs are involved. (There should be none.) Most important, evaluate the personal chemistry. If the future relationship is to be beneficial, both parties must be on a friendly, first-name basis. Insurance advice, even for a business, is just too personal for anything else. And, of course, also consider your overall impressions of competency and willingness to build a long-term relationship, not just to sell policies.

If you like what you see, ask him or her to go ahead; you've selected your agent. If you don't like the chemistry, or are uneasy about the agent's long-term interest in you and your business, keep looking.

What about a lawyer?

Unlike the need for an accountant and an insurance person, your company won't require a lawyer immediately unless you plan to enter into a partnership agreement or, in some cases, to incorporate. (As you'll see later, a lawyer is not absolutely necessary for incorporation.) Nonetheless, sooner or later you will probably need legal counsel, so it may help to shop now for a lawyer, and have him or her available when the need arises.

If the previously mentioned methods of finding a professional don't help when you are looking for a lawyer, try calling the legal referral service of the local bar association. Many larger metropolitan areas also have a legal referral service for arts-related organizations. A national directory is published by Volunteer Lawyers for the Arts. (Their website is www. VLANY.org.)

Once you have several names, call and determine over the telephone whether the lawyer is appropriate for, and interested in, your business. Then arrange for a personal interview to detail your needs. Ask if you will be charged for that meeting, and if so, how much. Before the meeting, prepare by organizing as precisely as possible what your needs, present and future, will be. For example, will you need a partnership contract drawn up, will you need assistance in setting up a corporation, or are you only interested now in establishing a relationship for unspecified future needs?

Remember, lawyers spend years in law school learning to be as analytical as humanly possible. Most of us in the creative professions, however, have been trained to think less empirically. So a successful relationship requires you to make an extra effort in being organized and precise. It also requires the lawyer to understand how you think and work, to meet you halfway.

At the interview ask specific questions: how many similar clients are there? Will the lawyer actually be working on your business, or will an associate or clerk actually do most of the work? If you are discussing a specific need, such as the drawing up of a partnership agreement, ask for a timetable of when things will happen. The law is a slow, deliberative process, and lawyers often develop a similar working pace. It helps if you apply gentle pressure to speed things up. Ask about charges and billing procedures. Be wary of standard charges for certain services. You want a lawyer who will give your needs all the attention and time they need. Good law is not prepackaged, and good lawyers expect to be well compensated for their time. Ask for estimates, but remember that as in your business, an estimate is only as good as the information on which it is based. Also ask what the normal billing procedure is, especially for things such as legal advice given over the phone. Finally, look the lawyer up in *Martindale Hubbell Law Directory,* a reference that rates lawyers and is available in most large libraries. (Their website is www.martindalehubble.com.) Then make your decision based on personal chemistry, related experience, rating, and fees—in that order.

Expect a good, not high-priced, lawyer to bill in the range of $200 to $400 an hour. For miscellaneous work and advice you may be asked for a retainer of a few hundred dollars—a sum held in escrow against future billings. Barring unusually complex situations, doing a partnership agreement will probably cost about $1,000 plus expenses; drawing up simple incorporation papers will also cost about $1,000.

Getting prepared

A successful creative business—freelance and multiperson—is built primarily upon contacts. Nothing, including your talent and your experience, is as important to your future as the right contacts. It follows that the more of the right contacts you start out with, the faster your business will become successful.

There is no better time or place to build the contacts you'll need than right now—especially if you are still employed and have the facilities and prestige of your present position. Your objective should be to do everything you can now to get your name known among the people and companies that will generate your business in the future. Note, however, this should not mean contacting your employer's present clients and informing them of your plans. It is too early for that, and it is probably bad strategy to boot. At this point the worst thing you can do is to try to undermine your present employer's business. Rather, utilize this time to build upon the knowledge, make the contacts, and strengthen the credentials that will be indispensable to you when you actually do make your break. Here are some tips on things you can do.

Join appropriate organizations. It's no accident that the membership of most local business organizations includes a disproportionate number of people selling services, or that many of the individuals you run into at advertising and creative club meetings represent the media, or paper companies. Club meetings are a very good place to make business contacts in a pleasant, social atmosphere.

Your present employer may even subsidize your membership in some of these organizations. So joining now may cost you less; it will start giving you the visibility and contacts you'll eventually need, and it will introduce you to other professionals whose advice and friendship can prove invaluable later. Initially you may have to force yourself to attend, but it gets easier after you get to know the other members. Moreover, you should do more than just join. Be an active participant. Volunteer for committees. Make it your long-term goal to be an officer. If you start climbing through the ranks now, you'll be in a great position to take advantage of your organizational visibility and contacts later.

Strengthen your portfolio. The more variety of work in your portfolio, the stronger your business will be. As a freelance you will invariably run into clients who won't consider you because you have never done anything specifically in their field or haven't demonstrated the broadness of your talent. As illogical as this may seem to you, it's a fact of freelance life. So while you are still drawing a salary, do everything you can to add as much variety and sophistication to your portfolio as possible.

Ask your supervisor for a crack at an assignment that requires a different style or type of design or writing. Ask to be assigned to different accounts in different industries. Volunteer to do speculative campaigns. Accept public service work. Write and publish magazine articles, theater reviews, or novels. Teach. Do creative photography or fine art. The more business-related the better, but anything you can do to show talent and earn public recognition will help.

Win awards. This may be easier said than done, but what you don't enter you can't win. Start compiling a list of competitions and samples of your very best work. With your talent and the number of creative competitions now available, it should be possible to strengthen your credibility against the day when you go on your own as "an award-winning" writer, designer, web designer, art director, or illustrator.

Many clients will be impressed by any awards you have won no matter how insignificant you know them to be. Peers with whom you will later be dealing will be more discriminating, but you don't have to emphasize all your awards on every call. In short, get as many awards as you can now, because they can't hurt later. Not only are awards useful for convincing skeptical clients, but they make nice decorations for your new office, too.

Entering competitions is, however, expensive. So get your employer to pay, if possible. Remind the other members of a creative team of the importance of awards to their future, too. Then call upon their support in lobbying your employer to fund the entry based on the value of award winning to the company or agency. If you can't get your employer to pay, be more selective, but still enter a few competitions. Pick your very best pieces and enter them where you have a good chance of winning. Ask any other creative team members to contribute.

Make client calls. This is also the time to increase your business acumen. The best way to do that is to get out from behind your computer and into the real world. Like it or not, you will be your own account executive in the future, so it is important that you not only know what is expected, but feel comfortable in the role. If you aren't at ease in soliciting business, estimating costs, scheduling work, and relating to diverse client needs, develop these skills now at someone else's expense.

Convincing your present employer to allow you to make more calls and take a greater role in business decisions shouldn't be difficult if you go about it right. Common complaints of many account executives are that creative staff live in ivory towers isolated from tough business issues and that clients often resent not meeting or working more closely with them. Make it known that you, perhaps alone among your colleagues, share these concerns and want to do something about it. Indicate that you would be better informed and more creative if you were allowed "out where the bullets fly" more frequently, and that it would be beneficial to everyone if you could observe and participate more in making sales calls and putting together estimates.

Establish credit. All financial institutions are wary of self-employed individuals. They are most wary of those who are just starting out with no history of success. So, the time to establish as much credit as possible is while you are still employed. At this point there is no need to share your future plans with the financial institutions. Simply increase your credit to the limit each institution will allow to persons of your means.

Talk to your present bank about overdraft protection on your checking account. If necessary, change banks to get it. Ask your bank about loan privileges based upon your savings account. Apply for several general credit cards—American Express, MasterCard, Visa, Discover. And if you own your own home, consider a second mortgage or home-equity loan.

Consider borrowing? In general, it is probably not a good idea to borrow a significant sum of money to finance your business venture. If tempted, talk to your accountant about how large the risk is, and the ramifications, positive and negative. If borrowing does make sense, you should know about the Federal Government's Small Business Administration (SBA) loans. As with any government program, this one is subject to change. What follows is how things stand at this writing.

There are two types of SBA loans—those guaranteed by the agency, and those it provides itself. Loans the SBA provides, direct loans, are almost exclusively for specially defined borrowers such as disabled persons and minorities in economically depressed communities. The other type, SBA-guaranteed loans, are made by a participating bank and allow businesses that wouldn't otherwise be eligible to borrow.

Most profit-making organizations qualify for SBA loan assistance. However, loans cannot be made to those involved in the creation or distribution of ideas or opinions. This provision is normally interpreted to mean that publications aren't eligible, but that companies engaged in producing communications for others are. Certain other communications-type activities, such as desktop publishing, probably qualify, but applications may be challenged. Other qualifications are that the applicant be of good character, have already invested personal capital (usually 20 to 30 percent of the need), and be able to show that the loan is a sound and necessary investment for growth.

You can get a loan for most business purposes, including working capital and new equipment. Interest rates vary, but are typically prime rate plus 1.5 to 2.75 percent. Many banks also charge an SBA processing or loan packaging fee that adds several hundred dollars. SBA assesses a guarantee fee of 1 to 2 percent. Terms of repayment vary as well, but seven to ten years is typical. Virtually any bank can make SBA-guaranteed loans. However, it is often a lengthy process. For faster processing (less than three weeks), look for a bank that is either an SBA Certified

Lender or SBA Preferred Lender. There are about 600 certified lenders and 100 preferred lenders nationwide. For the names of SBA approved lenders in your area, call your local SBA office or visit their website: www.SBA.gov.

Schedule rest and recreation. A change of pace, relaxation, provides the refreshment most individuals occasionally need to continue thinking and acting clearly and creatively. Indeed, "getting away from it all" is recognized by some large corporations as being so important that they insist their employees take their annual vacations each and every year. Chances are you don't work for an organization like that, but that doesn't make the need any less important.

You are about to enter a business in which it will be even more difficult than it is today to take regular vacations, especially during your first year or two. Yet, paradoxically, your income will be even more dependent upon your ability to be creative and make sound decisions. So vacation time will actually be more important than ever. Most important, there is your long-term health to consider.

One answer to this dilemma is to start your own business completely relaxed and refreshed. The best way to do this is to take all the vacation time, business trips, long weekends, and sick days possible while you are still employed by someone else, and you are still being paid for the time you take off.

Roughing out a business plan

The next step on your road to financial independence and success is to develop a rough business plan. Even when starting out as a one-person operation, you are still founding a business and you must approach it like one. Like every other business, yours will benefit from an objective view of its market, a set of clear objectives, and a strategy for obtaining them—a business plan. Don't be put off by the sound of this; at this stage a business plan won't be all that complicated. It needn't be formal, nor be seen by anyone but the president—you. However, it will start to discipline your thinking and provide benchmarks against which to measure your progress. You'll be very surprised at how even the simplest plan can help.

Given the importance of business planning, two types—basic and formal—are shown in Appendix 2. Turn to it now. Everything that follows should be undertaken only after you have first roughed out a very basic business plan for your company.

What type of company?

There are four basic business structures—sole proprietorships, partnerships, limited liability companies, and corporations. Your legal obligations and protection, the type of taxes and the way you pay them, and your ability to build financial equity are directly affected by which one you choose. There is no right or wrong structure. Which one will be right for you is a decision that is best worked out in consultation with your accountant. Moreover, it is possible to change the structure later if it becomes appropriate. The following summary provides the basics, enough to speak somewhat knowledgeably with your accountant. More detailed information on forming partnerships, limited liability companies, and corporations is in Appendix 1.

Sole proprietorship. This is what your company will be considered if you never organize it in any formal way. It is the simplest kind of business structure because it has no existence apart from its proprietor. All the assets and liabilities that accrue to the company are also the personal assets and liabilities of its proprietor.

With a sole proprietorship there's no complicated paperwork involved in setting up the business, although most states or municipalities do require all businesses to be registered. Once operating, bookkeeping and taxes are also simple: all income is recorded, all business-related expenses are deductible from that income. What remains is taxable. Tax reporting is relatively easy (Schedule "C," Self-Employment Income). The major disadvantages of a sole proprietorship are personal financial exposure (all business obligations are also your personal obligations), somewhat fewer tax benefits, and the inability to share ownership risks. (See "Corporation" below.)

Partnership. This is one step up from a sole proprietorship, a business arrangement where two or more individuals share income, expenses, and risks. It is essentially a proprietorship involving more than one proprietor. Although expenses can be cut by half or more and income potential multiplied, financial risk and personal stress increase many, many times. The result is that most partnerships break up, often acrimoniously.

Limited liability companies and partnerships (LLCs & LLPs). These are relatively new, increasingly popular types of business structures. They provide most of the organizational and taxing simplicity of sole proprietorships and partnerships with a limitation of personal financial liability similar to that of a corporation.

Corporation. Incorporation establishes a company that is differentiated in the eyes of the law from its owner(s). It must be organized and chartered in accordance with the laws of a particular state, but can operate in any state as long as it registers to do business there.

As a separate legal entity, a corporation owns all the assets of its business, everything from accounts receivable to computers to pencils. It is also responsible for its actions and its debts. One or more individuals (shareowners) own the corporation. Shares (stock) are issued to the owners in proportion to capital investment and other contributions. Closely held corporations (the kind appropriate for us) issue stock privately; publicly held corporations list their stock for sale on the open market (stock exchanges). One of a corporation's business expenses is the salaries of its employees, even when its employees are also its shareowners.

A major advantage of the corporate structure is its independent identity. If properly chartered, any action taken against it does not jeopardize its shareowner(s) beyond their investment. In addition, there are tax benefits that are not available to nonincorporated companies. The disadvantages of the corporate structure are the initial cost of incorporating, the ongoing costs of additional record keeping, and some loss of business flexibility.

Getting necessary permits

As covered previously (see "Picking a good name"), most creative businesses, including freelance ones, are required to register with one or more city, county, or state agencies. Sometimes nothing more than registration is necessary; sometimes a fee is required and a license or permit issued.

Most states now have sales and use taxes, as do some cities. What is covered, and who collects how much and when, vary widely. In many parts of the country, freelances are considered to provide an "intermediate," nontaxable product that will later be turned into a "final," taxable product, such as a printed brochure. However, some states interpret some or all types of tangible creative work (specifically final art, photographs, manuscripts, and computer files) as taxable. The best way to find out what you will be required to do in your community is to check with other creative suppliers or the local creative club. Simply, "When in Rome, do as the Romans do." Also ask your local state or city Department of Revenue for a copy of sales and use tax rules and regulations.

Sales and use taxes are taxes on clients, not on you. However, when appropriate, you are responsible for collecting and remitting them unless a client provides you with a resale or exempt use certificate. *Failure to collect may make you liable for uncollected taxes, plus penalties, plus interest.* So, if there is any doubt about whether your services are taxable, it is probably better to collect the tax. To collect and remit sales taxes in most areas requires registration and a permit. Finally, unless you collect sales tax on the work you do, you will be ineligible for any exemption from paying sales taxes on any purchases you make. For help in the procedures required to collect and remit sales taxes, see your accountant.

Setting up the books

When it comes to bookkeeping, there is probably no business simpler than freelancing. Nonetheless, it is a little more involved than balancing your personal checkbook; there are some things that you need to set up.

Get the advice of your accountant. What's covered here is necessarily general and just the essentials. As an individual you have a highly specific tax situation that may be directly affected by the way in which you set up your books. Also, if you have plans to grow your company, it may be best to set up more complex procedures now to make bookkeeping simpler later.

Get contact management software and a good desk diary. Use them to keep track of and record all appointments, assignments, and work hours, and all reimbursable or tax-deductible cash expenditures. Do this religiously, each and every day. This simple procedure should be the basic element in your record keeping. It conforms to the IRS guidelines for a "contemporaneous log of expenses" and it is all you need to ensure that you bill your clients accurately for the time spent on each project.

Get company checking accounts. You should keep personal and company expenses and check writing separate. So the next thing to attend to is company checking accounts and checkbooks. To open commercial checking accounts, most banks require an "employer identification number" or EIN, even though you don't have employees. It is simply a way to report interest income and other information to the IRS.

Many banks will do the paperwork for you, or you can ask your accountant or get the forms from the IRS directly. There is no charge.

Two company checking accounts, one a straight no-interest commercial account for paying regular bills, the other a "money market" account with check writing privileges where you can store excess cash at high interest, are best. Whether you incorporate or not, having two accounts—one for routine deposits and check writing, the other to ensure high interest on capital assets—is important once you don't have a routine paycheck to count on. Move money back and forth between the two accounts as appropriate.

For your checking account you should have a system that records checks as they are written and allows you to allocate the expenditure to a specific bookkeeping account. There are several inexpensive computer programs that will do this electronically, the most popular being Quicken (www.quicken.com).

Picking a date

Now comes the toughest decision of all. Select a date—call it "My Independence Day"—when you will actually start working for yourself. Consider the selection carefully and be prepared to commit yourself to it—irrevocably. This is the final test. If you are not ready for this firm commitment, you are not ready to start freelancing at this time. Stop now before it is too late.

Ideally, My Independence Day will be three or so months in advance so as to give you adequate time to get organized and take care of the myriad of setting-up-the-business details. You can do this in less time if necessary, but chances are you will need at least a month to do everything the right way. Don't try doing it in less than a month unless you are forced by such circumstances as being fired.

On the other hand, don't set My Independence Day more than six months away. There are just too many things that can change for you to be firmly committed. Set a tentative date now for review later if you wish. But don't commit yourself to the future until you can see it on the horizon, and that's seldom longer than half a year away.

Although My Independence Day can be any day of the month, it may be most convenient to make it the first Monday. That way the pay from your old employer will end with one month, and the pay from your new employer (you) can start the next. Also, ending your present employment on good terms at the end of the month is a businesslike arrangement that sets a positive tone for the future.

Once you have established My Independence Day, circle it on every single calendar you own. It is a date you will remember and celebrate long into the future. Now start setting up your new business and counting down the days until it becomes a reality.

4. Running Your Freelance Business

Your goal of becoming a well-paid freelance is now within easy reach. You're prepared, aware of the trade-offs as well as the benefits. You've developed a viable business plan, selected professional counsel, established a business structure, obtained insurance, and set a date.

Now all that remains until you actually start working on your own— until your own, personal Independence Day—is to make a smooth transition from employee to self-employed. Now is the time to go ahead and take the final steps in setting up your new business.

Start by considering whether to set up an office in your home, or to rent an official office. You will have to make a decision based on what you can afford, or what will make you feel most like going to work every morning. You will also have to take the steps to ensure that your office is comfortable, reflects your personality, and is an efficient work space regardless of where it is located. You will have to install essential services such as telephone and an internet connection. And, finally, you will have to quit your present job in a way that reflects your professionalism and doesn't burn any bridges behind you.

You are about to pass the point of no return. From here on, much of what you do will be public and will affect positively or negatively perceptions of peers and colleagues. In turn, these perceptions will ultimately affect your reputation, what kind of future you will have, and how much money you will make. While this is the time to move decisively, it is also the time to move carefully and lay a solid foundation for the years ahead.

Crossing the bridge without burning it

There is nothing certain in the life of a freelance except death, taxes, and finding out that a past colleague, who you once told to stuff it, is now an influential potential client. Sometimes the insult proffered was well deserved and the price later paid well worth it; you'd do it again. But more often, telling off a business associate provides only the most fleeting of satisfactions while jeopardizing your reputation and opportunities long, long into the future.

Restraining your emotions can be especially tough if you are about to leave an employer who has treated you badly. Even so, letting your emotions win out is probably unwise. No matter how badly you feel you've been treated by your present employer and clients, most likely it will be in your best interest to part amicably. You never know when you might need a character or employment reference. Even if that seems unlikely, why give anyone the desire, opportunity, and ammunition to bad-mouth you? Besides, the single most disarming and perplexing thing you can do to an SOB is to react in the way most unexpected, the one way he or she can't deal with—forgiveness.

Even if you've been treated badly in the past, it is probably best to rise above it and quit with the style of a lady or gentleman: It's been a great experience, but now it's time for me to move on. As soon as you're ready, make the break. Give your employer at least two weeks notice, preferably more. Show your professionalism by helping to find and train your replacement, and by continuing to work hard, as difficult as that will be.

If your employer reacts immaturely and asks you to leave immediately, consider it a blessing. You are prepared to start freelancing now; all you are doing is biding your time. Starting a few weeks earlier will speed things up.

Also be careful about what, if any, client work or ideas you take with you when you leave. Ethics is not something that can be prescribed here, so your conscience is your only guide on what's appropriate in your particular situation. It is always best, however, to err on the side of conservatism. You are well prepared for the future, you are talented, and there is lots of work out there. So why take a chance on recriminations and possible legal liability by trying to take clients or assignments along with you? If you have worked particularly well with one or more of your present employer's clients and mutually wish to continue to work together in the next few months, it is best to consult a lawyer first. In general, it is wise to observe these two guidelines: 1) Don't actively solicit any of your present employer's clients while still on the payroll. 2) Don't undertake any project for a client of your ex-employer until you have been working on your own for at least several months.

You have the right to show portfolio samples of work that you have been involved with when working for ex-employers as long as it does not involve misrepresentation. Exceptions to the above would be if there were signed agreements prohibiting disclosure, proprietary information was divulged, the display went beyond copyright "fair use," or an individual or organization was being libeled. However, ex-employers have no obligation to provide you with samples. (For more on this subject from the employer's perspective, see "Employee noncompete agreements" in Chapter 17.)

Get an office or work at home?

Do you set up an office in your home or apartment, or do you look for space in an office building? The former is cheap, may provide tax benefits, and gives greater flexibility. The latter provides more credibility, better client convenience, and possibly greater personal satisfaction.

Most readers of this book will have a choice, and should weigh carefully the positives and negatives of each option as presented below. For others, however, there is no choice. Lack of working room at home may dictate the need for office space elsewhere, or the needs of parenting or a disability may require the convenience of a home office. As valid as these and other special considerations are, unfortunately they don't affect at all the advantages and disadvantages of each office option. So even if you don't have a choice, familiarize yourself with the limitations of your office location. That way you'll be prepared to cope with and overcome them.

An office at home—the goods and bads. There are only two advantages of a home office: it is cheap, and it is convenient. But, you might ask, with two advantages like these, who needs more? By working at home your office overhead will be next to nothing. Perhaps your electric bill will go up, but not much else. There will be no commuting or parking costs. Since your home office will be, literally, next door, commuting time is zero, allowing you to work more. You can work when the mood strikes you, even at three on Sunday morning. Being handy and having flexible work hours will also give you a lot more time to spend on recreation, or with the kids. You may also qualify for tax benefits. (See "Deducting everything you can" in Chapter 9.)

The negatives of a home office are not so immediately apparent. Many of us need the intellectual stimulation of getting up and getting out of the house. Others need the social stimulation of commuting, stopping by the deli for coffee, meeting others, and going out to lunch. Still others need the stimulation of a metropolitan environment; if your home is in the country, you may find the atmosphere great for writing fiction or painting landscapes, but not conducive to commercial creativity. Although a one-person office anywhere can be a lonely place, there is none lonelier than the one at home. A home office can also be a very distracting place if you have to share it with kids, pets, and cooking smells. Finally, if your home is not conveniently located, you may have problems getting to last-minute meetings, and obtaining such essential services as deliveries and proofs.

An official office — the goods and bads. What greater fulfillment of an entrepreneurial dream can there be than your own company's name on a lobby directory, and lettered in gold leaf on an office door? What more effective way to demonstrate to skeptical potential clients that your new company is serious about its future, too?

An official office gives you a place to head for each morning, provides the psychological reaffirmation that you have taken the first step into the future, lets you meet clients in an atmosphere conducive to business, makes it easier to employ help, and provides the businesslike environment often needed to do your best work. With an official office you will have a choice of where to locate, so you can pick a location that is convenient for suppliers and clients, one that also allows you to be more productive.

The main disadvantage of an official office is cost; it always raises your overhead. The secondary disadvantage is inconvenience; it often means time wasted in traveling. So the question to ask yourself when considering an official office is whether it will increase efficiency, quality, or business to a degree that more than compensates for its expense. In doing this, take into account the home office alternative, examine your psychological needs and work habits, and don't forget to factor in such hidden office costs as parking and cleaning services. Finally, getting an official office involves taking the long view of your business, not the short view. It usually involves signing a lease, so if you are not sure where you want to locate, or are short of capital, it may be best to wait until your business is more stable before committing yourself.

The bottom line. You must feel good about where you are going to work—both economically and creatively. If you are a disciplined, self-motivated individual who does not need social interaction and has a conveniently located home or apartment with sufficient room free from distractions, it is probably best to start your business with a home office. The savings will be substantial.

Today many professionals work out of a home office, and it doesn't carry the stigma it used to. Many of today's large and well-known corporations started at home, within recent memory. Some large companies now allow employees to work at least some of their time at home, linked electronically with a central office. Many more small firms have home-based cottage industry employees.

Despite all this, however, recognize that there may be skepticism about the stability of a home-based business (from both clients and bankers), and that no home has the business-generating credibility of an office building address. By establishing your office in your home, your new company probably won't be considered for as many high-level (read: profitable) jobs as it would if the company were located in an office building.

The conditions given above, which make a home office attractive when first starting out, are rather difficult ones to meet. If you don't have the right kind of space, or need the motivation of getting up and getting out in the morning, don't suddenly be concerned about the viability of your new business. You must do what is right for you. Starting your business in a rented office is simply part of your individual formula for success. What is good for you isn't good for everyone else, and vice versa. Further, your professionalism will be enhanced by your office location, and you'll have a better chance at the best business. Take pleasure in the fact that most successful freelance businesses eventually end up renting office space anyway, so you are just ahead of schedule.

Arranging the home office

Almost without exception, everyone who has done it comments on the difficulty of working at home, even though most master it. For some of us, our early conditioning tells us that home is a refuge, a place to escape from work, not do it. For all of us, the proximity of living/recreational/family space, and the obligations and temptations that go with it, makes concentration tough. Because creating is such hard work, most of us will willingly accept any excuse to delay it.

It is important to recognize all the foregoing before establishing your home office, because the resulting lack of motivation can kill a new free-lance business very fast. Your home office must be set up to minimize the inherent and unavoidable difficulties of working at home, not exaggerate and enlarge them.

In planning your home office, the space you choose should be dedicated exclusively to your business, have adequate working room, be comfortable, and be isolated as much as possible from the rest of your living facilities. By so doing you can go a long way toward reducing the negative effects on your business of interruptions, loneliness, temptations, and family tensions.

If the only way you can work at home is on the kitchen table, your chances of becoming successful are very, very limited. Your chances improve to maybe 50/50 if you can take over a corner of a bedroom and make it into your private, permanent work space. You're an odds-on favorite to succeed if you can convert a whole room—an unused bedroom, a family room, or the basement—into an office. And if you can convert your garage, or add an addition on to your house, you'll have the ideal home environment for success.

Creating an isolated space that is used solely for business and decorating it to reflect your personal, professional tastes will also help ensure that you will be able to combat the inevitable psychological difficulties of working at home. Every time you enter your office you will be entering a world separate from the rest of the house, a world in which your professionalism, your past successes, and your present assignments are very visible. These reminders provide the necessary reinforcement to self-worth that most creative individuals find absolutely essential when not working with peers.

As for zoning prohibitions against offices in residential neighborhoods, you should have no problem as long as you work alone, don't hang out a sign identifying your home as a business location, and don't create a large volume of traffic. In some states your ability to work in your own home is even protected by law. If, however, you are planning to add an addition to your home for use as an office, or have plans to employ help someday, it will pay to get the advice of a lawyer first.

Finding an official office

Renting an office involves some complicated and expensive decisions, perhaps the most complicated and expensive you'll face as a freelance. You have to consider the effect of location, size, and comfort, and, most of all, expense.

Only you can determine what is the right location. Size and comfort depend mostly on personal factors. As a general rule, however, the smallest office that an individual can work out of without feeling claustrophobic is about 10 by 12, or 120 square feet. This size assumes cleanliness, a window, plenty of light (preferably natural), good ventilation, a pleasant hallway outside, and nearby toilet facilities. The absence of any of these increases the need for space substantially. The best size for a freelance is usually around 200 square feet. At the other extreme, 400 square feet and over, even if you can afford it, will probably make you feel and look like the last survivor in an office purge.

What office space will cost varies, of course, according to market and amenities. Luxurious space in a small city won't cost much more than barely tolerable space in midtown Manhattan. You'll probably get electricity, heat/AC, an internet connection, cleaning service, and parking in a small city as well. Unfortunately, there's an economy of scale in renting office space, which discriminates against the small-space renter. As a guideline, single-person, quality, unfurnished office space runs from a low of $15 per square foot per year to well over $75. This means a 150-square-foot office can cost from $225 to $1,000 or more a month.

It is also unfortunate but true that the best deal usually comes with the longest lease. Property that rents for $40 a square foot with a six-month lease may rent for $35 with a one-year lease and $25 with a two-year lease. This is especially true in locations where the office rental market is tight. If you can afford it, it is probably best to take a one-year lease with a renewal option that limits the amount of rent increase. In any case, don't take a lease with the idea that you will be able to break it if things don't work out. Check with a lawyer before signing anything.

As a way of minimizing rental costs, consider sharing facilities with a freelance with complementary talents—copywriter, designer/art director, or web developer. Because two don't need twice as much space as one, doing so can reduce expenses for both. It may also result in some referral business: copy clients often need design/art direction, and design/art direction clients often need copy. To find someone who has room to share, or who is also out looking, ask among colleagues. If that doesn't work, place an ad in an industry trade magazine such as the local edition of *AdWeek*, or a creative club newsletter. You may also wish to consider sharing with another person with your skills, but for obvious personal and professional reasons, that arrangement may not be satisfactory. (For more on renting space, see "Evaluating new office or studio space" in Chapter 16.)

A third option is to rent a turnkey office from one of the companies that specialize in providing fully equipped offices to individuals and small businesses. They operate on the idea of clustering many small offices around central, shared facilities. Called executive suites, they are organized around the needs of entrepreneurs and sales people, and provide telephones with answering service, a receptionist, internet connection, on-call secretarial help, copy and fax machines, and conference facilities. With an executive-suite office you may pay for style and amenities that are inappropriate when you spend much of your day behind a computer. On the other hand, they do provide impressive space if you meet with clients; they often result in new business contacts; you get on-call secretarial service; and you won't have to get your own office furniture, internet connection, or telephone-answering, fax, and copying equipment. Prices are 50 percent higher or more per square foot than for regular office space. To find companies renting executive suites, look under Office and Desk Space Rental Services online. (There is more on this subject in Chapter 16.)

Finally, if you can afford it, the best alternative is to purchase an office condominium and pay yourself the rent. There are significant tax-sheltering advantages. How to do it and what you can expect are covered under "Purchasing commercial space" in Chapter 16.

Wherever you decide to locate your office, remember that you will be spending a lot of time there, so scrimping on comfort or amenities isn't wise. The way you decorate your space is at least as important as where it is. Let the furnishings and decoration reflect your personality and your creativity. Even if no one else ever visits your office, surrounding yourself with your good work will help in those inevitable times when you have an attack of the lonelies, or question your creativity. Make sure your office is more than just a place to work; make sure it also is a place that works by providing motivation and inspiration.

Office necessities

Equally important is making sure your office is functional. This isn't as elementary as it may sound. You may find yourself putting in more office time than ever before, or you may spend more uninterrupted hours behind a desk than ever before. In either case, the functionality of your space—how comfortable it is and how well it is laid out for working—can be critical in warding off fatigue, and in keeping you alert and creative.

Quality office furniture provides an excellent return on investment. It will pay itself back many times in comfort and increased efficiency. Since your company will grow and prosper, it is probably better to start off with a few good pieces than with more pieces of lesser quality. Furniture from discount office supply stores will wear out fast and have little style and comfort. Don't confuse quality with design-y, however. For personal and business reasons you may feel that your office furniture has to make an aesthetic statement. If so, fine. Just don't get your priorities mixed up. Priority one has to be comfort. (For more on the crucial importance of comfort, see "Remembering to work smart" in Chapter 5.)

When shopping, you'll soon discover that quality office furniture is expensive. A run-of-the-mill desk can be well over $1,200, a small conference-room chair over $400; there is no price limit on designer pieces. The reason is that the market is relatively small, and the furniture is built to

take hard wear and abuse. But since your office will have very light wear it might make sense to buy what furniture you can—chairs and lamps, for example— from a home furnishings store. Also, check out warehouse office furniture outlets where odd pieces are sold off. Such pieces are often all that a small office needs.

Don't buy any furniture until you have checked the possibility of renting it. Although renting raises your monthly overhead, it keeps you from tying up precious capital. There are office rental furniture outlets in most metropolitan areas.

As for office layout, your work surfaces should be large enough and laid out in such a way as to keep essentials handy, minimize clutter, and reduce unnecessary movement. They should also be of the right height to avoid arm and shoulder fatigue. Your chair should keep your back comfortable, even during those long stretches when you are working to beat a deadline. Your telephone should be within easy reach. And, speaking of telephones, a cell phone is not enough. Your office needs a traditional landline, not only for the business listing that comes with it, but also for reliability and transmission clarity. Use your cell phone only when necessary to maintain connections out of the office.

The location of office furniture relative to light is critical. If you have a window, it is probably best to place your primary working surface at right angles to it. Facing the window will probably be distracting; putting your back to it will cut off light. Most plants need some natural light. If you have track or built-in lights, they have to be over your primary work area. Position lamps where they illuminate without creating glare, especially on computer screens. Chairs for visitors have to be in a well-lit area, or have separate lamps. Keep cords out of traffic areas. You probably won't want to sit too close to heating or air-conditioning units; sit where you can get fresh air, and where you can see the door, especially if your office is in the city or in a building open to the public.

Much of the arranging to assure that your office is comfortable can only be accomplished by trial and error after you move in. But you can experiment beforehand by getting an outline of the space and testing various floor plans. Using a scale of 1" = 1' and some graph paper, cut out outlines of furniture shapes and move them around. See what fits best. Use this layout when you first move in to your office, then spend the next week or two adjusting, improving the layout to assure the maximum in comfort and efficiency. Or get one of the software programs that will let you accomplish the same thing on your computer.

Before you move in, have the office freshly painted. This will usually be part of any rental agreement. Even if you are setting up a home office, painting the area in new colors will help reinforce the psychological aspect of starting over. Pick light, flat, pastel colors—they are easier on the eyes, help keep you alert, and visually increase the size of an otherwise small area.

Buying insurance

For an individual, having enough of the right kind of insurance is simply wise. For the principal/president/creative director of a small business, it is more than just wise—it is necessary to ensure economic survival. But what exactly is enough? What is the right kind? How much should it cost? And how do you go about getting it?

First, the scare tactic: without proper insurance, the cost of a business loss, major accident, or medical problem can wipe you out. Even minor losses, accidents, or medical problems can devastate an otherwise prosperous individual and his or her business. Sooner or later a little rain is going to fall in your financial life and you'd best be well covered. Here we look at how to go about buying the right insurance umbrella—one big enough to cover the essentials, one small enough to afford.

If you've left an organization with more than twenty employees that offered full or partial company-paid group insurance, you are entitled by Federal law (COBRA) to continue that coverage for up to 18 months if you left voluntarily (quit), or 36 months if you left involuntarily (were laid off, but not fired). Such group plans provide coverage that is much more comprehensive and costs less than what can be obtained individually. Some states require ex-employers to provide additional protection as well. Contact your former employer, the insurance carrier, or your state's department of insurance about these rights.

Health (medical) insurance. How much insurance you'll need, how much it will cost, and where you should purchase it depends on four interrelated factors: 1) the number of dependents covered by the policy; 2) your dependents and your age and medical conditions; 3) what the policy does or doesn't cover (excluded procedures and type of deductible); and 4) the size and buying power of the organization contracting for the coverage.

Required coverage. All U.S. citizens must have basic health insurance. If your health insurance was previously provided by your employer or family, ask your insurance agent for advice. (See Chapter 3 about selecting an agent.) Insurance requirements and assistance is selecting coverage can also be obtained from your state's health insurance exchange, which is required by the Federal government to help citizens obtain affordable health care. (Firms with fewer than fifty employees are not required to provide health insurance to employees.)

Health Maintenance, Preferred Provider, and Exclusive Provider Organizations (HMOs, PPOs, & EPOs). Generally speaking, HMOs require you to use their physicians and facilities; EPOs want you to join one of their networks of physicians and facilities; PPOs provide a choice among a large group of physicians and facilities. The most affordable coverage is usually through a group plan sponsored by a trade association or business group.

Private carrier insurance. This is coverage offered by national insurance companies through their local ("captive") agents, or by independent agents. These policies are also sometimes called indemnity plans. You choose the extent of your coverage and can obtain treatment by any physician or facility. This makes these plans the most flexible. They may also be the least expensive if you opt for high-deductible coverage. Private carrier health insurance is sometimes difficult to obtain, and coverage is also affected by an individual's age and physical condition. There's a nuisance factor, too—you'll likely have to pay first, then to get reimbursed you must obtain the physician's signature on a form you have to submit to the insurance company. There is little or no regulation or control over future cost increases.

Health savings accounts. These combine a high-deductible insurance policy with an opportunity to put aside tax-deferred income in a special savings account to cover routine medical expenses. For healthy individuals with stable businesses they offer a possible way to cut medical insurance costs while also saving additional money for retirement. Individual insurance premium reductions of 10 percent to 30 percent over traditional health insurance are promoted.

Health insurance cost. It varies throughout the country, but at this writing the average national cost for an individual with no dependents is $425 a month; family coverage is $1,200 monthly.

Dental insurance. It is affordable only as part of a group health insurance plan and often requires 100 percent group participation. There is often a one-year wait before anything other than preventive benefits (teeth cleaning, etc.) take effect, and orthodontics aren't covered. Group premiums average $40 to $60 a month for individual coverage; $75 to $120 a month for family coverage. (Dental injury caused by accidents is normally covered by health insurance policies.)

Tax deductibility. Health and dental insurance premiums paid by employers are fully tax-deductible for C corporations, even for an employee owner. For S corporations employee premiums are fully deductible, but not those of owners. At this writing 60 percent of premiums are deductible for S corporation owners, sole proprietors, and LLC partners. Because tax deductibility constantly changes, check with your accountant.

Disability insurance. This is the second most important type of business insurance. It is your (or any employees') assurance of an income in the event an illness or disability makes working impossible. Think of it as protecting your company's principal asset—your income-producing abilities.

Unlike the lack of health insurance, which is noticeable with every illness, lack of disability insurance doesn't become important until it's too late—incapacitation. Therefore, and put mildly, an individual without disability insurance is playing a game of Russian roulette with his or her future. The only exception is individuals who have adequate financial resources to cover a loss of income. (Disability insurance should not be confused with Workers Compensation Insurance, which is an employer requirement and whose benefits apply to only on-the-job injuries. Also, "wage replacement" insurance, mandated by some states, is not comparable.)

Anyone self-employed should get what is referred to as a "secured" or "noncancelable" disability policy. As the name implies, these non-group policies can remain in effect despite the employment status of the insured. They also offer the opportunity to define terms of disablement and to custom-tailor benefits.

Determining benefits. The first thing to contemplate is how soon after disablement you'll require income. The longer the deductible or elimination period, the cheaper the policy will be. Consider your accounts receivable and whatever assets you can easily liquidate. A 90-day wait for benefits (the deductible) is most common. As for long-term need, keep in mind that payouts could be tax-free (see "Payment of premiums" below), you could do away with most work-related expenses, and you could scrimp on many personal pleasures. As a guideline, insurance companies figure that 50 to 60 percent of present income will be necessary. You may come up with a lower figure, but be realistic.

Determining disablement. The policy should provide for at least partial disablement if you cannot perform all your present work functions, including calling on clients, even if all your creative faculties or management activities are unimpaired. Set your own definitions of disablement and ask your insurance agent to shop around to find a policy that matches them as closely as possible. Remember, what might not be disabling to a normal white-collar worker could be to a creative person (e.g., a hand tremor could put an illustrator out of work, but have no impact on a data processor).

Other considerations. Check to confirm that the policy has the following: A residual benefits provision (partial benefits without total disability), coverage for both accident and illness disability, a cost of living (inflation) rider, is "guaranteed renewable" (can't be canceled, but premiums can rise) rather than being "noncancelable" (no changes possible), and, if available, an "own occupation" provision rather than "reasonable occupation."

Cost. A typical disability insurance policy providing $4,000 a month until age 65 and starting 90 days after declared disability will run a 35-year-old male freelance about $130 a month ($1,560 yearly) at this writing. Half this coverage equals half the premium—$2,000 for about $65 a month. Premiums on policies for females are often 25 to 30 percent more.

Payment of premiums. When disability premiums are paid by the business (before taxes), any disability payouts will be taxable. If paid for by private funds (after taxes), payouts will not be taxable.

Tax deductibility. The same rules apply as for health and dental insurance premiums.

Life insurance. We often think of it only in a personal context, but adequate life insurance is also a business issue. It can help provide protection to your dependents, as well as ensure an orderly transition of your business interests. Some policies can also provide tax-deferred retirement money. How much money your beneficiaries will need, how much if any retirement funding is desired, and how big a monthly premium is affordable are all personal issues. As one guideline, the insurance industry recommends a policy that pays a lump sum of five to eight times the annual income for a family wage earner with average indebtedness. You may need more or less.

Cost. Life insurance rates are based on an individual's age, sex, and health, so cost-estimating is difficult. As an example, however, a 35-year-old, nonsmoking female can usually purchase straight term (no cash value) life insurance for about $1 per year per $1,000 of death benefits plus an additional $25 to $75 policy fee. In other words, a $100,000 policy will have an annual cost of $125 to $175.

The same individual purchasing whole-life insurance (insurance with cash value) will pay from $2.50 to $7.00 per $1,000 (depending on the cash buildup) plus the policy fee, or from $250 to $700 yearly for a $100,000 policy. As for how much cash will build up, a rule of thumb is that the total premiums should at least equal the cash value of the policy in ten years or less.

Tax deductibility. Insurance policies are not normally tax-deductible.

Key person/buy-sell insurance. This is important insurance when you have a partner or employees. It makes it possible for remaining owners to come up with the cash to buy out a deceased or disabled owner. It can also be used to fund the buyout of a departing owner or the death or disablement of a valued employee. An optional addition to key person life insurance can provide protection from suits arising from the actions of partners. Key person policies should be written in conjunction with a buy-sell agreement controlling distribution of business assets.

When there are only two principals, each usually takes out a life insurance policy on the other. He or she is responsible for its premiums and is its beneficiary. When there are more than two principals, policy premiums are usually paid by the company, which is the beneficiary.

Term insurance is the least expensive option, although premiums become increasingly expensive as insureds grow older. There is also no buildup of cash value. Variable universal life insurance is more expensive, but premiums do not increase with age, and policies offer a buildup of cash value, which might be used to fund a buyout. It may be the appropriate choice in some cases.

In addition, it is wise for every principal and crucial employee to be covered by a similar disability policy. This policy, funded like life insurance, is in addition to a disability policy that an insured person may carry on him- or herself to ensure income.

Cost. The same as life and disability policies written for traditional purposes.

Tax deductibility. Depends on who pays and who benefits.

General coverage for home-based businesses. One of the benefits of freelancing out of your home is that business insurance needs are minimal. Tangible assets are few and there are few situations that would expose one to liability.

Equipment. Most routine business items, such as desks, computers, and peripherals will most likely be covered for up to $2,500 against fire, theft, or other common loss by a standard "homeowner's," or "renter's," insurance policy.

Of course, $2,500 won't buy you much equipment today, so if you don't want to take a risk you may want additional protection. Inquire whether it can be obtained through a rider to your homeowner's or renter's policy. Such riders are typically available for $1.50 to $2.00 per $100 of additional coverage. For example, to bring coverage to $15,000 from $2,500 would cost from $187.50 to $250.00 extra each year (12.5 x $1.50 or $2.00).

Since electronic stuff comprises most of your risk, if adequate coverage is not available or very expensive, you may also want to investigate specific computer (electronic) coverage as described below.

Liability. If you have clients or businesspeople coming to your home office or studio, you'll also need to increase and redefine the comprehensive personal liability (CPL) coverage in your homeowner's or renter's policy. An endorsement adding coverage of $500,000 (recommended) will run from $15 to $50 per year depending on office location.

Home-office insurance. Some insurers offer special work-at-home riders to homeowner's insurance. They provide business property, liability, income loss, and other traditional commercial coverages. A typical add-on premium is about $200.

General coverage when renting space. The most economical insurance coverage for businesses renting commercial space almost always comes from a multifaceted business owner's policy (BOP). This might also be true if you have an extensive home office, especially if employees work there.

BOPs typically include the three common needs of small businesses described below —general contents, commercial general liability, and business interruption insurance. Most BOPs have a minimum premium of $300 to $500 yearly. If your needs are modest, ask your agent if it's possible to add coverage without raising the premium.

General contents coverage. It can be specified as "all risk," which includes everything not specifically excluded, or "named peril," which covers only things specifically identified. All-risk coverage with no exclusions might be difficult or expensive to obtain, depending on the location of your business. Coverage that excludes specific damage, such as that by floods or earthquakes, might be all that's possible. In some situations, named

RUNNING YOUR FREELANCE BUSINESS

peril coverage that specifies a dozen or so coverages, no more, will be all that's obtainable.

Commercial general liability (CGL) insurance. It covers bodily injury to others (e.g., an accident in your office). Also, damage to someone else's property (e.g., causing a fire that damages other offices in the building). Many landlords will insist on "in force CGL insurance" before renting space.

Business interruption (business income) insurance. It provides compensation based on your financial history for twelve months if your business is unable to function resulting from circumstances (not personal or medical) beyond your control.

Specific business coverage. In addition to a BOP, many creative firms also have a need for one or more additional policies to cover risks excluded or limited in a BOP.

Computer insurance. Most homeowner's and BOP policies will cover all the equipment of a small creative firm. Registered software is also covered by most policies up to 20 percent of the hardware value. Be sure to check with your agent to determine the extent of coverage, particularly if your business is electronic-intensive. Also note that work in progress is never covered by commercial or homeowner policies. The best (sometimes only) protection is to back up files and store them offsite.

Adequate computer coverage for mid- to large-size firms often requires a separate Business Electronic Equipment policy.

Cost. Typically $550 to $750 for $30,000 of equipment and $100,000 of "extra expense" or reconstruction (work in progress) coverage.

Errors and omissions insurance. This coverage protects you against liability arising from mistakes. Because of the expense, most freelances and small firms rely on the protection afforded by client sign-offs and, ultimately, by incorporation. If necessary to have it for a particular, high-risk project, try to get "one-shot" coverage and bill the premium to the client as a job expense.

Cost. Typically $1,200 to $1,500 annually for $100,000 of coverage. The exact type of coverage must be carefully specified, too.

Umbrella liability coverage. It protects your business from the high awards often assessed by juries for accidents because of negligence.

Cost. From $250 to $500 annually for $2 million coverage.

Bailees coverage. It covers the value of client or supplier items in your possession that may be lost, stolen, or damaged, such as stock photos.

Cost. From $50 to $75 annually per $10,000 of coverage.

Valuable papers coverage. It covers artwork stolen, damaged, or destroyed (except in transit).

Cost. From $20 to $40 per year per $10,000 of coverage when added to a BOP. The same coverage would cost about $150 if purchased independently.

Transit coverage. Maximum liability for most express delivery services is $500. Additional coverage can usually be purchased. Be sure, however, to identify the insured material as "commercial" instead of "fine" art. If you do a lot of shipping, investigate a blanket transit coverage policy.

Flood, earthquake, and natural disaster insurance. It extends coverage to these otherwise uninsured risks.

Cost. It is based on probability, so premiums vary widely depending on the business location.

Automobile insurance. You're probably aware of most of what you need and its costs. But you may not know that your present auto insurance could be insufficient when you're engaged in commercial activity. So make sure your auto policy also reflects any business use of your vehicle.

Cost. Most insurance agents recommend liability coverage (bodily injury to others) of at least $250,000 per person, or $500,000 per accident for autos regularly engaged in commercial activity. Such coverage will cost $100 to $200 yearly, depending on state, location, and driving history. It is also important to have uninsured and underinsured motorist coverage to cover you if hit by others with little or no insurance. The former costs about $100 to $150 extra yearly; the latter $30 to $50.

Final thoughts. Insurance is only one aspect of emergency planning. You should keep an up-to-date inventory of insured items. You should also have a plan for coping with the other disruptive aspects of an emergency—who should be notified, what will need immediate attention and what won't, and who is responsible for what actions. And as business conditions change, so should your coverage. Insurance coverage should never be static. It should be evaluated and adjusted at least yearly—the reason you should have an independent agent/consultant to advise you. (See Chapter 3.)

5. Long-Term Success

The minute you become self-employed, you start competing against other, established freelances. You also begin competing against well-known creative suppliers, such as advertising agencies and design firms. You compete against entrenched, in-house creative departments in larger companies, too. For all these reasons it is critically important that as you start your new business you not only hit the deck running, but hit it running at high speed.

The first six months are the most important in the life of any business. This is the time when you will prove that you are as good as, or better than, the competition. If you do things right, if these six months are active, fun, and rewarding, you will be in business for good, or at least until a better opportunity comes along. On the other hand, if they aren't, you probably won't have the enthusiasm or wherewithal to continue. If this should happen, it could have a devastating effect on your sense of self worth, regardless of where you work in the future.

Your first six months in business will undoubtedly determine the extent of your success. During this time you will establish work patterns, decide what business to pursue, and position yourself in the eyes of potential clients. Simply put, this is the time when you head off either in the right, or the wrong, direction.

Be disciplined in how you work

Working discipline is the first subject covered in this chapter for an elementary reason: *working discipline is the single most important determinant of freelance success.* Stop. Go back and read that sentence again. Now repeat it to yourself. Then make sure you remember it today, tomorrow, and every single day you continue to work for yourself. Because the first day you forget it, the first day you put laziness, recreation, or personal creativity ahead of working, will be the first day of the decline of your fledgling business.

Does this mean you are about to become a creative automaton, a workaholic always questing for rewards never to be enjoyed? Not at all. All it means is that your new freelance job must be treated like every other job you ever had—as serious work. Most people who are successful work hard at what they do. For them, work comes first and foremost during the hours allotted for it. The fact that you are now one of the self-employed doesn't change that basic fact, it just makes it easier to forget, as well as more important to remember.

As crass as it sounds, working discipline, the process of attending first to the all-important task of making a living, is far more critical to your future happiness than finding the right clients, or producing award-winning creativity. All this and more will come in due time, but how much and for how long will depend in large measure upon the work habits you establish now and adhere to throughout your self-employed career.

The problem is this: when you work for yourself it is easy to excuse yourself from working. As prominent and well identified as this danger is, it is the shoal upon which many businesses founder. Sometimes lack of motivation is caused by a phone that doesn't ring—it is hard to work hard when no one else cares. Other times, bad personal habits, such as a tendency to procrastinate, sap productivity. Still other times, it is easy to succumb to pure laziness, to put off until tomorrow what could easily be done today, especially if the sun is shining or the fish are biting. Regardless of the cause, however, if you are to succeed you must fight this battle with strength and conviction.

Work discipline is not something you should have; it is something you must have. You must keep busy for psychological reasons, to constantly replace clients who will leave, to generate growth capital, to improve yourself professionally, to pay the bills. In a larger organization, the effects of a single individual's bad work habits and occasional bad days are easily made up by others. In a group of eight, losing one employee for a day reduces overall productivity by only 12 percent; in a group of one, 100 percent of productivity is lost.

Presented below are the five basic and essential elements of working discipline for the freelancer. Review them, remember them, practice them. Yes, it will be possible for you to make it as a freelance without practicing every one, every day. But make no mistake, your long-term success is directly related to how well you understand and practice the spirit each encompasses.

Work regularly. Most of us have done freelance assignments before. Chances are we did them in our free time; they were fun, and they put a little extra into the rainy day kitty. We could afford to be relaxed about when we worked, when we delivered, and what we charged. No more. Once freelancing becomes a vocation rather than an avocation, the work rules change. The biggest difference between occasional and full-time freelancing is the need for regular work habits.

The primary reason for regularity is client expectations that commitments and deadlines will be met. But nearly as important is the psychological need most of us have for a normal job. Because of cultural conditioning, most of us associate normal with regular, and regular with good. We find it hard to do good commercial work when isolated from the disciplines we associate with regular commercial activity. When we do feel normal about what we are doing, we are better able to draw upon our past experience and talents, the reasons clients hire us.

This does not necessarily mean that you have to do your work when others do theirs, although it often helps. You must be available to meet clients when they want, but otherwise when you work is your choice. Some freelances feel most comfortable working the office hours to which they have become accustomed—9 to whenever. Others find early in the morning the best time to be creative, and afternoons the best time to make calls. Still others sleep late, make calls in the afternoon, and create all evening. And so forth. The point is that successful freelances keep regular hours— i.e., they do their creating at more or less the same time every day, and they take care of business needs at more or less the same time every day.

It is possible that you may be different, that you can be successful by being creative whenever the mood strikes you, and using your noncreative time to otherwise take care of business. If so, freelancing will be more than a good living; it will be creative nirvana. Still, I wouldn't bet my future on it if I were you.

Value time. Closely related to keeping regular working hours is developing an appreciation for time. It may be a cliché, but time really is money. Now that you work for yourself, you can no longer afford to confuse being at work with working. You must not only be at the computer regularly, but you must also be productive when there. Interruptions such as socializing, attending to personal matters, family crises, daydreaming, even lunch, don't count as work time. Be tough about this. Remember, you're the boss.

Perhaps the best way to develop an appreciation for the value of time is to start charging yourself for every hour in a normal work day. Assign a dollar value to work hours based on a forty-hour week and your financial needs. Then at the end of each day, add up the charges you will actually be billing to clients. Over an extended period, say several weeks, you should be billing a substantial portion of what you owe yourself. (Billing must be at least 50 percent on average for most freelancers to have a viable business.)

Always meet your deadlines. Being a freelance is a service business. Being a freelance is a service business. Being a freelance is a service business. No, the computer didn't get stuck; the repetition is intentional. Nonetheless, this point will still be forgotten by some freelances when they face the pressures of multiple clients and their demands. These freelances will be among the ones whose business eventually atrophies. Just as location, location, location is everything in retailing, service, service, service is everything in freelancing.

Your very *raison d'être* is to do for others what they cannot, or will not, do for themselves. When you accept an assignment, the client expects you to be competent, professional, and most of all a fanatic about meeting his or her deadlines, your obligations. Often for good reason, too, because dozens of other people's functions and thousands of dollars ride upon getting your material on time. Even when the clients' deadlines are only dictated by whim, by accepting the assignment you agreed to meet whatever schedule was established. If you don't meet it, no matter how legitimate the reason, the experience can only reflect negatively on you; likewise, meeting a deadline but compromising quality in the process.

Unfortunately, missed deadlines caused by sickness, death in the family, work overload, nonperformance of suppliers, and the escape of your pet canary will probably be viewed the same way, as excuses.

When you've used too many excuses with too many clients, the phone will gradually stop ringing. So whenever accepting a project, always give yourself more than enough time to do it well, and keep in mind Murphy's Law: If anything can go wrong, it will.

Make work when you have to. The fact that you have decided to stake your future on freelancing shows you to be a person with high energy and an entrepreneurial spirit. It also marks you as the type of person whose self-worth depends in large measure on keeping productively busy. You are a Type A personality—compulsive and driven by a need to succeed. One of the most destructive things that can happen to you is to have nothing to do, and no one to care. If that happens, you not only question your decision to freelance; you question your whole future and ultimately your creative ability.

Nonetheless, it is a fact of freelance life that in the best of times business will come in spurts; in the worst of times there will be a long wait between spurts. That there will be times when you will be unemployed is an occupational hazard you should recognize right from the start. That's why you should devise a plan to combat the effects of inactivity now, while you are still in the flush of enthusiasm for your new career.

Until your business is firmly established, the only way to fill nonassignment working hours is by soliciting work—writing letters, setting up appointments, showing your portfolio. Later, after your business is well established, you will still want to use some of your downtime to find new, better clients. As discussed in Section Three, constant promotion is essential if you are to prosper. Despite your best promotional efforts, however, chances are you will still wake up some mornings with nothing to do. These are the times when your mental health requires one or more potentially productive long-term projects. These might include a plan for the development of new business, or the preparation of a pitch to a new type of client. If you are a writer, perhaps you want to try your hand at writing something different—unsolicited magazine articles or the book you have long planned. If you are an illustrator or designer, this could be the time you need to do some speculative pieces to round out your portfolio, or to pursue a latent talent in fine art.

The important point is that you get up, dress, go to your workplace, sit by the phone, and work, regardless of whether or not you have revenue-producing assignments. Do this with the same unvarying regularity every single business day.

Don't forgo relaxation. Everyone's metabolism and tolerance of stress is different. What's a killer work load for some will be a challenge to others, and vice versa. Nonetheless, freelancing is a very stressful way to make a living. Every time you show your creative output you expose yourself to criticism. Every new client requires a different exercise in tact and diplomacy. Topping it all off is great unpredictability of income.

For these and more reasons, every one of us requires some time away from the pressures that make up our daily work life. It may be true that it's better to burn out than to rust out, but you don't want out. You want to stay in the game until you decide there is something better to do with your life. The best way to ensure this is to build ample time for relaxation into your work schedule.

Taking time off to relax is nothing more than making a sound investment in your long-term success. Benefit from the decades of experience compiled by large corporations, many of which now require executive employees to take a set minimum vacation each year. They know that time off usually more than pays for itself in increased creativity and productivity. As the senior executive of your company you, too, should be required to take vacations and holidays. Charging one's personal batteries is a very important, and very often neglected, element of long-term success. Besides, you can't spend your success in heaven, so why wait?

Taking time off—nights, weekends, vacations—requires personal work discipline and planning. It is one more reason why you should set regular working hours, and it is why now, as you start your new lifestyle, you should already be thinking about your first vacation. Don't wait. Plan now to mark your first anniversary as a freelance with a vacation trip to celebrate your success. Then get in the habit of celebrating at least once a year. Believe me, you'll earn every hour of it.

To take nights, weekends, and occasional weeks off takes a great deal of tact and firmness with clients. As a single individual in a service business it means that there will be times when you cannot respond to client requests. In a few cases, this will mean unhappy clients and the loss of business, but more often it won't. You will be surprised at just how many rush jobs turn out not to be. In the long run, not accepting every job, and particularly not accepting jobs with unrealistic delivery dates, will work in your interest. You want to slowly and carefully build a reputation as a top-notch creative resource. To deliver work of quality takes thought and time. You don't want to be perceived by clients as some type of creative mechanic who is on twenty-four-hour call. Always remember, when you start jumping through hoops on request, you can be replaced by a well-trained seal.

Start marketing yourself right away

After working (and relaxing) discipline, the second most important determinant of success is to make a large group of potential clients aware of the quality of your work, and your availability. In short, market your services. Don't make the common mistake of believing that marketing activity isn't essential. Or that it will only be necessary until you get established. *To be successful today (and tomorrow), you must devote considerable and continuous energy to marketing your services.* What and how much is covered in detail in Section Three.

The object of marketing is not only to keep busy (get assignments), but to allow you to develop your business in the most personally satisfying and profitable manner. Equally important, marketing can provide the client and assignment variety that will give your business stability. Initially, you may have to depend upon a few clients and types of work to assure cash flow. Nonetheless, your long-term goal should be developing the broadness of business that will keep you from being too dependent on a few clients or types of assignments. After inadequate capitalization and lack of working discipline, dependence on too few clients sinks the most freelance businesses.

The ideal situation for most freelances is one or two large, steady clients along with a variety of others who call occasionally as their needs dictate. One large client who contributes up to 25 percent of gross income or two who contribute up to 50 percent is perfect. With more of your income dependent on a couple of clients, you are at considerable risk; with no steady clients you place yourself on something of an income roller coaster. In addition, variety is usually an important element in personal contentment, and is always a critical element in sustaining excellence. Variety is more than the mere spice of creativity; it is the very essence of creativity.

Maintaining your professionalism

Being a one-person organization often necessitates cutting financial corners, making hasty creative decisions, and forgoing social pleasantries—all things that chip away at professionalism, the bedrock of any freelance's appeal. Be aware of it when it happens, and keep it to a minimum. Despite how hectic things occasionally become, fight the temptation to make compromises; maintain your standards at all costs.

Think of professionalism as a combination of experience and attitude, two attributes with which you are now amply endowed. Over the months and years ahead you will continue to make deposits in your bank of experience. At the same time, you must be careful not to start withdrawing from your attitude bank. Attitude is the very thing that made you an ideal candidate to become a freelance.

Attitude is largely formed by routine. So now, as you start your new business, establish the procedures that will allow you to continue to positively address each new challenge. Unfortunately, when you work for yourself it's easy to slip into bad habits and to gradually lose the all-important polish you started with.

Creative standards. There will be times in the months and years to come when the pressures of meeting multiple deadlines for multiple clients will force you to do things differently than you did before. This can be good because change can bring growth. But not always.

It is, for instance, easy for the pressured writer to pick up previously written boilerplate copy to flesh out a brochure. Or for the pressured designer to apply a previously worked out solution to a different type of branding need. Or for a writer, designer, or illustrator to steal a concept from the pages of *Communication Arts*. All are creative cop-outs, even if the client never knows the difference.

Other times, you will be asked to do a job with inadequate information, or a budget that makes quality impossible. When it happens, remember this: six months after the fact, no one will remember the conditions under which the work was done. However, for many years everyone will continue to note the poor quality, and associate your name with it.

As you become increasingly successful, as clients respond to your particular style, you will be tempted to experiment less and less. If so, someday clients will discover that your work all looks the same, and quite dated. That is when they will start looking for new creative sources, ones without a formula appearance. Once you start letting external factors, such as success or everyday time pressures, dictate your creativity, you've stopped growing. Worse, you are on the downhill slope of what was once a promising career.

Business standards. Freelancing is unlike other businesses in that its personal nature makes it hard to maintain objectivity. This is especially so given the fact that you become involved in every aspect of the business, and have little or no other input. Yet subjective decision-making is the bane of any business, and the smaller the business is, the more devastating it can be.

You have to work hard at not letting your personal feelings and preferences cloud your judgment and interfere with rational decision making.

Even a dumb client is usually right, at least if you want to keep him or her as a client. You must do what others want to be done, not necessarily what you think is right. No matter how much you may want to be a nice person, you can't take much work that doesn't pay, even for old friends.

You will also find it difficult to be both creative and a clerk, often at different times in the same day. But to put off bookkeeping or not to keep accurate account of your time can lead to over- or under-billing. In one case you risk losing a customer, in the other you risk losing your income.

Finally, you can never afford to take any client for granted. As soon as you do, the client is lost. Everyone wants to be appreciated. The longest, most stable relationships sour the minute a client suspects he or she is being taken for granted, old friends included. So, always return phone calls promptly.

Personal standards. The longer you are away from the formal world of office and organized work, the easier it will be to slip into personal habits that are potentially destructive. Why dress just to sit all day at the computer? Why solicit new clients when you are so busy? Why be polite to rude clients? Why take good clients to lunch? Why attend creative club functions? Why stop by to chat with old friends? Because if you don't, your sense of personal self-esteem will surely start to slip, and a slip will eventually become a slide. You will gradually lose the positive mental attitude that is at least half of your professionalism, and is wholly essential to your continued success.

Learning to deal with problem clients

This is perhaps the greatest ongoing challenge to your long-term success. It would be great if every client was ideal—knowledgeable, not demanding, fun to work with, a speedy payer. But, being human, most are not. Yet, you must deal with them anyway, and you must learn to do so in a way that leaves both of you satisfied. What follows are some rather common client imperfections, how they usually surface, and how to deal best with each. These tips can help you educate your clients on specific working relationships, and increase your professional stature in the process.

"They waste my time." *Problem:* You make an appointment and arrive on time, but you're kept waiting forty-five minutes in the lobby. Or, after arriving you find that the client called in sick and no one remembered to call you. Or the scheduled one-hour meeting turns into three hours. Or a client discusses changes ad nauseam over the telephone. How can you protect your time without offending the client?

Solutions: A busy, successful individual, one who charges a high rate for his or her time, doesn't waste it. When clients recognize this, your professionalism is enhanced, and you become more efficient as well. Try these techniques to convey just how important your time really is: Seldom wait more than thirty minutes to see anyone. After that, tell a receptionist/secretary you'll have to leave to ensure that you can keep your other commitments, and that you'll call to reschedule. When making the rescheduling call, tactfully make the point about being kept waiting by asking the client to pick a new time that might be less of a problem.

In cases where you've been stood up, call the very next day to reschedule. Say something to the effect of, "Fortunately, yesterday wasn't a big problem after all because my next appointment was very flexible." In other words, lay a little guilt trip on the client. If an appointment was in conjunction with a job you're already working on, you may also want to inform the client that you will have to charge for the aborted meeting.

Whenever you believe there is a possibility a client meeting will run long, explain that you can't stay beyond a certain time because it will conflict with another appointment. Then, at the appointed time, excuse yourself. Whenever a meeting runs more than an hour longer than scheduled, tell the client you'll have to leave because you're running into a scheduling conflict. Whenever a client ties you up for long periods on the telephone, cut the conversation short by saying you'll have to call back later because you need to leave shortly for a meeting.

"They think they own me." *Problem:* You have steady clients who provide lots of work, but who also treat you like an on-call servant. They expect you to drop everything and come in for a meeting on a couple of hours notice. Or they call you in the evening or on the weekend to discuss business. Or everything they do is on an almost impossible deadline. How can you get them to back off without losing them?

Solutions: The more business that is tied up with one client, the more of an issue this becomes. It is unwise in the long-term to have too much of your future tied to the whims and fortunes of any client. To keep from being financially blackmailed, never get more than 25 percent of your income from one source.

To get and keep respect, you should maintain a certain professional distance from every client. Be casual and friendly, but be careful not to get too close, or be too informal. Too much familiarity keeps you from being taken seriously, can trivialize your efforts, and often breeds disrespect.

As for discouraging abuse, there are several things to do. Most important, never answer your business phone after hours or on weekends, never give out your home telephone number, and avoid giving out your cell phone number. If the client already has your home number, have someone else answer evening and weekend calls, or screen these or cell-phone calls. Wait several hours, perhaps all day, before returning a call. Use the excuse that you were out for the day or evening. The next time the problem client calls during regular office hours, say you'll have to call back because you're in the midst of a meeting, or just going out to see another client. In short, get the client used to thinking you've become a very busy (in-demand) individual who can no longer respond at the drop of a hat.

As for short-deadline work and unreasonable requests, use the same psychology. When called with such an assignment, tell the client it will be difficult to respond because you are booked with other work, but you'll manage to squeeze it in somehow. On the next call, say you'll have to check first with another client to see if it's okay to reschedule his or her job. Then call back and say that the other client was very generous and allowed you to reschedule their work. Sometime in the future, you may even want to turn down a small assignment. Say you're booked. Although it is always difficult to refuse work, it probably will be best in the long-term.

Remember, the more successful a client believes you are, the more they will be willing to pay for your work, and the more respect you'll receive.

"They want to pick my brain." *Problem:* Clients expect you to come up with ideas or creative approaches at lunch, sketched out on the back of a napkin, like they see in the movies. Or expect you to come back with multiple computer variations from which to pick and choose. Sometimes they expect ideas before they even give you the assignment. How do you say, I can't do this without appearing uncooperative or uncreative?

Solutions: Say the only ideas that are any good are those that are the result of some serious thought, and that takes time. Contrary to popular belief, good creativity—that which works in the marketplace—does not usually come in a flash of inspiration. Rather, it comes from a process that requires a definition of objectives, followed by information gathering, followed by a lot of analysis and thinking, followed by lots of trial and error. Metaphorically: good ideas aren't like bananas; they don't grow rapidly or in bunches. They're more like a single fruit that comes from a well-sown seed, and a plant nurtured and pruned to perfection. Therefore, doing fast, multiple concepts is an unprofessional approach that you don't practice.

Remember, too, that if you do throw out many quick ideas, or show many concepts, chances are none will be developed thoroughly enough to impress the client. Most clients are very literal in their thinking. The process of providing multiple approaches also can confuse them and make it appear as though you have no strong opinion on what works best. Always keep in mind that the value of any product, creativity included, is usually equated with how much work and effort is perceived by the customer to have gone into it. Top-of-the-head ideas and fast concepts, no matter how good, usually are not viewed as being very valuable.

If the client asks for ideas before you get the assignment, say all that is above, and add that you'll be happy to get started as soon as they give you the okay. If they are looking for ideas as proof of your creativity, indicate that your portfolio is ample evidence of your capability. Finally, when presenting any idea, make sure you enhance it and protect it by going over the process by which you arrived at it, step by step.

"They make too many changes." *Problem:* The client shows your work to everyone, and everyone has an opinion on how to make it better. Your efforts are always bastardized. You have to work overtime to make all the changes and keep to the schedule, and this reduces or eliminates most of your profit. How can you keep the changes down to a manageable number?

Solutions: Insist that any concept be reviewed first by the person who gave you the assignment and at most one or two others. No more. When presenting, go over the input you received and how your concept addresses each and every objective. If appropriate, tell the client how good his or her input was and how it made addressing the creative challenge so much easier, and the result so much better. Get the client to commit on the effectiveness of your effort.

As for further review, remind the client that good creativity is often ruined by too much input. Again, compliment him or her on good direction and indicate that you wouldn't want to see "our" approach vitiated by others not in on all phases of the process. Indicate that with most of your other clients, once the project manager approves a concept, the only additional review is for information only or technical accuracy. If he or she still wants to show the concept to others who may make changes, insist on being there to explain why you did what you did. Also tell the client that only one such meeting was included in your estimate/schedule and that any other ones will probably result in delay and additional charges.

How well do you meet client expectations?

Lest you forget, a client/freelance relationship is a two-way street. Not all the problems are theirs. They have concerns, too. Of all the various characteristics that make up the way a creative assignment is handled, which do clients think are most important, rate most highly? The better you can answer this question, the happier your clients will be, and the more prosperous your freelance activity should become.

Of course, for every client, every job, different factors are important. Further, it's safe to say that every client wants every job done at the lowest possible price, with the highest possible quality. Nonetheless, some things are more critical than others. It takes some freelances a long time to discover that what they've been focusing on may or may not be what their clients are actually concerned about. How relatively important is your distinctive style? Your innovative creativity? Your absolute reliability? Your speed? Your ability to get it right the first time? Your attention to details? Your years of experience? Your chemistry with the client? A mix of these characteristics is what every client feels is important when considering a creative supplier, either freelance or multiperson shop.

Style. That subjective element best described as the distinctive look, feel, or sound of your work. In a portfolio, it is the similarity and recognizability of the samples. Although most creative individuals feel that the stronger their style the better, clients often view style differently. For certain assignments, too strong a style often implies a lack of flexibility some clients find discomforting.

Creativity. Your ability to provide unique, one-of-a-kind solutions to specific problems. In other words, the degree of innovation with which you address a challenge. This, too, is an attribute highly valued by most creative individuals, but not necessarily by all clients. For some straightforward assignments, too strong an emphasis on creativity gets in the way. Stressing creativity too highly to the wrong clients, especially if it appears gratuitous, can result in being passed over for many routine, rent-paying jobs.

Reliability. Your ability to keep commitments, to deliver what is promised, when it is promised. Although most of us understand that reliability is important, few appreciate how much so. Fact is, most clients are concerned more about reliability than creativity. As indicated below, reliability rates higher on average than anything else.

Speed. Your ability to deliver work fast. Although always related to work load, quick turnaround is also a function of how rapidly you conceive and execute ideas. For some deadline-oriented clients and types of work it is very important; other times, it is only a bonus.

Getting it right (GIR). Your ability to grasp quickly what the client wants and provide it, ideally the first time around. As creatives, we often consider multiple refinements of a concept or idea to be the norm; some clients have little or no tolerance for this process.

Attention to detail (ATD). Your enthusiasm and ability when it comes to handling minutiae and following up. Obviously, this is more important for some types of assignments than others, and to some clients more than others. Nonetheless, it's usually a higher client priority than many creatives—those who focus on the concept, not the execution—appreciate.

Experience. Your background or talent in a particular field or type of work. Most creative individuals feel, rightly, that their talent and experiences are transferrable to any challenge, any type of business. Unfortunately, clients often don't feel the same way. Many feel secure only with someone who has previously faced a similar challenge, so they insist on prior experience as a prerequisite.

Chemistry. Your ability to relate to a client on a personal level. In situations requiring close interaction, it can be crucial to success. How smoothly a job proceeds often depends upon how well everyone gets along. Clients are very forgiving of individuals they like, very unforgiving of those they don't.

The table on the next page shows how a broad cross section of typical clients—creative directors, art buyers, webmasters, and advertising/sales managers across the country—ranked the above traits on a scale of 1 to 10 in a *Creative Business* survey. It provides a rating of the relative importance (sensitivity) typical clients ascribe to individual and job characteristics. Put another way, everything on this list is important to every client, every time; the rankings merely show what is more or less important.

Note that this shows only nationwide averages. Your local clients may have somewhat different priorities. It does not account for any personal idiosyncrasies. Also, most clients consider price and quality paramount.

Finally, note what may be a pleasant surprise—the relatively small differences in the total scores. Although differences in individual categories are substantial, overall they come close to averaging out. In short, the grass isn't greener; most of your fellow creatives with different talents have just as difficult a job dealing with clients as you do.

	Style	Creativity	Reliability	Speed	GIT	ATD	Experience	Chemistry	Total
Art Direction	7	9	6	9	9	9	5	6	60
Copy (promotional)	8	9	7	8	6	7	7	8	60
Copy (descriptive)	6	6	8	6	8	9	9	9	61
Copy (technical)	5	4	10	7	6	10	10	6	58
Design (interactive)	4	6	10	9	9	9	6	6	59
Design (print)	7	8	8	7	6	6	6	8	56
Design (ID)	9	9	7	7	6	6	6	7	57
Illust. (general)	10	10	7	5	6	7	9	4	58
Illust. (technical)	7	5	7	6	8	10	9	4	56
Photography	8	7	9	9	10	8	5	5	61

How well can you manage your most precious resource?

Wise freelances, those concerned about long-term success and satisfaction, soon discover that they can never really save time. They can only spend it. So, how effectively do you spend time? Do you plan carefully, treating minutes and hours as the precious resources they are? Even more important, do you spend your time achieving the personal and professional goals most important to you? To answer—and to brush up on the key principles of time management and your long-term success potential—grab a pencil and take this brief test.

Circle 3, 2, 1, or 0, according to the following scoring key, as you answer each question. If you answer always, circle 3; if you answer usually, circle 2; if you answer sometimes, circle 1; and if you answer never or rarely, circle 0.

1) Do you have short- and long-range goals? 3 2 1 0

2) Do you have a business plan, and do you revise it? 3 2 1 0

3) Do you spend a few minutes planning each day? 3 2 1 0

4) Do you list daily tasks by priority and concentrate on the top? 3 2 1 0

5) Do you assign noncreative tasks as high a priority? 3 2 1 0

6) Do you keep an ongoing to do list of undone tasks? 3 2 1 0

7) Do you handle the important tasks when you feel alert? 3 2 1 0

8) Do you group similar tasks together? 3 2 1 0

9) When you get messages or mail, do you prioritize them? 3 2 1 0

10) Can you break large projects down into small chunks? 3 2 1 0

11) Do you isolate yourself when you create? 3 2 1 0

12) Is your office or studio neat and efficiently organized? 3 2 1 0

13) Is your office or studio a pleasant working environment? 3 2 1 0

14) Do you have a system for easily filing/retrieving work? 3 2 1 0

15) Do you have a way of saving or recording thoughts? 3 2 1 0

16) Do you skim-read to obtain key information? 3 2 1 0

17) Do you use waiting/travel time to read? 3 2 1 0

18) Can you make rational decisions quickly? 3 2 1 0

19) Do you have backups if your concepts aren't accepted? 3 2 1 0

20) Do you keep team members informed? 3 2 1 0

21) Are you well organized for brainstorming sessions? 3 2 1 0

22) Do you have a clear agenda for client meetings? 3 2 1 0

23) Do you stop when you feel stress or loss of creativity? 3 2 1 0

24) Do you keep a log that shows how you spend you time? 3 2 1 0

25) Are you always looking for ways to be more efficient? 3 2 1 0

Total points _____

If your score comes out between 65 and 75, you're a fine time manager. If it's between 46 and 64, you need a few modest improvements to become even more productive each day. If it's between 25 and 44, you're on the right track, but need to think a lot more about using your limited time more efficiently. If your score is below 25, you've exhibited an inefficiency that is truly business-threatening—make changes now before it's too late!

Remembering to work smart

The very nature of creative work today means that you are likely to be sitting in one place—before a computer—most of the day, and most of the activities you perform there are both minimal and highly repetitive. These conditions are conducive to painful, sometimes debilitating, physical damage—cumulative stress injuries, sometimes called repetitive motion injuries. They range from the neck pain a designer experiences when sitting down at a computer, to the "frozen" two fingers of a writer's hand, to the sudden inability of an illustrator to hold a pen, brush, or mouse steady. However they show up, they shouldn't be taken lightly. Your present and future income rely on your ability to execute your ideas. Here are some tips on how to avoid cumulative stress injuries:

Work ergonomically. You may spend 75 percent of your day sitting, so your chair should not only have a good seat, but firmly support the back's natural "S" shape. The keyboard and mouse pad you use should allow working with your forearms level and hands tilted down slightly. Grasp a mouse lightly, never tightly. Alternate digits when clicking. Use keyboard commands. Try switching hands occasionally. Looking up at a computer monitor is nearly always bad, looking straight ahead is okay, and looking down slightly is usually best. The bigger the monitor, the more of a problem this can be.

Watch your posture. The longer you sit every day, the more important good posture becomes. Stand and sit straight, shoulders back, chest out, and chin in.

Be wary of the telephone. If you cradle the telephone handset between your shoulder and ear, you are asking for trouble. If you do a lot of telephone talking (e.g., conducting telephone interviews), get a speaker phone.

Alternate tasks. The more variety in your work, the smaller the chance is that one group of muscles will become fatigued. Mix things up. Interrupt computer with noncomputer work as frequently as possible.

Take frequent breaks. Stand up, stretch, shrug your shoulders, and shake your arms for about a minute once every hour.

Exercise regularly. Hard physical exercise, at least twice a week, strengthens vulnerable muscles. It also produces endorphins, the body's natural tranquilizer. Together, stronger muscles and less tension provide a major defense against cumulative stress injuries.

Be alert for symptoms. No matter how studiously you try to avoid cumulative stress injuries, your work puts you at risk. Given the potential for problems, be concerned if you feel muscular discomfort for several days. Pay particular attention to the soreness of hands, wrists, arms, and fingers, and to pains in the shoulders, back, and neck. If discomfort continues, try changing your working positions and patterns. If change doesn't help, see a healthcare professional for diagnosis and treatment. Early intervention usually alleviates most cumulative stress injuries without expensive treatment. Putting it off could easily nip your career in the bud.

Are you really self-employed?

The final criterion for long-term success is making sure that you are considered self-employed by the authorities, as well as yourself. How so? Well, lets look at a hypothetical situation:

You've been offered a several-month assignment by a large advertising agency. It involves going to their offices every day for four hours of work. They agree to pay $60 an hour, much lower than your normal rate, but not bad considering how much steady work is involved. They will classify you as temporary, freelance help, so they won't be deducting income, Social Security, or unemployment taxes from your pay. Since you'll continue to remain self-employed, you'll still be able to deduct any business-related expenses, such as travel between the agency and your regular office. See any problem here?

If not, you may be riding for a big fall, courtesy of the Internal Revenue Service. Chances are high that, if audited, both you and the client company will be accused by the Feds of avoiding taxes and told to pay up, with penalties. Moreover, the chances of getting audited are high. The reason has to do with the IRS interpretation of who is self-employed and who is an employee; and an IRS initiative to pay closer attention to those taxpayers who use Schedule C (Self-employment Income) when filing their taxes.

There are strong reasons why you should want to protect your self-employment status and not be considered an employee. Likewise, there are strong reasons why clients don't want to classify you as an employee:

when you're treated as a self-employed individual, everyone gets a lower tax bill.

As a self-employed individual you can deduct all your business-related expenses (at this writing, employees can deduct nonreimbursed expenses only when they exceed 2 percent of adjusted gross income); you can more easily qualify for business deductions for computers, autos, and home offices; and you have more latitude in tax-favored retirement plans.

Employers like to classify workers as self-employed because doing so allows them to avoid withholding income taxes and paying Social Security and unemployment taxes and expensive fringe benefits.

The easiest solution is not to get in this situation in the first place—don't accept long-term, in-house assignments. Not only might you get an unpleasant tax surprise later, but, more important, in the long-term it's probably bad for business. It is difficult, perhaps impossible, to build a stable creative business without developing a very broad base of clients. You will never get to develop such a client base if you accept long-term assignments. Nonetheless, for some of us the easy solution is unrealistic. At least for now, we have to take what work is available. So here are some tips that will help you pass the IRS's self-employment test.

Elementary considerations. Conduct your affairs under a business name (e.g., Jane Smith & Associates) and have all the normal attributes of a business: letterhead and business cards; a separate, business checking account; a separate, business-listed telephone; and a business website. In addition, the more clients you have, the better. (If you have only one or two clients, there is a strong chance you'll be considered an employee, especially if you work on their premises. The IRS will probably consider it two part-time jobs.) Having a separate, non-home office helps, as does evidence of promotional or marketing effort and expenses. If you, in turn, employ help (including farming out work) that's good, as well.

On-the-job considerations. Always make sure you send an invoice on your letterhead for the work done, weekly if possible. If you get checks without asking, you'll almost certainly be considered an employee. Also, be careful that the company doesn't inadvertently treat you as they would regular staff. For example, you shouldn't be listed in the company phone book, or be eligible for any employee perks, including holidays. It will also be better if you keep irregular hours, and for longer-term assignments, occasionally change working locations and supervisors.

If you are concerned about the IRS later treating you as an employee and socking you for back taxes, discuss any questionable situation with your accountant or ask the IRS for a ruling now to avoid later problems.

Get IRS Form SS-8. It requires you to answer four pages of questions. Note, however, that if you send back the form and the ruling turns out not to be in your favor, you'll be stuck with it.

For more on this subject from the employer's perspective, see "The freelance option" in Chapter 17.

SECTION ONE
HIGHLIGHTS

- **This is a time of self-employment opportunity.** The growth of the communications industry, business outsourcing, and the ability to control your own future makes freelancing an increasingly attractive career option for many creative individuals.

- **Motivation is the foundation for success.** As important as creative talent is, much more important is what motivates you to work for yourself, and whether you have the right personality for it.

- **Freelancing is a business.** As in any other business, location, structure, permits, capital, and credit lines must all be considered. A business that fails to plan, plans to fail.

- **Organization is crucial.** Before making the big step, arrange for an accountant, buy insurance, set up your books, purchase what's necessary, and arrange your work space. Then hit the deck running.

- **Success is seldom an accident.** Discipline, professionalism, marketing, knowing how to deal with clients, keeping options open, and working smart are what separates the freelance winners from the also-rans.

Freelance norms

Start-up capital needed	3 months of present salary
Time needed to establish a secure business	2 years on average
Major short-term problem	Lack of working discipline
Major long-term problem	Lack of social contact
Average annual accounting costs	$1,200 plus annually
Average annual insurance costs	6–10% of yearly gross
Average first-year equipment cost	10% of income
Average annual cost of software upgrades	25% of equipment value

PRICING, COLLECTING & TAXATION

*"The value of money
is that with it we can
tell any man to go to
the devil. It is the sixth
sense which enables us
to enjoy the other five."*

SOMERSET MAUGHAM

How do you go about pricing your services? How comfortable and professional are you in talking about pricing to clients, and preparing job estimates and proposals? How efficiently do you collect the money that's owed you?

If you are unsure about your methods, you're not alone. What to charge, how to prepare job estimates, and how to collect on time are among the biggest concerns among freelances and small creative businesses. For good reason, too. After lack of working discipline and adequate capital, nothing accounts for the failure of more creative businesses than pricing and collecting practices.

The subject of this section is how to make money, how to keep it, how to protect it, and how to grow it.

Of course, money isn't the only reason to be self-employed. But it is certainly the most important reason. There are other ways to obtain creative satisfaction, job variety, and working freedom. Only working for yourself combines all this with the opportunity to make more money.

This book is dedicated to the proposition that by combining talent, motivation, and business sense, an experienced and talented individual can make enough money to enjoy life thoroughly—from $60,000 to well over $120,000 a year—as either a freelance or a principal of a small studio or agency. Moreover, because of tax benefits, money earned this way will actually be worth about 10 percent or more than a salary paid by an employer, depending upon individual circumstances. To put this in the perspective of your peers, as this is written, senior art directors and copywriters in large advertising agencies have (highly taxed) incomes averaging about $100,000 a year. The average salary for a graphic designer of ten years experience is about $55,000. And U.S. Department of Labor statistics record that about 6 percent of American wage earners make over $100,000 per year.

6. Establishing How Much to Charge

Before sitting down to determine how much to charge, you should look at the big picture. Many individuals assume that pricing is the most important factor in business success. Given this orientation, they often tend to underprice to ensure they'll get work. The logic is: By being more competitive and busier, I'll make up with higher volume what I lose through lower rates.

Unfortunately, there are two fatal flaws in this thinking. First, working harder at lower prices often results in creative burnout. You may be financially successful, but for how long and at what price?

Second, a reputation for low-price work attracts smaller, less sophisticated, and more demanding clients, while repelling the larger clients with the good assignments. Jobs are often lost, or an individual or shop not even considered, because of the bargain-basement image low price conveys. And since price is often equated with quality, once any business gains a reputation for low-price (read low-quality) work, it is exceedingly difficult to shake that perception and raise prices.

So, the first rule in pricing is not to overemphasize its importance in obtaining work. Price alone is seldom the determining factor in getting or losing a good job, and the way you price your services is not the most important factor in long-term success.

The right attitude

After considering your qualifications, the next thing any *good* potential new client will consider is the freshness and enthusiasm you exhibit. Only after that will how much you charge be considered. The reason is, good clients—the ones who have large, interesting assignments and who pay on time—realize that the quality of creativity depends mostly on an individual's understanding of a problem and enthusiasm for a challenge.

This is not to say that cost isn't important to good clients; just that cost is only important in the context of value received. Given a choice, any smart client would rather overspend slightly on really good work than underspend on work that isn't effective.

The point is that successful individuals worry more about their perceived qualifications and attitude than about how their work is priced. It is, of course, true that plum assignments can be lost because of what a client considers to be inappropriate pricing, but it is more often true that they are lost because of a perceived lack of experience, ability, or attitude. So when calling upon clients, concentrate on convincing them that you have the experience they're looking for, the discipline to get the work done on time, and fresh enthusiasm for their assignment.

There's another point worth considering at this time: the personal satisfaction one gets out of being self-employed is closely linked to one's attitude about money. This requires a tacit recognition that what you do for clients doesn't cost them money; it makes them money. Moreover, the higher the client's return on an investment in your talent, skills, and experience, the more you are worth to them. Thus, well-adjusted creatives never feel guilty or apologize for what they charge because they know that clients get back many times their fees in increased business opportunities.

Finally, recognize that the money you make is more than just a purchasing medium. It also functions as a yardstick of accomplishment. Even if you are both wealthy and pure, and few of us are either, it still provides the best possible measurement of progress—equally appropriate for assessing how we are doing relative to others, and to our own standards and aspirations.

Earnings mathematics

Lets start with a hypothetical question and a goal. What would it take for you to make $100,000 a year (gross income) working for yourself? Now, you don't have to be a mathematician to figure out that if you work fifty weeks a year and bill $2,000 a week you will make $100,000. Breaking this down, $2,000 a week is $400 per day, or $50 per hour for eight hours. (This math is most appropriate for freelances. If you have employees, see "Salary and profitability norms" in Chapter 19.)

You may see a problem here, however. Realistically you can't work every hour of every day, fifty weeks a year. In fact, the actual time you will probably be working on income-producing (billable) work is only 50 to 75 percent. Why this range? Because if, on average, you work less than 50 percent of the time, you probably don't have the continuity of workflow a service business needs to be viable, or a creative person needs to be stimulated. If you're in this position, examine your time accounting and billing procedures, or start to promote your services more heavily. (See Section Three for promotional assistance.) Either way, you are on your way out of business unless you take action.

Why is the upper range of billable time about 75 percent? Because if you consider the many nonbillable (overhead) tasks of running a small creative business, it is unrealistic to bill more than than this on average. A small service business that does not devote 25 percent or so of each week to such activities as planning, marketing, and record keeping will implode from its own success sooner or later. When billable hours are more than 75 percent for more than six months and there is no sign of letup, it is time to hire staff, farm out assignments, raise prices to lower demand, or turn work down.

Given, then, the reality of working an average of 50 to 75 percent on income-producing work, lets run some numbers. If, for example, you are busy, on average, 50 percent of the time with billable activity, it will be necessary for you to charge $100 per hour to gross $100,000 annually. On the other hand, if you average 75 percent busy, it is only necessary to charge $75 per hour. If you charge $50 per hour and are only 50 percent busy, you can expect to gross $50,000.

We live in a time when auto mechanics, plumbers, and electricians charge $50 to $80 per hour. More relevant, most other midlevel professionals, accountants, lawyers, etc., charge $125 to $250. And larger companies in the business of providing creative services, ad agencies, design firms, and so forth, charge in the range of $150 to over $250 for creative time.

Any talented designer, illustrator, or copywriter should feel comfortable charging between $75 and $125 per hour, depending on whether he or she works independently or runs a studio. The more experienced you are, the larger your firm, the larger the metropolitan market, and the larger your clients, the higher your hourly fees should probably be.

The proper range

Pricing norms. As discussed above, larger companies in the business of providing creative services, agencies, major design firms, and such, charge in the range of $150 to over $250 per hour for creative time. If you are a freelance or small shop, your pricing should probably be in the range of 75 percent of what large shops and agencies in your market charge for similar talent and experience. Why less? Because purchasing psychology works against you. Clients expect to pay less when dealing with freelances and small shops because of the perception that individuals and smaller organizations possess less in the way of skills, talent, stability, and business acumen. This means the range for most freelances and small shops is between $90 and $150 per hour.

Minimum wages. As reported in numerous *Creative Business* surveys, the consensus of individuals working as full-time freelances or running small creative businesses is that given the overhead expenses and variability of workload, the *minimum* hourly rate charged should be $90. Successful and prosperous individuals and firms often charge more than twice as much.

Gross income. Government statistics show that a combination of living costs and the need to fund long-term security requires an income of about $60,000 a year for a single individual to live in comfort in most metropolitan areas of the United States. Those living in a rural area can often get by on less, but they will probably have to work harder because creative fees are lower and assignments fewer.

Thus, if the combination of what you charge, multiplied by the average hours worked, does not make $60,000 a year possible after business expenses are deducted, your chances of living comfortably, not suffering from creative burnout, continuing in business for many years, and putting away enough for future security are slim.

The recommended method: costs + profits

The best way to establish an hourly fee is to first calculate actual business costs (labor + overhead) and make it the basis for determining the minimum hourly rate that must be charged if a business is to be viable. Then, knowing this figure, what is actually billed per hour should be the minimum, plus an additional profit margin, plus (or minus) any modifications required by the competitive environment. Although this method is seldom appropriate to someone just starting in business, it is the only way to provide a good fix on how profitable (or not) a business actually is. This process is crucial for creative firms with employees.

First calculate labor costs. Start by adding up all salaries, including noncreative staff. Then, add to this figure all other costs associated with them—unemployment taxes, FICA taxes, payroll processing, health insurance, 401(k) sponsorship, etc. For easy illustration purposes, let's say you have two employees, one whom you pay $45,000, one $55,000. You pay yourself a salary of $55,000. Benefit and other costs add up to about 30 percent of payroll. Thus, your annual labor costs are $202,000. (Salaries of $45 + $55 + $55 = $155 + $47 benefits (30 percent of $155) = $202.)

Take the above number and divide it by the total number of employee labor hours in a year. If you wish to be precise, add up actual working hours. Or, for simplicity, use 1,920 hours for each employee, which assumes 48 working weeks, with 4 nonworking weeks for vacations, holidays, and sick time. (48 weeks x 5 days x 8 hours = 1,920 hours.) In our example 1,920 hours per employee times 3 employees equals 5,760 available hours. However, even if your firm is constantly busy, at least 25 percent of working hours will be nonbillable. If business is slow, the average can easily grow to 50 percent or more. For our purposes, we'll assume 40 percent of working hours are nonbillable (60 percent billable), reducing your firm's average yearly billable hours to 3,456 (5,760 x .60). Divide your total labor expenses by the total average billable hours to arrive at your hourly labor expenses. In our example, $202,000 ÷ 3,456 = $60 per hour.

Now, calculate overhead costs. They are all the nonlabor expenses of running a business that aren't directly billable to clients. Include most items for which you have written company checks, as well as daily miscellaneous expenses. Don't include pass-along charges such as delivery services, printing, or media charges that are purchased for resale. Examples of overhead costs are: rent, equipment leasing fees or amortized purchase prices, outside labor, business taxes, utilities, automobile ownership and use, travel and entertainment, office supplies, service fees, postage, telephone, and marketing expenditures. We'll assume a conservative yearly figure of $100,000 for a three-person firm. Dividing this figure by the actual number of hours worked (5,760) produces an hourly overhead cost of $17.

Operating cost = labor + overhead. Next, add your hourly overhead cost to your hourly labor cost to arrive at total hourly operating cost. In our example, the operating cost of $17 is added to the labor cost of $60 per hour. The resulting figure, $77, is approximately what our hypothetical firm must charge each hour to simply cover its expenses. In looking at this example, note that the $77 figure does not accommodate an attractive salary for the owner. Nor does it provide any provision for profit or capital growth. More significantly, the numbers used are conservative, and it relies on maintaining a billable efficiency of 60 percent. It would, in other words, be a challenge for most creative firms to attain.

Hourly rate should be operating cost + profit factor. Once you have a fix on what you must charge every hour (your operating cost), you can now go to the final step of determining how much you should charge. This figure (your hourly rate) should be a combination of your operating cost, plus an additional factor for profit or growth capital. Adding in an amount for profit or growth will compensate for many business expenses which otherwise might be overlooked. It will also allow you to build a reserve fund against times of slow business or for capital needs (e. g., replacing computers). It can build equity in the firm so that you have something of value to sell-off someday, and it will help determine just how successful your company is. Profitability, what remains after reasonable expenses, is the yardstick by which all outsiders (e.g., bankers) will judge the soundness of your company.

Therefore, now add 20 to 30 percent as a profit or growth factor to the operating cost above. A mid-range 25 percent of $77 is $19, which establishes an hourly rate of $98 per hour, the fee which, in this example, should be charged to cover costs and allow for business profitability and growth. Not coincidentally, this is slightly higher than the amount previously referred to as the minimum a viable creative firm should charge. It should also be apparent through this example why firms with higher costs—expensive facilities, competitive salaries, up-to-date software and hardware, and lower billable efficiency—must charge even more.

Job quotes versus job estimates

A job price can be submitted to a client as a quotation (price will not change) or as an estimate (what the name implies).

Generally, clients prefer job quotes because they provide firm figures around which budgets can be developed. They also provide protection against billing surprises. Job quotations are similar to the way most other products and services are bought and sold; for many organizations, this is also a more familiar way of working. For us, an up-front job quotation also ensures there will be no after-the-fact discussion about a bill's appropriateness when it lands on the client's desk. Further, it provides an opportunity to price what the market will bear when there is little competition or price sensitivity. It allows you to make an occasional killing on those assignments where working fast and efficiently is possible.

Generally, the more routine the project is, the easier and safer it is to provide a job quotation. Design and illustration lend themselves more to it than does writing or interactive development. (Art time, even the most conceptual, varies less from job to job than does writing or interactive development, which tend to be open-ended.)

Despite these attractions, it is probably unwise to provide job quotations, except for routine assignments for well-known clients. It is particularly risky for those who are relatively inexperienced or are just starting out in business. The reason is simply that most creative assignments change from the time they are first priced until the time they are finally delivered. In such situations, estimates provide a degree of flexibility and insurance that is lacking in job quotations.

Whenever possible, it is better to provide clients with a job estimate— a close approximation, but not necessarily an exact price. Make the estimate as tight as possible given the information supplied. Inform the client that if conditions change, the final price will change either up (higher), or down (lower). Once the job is under way, inform the client periodically of progress against the estimate. (Example: "I'm about halfway through the job and have used approximately half of the estimated time, so I should be able to make the estimate okay.") Unless you inform the client otherwise, you should deliver the job at the estimated price.

By keeping the client informed, you allow ample opportunity to make any budget adjustments that may be needed later, or ample time to change the job specifications if necessary to meet a budget. In short, you eliminate the end-of-job surprises that are the concerns most clients have with estimates versus job quotations. The procedure for preparing and presenting estimates is covered in Chapters 7 and 8.

Practices to (usually) avoid

Any pricing method that works consistently well for you is, by definition, good. All three of the methods presented below have their proponents. Nonetheless, the experience of most individuals is that problems usually outweigh benefits. Consider each of the below with considerable caution.

Different rates depending on busyness. Considered logically, this seems to make sense: when you're busy you should charge higher rates; when not, you lower them to get work. After all, any work is better than no work. Right? Maybe not. When a business becomes known for cutting prices, it attracts undesirable clients, and once a client has gotten services on the cheap, it will be hard for them to accept normal prices later. It is normal for any firm to adjust prices from project to project based on internal and external conditions, but adjustments should be transparent. When clients believe that a creative firm cuts prices to stay busy, it encourages pricing blackmail.

Different rates for different clients. It is bad business to discriminate either for or against any type of organization or company. Treating every client the same is both fairer and easier. Charging lesser fees to favorite clients, small firms, start-up companies, or "poor" organizations can only be justified in those rare cases where a potentially profitable relationship wouldn't be established otherwise. Be particularly wary of providing a price break now in the hopes of getting more business in the future. Once a pricing norm has been established, it is tough to break. Moreover, small companies seldom stay with their original suppliers once they get larger.

Giving a break to not-for-profits. The impulse to give something back to organizations we benefit from is admirable. But don't be naive. Most other suppliers do not provide discounts to not-for-profit organizations. (Example: local utilities and those providing routine services and supplies.) Like them, your firm's overhead and labor costs are the same regardless of whom you work for, so any discount comes directly out of your pocket. In actuality, a price reduction for a not-for-profit is a charitable donation. But unlike charitable cash donations, the value of a pricing discount is not tax deductible. Further, the organization may not be a charity you would otherwise support. Charitable activities and business activities should be kept separate.

Work for hire

Under the U. S. Copyright Act, in most cases an artist or author owns the copyright to any work he or she creates. That is, he or she owns the exclusive right to reproduce it. The major exception is work produced under what is called work for hire. In these cases, reproduction rights ownership (copyright) belongs to the party paying for the work.

There are only two clearly defined work-for-hire situations: 1) where the creator is an employee of the party receiving the work; and 2) where the creator signs a work-for-hire agreement indicating willingness to waive copyright ownership. All other situations are subject to interpretation and possible confusion.

While this definition of copyright ownership and work-for-hire exceptions largely accomplishes what Congress intended—to protect artists from exploitation and artistic works from unauthorized reproduction—it also raises some questions, particularly as regards commercial creativity. For example, does it also mean that a logo designed for a client is actually owned by the designer, to be reproduced only with his or her permission? What about brochure copy? Is it actually owned by the writer? Can only the originator make changes to a client's website?

Until over two decades ago courts had ruled that anyone who controlled the input of an artistic work (as is the case with most commercial creativity) was, in effect, acting as an employer. Thus, once payment had passed, so had ownership, inasmuch as the work created fell under the work-for-hire employee definition. A 1989 Supreme Court decision (CCNV v. Reid) altered this. It applied a new, tougher standard of what constitutes an employment (work-for-hire) relationship. This standard relies on some thirteen separate tests to determine whether an employee relationship does exist. No one test is conclusive; it is the courts' interpretation of all the tests that's determinative.

This tougher standard didn't affect copyright transfer on most clearly commercial, multifaceted projects (logos, brochures, websites, copy etc.). However, it had a great effect on the ownership of more purely artistic works such as illustrations, cartoons, poetry, and surface designs. For this type of art, the firm or individual commissioning it could no longer take for granted a work-for-hire ruling and the ownership rights that came with it. Everyone commissioning art—including designers, ad agencies, and PR firms, as well as client companies—suddenly had more cause to be concerned about copyright ownership.

The post-1989 work-for-hire standard has, indeed, kept some fine artists from being exploited. But for most commercial artists it is, at best, a mixed bag. The reason is that many art buyers have, in light of the Supreme Court's decision, been advised by lawyers to play it safe—not to commission any artwork without first having the creator sign a work-for-hire agreement. This eliminates any possibility of using the artwork without proper authorization. It also eliminates any need for future artist negotiations, a not insignificant factor given the speed and flexibility with which businesses like to operate today.

As would be expected, the larger the art-buyer's company, the more that's at stake, the more rigidly this no agreement, no assignment rule has been enforced. Thus, many artists who once negotiated usage rights assignment-by-assignment now face a new, unpleasant business reality: be willing to sign away all future rights up front, or be prepared to forgo many assignments.

It is ironic that the Supreme Court's attempt to strengthen artists' rights has in many instances had a profoundly negative impact on artists' pocketbooks. The Court's decision is also having another effect. By encouraging those commissioning commercial art to accept nothing less than full ownership (through requiring a work-for-hire agreement), a new norm has also been established. Once an art buyer has successfully used work-for-hire agreements, it is unlikely that he or she will want to revert back to the old negotiation-of-usage process. By simplifying everything, work-for-hire agreements have made art purchasing more or less like other purchasing. Finally, when commissioning artwork for use in a third-party piece (e.g., a client brochure), work-for-hire agreements avoid any concern about unauthorized client use in the future. Eliminated is any need to explain why artwork can't later be used for other purposes without additional negotiation and compensation.

Whether you agree with, oppose, or are neutral about work-for-hire agreements, they have become a factor in today's creative services business.

Price by value?

Most creative firms, freelance and multiperson, price their work based on how many labor hours will be involved, modified by market conditions. But why not price it based on the actual value of the work to the client? There are several reasons why it is not normally possible. (The exception is more purely artistic work, such as illustration and photography, as covered in "Use-based pricing" on page 110.)

There must be a mutual agreement on measuring value. Unfortunately, every method for evaluating a creative effort is ambiguous. It is next to impossible to base value on creativity or impact alone because of its subjective nature. Tracking sales is only a valid measure when all the influences beyond your control—pricing, distribution, sales force activity, etc.—are neutralized. Evaluating readership scores or web hits requires a base line for comparison and is affected by numerous external factors, such as media environment, placement, and website promotion. In short, there is no certain, quantifiable way to determine and

measure the value of a creative effort, and what means do exist require sophisticated tools and techniques beyond the reach of all but the largest firms and clients.

There must be a fair procedure for compensation. Even when value is agreed upon, there are still issues of regular monitoring and payment. Only in the publishing and entertainment industries do clear precedents for royalty payments based on sales exist. (Publishers' royalties vary widely, but average 10 percent of the list price of the item.) Moreover, authors are dependent on their publisher's honesty, since verifying sales and royalty accounting is time-consuming and costly. For a client this pricing approach involves unfamiliar monitoring and payment systems; for a supplier it poses legitimate concerns about dependability and trust.

It must be reciprocal. Clients agreeing to pay a premium for very effective work would probably also want a refund for work that turned out to be ineffective. Would you really prefer to work under these conditions, especially when there are so many variables? There is a chance it would produce more income, but there is an equally strong chance it would produce less.

The bottom line. Occasionally a creative effort will create far more impact than a client pays for. Occasionally it will bomb and produce far less impact than the client pays for. But fairly-priced creative efforts do what they are supposed to—produce a good value for the client's money at a good profit for the creative firm.

Commission pricing

Developing and placing ads is often partly or wholly covered by media commissions. The traditional media commission is 15 percent. For example—and assuming a previous arrangement with the publication for an agency discount—if your firm prepares and places an ad whose space cost is $2,000 (rate card), it should be billed $1,700 by the publication. In turn, your firm bills the client for $2,000, taking a $300 or 15 percent commission. (Note: The $300 commission in this case is 15 percent when figured as a mark down, but is 17.65 percent when figured as a mark up.) An agency commission typically covers only account service time. The agency bills the client on an hourly basis for creative, production, and ancillary services, as well as all expenses. (With large-budget accounts some creativity is often covered, and with small-budget accounts some service time is often not covered.)

Use-based pricing

Should the use of creative work affect what is charged for it? If so, how much? These questions have perplexed creative individuals for well over a century. Changes and growth in the communications industry have further complicated the situation with both practical and legal issues.

For most graphic design and copywriting assignments. Clients expect to pay the creator and own the work. Period. Most, especially those with concerns about reacting quickly to market conditions and maintaining competitive uniqueness, would look askance at anyone desiring a use-based fee.

For many illustrations and literary works. Selling one-time rights, pricing according to exposure, and royalty fee arrangements are common. Today's accepted practice is to arrive at a base price (usually the time involved in creating, multiplied by the hourly rate, plus expenses) and consider it as normal for one-time rights, and/or local exposure in major media or national exposure in minor media. After that, everything is negotiable, with the upper limit normally being half again the base price (50 percent more). For small jobs or exceptional circumstances, the original price is sometimes doubled (100 percent more).

Royalty fees. Royalties are an exception to the above; everything— initial payment and royalty fee—is negotiable. When negotiating a royalty fee arrangement, try to get as much money up front (the initial payment, or advance) as possible. Also, make sure that the royalty fee is figured on gross receipts (total income) not on net receipts (income after expenses). Never enter into a royalty arrangement with a firm that does not have strong reputation for honesty. It is common for an advance payment of several thousand dollars to be offered, along with royalties of 10 to 15 percent of gross receipts, paid quarterly.

Exposure fees. Such arrangements—a base price plus an additional charge based on exposure—is a common practice for certain assignments with high market impact. The same considerations as with royalty fee arrangements (see above) apply.

The trend. The competitive pressures of dealing in a fast-paced, often worldwide market mean that each year fewer and fewer clients are willing to negotiate usage fees for creative work. Doing so is time-consuming and leaves them potentially vulnerable.

Should you have a minimum fee?

Sooner or later, almost every viable business comes to an inescapable conclusion: at some level the cost of doing business can be greater than the income it generates. Should your business be any different? Probably not, especially if it is small now and you want it to grow and prosper in the future. This will require a certain volume of activity, a certain level of operating efficiency.

What's appropriate? A per-job minimum of one day's billable work (eight hours) or its equivalent is recommended for both freelances and multiperson shops. As your firm prospers, the per-job minimum probably should go up (two days work, three days work, four days work, etc.), although there's no formula for doing so. Likewise, there's no upper limit. The more talented and prosperous you are, the more latitude you have.

There are, of course, common-sense exceptions to minimum fees, especially for good clients. When making an exception, however, try (tactfully) to ensure that it's recognized as such. For example, say something like: "We don't usually accept jobs this small, but in this particular case we'd be happy to make an exception. Writing the invitation to your company picnic will be an interesting and enjoyable change of pace."

It is also a good idea to publish your minimum per-job charge in any information you send out to prospective clients. ("Our minimum project charge, based on one billable day of our time, is $000.") Doing so will help filter out underbudgeted window shoppers. In addition, it will enhance your professionalism and the value of your time among those clients who can afford you.

Add an administrative expense to estimates? To coin a phrase, small jobs mean small profits, especially in a service business. This is because it often takes as much time to sell the client on a small job as a large one. Client contact time—getting input, showing concepts, and making changes—also takes proportionally more time for small than large jobs. Administrative tasks—time keeping, bookkeeping, and invoicing—take about as long, regardless of job size.

To compensate somewhat when there is a lack of strong price pressure, it is advisable to add an additional 5 to 10 percent to a job estimate as an administrative expense. On the other hand, when there is strong price pressure and any work would be welcome, it can simply be omitted. (See the Estimating Worksheet in Appendix 3.)

What about jobs in progress? A general rule is in order here as well: no in-progress job should be billed for less than one hour of work.

In some cases, this will mean saving up client changes and AAs until there is more than an hour's worth. In other cases, it will mean billing for one hour, even though the changes take only ten minutes to accomplish. Whichever the case, it is a necessary discipline because of the time-wasting inefficiencies that always accompany switching from one job to another—finding materials, opening files, getting in the right mind set, and closing and saving files.

Here, too, of course, there are common-sense exceptions: tight-deadline work can't be saved up, and good clients should never be kept waiting. In the latter case, computer programs notwithstanding, it may not even be cost-effective to record small blocks of time. Especially with large jobs, it may be better to ensure that the estimate is loose enough to accommodate a few uncounted minutes here and there.

As for work of more than an hour's duration, production work should probably be billed in increments of 15 minutes (a quarter hour). For creative (conceptual) work, most multiperson shops bill in hourly chunks; many freelances and shop principals bill for creative work in minimum chunks of four hours (half day). Whatever the timekeeping basis, the minimum-charge discipline is important whether it will actually affect the bill the client pays, or will only be used to compare estimated costs to actual costs.

Finally, recognize that minimum charges are only as effective as your and your employees' ability to keep and submit accurate time sheets. Although computer time-tracking programs have provided great assistance in this area, failure to keep track of job time is still a major problem. (For more on this subject, see "The importance of time tracking" in Chapter 19.)

7. Coming Up with a Job Price

As with any service business, the first step in pricing creative services consists of knowing your true hourly costs and being comfortable with what you must charge to maintain profitability. This was covered in the preceding chapter.

The second step is to know how to estimate how much time a specific assignment will take. That's the subject covered here.

Dodging the ten pitfalls of preparing estimates

No matter how long we do it, most of us never become totally comfortable with the estimating process. Guessing, scheduling, and number crunching aren't very exciting. In addition, accumulating experience takes years because every new job has dozens of variables. Then there's the high-stakes pressure: do it wrong and at best you'll end up losing the job; at worst you'll end up losing your shirt!

So about the most positive thing one can say about estimating is that it's a necessary evil. It may never be enjoyable, but it does have to be done right. Unfortunately, as much as everyone would like a magic formula, there isn't one. Learning to estimate accurately takes a large dose of trial-and-error experience. There are few shortcuts, and only practice makes it (somewhat) perfect. It is, however, possible to shorten the learning curve. Listed below are the ten mistakes most newcomers (and many experienced hands) make. A worksheet is also provided in Appendix 3 to help ensure that all potential time and expense costs of an assignment are counted.

Pitfall #1: Too much guesswork. How deep is the ocean? How blue is the sky? How long is forever? These questions are about as difficult to answer as the one often asked by clients: how much will my (brochure/annual report/ad/speech/website) cost? In all cases, the answer is the same: it all depends. Specifically, in our case, it depends on the problems or opportunities to be addressed, the timing for doing so, the medium to be used and its specifications, and the client's desires, taste, style, sophistication, and budget.

Without knowing all this, in detail, it is impossible to produce a valid estimate. Although this may seem elementary, preparing estimates on insufficient information remains the biggest single estimating problem. It stems primarily from either of two sources: not considering everything, or not admitting the impossible.

Not considering everything. The information needed for every assignment is, of course, different. Nonetheless, use of a basic checklist such as the *Creative Business* Estimating Worksheet (see Appendix 3) can help reduce the odds of missing the familiar and the obvious. Equally important, such a form will improve the consistency of estimating. Use it in conjunction with a form like the *Creative Business* Assignment Questionnaire (also see Appendix 3), and keep both as part of the permanent job record.

Not admitting the impossible. What about situations that simply can't be well enough defined for an estimate? First, have the courage to say: "As much as I'd like to, I just can't give you an answer without more information. All I can tell you is my experience is that such projects normally run anywhere from $0,000 to $0,000." (Provide a 50 to 100 percent range.) Always keep in mind that it is usually better to lose an assignment than to get trapped into a price without an up-front agreement on its scope.

Now offer the client an alternative. The least risky one for you (and the one least acceptable to many clients) is to quote your hourly or daily fee and say that you'll be happy to work on the project at that rate until it can be better defined. At that later time you will be able to prepare an estimate of costs for the balance of the project. Another alternative, one that's more time-consuming but easier for many clients to accept, is to prepare one or more "rough" estimates based on certain assumptions, as described next. (For more, see "How to estimate the not-definable" later in this chapter.)

Pitfall #2: Fear of making some assumptions. Because most clients are not communications professionals, they often don't know or can't articulate what they need. They look to us for help in defining it. When you sense this is the case, it may be wise to prepare something they can react to, either positively or negatively.

First get a feeling for their budget. ("Is the $0,000 to $0,000 range I indicated what you anticipated?") Then spend a few (no more) hours coming up with up to three hypothetical approaches to the problem as

best you understand it. Ideally, an economical (good), moderate (better), and quality (best) solution. Find previously produced examples of each type of approach, or do some very rough pencil sketches, so the client can visualize what you have in mind. Prepare a single-page "ballpark" estimate for each example. Then explain the positioning/cost/quality trade-offs of each approach to the client.

Note that this should probably not include preparing concepts (new ideas). This additional step crosses the line into spec work, which is not only considerably more risky, but usually diminishes rather than enhances your professional image.

Pitfall #3: Confusing quotes with estimates. A quote is a fixed price based on fixed conditions; an estimate is an approximate price, based on flexible conditions. This is not just legal hairsplitting. Clients asking for a quote may be expecting just that—a price that's locked in up front. There are certain situations where providing quotes may be appropriate, such as routine and highly predictable assignments, but by and large, the strong likelihood of changes occurring between cost estimating and final delivery make it better not to provide them. Quotes should be limited, in most cases, to individuals who are gamblers willing to take the risk of winning big or losing big. Moreover, unless you are actually providing a "quote," avoid using the word. Most clients will be satisfied with an estimate (the right word to use) presented either as a proposal or letter of agreement, especially if they're assured that the price will not change unless they are notified first that job conditions have changed. (For more, see "Job quotes versus job estimates" in Chapter 6.)

Pitfall #4: Not breaking it down. The bigger a project, the harder it is to estimate—unless you think of it as several interconnected tasks.

Even with small projects (a "slim Jim" brochure), the more discrete steps you can identify, the easier it is to figure how much time each will take, and the less likely you are to overlook any steps.

Although every project differs, most assignments can be broken into at least the following tasks: gathering input (initial client meetings), evaluating input (reading, digesting, and thinking), conceptualizing (working out ideas), computer time (writing, sketching, or designing), approval (client reviews), changes (client alterations), service bureau involvement (time and charges), production (press checks, or "going live"), and administrative time (traveling, billing, etc.). Each of these tasks is assigned a time value, which is multiplied by an hourly rate. Adding the results produces the estimated price. (When estimating, use only whole hours, not fractions.) While it is probably better not to provide the client with this level of detail, compiling it is necessary. It is the only way to arrive at a price that covers all the time the job will probably take.

Pitfall #5: No padding, no checkpoint. No matter how long you've been doing them, and how finely you break down all the tasks, assignments nearly always take more time then anticipated. If you're new to estimating, they end up taking a lot more time. One reason is the optimism most of us have about our own (and our clients') efficiency. Another is our desire to hold prices down to be more competitive. Whatever the cause, be aware of this universal tendency.

One cure for underestimating is to add a little padding to discount the "optimism factor." If you're inexperienced, increase estimated time by up to 20 percent; even if experienced, increase it by at least 10 percent. Granted, this may affect your competitiveness, but don't forget that it's not smart to prepare a "competitive" price estimate if you end up making little or no money on the job.

Another underestimating cure is building in one or more checkpoints for fine-tuning the estimate as the job progresses. The most logical place is after the concepts/first draft/rough sketch are approved. If you inform the client at this time that you'll be able to beat the estimate, you'll look like a hero. Even if you must inform him or her that changes have made the estimate no longer valid, it is still better to face the situation sooner rather than later. The client's better understanding will allow a more rational discussion of the situation.

Pitfall #6: Sloppy or inaccurate time-keeping. Even under ideal circumstances, estimating job time is largely a trial-and-error, learn-from-past-mistakes process. Thus, the most accurate estimates usually come from individuals and shops with the best reporting procedures and most complete time sheets to draw upon.

Every hour spent on every job should be logged and all records archived. Even if you occasionally decide not to charge a client for all of your time (e.g., the extra effort to create a "portfolio" piece, or the extra hours spent working out a computer glitch), it is still important to have complete time records. The accuracy of future estimates depends on the accuracy of records compiled today.

Pitfall #7: Sloppy or inaccurate expense-accounting. Estimating job-related miscellaneous expenses is not as problematic as time estimating, but experience and accurate records are still very beneficial. Anticipated expenses should be included in estimates as a separate item. Except for unusually significant ones, it is probably not appropriate to break them down at this time, although it may be preferable to do so when invoicing. (For example: "We estimate miscellaneous expenses—delivery charges, reference materials, etc.—will be approximately $000.") Additional services such as writing or design help, service bureau charges, photography and illustration, and printing or postproduction should also be treated as separate items in the estimate. When doing so, be sure to include (but not necessarily identify) your markup. (For guidelines, see "What to charge for" later in this chapter.) Another option is to have invoices for major outside services and expenses billed directly to the client. This eliminates the risk of carrying large invoices, but also eliminates some profit. If done, the projected cost should be included in the estimate but clearly labeled as a direct-bill item.

Pitfall #8: Too many rates. It used to be that every firm, and most freelances, had several different billing rates, depending on the task performed. No more. The world has changed.

For freelancers and small firms. As a rule of thumb, it is usually best to estimate (and bill for) all time—meetings, consultation, creative, and production—at the same rate. A single billing rate regardless of the task performed makes time-accounting and bookkeeping much easier. Equally important, it is more consistent with professionalism. The actual value of your time (the labor cost component of the hourly rate) doesn't change based on the function you perform, so why should its price?

In this electronic age whatever distinctions used to exist between "creative" and "production" work have almost disappeared anyway. And finally, high capital equipment and operating costs (computers, software, training time, etc.) are making overhead an increasingly large component of the hourly rate. Overhead remains a constant, regardless of the function, or the person performing it.

There is, however, one possible exception. In some states creative time is not sales-taxable, while production time, which is often defined as involving the creation of tangible materials—primarily disks, files, or artwork—is. In these situations it may be better to define and break out production time and bill for it at a lower rate. This may decrease the portion of the job upon which you are required to collect sales tax. (Caution: Every state, and some localities, have different rules. Check with your accountant to determine the safest procedure to follow.)

For larger firms. Because larger firms have different levels (costs) of talent, it usually makes sense to have different billing rates. This allows the shop to compete profitably on several different assignment levels. Demanding, high-budget jobs can be assigned to senior talent (higher rate); less demanding, low-budget jobs can be assigned to lesser talent (lower rate).

The trend today is to standardize around three rates: one for principals and senior creative staff (high); one for midlevel creative staff (medium); one for junior creative and administrative staff (low). When setting different hourly rates, it is important that they be assigned to individuals based on their talent and salaries, not to specific functions. Further, when estimating (and also when project-managing) special care must be taken to ensure that the right task is assigned to the right individual. To ensure profitability, an employee's billing rate usually has to be at least three times his or her salary.

Pitfall #9: Different rules for different clients. Even though most clients are only interested in the bottom-line cost of a project, it's usually better to be open with them about how an estimated price is arrived at. ("This estimate is based on approximately hours of work at $000 per hour.")

It is also usually best to estimate all jobs on the same hourly-rate(s) multiplied-by-anticipated-time basis, regardless of how busy you are or who the client is. This keeps the estimating process relatively simple. It also makes the estimate easier to defend, eliminates any potentially embarrassing inconsistencies from job to job, year to year, and client to client, and avoids any impression that you may be charging "whatever the traffic will bear." If the job actually turns out to be different from the one you estimated—a typical situation—estimating consistency makes it easier for you to come up with a new estimate, and easier for the client to accept it.

If it is necessary to lower costs to be more competitive, do so by reducing the estimated hours the job will take, *not* your hourly fee(s).

Pitfall #10: Gilding the lily. Finally, as much as we'd all like to do "perfect" work for our clients, we should recognize that it's an impossible objective to achieve. The closer we get to perfection, the more time and expense is involved in attempting to achieve it, and the more elusive it becomes. To estimate a job based on "perfection" is to set a trap that will snare us every single time.

As an example, let's say that giving a client a creative solution that's 90 percent of "perfection" (your definition) will take ninety hours. To go from 90 to 95 percent won't take a proportional five more hours; it will probably take ten. And to go from 95 to 97 percent of perfection will probably take an additional twenty hours! And so forth.

Does this mean that you shouldn't give your clients your very best efforts? Not at all! It simply recognizes that at some point the quest for perfection will outpace either the client's budget or your profit on the job. In other words, at some point extra effort has no meaningful benefit other than your personal and possibly expensive sense of satisfaction. So prepare your estimates based on the best possible solution in keeping with a reasonable creative effort and the client's budget and sophistication. If you do this every time, profit and satisfaction will surely follow.

How to estimate the non-definable

A client calls, asking for a proposal on a complex and exciting new project. You want the assignment, but it turns out that the full extent of it can't be determined without actually doing some homework and using more than a little creativity. If you decide to do some work before estimating—that is, to spend time thinking and developing concepts around which to estimate—you may end up working for free, not to mention giving away good ideas. If you opt not to do this—that is, to prepare the proposal around incomplete information and undeveloped ideas—you risk estimating high and losing the assignment, or estimating low and losing money if you do get it. How do you address this? There are no sure-fire answers, and every situation is different, but here are some approaches that might prove helpful:

How much is the job worth to you? Set some time parameters. As a guide: most normal estimating and proposal writing should "cost" (the value of your figuring and writing time only, not sales-call time) between 1 and 2 percent of the job estimate (your gross income). Depending upon circumstances (how bad business is and how much you'd like the assignment), most creative individuals and firms consider it acceptable to expand this up to 8 percent of an anticipated estimate, but seldom more.

At 10 percent and beyond you are essentially working on speculation, an unhealthy business practice.

Charge for the proposal. If you require more time than is normal to put together a good proposal, inform the client. Say that you would like to provide the most detailed and accurate proposal possible, and that the only way to do so in this specific and unusual situation is to devote additional time (state approximately how many hours) to research and conceptual development activity. Then, without apology, ask the client if he or she would agree to split the cost of this development activity with you 50/50 (or name a small amount, typically a few hundred dollars). Be sure to also state that this cost will be fully credited (deducted from your creative fees) if you are awarded the assignment.

Will the client go for it? Maybe yes, maybe no. Although somewhat unusual for nonadvertising assignments, this practice is growing in popularity in the advertising world. There, providing an agency with a "development fee" is seen by many clients as good business—a means of eliminating the artificial environment surrounding most speculative work.

If the client agrees, you not only get reimbursed for some of your pre-assignment efforts, but you'll probably also do better work and gain an inside track. If the client declines, you can now decide whether the proposal effort required is in keeping with the chances of getting the job. Either way, simply asking for a "development fee" shows you to be a professional who is interested in taking the time to do things right, and a good businessperson. This is similar to a concept development fee in lieu of spec work. (If a proposal development fee is extended to include the development of a concept, the client will own what's developed.)

Use time-based pricing. What about situations that simply can't be well enough defined in advance to provide an accurate proposal? For example, writing a technical manual whose length depends on the features of a product still under development, or designing a kit of sales materials when the product's distribution hasn't been decided. The only appropriate way to price such projects is to quote an hourly or daily fee to be applied against an open purchase order. However, to assure the client that he or she will not be simply writing blank checks to you, it is also important to state that you will invoice monthly (or more often, if appropriate) and include with each invoice a breakdown of the work done, along with a best estimate of the work remaining. In other words, there will be no surprises for the client.

Ask lots of questions; don't give many answers. When clients pick your brains before you know whether you'll get the assignment, you can often subtly disarm them by taking the offensive. Ask them questions (it's an old politician's trick). For example, say to them, "What type of approach do you have in mind?" or "Which of your competitors' brochures do you like best?" Don't wait for them to say, "What do you think we should do?" or "What do you think of this competitive brochure?" By taking the initiative, you won't be put on the spot or give away ideas. You appear much more flexible and interested in their opinions and needs.

If a client asks, directly or indirectly, for advice or solutions before committing to the assignment, try saying no tactfully: "As much as I'd like to, I just can't answer that on the spot." If the client persists, be more definitive in an informal, non-threatening way: "I'm sorry, but if I answered that now, there would be no reason for you to hire me, would there?"

Handling price inquiries

When a potential client asks up front. If the query is by phone or mail, provide a "ballpark" job figure, a price range, and/or your hourly/daily rate. Never be more specific without actual job specifications and, preferably, a client interview. In other words, provide enough information to qualify the potential client as serious, but no more. Keep in mind that a client this concerned about money up front probably either has no idea of what good creative talent costs, or knows and is searching for a bargain. In either case, be wary.

Before making a presentation. The quality of your work and the impression you make is much more important to any good client than how much you charge. Concentrate on convincing the client that you have the experience needed, the discipline to get the work done on time, and enthusiasm for the assignment.

To get yourself psyched for a presentation, adopt a positive mental attitude: your work is the absolute best, or at least the absolute best at the prices you charge. Remember, you are doing the client a favor by showing how you can solve problems or create opportunities.

Be wary of any client who asks about price as you are about to begin a presentation. This may be a signal that money is a higher priority than quality. The way to answer such a query is to say that it will be better if you discussed pricing more completely after showing your work. In other words, dodge the subject until you've had a chance to show why the quality of your work makes whatever you charge a bargain.

In the context of a presentation. Focus your presentation on how you have solved problems for other, similar clients; all the ways you can help a client produce better work, faster, are strong positives. Think about them, memorize them, believe in them, show them.

Don't bring up pricing until the very last thing. If you present a good portfolio well, cost is the only negative part of the presentation. So delegate it to the end, after you have had ample opportunity to show why the work you do is inexpensive at any price. If you have done a good job presenting, then price will be the smallest of factors in deciding whether or not to employ your talents. (For more, see "How to cover pricing" in Chapter 14.)

When you're asked about how much you charge during a presentation, it's best to say something to the effect of, "I'll cover that completely in just a few minutes." Again, dodge the subject until you've had a chance to show why the quality of your work makes whatever it costs well worth the price.

When asked about the price of a specific job, never be specific. Always say something to the effect of, "I can't remember exactly. It seems to me this was in the range of $2,500 to $4,000 (give up to a 100 percent range), but I'll be happy to look it up and get back to you." If the client asks you to call back with an answer, make sure that when you do, you preface your reply by saying that not only is every job different, but since this particular one was produced many prices (service bureau charges, paper, etc.) have risen. In other words, it's only an approximate guide.

If the subject of price doesn't come up after you've discussed and shown your work, ask if there are any questions about your capabilities or how you price. If the client has called you in with a specific project in mind, say something like, "Is there anything I can tell you regarding our (my) capability to handle the project you have in mind?"

Now, briefly and without embarrassment or apology, describe how you charge. For example: "We (I) charge $125 per hour for our (my) time. What this means is that the design of an eight-page brochure normally runs from $3,500 to $6,000, depending upon complexity. Of course, we (I) always give a specific estimate as soon as a job is clearly defined and before starting work."

Be wary of any potential client who wants to negotiate a special price, or who asks you to meet a budgeted price lower than what you estimate the job will cost. The request may be legitimate and you may want to accept, but recognize that by so doing you compromise somewhat your professional image, and you leave yourself financially exposed. In addition, the clients who make the most financial demands usually end up being the most difficult to work with.

When discussing price, be decisive; never apologize for what you charge. You are a communications professional with years of experience who provides à la carte creative services at competitive prices with outstanding value. If your prices are too high for a particular client or job, consider that the client's problem, not yours. Not every client should be able to afford you. It is probably better for a potential client to raise his or her standards than for you to lower yours to meet some arbitrarily derived budget figure.

The best way to meet a tight budget is to work with the client to modify the job specification, and, if necessary, to reduce the number of hours you will need to work. Although it is always tough to turn down work, especially when you're not busy, it will be best in the long run if you don't negotiate basic rates. To do so may make you look struggling and badly in need of work, or like a consultant whose pricing is arbitrarily derived, or like a pseudo-professional who doesn't have high standards. Almost without exception you'll find that any client who hassles you on price will also hassle you later on your procedures, the quality of your work, or the way you schedule jobs. If you do decide that it's in your best interest to accept a lower job price, always do it on an exceptional basis. Make sure the client understands that you are making an unusual exception, and why. For example: "This is below what we usually charge for this type of work, but it will provide a great portfolio piece for us. So we'll be happy to handle it under these terms if you'll allow us to also use it for promotional purposes."

Providing a firm quote. As noted before, it is very risky to submit a hard-and-fast quote (versus estimate) on a job. If you do, and you get the assignment, you will either make lots of money, or (equally likely) lose your shirt. The creative process can't be specified with the same precision as manufacturing, where quotes are appropriate. It is next to impossible to define a service assignment well enough to make a quote risk-free.

To work on a quoted fee basis is always to take a financial gamble because of the subjectivity with which service work is judged. When the service provided also involves ideas and their creativity, it becomes doubly difficult to be precise. When assignment conditions change, as they do for most communications projects, precision becomes even more difficult. Nonetheless, a request for a quote ("RFQ" in government lingo) is common among governmental agencies and some publications. Only you can decide whether you want to accept the risk that comes with such a request.

Trying to talk a client up. If the client has a budget lower than your estimate, don't make the mistake of trying to talk him or her into raising it. It's okay if the client comes to this conclusion independently— that is, that you are worth more than what has been budgeted. But a client persuaded to up a budget may try to justify the extra cost by making extra demands upon your time and the quality of your work. This puts you in a no-win situation. Every salesperson knows that the only satisfied customers are those who make up their own minds. Since your future depends in large measure upon repeat business and complimentary word-of-mouth publicity, the only customers you can afford are satisfied ones.

Rush fees and overtime charges. Although often justified, especially when late hours and weekend work are involved, to many clients adding an extra fee (10 to 25 percent) for rushing completion of their job sounds like punishment for their lateness (read incompetence). You can usually accomplish the same end (additional compensation for your extraordinary effort) by adding a fee for "additional help" to get the job (or other previous commitments) done on schedule. This always sounds better to the client than "rush fee," and it enhances, rather than compromises, your professional image. (See "What about cancellation provisions" in Chapter 8.)

What to charge for

As indicated previously, one of the more common mistakes made when estimating or billing a job is not considering all the expenses incurred or services performed. Sometimes these omissions only cut into short-term profitability; other times they affect long-term viability. To make sure you don't fall into this trap, remember to pay particular attention to the following when preparing an estimate or doing your final billing.

Time. When you call on a prospective client, the standard should be one presentation (sales pitch) per assignment. Make exceptions, of course, for assignments that hold unusual promise, but they should be just that— exceptions. Without this one-call/one-job discipline it is very easy to waste time on clients who turn out to be only window-shopping. After getting the assignment, all job time—travel, waiting in lobbies, meetings, creating, revisions, press checks, etc.—should be considered billable.

Travel. Travel time to local clients (within 50 or so miles) is normally considered an overhead expense. Beyond 50 or so miles, travel time is usually billed to the client as work time, except in cases where it might be appropriate to make an exception in order to compete with other suppliers located closer. As for other travel billing arrangements: some individuals and firms bill at two-thirds their normal hourly rate; some bill at their normal hourly rate, but make sure they also do client work when sitting on an airplane; some travel in the evening and charge half their normal rate.

All major travel expenses—plane fares, hotel accommodations, airport transportation, meals—should be itemized and billed at cost. Receipts for expenditures over $25 should be submitted with invoices. It is your choice whether or not to break out and bill minor travel expenses. Some individuals and firms consider parking fees, automobile mileage, and cabs to meetings to be separately billable. Others consider accounting for such minor expenses to be too troublesome, and consider travel expenses within a certain radius of their office to be part of their nonbillable overhead.

Whichever way you choose to account for local travel expenses, make sure you consider them, and make sure the client understands in advance how they will be covered. This is especially important if there's a competitive advantage to not charging for them separately. (Example: "My fees are all-inclusive. I don't charge additional for local travel time or minor expenses.")

Expenses and markups. As with travel, all major miscellaneous expenses—delivery charges, reference materials, unique supplies— should be billed.

If you purchase a lot of expensive outside materials and services—such as writing, design, programming, photography, and printing—you will probably want to mark up these bills before including them in your invoice to the client. The lowest markup should be 15 percent (except in the case of high volume/cost printing), the highest 30 percent; average is 25 percent. Do what is most common in your community. Marking up large expenses is a fair procedure, reflecting your handling of the work and the fact that you must pay the invoice before being paid by the client.

The other option is to have invoices for outside services and supplies sent directly to the client. This eliminates the markup and possibly the profitability that comes with it (see below), but it also eliminates any risk of having to cover large bills if the client is late in paying your invoice. Many cost-conscious clients like it better this way, too. When working with a printer who will invoice the client directly, you may wish to suggest a "finder's fee." Many individuals and firms feel a fee of up to 5 percent is appropriate since most larger printers pay their salespeople a commission. Others prefer not to ask for money, instead building up "goodwill credits" that they can cash in when a favor is needed, such as getting promotional material printed free.

What to give away

In a phrase, as little as possible. Over two hundred years ago, Samuel Johnson wrote, "No man but a blockhead ever wrote except for money," a sentiment equally appropriate today, and to all creative services, as well. Some investment of your time in projects that are not financially rewarding may pay off in increased exposure and publicity, but probably less than you think. You may also want to consider contributing your talent to worthy causes, but restrict your altruism unless you can truly afford it.

Don't be conned. Freelances and small firms are targets for people who want something for nothing. Often this is out of naiveté, but sometimes it is malicious. If you haven't already, sooner or later you will be approached by small firms who will ask you to work for little payment now on the promise of "lots of big jobs" when the company grows. You'll be asked to exchange your services for a "piece of the action," or some other noncash reward. You'll be invited to show concepts and ideas in order to be considered for an assignment (speculative work). You'll bust your butt to get a job done on time, only to have every item on your invoice challenged.

So recognize these truths beforehand: Most companies who want you to work now for future payoff won't be around in the future. A "piece of the action" won't provide what you probably need most—cash flow. Every idea and concept you show before you get an assignment may be appropriated (stolen). It is a rite of passage among some ladder-climbing individuals to prove themselves by "beating up" their suppliers.

Regardless of whether or not the source of the abuse is honest, your only protection is your own diligence. Don't accept low-paying jobs; you haven't the resources to do so. Work only for money backed up by a purchase order. Decline speculative presentations; you can't afford to do them. Make your terms and conditions crystal clear before you start work. Perhaps most important, work to build a client list of reputable companies who know how the game is played, and who honor and protect their suppliers.

Limit freebies. Because you possess a talent that friends, neighbors, and relatives occasionally need, no doubt you are asked to produce materials for local clubs, small retailers, church groups, or civic organizations. In some cases, the individuals requesting your help will be prepared to pay, and will believe that they are doing you a favor by providing work. In other cases, you are just a more visible source for talent donations.

The unfortunate reality, however, is that when you are self-employed you have far less time to donate, even to worthy causes. It is much easier to bat out a brochure for a local club when you are employed by someone else than when you are working by yourself, or are responsible for the future of a struggling organization. Charging your normal rates will probably insult the people who offer to pay. How much work of this type you accept is a personal decision. You should take your social obligation to your community seriously, and doing friends a favor will probably repay itself many times in many ways. But never lose track of the fact that you are in business to make money, not to make friends.

Perhaps the best response to those soliciting your talents is frankness and honesty. Explain your financial or workload situation, offer to work on an as-time-is-available basis and to do the work free, or barter for something they have that you need. Stay away from reduced-rate pricing. Chances are it will only encourage more requests.

Be protective of your time. Time and effort may be money to you, but they aren't to many prospective clients. You may be requested to make presentations at very inappropriate times, such as 8:00 a.m. in a city hours away. You may be asked to drop everything and come in for an interview, or "rush over" samples for evaluation. You can be kept waiting in reception areas. You get stood up. Sometimes it is all worthwhile, because the payoff will be big. But often it isn't. So you must learn to discriminate between potential clients who waste your time, and those who provide jobs.

Establish rules and stick by them. Determine the extent of a potential client's work before visiting. Don't go if it isn't large enough; ask the client to come to your office. Never drop everything to meet a potential client's requests; it gives the appearance that you will shortchange an existing client to win a new one. Discourage providing unaccompanied samples (drop-offs); insist that they are meaningless without you there to explain them. (See "What about 'drop-offs'?" in Chapter 14.) Limit your presentation to one meeting; after that charge for your time. The best overall advice is this: clients will respect your time in direct proportion to what they pay for it.

Terms and conditions

Since cash flow is an important aspect of profitability, the following terms should be part of the basis upon which your estimates are figured. They should be written into each estimate presented to the client (see Chapter 8).

Payment in thirds. An increasingly used, almost "standard," pricing and billing procedure for creative work is one third of the estimate upon acceptance of an assignment, one third upon client approval of the first creative submission, and one third upon satisfactory job completion. Some individuals and firms ask for half (50 percent) up front, especially with unknown clients, or whenever there will be a large cash outlay before final payment.

Although how strongly you choose to encourage this arrangement depends upon your competitive situation, don't be overly concerned about client sensitivity. It is probably less of a consideration than you believe. Most clients will agree. If a client balks at giving you money up front, you can always make "special arrangements" as a compliment. (Example: "Although progress payments are my normal procedure, because I would like to have the opportunity to work with you, I will make an exception in your case.")

Net 30. The accepted payment standard for business invoices is, as it has been for decades, thirty days. This is usually expressed as "Net 30." Never let a client tell you that times have changed, that, say, "Net 60" is now normal. This may be the way a particular client chooses to operate (and you may opt to accept it), but it is not the business norm.

You should inform each potential client by a clear statement on every proposal, estimate, and invoice that "Net 30" is your payment standard. Also make sure "Net 30" appears on the client's purchase order or other internal payment authorization. If it does not, ask why.

How accurate is *Pricing and Ethical Guidelines?*

Wouldn't it be nice if there was a source you could easily turn to whenever you had a question about how much to charge? For designers *Pricing and Ethical Guidelines*—published occasionally by the Graphic Artists Guild (www.gag.org)—provides such a source. *Pricing and Ethical Guidelines* (PEG) sells for around $35, or is supplied free with membership in the Guild.

Fulfilling a need. *Creative Business* surveys indicate that most designers and illustrators question the prices reported in PEG, believing them to be "New York based" and, therefore, much too high. (Interestingly, the same "too high" comment also comes from designers and illustrators in New York.) The *Creative Business* database confirms that the prices quoted in PEG are on the high side; an average of 10 to 15 percent too high for most areas of the country, although occasionally more or less.

When to refer to it. What you charge for a given job should depend upon several factors unique to you and the assignment: your experience and talent, your costs of doing business, what the local market will support, who the competition is, and (perhaps) how badly you need the work. There is no way PEG or any other source can shortcut this process. Thus, PEG should never be used to price a job.

The time to use PEG is after you have determined what to charge. Then, and only then, take it down from the bookshelf and look up a similar type of work. In the unlikely event that your price is higher than that shown, and it was carefully determined, don't worry about it. In the more likely event that your price is lower, don't necessarily change it, but do reconsider whether you have accurately estimated the time involved, or whether your hourly rate is too low for someone with your talent, experience, and overhead costs.

If your price is lower than that shown by PEG, note the difference and use it to your advantage when discussing the estimate with the client. For example: "I think you'll be pleasantly surprised with the price we've been able to come up with. Because of (reasons) we were able to come in several thousand dollars under the Graphic Artists Guild guidelines for this type of work" or, in answer to a negative comment, "Actually, before I came over today I did check the estimate against the prices provided by the Graphic Artists Guild for similar work, and our price is several thousand dollars less than they recommend."

How accurate are *Writer's Market* and *Artist's Market?*

Writer's Market and *Artist's Market*—published yearly by F&W Publications (www.f&wpublications.com)—also provide job prices. However, most of the content is devoted to journalistic freelancing and the prices paid by magazines. Unfortunately, these prices are probably accurate (see "Publications—low pay, high prestige" in Chapter 11). As for the advice and prices reported for commercial writing, design, and illustration, they are incredibly broad and in many cases substantially below the rates actually charged by successful individuals. My advice is to take these books seriously only if you wish to pursue the editorial market.

8. Presenting Estimates to Clients

When is an estimate letter more appropriate than a proposal? Is a formal contract better than a letter of agreement? What should be covered, and how much detail provided? What is the best way to protect yourself? To what do clients react most and least favorably? These are not easy questions to answer. What is appropriate for one client may be totally inappropriate for another. Nonetheless, assignment "paperwork" is an important component of developing professional client relations, ensuring adequate compensation, and maintaining the records that allow you to constantly improve your profitability.

The two-step process

The best way to conserve your time, protect your interests, and keep clients happy all at once is to make estimating and preparing proposals a two-step process. Think of the first step as a basic definition of the ground rules. Think of the second step as a more detailed application of the rules to a specific situation.

1. A "how we charge" statement. Here's how the first step works: Prepare a short, no more than two-page, statement of your general billing procedures. The primary use of the statement will be as a leave-behind after you make an initial presentation to a potential new client. In addition, it can be used during the presentation as a way to deflect questions about pricing ("Before I leave, I'll give you a sheet that describes how I price my services") and as a way to close the presentation ("This sheet summarizes my billing procedures. I hope you'll file it, and give me a call when appropriate"). Also use the statement to answer general telephone inquiries about pricing and to screen out clients with inadequate budgets.

Such a statement will differentiate you from the competition because few freelances and small firms provide clients with any advance pricing or working guidelines. For an example of such a statement, see "Working description" in Appendix 3. Use it as a guide, or prepare something from scratch that suits your organization and style. When you get a call from a known client, you'll know the ground rules have already been established. This makes the subsequent proposal writing much faster and easier.

What if you get a proposal request from a prospective client you've never called upon? Use the sheet as a preface to the proposal, or attach it to the cover letter you send along.

2. An estimate, letter of agreement, or proposal. Now we're ready to consider the second step of the process: the paperwork necessary to turn a prospective client's interest into a paying project. It is the service agreement or contract that typically takes the form of an estimate, letter of agreement, or proposal, depending on the circumstances.

Not too little, but not too much

Whatever the format, what is sent to prospective clients for approval should be custom-tailored to the specific circumstances of the job and the prospect's needs. There's no one size that fits all. The shorter and simpler, the better.

The three criteria. Three objectives need to be met. One is to address prospects' questions about procedures, pricing, and schedules. The second is to make them comfortable with your knowledge, experience, and capabilities. And the third is to summarize your processes—creative, production, and billing. All three are necessary because no matter how good the prospect, or how detailed prior discussions, it's difficult to verbally cover the key aspects of the production process. A written agreement stating what will happen, when, and for how much avoids simple misunderstandings now, and can serve to refresh lapsed memories in the future.

Yet as important as such agreements usually are, they seldom provide as much legal protection as most of us would like. That's because the "product"—creative executions—is always unique, hard to define precisely, and subjectively evaluated. The upshot is that there are so many potential loopholes clients who look to find one usually can, especially if they have legal staff on retainer. So while having something written and signed is important, it can't be counted on for anything other than rudimentary legal protection. It is legally powerful only in clear violations involving substantial sums of money. The reason for mentioning this while simultaneously stressing the necessity is to discourage spending an excessive amount of time on preparation.

How much time? The fact is, every hour spent on new business paperwork is potentially nonbillable overhead. Only when it results in actually getting the project is there an opportunity to recoup the cost, and even in these cases it requires discipline. Thus, a paradox: the less time you spend, the more money you can make. On the other hand, the less time you spend, the less your chances of getting the job. So there's a strong incentive to strike the right balance, to be as efficient as possible.

Matching effort to potential. *Creative Business* newsletter surveys indicate that the average dollar value of crunching the numbers and preparing new business paperwork (but not including the time and costs of making the presentation) should probably not exceed 2 percent of a job's estimated fee billing. As an example, the cost of estimating and preparing a proposal for a job estimated to bill out at $15,000 would be $300 or lower, or a couple hours of time. This assumes normal information and procedures as well as the use of templates and copy that can be easily customized.

Handshake only? Considering cost, might a handshake be all that's necessary with some long-standing client relationships? Also, perhaps it would be all that's needed for fast-turnaround jobs when there isn't time to put something in writing? In both situations, a lack of paperwork would save time and lower costs. In fact, design industry studies in the past have shown that less than half of all design projects are covered by any paperwork. This is, in many cases, the result of trusting long-term clients, in some others an avoidance of inconvenience, and in still others a fear that being too detailed might raise better-left-unaware-of issues. Whatever the cause might be, all it takes is being burned once, after which having something in writing takes on new importance.

Preparation costs should, of course, always be weighed. But naiveté can be very costly. Without having things written down, you're vulnerable not only to an honest client's imperfect memory, but also to being taken advantage of by dishonest ones. Both present great risks when substantial amounts of time and money are involved.

The problem with formal legal contracts

All agreements are equally binding. The only difference in enforceability is their specificity. One way to get some of this without seeking a lawyer's services is to adopt the wording and appearance of standard or customized legal contracts.

PRESENTING ESTIMATES TO CLIENTS

Standard legal contracts. They are available for downloading off the web (search under legal contracts for designers, web designers, copywriters, etc.). Several are also available in the book *Pricing and Ethical Guidelines*, available from the Graphic Artists Guild (www.gag.org). Yet, while such contracts do provide legal formatting and language, they're usually also off-putting to clients.

Customized legal contracts. An alternative is to custom-tailor a contract by taking paragraph modules from the "Standard Form of Agreement for Design Services," available through the American Institute for Graphic Arts (www.aiga.org). It is less legalistic (more client-friendly), but it does tend to encourage including more terms and conditions than are normally necessary or suitable.

Bottom line. Legalistic contracts should be avoided in most circumstances. They undermine one of the major objectives when soliciting a prospect's work—that is, establishing a sense of comfort in being able to work together informally in addressing a project's needs. Not least of all, contracts don't provide that much additional legal protection in the situations most of us face anyway. The only regular exceptions are long-term, large-dollar design or interactive projects, such as ongoing branding or extensive site development and management, or illustration projects with a new or difficult client where there is no personal contact.

Three recommended formats

Okay, if that is what doesn't make sense in most situations, what does? For most situations faced by most readers, one of three "plain English" formats is best, depending on project size: 1) a simple one- or two-page estimate, 2) a several-page letter of agreement, or 3) a multi-page detailed proposal. Templates and boilerplate copy can be prepared in advance, vetted by a lawyer where appropriate, stored away, then easily customized for a project at hand. Examples of each of the three formats are in Appendix 3.

Each of these formats provides detail appropriate to the size and scope of the project. That is, it is enough for a client to make a decision but won't unnecessarily consume too much time. Each also includes the four essentials for any project agreement: 1) describing what will be done and when, 2) stating the price for doing it, 3), the terms and conditions, and 4) a prospect's approving signature.

A simple estimate for small jobs. This is recommended for projects under $3,000. Most projects under about $3,000 need nothing more than a simple one- or two-page estimate. They are quick to prepare and will provide all the paperwork most prospects need. When signed, they are authorization to begin work. Note, however, that here, as with other formats, a purchase order should be requested. While a signed estimate is adequate to begin work, a purchase order number is often necessary for an invoice to get paid, especially with larger clients. (See "Purchase orders and work that can't be defined" below.)

A letter of agreement for midsize jobs. This is recommended for projects between $3,000 and $12,000. For projects of this size, a little more detail is normally appropriate. It can usually be covered in a two- or three-page letter of agreement. Delivery should be in person or by mail (not e-mail). When directed to a new prospect, it is best to enclose the letter in a presentation folder also containing a brief biographical sketch or capability brochure, an up-to-date client list, a business card, and any samples of similar work that could help the prospect assess your capabilities.

For larger jobs, a detailed proposal. This is recommended for projects $12,000 and up. Most projects of this size require a proposal of several pages. Except in cases of very large, multi-job or multi-month projects, it is usually best not to exceed a dozen or so pages. The best proposals not only provide a description of what will happen, and how much it will cost, but also reassure the prospect that there is a clear understanding of the problems or opportunities they are facing and that you are competent to deal with them.

Segmentation. The key to composing a good proposal is to segment the project into a few phases (steps) of more or less similar activity. Doing this makes it easy for prospects to read and understand, and it provides the detail most want. How many phases and how much detail is always a judgment call, but three to five is usually sufficient. For example, Phase I might be orientation and information gathering; Phase II, concept development, wireframing, and copy/design approvals; Phase III, art direction of photography; Phase IV, creative production and programming; and Phase V, print supervision, delivery, and going live.

Although some firms include a breakdown of costs with the description of each phase, it is more common to put the costs of each phase, along with their total, in a separate section. When done this way, the proposal essentially has two sections: one on creative and process, the other on costs. For progress payment invoicing, the costs for several phrases are often lumped together. Separating costs also makes a presentation less likely to get bogged down in price discussions when going over the project's creative and process aspects. In addition, it is usually helpful to indicate other costs separately (expenses, subcontracting, etc.). This provides the total cost picture without exaggerating the amount that actually stays with the firm.

Length. When a proposal grows to be twenty pages or so, as might be the case with very large or long-term projects, it should be broken down into three or more sections. In such cases, Section One describes and schedules activity in the several phases indicated above, including separate phases for each individual component. Section Two contains cost breakdowns. And Section Three usually provides material to help the prospect be totally comfortable with your ability to handle all aspects. Examples of what to include in Section Three are a brief description of the firm and its history; relevant project or industry experience; a list of past clients; biographical sketches of team members working on the project; relevant awards; and client references.

What about cancellation provisions?

A cancellation provision, sometimes called a "kill fee," is inserted in client agreements by many creative suppliers for protection against the project being cancelled before completion. A figure of 50 percent of the estimated fee is often used. Although this approach works reasonably well for illustration and literary assignments where there is a minimum of client interaction, it is inappropriate for most graphic design, advertising, copywriting, and interactive projects. A better way is to base cancellation or kill fees on how much work has actually been done. Here's what I recommend you put in your prospect paperwork. "In the event of the cancellation of this assignment, or any delay of more than three months, we will invoice you for the greater of either: 1) all work completed up to the date of notification, including expenses; or 2) 20 percent of the agreed upon estimate plus expenses. All incomplete work will remain the property of (creative firm)."

Getting paid for work completed in the event of a client delay or cancellation is only fair. The arbitrary figure of at least 20 percent of the estimate is justified as a fee for reserving your time. Retaining the ownership of incomplete work is to protect any of your partially developed ideas and concepts. One note of caution, though: Before sending a client an invoice for a cancelled or delayed job be sure to explain to them that creative time is often expended long before there are tangible results to show for it. For instance, it is possible that 50 percent of a job's estimated hours could be used up when a client has seen only a few very rough ideas. Unless they understand this, they will probably question the invoice.

Purchase orders and work that can't be defined

In most client organizations an accepted estimate, letter of agreement, or proposal will generate a purchase order (PO), authorization to begin work. In fact, in many larger organizations no payment greater than several hundred dollars is allowed without a purchase order. Thus, to ensure timely payment it is important to understand how the purchase order system works.

A purchase order is a way of allocating payment against a specific budget account. It is also an official authorization for a vendor (you) to do work, and it provides official delivery and payment terms. POs are usually written by an organization's purchasing or accounting department upon the written request of a company executive (your client contact), supported by written documentation (your paperwork). If there is no documentation, there may be no request, no purchase order, and no payment.

After approval, usually by a senior executive, the purchase order is entered into the organization's computer system and the vendor is sent a copy. This procedure normally takes one to two weeks. Once a purchase order has been entered into the organization's computer system, any invoice submitted usually goes through these steps before payment: First, it must be approved by the person who initiated the PO. Then it must be sent to Purchasing or Accounting to "log" against the PO. Finally, Purchasing or Accounting must forward it to the organization's Accounts Payable department for check clearance and issuance.

From invoice approval to check clearance typically takes two weeks or so. Actual check issuance is somewhat later, depending on the PO payment terms and the dates the company actually issues checks. For example, if the payment terms are "Net 30" (payment 30 days after invoice receipt) and checks are issued to vendors on Wednesdays, a check would actually be issued on the next Wednesday, more than 30 days after the invoice had been received. When there is no prior purchase order authorizing work, an approved invoice will often trigger one. Payment will likely be delayed for several additional weeks because the PO will have to be routed for approval and entered into the system first. Only then can the waiting invoice be processed and a check issued.

Not every project, however, falls neatly into the category of work that is easily defined. Some projects, for instance, haven't been fully worked out by the prospect, but work still needs to get started to make a deadline. Then, too, there's long-term, multifaceted work where the course(s) of action can't always be predicted in advance, such as a major rebranding. Nonetheless, work that is not well defined is a leading cause of lack of success or later problems. So how can you satisfy a prospect's need for purchasing documentation with your need to get one or more payments before things are fully resolved?

Ask for a purchase order for partial development. POs don't have to cover an entire project. When the full scope of what will be done and what it will cost can't be determined, ask for a PO of a modest amount to cover "project definition." At the conclusion of this activity, details and further costs can be presented for reaction and negotiation. A new PO can then be written, or the current one amended, to cover the newly defined project. Should, for whatever reason, the client decide not to proceed, they will be out only the cost of this preliminary work.

There are, though, two potential cautions in going this route. One is to make sure that whatever time is spent on this activity will be priced at normal rates. Don't make the mistake of asking for a lowball PO in order to get things defined, only to discover later on that you've lost money on what turned out to be one of the more crucial phases of the project. The other caution is the possibility of getting into an ownership dispute about what has been developed should the client decide not to proceed. The PO should clearly state that the copyright and native files of anything produced remain your property.

Ask for a "blanket purchase order." This is another route that can be taken when projects can't be clearly defined. It is even more suitable when they are ongoing. A client's blanket PO authorizes a supplier to provide loosely defined goods or services during a given period for a total price not to exceed a stated amount. One can also be authorized for purchases of multiple items within a specified field over an extended period.

A blanket PO will enable a client's Accounts Payable department to honor invoices before a project has been completely defined or priced. It will also enable regular payments for extended projects or activities, such as retainer disbursements. In such situations, only a single PO will be needed. The amount of each invoice will be deducted from what it authorizes. As long as the total does not exceed this amount, there will be no need for further paperwork.

There may, however, be a prerequisite before some larger clients will issue a blanket PO. Since it involves an open-ended commitment, a firm might have to first qualify for the Purchasing department's "approved supplier" list. Ask your contact person whether they have such a list and, if so, how to get on it. Don't be reluctant to ask about a blanket PO. The benefits are not all one-sided. They reduce paperwork and the cost of invoice authorization. They also make accounts payable more efficient for routine purchases or ongoing commitments.

The psychology of price acceptance

The pre-project paperwork presented to a prospective client is their first solid indication of what their project will actually cost. Even when there is no "sticker shock," there is a natural, self-interest tendency to want the price lowered. Successfully avoiding or responding to a "this is very expensive" reaction requires confidence in your own procedures and worth. And it also takes some understanding of the role psychology always plays in pricing acceptance.

Perceptions affect reality. Whether a project's cost will be perceived as over-, under-, or appropriately priced is strongly affected by what a prospective client sees when he or she looks at you. The quality of work in your portfolio aside, a well-dressed, personable, and articulate professional is worth more than someone lacking these qualities. Consider this analogy: Lord & Taylor can charge higher prices than Walmart. Further, it is very difficult to get rich in a service business adopting a volume discount (Walmart) strategy. So to be financially successful, think of and present yourself as the Lord & Taylor (or Brooks Brothers or Ann Taylor) of creative services.

You get what you pay for. It's a cliché, but most people, clients included, believe it. Your task is to convince them that while your pricing might be just a bit higher, the value provided is a lot higher. Another way of looking at this is that you can never be overpriced; the worst you can ever be is too expensive for a particular client's needs.

There is always someone cheaper. Clients looking for lower prices can always find them, and unscrupulous ones will use this ploy to try to lower what you charge. Don't play their game. What no client can ever get elsewhere is your quality, service, and dependability. The only pricing competition you should ever acknowledge is from other suppliers of equal quality.

Professionals don't haggle. Assuming you've done your homework and figured your pricing carefully, it should be largely non-negotiable. If you haggle over price and arbitrarily lower it, the client will believe it was inflated. If price is a problem, try to modify the job specifications, or find a way to produce the job without requiring as much of your time. (Also see "Let me see what I can do to meet your budget" in the next section.)

There is no "right" price. Ours is a business where every job is a different challenge that can be addressed in a multitude of different ways. The only appropriate price is what is agreeable to both you and the client. If the client has an unrealistic budget, that's their problem, not yours. Many budgets are arbitrarily set with little or no serious consideration for just how much actual work is required. Don't let a client's ignorance of the process or work involved cause you to give up your profit.

Handling price objections

Being able to also counter specific pricing objections is the step beyond understanding pricing psychology. If there's one thing that marks an individual's painful initiation to the real world of commerce, it's being hit for the first time with a strong pricing objection. Being able to handle such objections easily and successfully is the mark of an experienced pro.

Never assume that your price will be high. It's self-defeating. When a client challenges a project price or your hourly rate, act genuinely surprised. Never, ever apologize. No professional apologizes for charging an honest fee, and neither should you. If a client comments that your price is high, don't argue or disagree. Explain. Respond quickly by explaining in detail how you arrived at it (the many hours and components that will actually be involved in the job) and/or why your hourly rate is appropriate (talent, experience, industry norms). Also say that your past experience is that when clients consider your fees in the context of quality, experience, or service (pick whatever your strengths are) most find your charges quite reasonable. In short, when value rather than just pure cost is considered, you are very competitive. Then, in addition, immediately use one or more of the following responses (counters):

"Actually, my prices are lower than others for similar quality work." Say this with a straight face, and mean it. It is probably true. Besides, who really knows? By saying it, you challenge the client in a friendly way to think again. You also introduce the notion that low price isn't as important as high value (cost divided by the end result).

"Yes, my prices are a bit higher up front, but you'll find me to be less expensive to work with." The value of the many intangible benefits you offer probably far outweighs your slightly higher prices. Just how much, for example, are your greater efficiency and increased dependability really worth? For any busy client or important job, it probably is much more than your small additional fee. Say so.

"It's a small percentage of the total cost." Whenever a client compares your (higher) price with another (lower) price, put the difference in a larger context. Tactfully reduce the discussion to the level of the inconsequential. For example: "You know, if you think about it, when figured on a unit cost basis, the $500 difference between my fee and the competitor's is only about a half penny a brochure, a small price to pay for my additional quality and service" or "The $500 difference is something less than 1 percent of the total cost of the job."

"Let me see what I can do to meet your budget." Be helpful. Tell the client you would like to go back to your office and do some careful refiguring. Then come back a few days later with a new proposal that shows how the objectives and budget can be obtained by altering the job's specifications ("I've found I can give you the same impact by innovative use of two-color rather than four-color printing" or "I think we can lose the costly animation on site pages x and y, without any negligible effect").

If, however, the client is firm on his or her specifications and you decide that it's in your best interest to negotiate a price that is somewhat lower than your initial estimate, always do it on an exceptional basis. Make sure that the client understands that you are making an exception, and why ("Although your budget is well below what I normally charge, I would like to have more of this [type of] work in my portfolio. Therefore . . ."). Never appear to lower your price just because you need the work.

Six price presentation essentials

1. Put it in writing. If you don't, you're totally reliant upon the client's (not your) memory.

2. **Describe what will happen and when.** Insist upon enough input to prepare an appropriately detailed description of the project's processes and schedule. Don't submit anything until you are comfortable.

3. **Use the term "estimate," not "quote," in most situations.** A quote is a fixed price based on fixed conditions; an estimate is a flexible price based upon flexible conditions. Although quotes are widely used in businesses where specifications can be precisely defined (e.g., printing), they are seldom appropriate for creative projects where subjective judgments, interpretations, and revisions play important roles. Unless you are a gambler, decline any job where the client insists on a firm quote.

4. **Provide a firm but flexible schedule.** Clients want you to take charge. Tell them not only what will happen and when, but the production and financial consequences of not meeting the schedule.

5. **Include a clear statement of your terms and conditions.** Ideally, a third of the estimated cost should be paid up front, a third at creative submission, a third plus miscellaneous charges and expenses upon delivery. All invoices should be "Net 30" (payment due 30 days after invoicing) unless other arrangements are made in advance.

6. **Obtain the client's signature of approval.** It may not be complete protection against future misunderstandings and difficulties, but it beats having nothing.

9. Keeping More of What You Get

Freelancing or running a creative shop successfully requires an entirely different mindset about money than when one is conventionally employed. Chances are, when you were employed you measured your career progress by the growth of your paycheck. Now, however, keeping track of your progress is more difficult, so it should force you to think in terms of the true measure of financial success: the amount of money you get to keep.

In the broadest sense, what you keep is the difference between your income and what's left after subtracting all living costs. But that's at least as much a measure of lifestyle preferences as financial success. A much better measure of relative career progress is the difference between gross and net income. This is affected in just two ways: by your business expenses, and by your tax obligations. This chapter provides norms for both.

Measuring with a new scale

There is one generalization about self-employed income that is universally true: the dollars you make working for yourself are more valuable than those you made working for someone else. The reason is that many items that were previously considered as personal expenses are now legitimate (and sometimes not so legitimate) business expenses. All other things being equal, this lowers your personal tax obligation and raises your net income. Although you also encounter many new expenses, the bottom-line effect on a given gross income will be a higher net income, and/or a much better lifestyle.

How much positive change self-employment will bring to your net income is a function of many individual factors. Typically, however, a dollar earned while you are self-employed tends to be from 10 to 15 percent

more valuable. Put another way, if your annual income is $50,000, it will buy a life-style equivalent to $55,000 in straight salary.

In some cases it is even possible to have gross receipts that exceed $100,000, and live the lifestyle appropriate to that level, yet pay taxes on a net income of less than half that figure. How? How can you make sure that you squeeze every bit of the good life out of your gross income? First, you must have a good accountant to guide your activities and prepare what will often appear to be quite complicated tax strategies. As explained in Chapter 3, a good accountant is not a luxury but a business necessity.

Second, as noted in both Chapters 3 and 10, you must diligently keep complete and accurate records of your income and business expenses. Records are what will be used to determine the extent of your obligations and, thus, your profitability. Without good records even the best accountant in the world is powerless.

Finally, you must know the rules of the game and how it is normally played—specifically, how to judge what things really cost, and what legitimate tax strategies and business expenses are.

Setting the right priorities

Let's start developing your income-keeping strategy by reviewing three rather obvious points—three things that, experience shows, have a tendency to get lost in the euphoria that often accompanies "doing your own thing" for the first time, or later in the everyday grind of making a living.

You can't save what you don't make. Your first priority always has to be developing the ongoing business that will generate regular, sufficient income. Keeping more of that income is important only after you receive it. As self-evident as this would seem to be, it may, nonetheless, be a fight to keep yourself from concentrating too heavily on the financial advantages of business ownership, just as it may be difficult not to concentrate too heavily on such things as designing your stationery and styling your office. Always remember, if your first priority isn't getting paying business, sooner or later your first priority will become looking for a new job.

A dollar saved is worth several earned. Also remember that reducing your expenses, your overhead, is far easier than increasing your sales, and has both a faster and more lasting effect on net income. While it is true that you have to spend money to make it, it is even more true that self-employed individuals can't afford to waste money. You are a creative person, not a bookkeeper; continually keeping an eye on expenses will probably be a challenge. It is, however, absolutely necessary. There are,

after all, only two ways that any company can improve its profitability: by increasing sales, or by reducing expenses. To concentrate on one to the exclusion of the other is always poor business.

Don't get carried away with the tax deductibility of the expenses you incur. Nothing you buy or do in your own business is free; it is just a little less expensive than when you worked for someone else. In fact, you can think of the tax deductibility of expenses as something akin to buying at discount. For example, and to oversimplify things a bit, when you buy lunch for a client, rather than paying for the whole tab, Uncle Sam may (under current tax law when this was written) pay for up to 18 percent of it (50 percent of the tab is tax deductible; your income can be taxed at up to 36 percent, and 50% x 36% = 18%.) In other words, you'll still end up actually footing at least 80 percent of the tab, an expense you didn't have when you worked for someone else. So don't be quick to reach for the check, thinking that from now on expenses are some type of mysterious "tax write-off." Whenever tempted, think of this old business proverb: you don't get rich on volume when an activity costs you money.

Understanding the tax system

The tax man is the guy all small-business people love to hate. Just thinking about the endless forms to be filled out, the expensive accountants who have to be employed, and the hard-earned money that "disappears" into government coffers is enough to give most small-business people apoplexy. Sometimes it seems that growth and success are impossible in

such an "anti-business" environment. Wouldn't business be much more efficient and productive without the paper work and expenses necessitated by taxes? Wouldn't we all be richer, too?

Maybe, but that's a grossly simplistic attitude. The personal and business taxes you pay as a self-employed individual make possible services that are essential to the business community, and they also pay for social programs that most of us wouldn't want our modern society to be without. Of course, how many of these services and programs are actually necessary, and how efficiently the government provides them, are endlessly debatable. It is a subject you should, as a member of the entrepreneurial class, take an active interest in.

Regardless of your personal feelings about business taxation, it is possible to build a successful small business under the present tax codes. It's done every day of the week by people a lot less smart than you. Also, keep in mind that your feelings about the equity of the tax system have little or no effect on the amount of taxes you end up paying anyway. So rather than just grumble about how difficult taxes make your life, adopt a positive attitude and learn everything you can about them. Like it or not, the only thing that will immediately lower your tax burden is understanding enough about the system to take advantage of every tax-saving opportunity.

For a general understanding of tax matters, see IRS publication #334, "Tax Guide for Small Business." It is a roundup of the rules for deductions, payroll taxes, record keeping, and other issues that affect self-employed people and owners of small companies. For a list of other helpful publications, visit www.IRS.gov.

This said, a note of caution also has to be included. Sometimes a little knowledge is dangerous. Learning more about the business taxation system is very beneficial providing you use the information only as the basis for discussions with your accountant. Don't attempt to act directly on any of your newfound knowledge; there's too much at risk.

Deducting everything you can

In general terms, the basis for business taxation—for sole proprietors, partnerships, LLCs, and corporations—is simple: all income should be recorded, and all expenses related to generating that income should be deducted (subtracted) from it. What remains is the basis for taxation. Thus, it is obvious that the higher the expense deductions, the lower the basis on which your tax will be figured, and the lower your taxes. So don't let expenses go unrecorded.

Routine operating expenses. They are defined somewhat differently by municipal, state, and federal tax authorities. For our purposes here, however, a good guideline to follow is what the IRS calls its "Rule of Four."

Expenses must be directly incurred in connection with your business; they cannot be for personal or non-business-related items or services.

Expenses must be ordinary and necessary. That is, they must be accepted practice among other similar businesses, and must be appropriate to developing or maintaining your business.

Expenses must be for immediate services or items with a short effective life. For example, rent, office supplies, delivery services, taxi fares, etc.

The expense may be for any amount, as long as it is reasonable.

Capital business expenses. They are the expensive, long-life items necessary for conducting business: computers, printers, copiers, office furniture, business automobiles, etc. The cost for such large-ticket items must be prorated over their useful lifetime according to guidelines established by the IRS (usually five or so years). The purpose of this is to spread the cost over the life of the asset and to keep tax deductions from fluctuating wildly depending upon whether or not expensive capital goods were bought during the tax year.

All expenses incurred in operating the capital equipment—for example, paper for copiers, gasoline for automobiles, or repair service for either—are, however, treated as routine operating expenses.

To qualify as a legitimate capital business expense, an item must be a normal and regular component of doing business and be used a majority of the time (over 50 percent) for business purposes. In other words, a vacation home in the mountains or a company boat will take a lot of justifying. Further, if the item is not used 100 percent for business, you will be expected to prorate its routine operating expenses. For example, if you use a business car for pleasure every weekend (two days out of seven), the maximum you are entitled to deduct is five-sevenths of its costs, or that portion of its use that occurs for business.

Leasing. This is a way that businesses often obtain common capital equipment (automobiles, office equipment, etc.) but pay for it as an operating, not capital, expense. Basically, equipment leasing is just long-term rental, often with a provision that allows the lessee (you) to obtain ownership of the equipment at the end of the lease period when its cash value is low.

Leasing is appropriate in several circumstances. Since a down payment isn't always required, it permits you to obtain the use of equipment earlier than might otherwise be possible. It permits you to walk away from a given piece of equipment at the end of the lease period without worrying about how to dispose of it. Leasing also preserves your capital for emergencies. Perhaps most important, shifting the cost of equipment from a capital expense to an operating expense may have cash flow or tax benefits in some situations.

Be aware that leasing also has trade-offs. Monthly lease charges will probably be more than monthly purchase/finance charges. You won't have done much to help strengthen the credit rating of your business. At the end of the lease period you will have built little or no financial equity in the product. Raising operating expenses and reducing capital expenses might not be the proper tax strategy for your business. So while you should always consider leasing when thinking about obtaining capital equipment, don't make any decisions without first talking to your accountant.

Losses. The fair market value or original cost (whichever is less) of any business items lost or stolen is deductible from your business income. What is not deductible is anything you never actually had. For example, *you cannot deduct bills a client never paid,* although you can deduct the expenses incurred in trying to collect them. (An exception is possible if your company operates on an accrual, not cash, basis. This is unlikely for most small creative businesses, but may be the case with large agencies or design studios. Ask your accountant if you aren't sure.)

Business expenses that exceed business income may be used to off set income received from other sources if you are set up as a sole proprietorship, a partnership, LLC, or a Subchapter S corporation. So if you decide to freelance part time as a trial, and also happen to lose money in the process, you may be able to deduct these losses from your regular, salaried income. Note, however, that the IRS will be suspicious of your seriousness ("Is this just a hobby or real business?"), and will probably require some evidence that you are trying to make a profit, and actually achieve it in at least one year out of five.

Home-office expenses. Since many freelances work out of their home, one of the tax questions most often asked is, "How much of my household expenses is deductible as business expense?" Unfortunately, the answer is: not much. The IRS only allows you to deduct household expenses in proportion to the amount of space your business "regularly and exclusively" occupies in your residence.

For example, if you have an eight-room house, and you use one room exclusively as an office, then you may deduct for tax purposes one-eighth of your normal household expenses. If you have a four-room apartment and use one room exclusively as an office, you may deduct one fourth of your expenses. Normal household expenses that can be prorated include:

heat, electricity, telephone (all business long-distance charges are deductible if the calls are itemized), internet service, water, mortgage payments (exclusive of interest and taxes, which are 100 percent deductible), rent, and maintenance/cleaning/repair charges. The fact that you now also use the bathroom, kitchen, and hallways during business hours does not matter. Since these spaces are not used exclusively for business purposes, they cannot be a factor in prorating your expenses. In other words, if you do your work at the kitchen table, none of your household expenses are deductible. It may not seem fair, but that's the way it is. For further information, see IRS publication 587, "Business Use of Your Home."

Automobile expenses. This is an area of concern to freelancers, principals of multiperson firms, and sales reps alike. An automobile is an important piece of business equipment. It not only has to be replaced every so often, it also reflects on an individual and her or his company. Automobile expenses can be deducted for tax purposes in one of two ways.

Option one is through business ownership, in which the car is treated as a capital expense and its value depreciated over the length of ownership. In this method, all operating costs—gas, insurance, repairs, etc.— are tax deductible as business expenses.

To qualify, a "company car" must be used for business more than just occasionally. When it is also used for personal purposes, the depreciation allowance and expenses must be prorated. Any expenses for personal use picked up by the company must be reported as employee income.

Option two is through personal ownership, with a tax deduction for each mile driven for business purposes (commuting does not qualify). At the time of this writing, the IRS allowance was 56.5¢ per mile, a figure that has risen every year recently. No additional expenses are tax deductible, except for parking and tolls. Any car used for business qualifies.

Sole proprietors take the deduction directly on their personal tax returns, otherwise, the individual owning the car is reimbursed by the company, and the reimbursement is claimed as an expense on the company's tax returns. Nearly all firms use the IRS mileage allowance in reimbursing principals and employees, including commissioned sales people.

Whichever option is chosen, it must be used for the life of the vehicle. There is no switching from year to year.

The following example will show you how to figure the financial impact of each method. We'll assume that you will have the car for four years, that you drive 15,000 miles yearly, and that business use is 50 percent, or 7,500 miles annually.

If you select the personal ownership, mileage-reimbursement option, each year you will get a tax deduction of $4,237 (56.5¢ x 7,500 miles) for a total tax deduction of $16,950 over four years.

If you select the company ownership option, you'll have to know your yearly operating expenses—insurance, gas, oil, repairs, etc. For our purposes we'll estimate them at $5,000. This figure is then divided in half (the amount of business use) and the result multiplied by 4 (years of ownership). The total four-year deduction for operating expenses is $10,000.

Now do the depreciation calculation. Note that the IRS limits the amount of deductible depreciation. Currently, the first year maximum for a new car is $11,160, the second year $5,100, the third year $3,050, and the fourth and all succeeding years $1,875. Using this schedule, the total four-year depreciation is $21,185. Multiplying it by 0.5 (the percentage of your business use) gives a maximum four-year depreciation allowance of $10,592.

When this depreciation deduction is added to the operating expense deduction of $10,000, the total automobile tax deduction for four years becomes $20,592, or $3,692 more than what could be claimed under the straight mileage method.

There's more to consider, though. When financing is involved, loan interest is deductible for a company car, but not for a personal one. This could mean gaining hundreds of dollars in additional deductions each year.

On the other hand, insurance premiums for company cars are substantially higher than for personal cars, even when used only partially for business. In addition, more insurance is necessary because anyone injured in an accident with a company-owned vehicle is more likely to seek higher damages. Combined, these two factors can add several hundred dollars yearly to company-car costs. Only your insurance person can say how much.

Additionally, the low depreciation allowance for year four and after (currently $1,875) reduces the tax benefit of having an older company car.

Which way to deduct your business auto expenses comes down to a personal call based on finances and preferences.

As a guide, the best situation in which to have a company car is when you replace it every few years, don't actually use it a lot for business (despite what you claim), will pay high finance charges on the purchase, and are in an area with moderate insurance rates. Absent one or more of these conditions, it is probably better to stick to using a personal car and claiming the mileage deduction.

Be sure to check with your accountant before purchasing any car for business use. The above is for general information only.

Business travel and entertainment. You can also deduct travel and entertainment expenses reasonably related to the conducting of business. At this writing this includes 100 percent of all daily business expenses, except entertainment—example: client meals and event tickets—which is only 50 percent deductible.

In addition, if you wish to take a trip to Europe next summer for the sole purpose of taking photographs for a stock file, the expenses are probably deductible. Likewise, if you wish to attend a writer's conference, an art directors' seminar, or an animation trade show on the other side of the continent. As you might suspect, it is no accident that these activities are often held in resorts or attractive cities and that plenty of free time is scheduled. If you are incorporated, you can also schedule your next board of directors' meeting at a good restaurant and have the company pick up the tab.

You can legitimately include recreation/vacation into business trips, too, as long as 50 percent or more of the total time and expenses are business related and all expenses are prorated. As long as your business remains profitable, and you don't overdo it, you'll find that it is legally possible to take advantage of tax-deductible travel and entertainment benefits that will add considerably to the quality of your life.

Strategies for tax reduction

Once you understand the logic upon which your business taxes are based, and the critical importance of keeping track of all your business expenses, you are ready to consider long-term strategies to reduce your tax burden. These strategies can often make the difference between a marginally successful business, and one that will let you enjoy the good life and retire early enough to write novels or paint pictures. As a catalyst for your thinking, some ideas and strategies that are used by others are presented below.

But first, a dual note of caution and encouragement: every business situation is different. What works for another might not work for you; it might get you in financial or legal trouble. Conversely, what works very well for you might be disastrous for anyone else. So you should be both cautious in attempting to adapt "proven" strategies to your situation, and energetic in searching for unique ways to make the tax codes legally work to your advantage.

Cheating. Obviously, this is not a legitimate tax-reduction strategy. Nonetheless, there is no denying that cheating exists in our world. Fortunately or unfortunately, depending upon your point of view, it is relatively easy for a freelance or small shop to hide taxable income and inflate tax-deductible expenses. *Creative Business* surveys—admittedly unscientific because it's tough to get people to 'fess up—indicate that many self-employed individuals are guilty of one or more of the below sins. *But be advised that for just this reason, the IRS audits the returns of self-employed persons and small businesses more regularly and with more scrutiny than it does the returns of others. And if you are caught cheating the penalties can be high.*

When a company and an individual name are the same (Sam Smith/Sam Smith Design), it is easy for payment checks to be cashed and the money pocketed, or deposited directly into a personal checking account without being recorded in the company books as taxable income. The IRS's attempt to control this is the requirement that every company report on Form 1099 all payments to non-incorporated outside contractors of more than $600. In the real world, however, some clients forget to file 1099s (despite a potentially heavy penalty), some 1099s get filed under the wrong social security or employer identification numbers, and 1099s are not required for incorporated contractors. The result: the total on the 1099s the IRS receives seldom equals the actual income received by an individual. As long as the taxable income reported by an individual is more than the total of the 1099s, there will be no IRS audit on this basis.

Since the costs of doing business reduce taxable income, self-employed individuals often invent or inflate routine business expenses—for example, parking fees, taxi fares, postage costs, and client lunches. The IRS requires that expenses over $50 be supported with a receipt showing the business purpose, but those under $50 need only be recorded "contemporaneously" in a desk diary or daily log, although receipts are helpful if questioned. The result is that some individuals make sure that every day there are several dollars of miscellaneous business expenses recorded. There are no guidelines on how much in miscellaneous expenses the IRS will consider reasonable, but if 5 percent or less of total operating expenses ($2,500 out of $50,000) is claimed for a variety of recorded, non-invoiced expenses, it is doubtful this alone will provoke an audit.

Finally, self-employed individuals call personal purchases business expenses—for example, taking a friend out to dinner and calling it client entertainment; purchasing an expensive camera for personal use; taking a vacation trip to another city and calling it business; purchasing a painting for the office that ends up in your living room; using the "company" car mostly for personal use.

There is reason to be cautious. If you find any of the above tempting, also consider this: the IRS (and state and municipal tax agencies) can examine your bank accounts to see whether you've made deposits in excess of declared income. If found, you have to pay the avoided taxes, plus interest, plus a penalty (fine). They also can question the legitimacy of, and "disallow," any business expense. Expenses which are later disallowed will have to be paid, along with accumulated interest and penalty fees. Most important, criminal charges can be filed if the "mistakes" found in an audit—in either under-reporting income or overreporting expenses— exceed 25 percent or more of the total, or show a pattern consistent with attempts to defraud.

Buy in anticipation of freelancing. If you haven't yet gone into business on your own, it may make tax sense to incur many of the organizational costs of your new company—stationery, office furniture, telephone installation, etc.—during a year when you have primarily salaried income. Chances are, as a salaried employee you could use more tax deductions, and your income is probably higher than it will be initially as a freelance. In other words, tax deductions will probably be worth more to you sooner than later. In order to pass the IRS test on this one you should already have some income from freelancing, and it may be necessary to depreciate some of the costs over several years. Ask your accountant what is possible in your specific situation.

Barter when you can. Bartering—trading your services for someone else's goods or services—is technically considered by the IRS as taxable activity. The fair market value of the goods or services received should be declared as income by both parties. In reality however, nearly all small businesses forget to keep track of and declare such arrangements, and the IRS admits that bartering is almost impossible to detect unless done often, or in very large volume. So if you have an opportunity for a beneficial exchange of services—for example, bartering ad preparation for some of the goods or services being advertised—consider it. Such a cashless, taxless arrangement may be a very good deal for both parties. But don't lose sight of the fact that bartering only makes sense when you don't need cash, and when you do need the goods or services offered.

Employ the family. Money paid to a dependent child could qualify as a tax-deductible business expense if he or she performs meaningful work and is compensated realistically. (For example, you can't pay your child $50 an hour to empty wastebaskets.) You should keep track of work hours, or receive an invoice just as for a traditional employee or outside vendor. If a dependent child receives less than $600 (all sources), his or her income does not have to be reported and is not taxable. Earnings above this are taxed at a rate of 15 percent up to $22,750 at this writing. And if your child is under 18, the income is not subject to Social Security tax (FICA) or to federal unemployment tax (FUTA). State taxes may also be exempted.

Here's what this means: you get to claim the pay as a business tax deduction, lowering your taxable income. The child either pays no taxes on the money received, or pays at a more favorable rate than you would if you either kept the money (sole proprietorships and S corporations) or paid it to yourself as salary (C corporations). In other words, the amount of money the family earns is the same, but the taxes paid are less. Check with your accountant to see if this income-shifting strategy makes sense for you.

Buy and rent back. If you have a corporation and wish to make a solid investment, consider purchasing an office condominium rather than renting an office. This way you can stop working at home, reduce your individual tax burden, and make investment profit all at the same time. The procedure is very simple, absolutely legal, and quite lucrative. First purchase an office condominium in your own personal name, financing it in any way that is appropriate. Then, rather than looking for a tenant, simply rent it to your company. All the rent paid by your company to you will be a legitimate business expense. The rent you collect will be taxable personal income, but most of it can be offset by the tax-deductible expenses of investment property ownership. Such expenses include utilities, maintenance fees, repairs, taxes, and any financing charges. The result of this investment is the immediate opportunity to "shelter" some of your personal income and thus pay lower taxes, while at the same time accumulating equity due to any property appreciation. Of course, there may also be significant psychological benefits from owning your own office space. (See "Purchasing commercial space" in Chapter 16.)

Corporate advantages. Let's look at two specific tax advantages that every individual who has incorporated should know. (For other benefits and liabilities of incorporation, see Appendix 1.)

First, and probably most important, your corporation can legally pay the premiums for all health, disability, and life insurance policies of its employees. Further, if it is specifically recorded as an employee benefit in the bylaws, your corporation can also pick up any medical or dental bills not covered by health insurance. The only caveat is that when this benefit is made available to one employee (you), it must also be made available to all others (any staff).

A regular "C" corporation (not an "S" corporation) in a service business can also accumulate up to $250,000 that it is free to invest however it wishes. Building this type of equity in the corporation makes it more valuable for purposes of negotiating loans and for possible future sale and cushions against possible business downturns. If the corporation invests its excess money wisely, dividends are only taxed at 15 percent. To invest accumulated money by increasing corporate profits, rather than personal income, may bring greater returns through deferred or avoided taxes.

On the other hand, the profit of a corporation is also taxed. To avoid double taxation on eventual payout (unless you wish to accumulate money in the corporation for the reasons given above), your accountant will probably ensure that your corporation never shows more than minimal profitability.

Retirement planning

If you're a typical reader, retirement is probably the farthest thing from your mind right now. But you probably do occasionally think: wouldn't it be great to just accept those few projects you really want to work on? Or how about having the freedom to indulge personal interests, like going to an island all summer to paint, or to a cabin in the mountains to write?

This is what retirement planning is really all about: giving you the freedom to do what you want later (but not too late) in life. As such, it should be an important consideration for self-employed creatives even more than for most other people. Because we are not generally much given to analytical (left brain) thinking, planning is not something we do easily. Moreover, when we work for ourselves, we also don't have access to employer-sponsored retirement plans. Yet, being in a business prone to early burnout, we need some type of financial cushion for the future more than most other folks do. Unfortunately, there are few subjects more dry and boring than retirement planning. It requires deciphering acronyms like IRA, SEP, Keogh, and ESOP, and reeks of number-crunching. Then, too, there are all those financial types you have to deal with, individuals who can't understand anyone who doesn't eat, think, and sleep investment strategies. There is also the sure knowledge that we're never going to burn out or grow old anyway. So retirement planning is an easy task to put off—often until it is too late.

An encouragement. The above notwithstanding, setting up and maintaining a retirement plan is actually not that difficult. Particularly if you are still young, chances are you won't have to forgo many lifestyle pleasures in order to amass a stake significant enough to guarantee independence—i.e., your ability to do your own thing free from financial concerns—later on. If you have employees, the cost of sponsoring a retirement plan may pay for itself in an increased ability to attract and hold good individuals. If you can also afford to contribute to an employee plan, your competitiveness as an employer will take a quantum leap. Whatever your situation, some type of retirement plan is probably going to be necessary sooner or later. Even assuming that social security funding will be able to keep up with the increasing demands of a larger and older American population, to enjoy even a modestly comfortable life-style will take substantially more than the government's monthly check.

Financial benefits. Whether you work by yourself or have employees, the effect of a retirement plan on your business and personal bottom line can be substantial. The only negative is that once money has been saved in a tax-deferred plan it cannot be withdrawn without penalties until age 60.

For individuals. The first and most obvious benefit is accumulating savings for later years. The second benefit is both deferring taxes and shelling out less when you do pay. Income invested in government-approved plans is tax-free until the money is withdrawn. This usually follows retirement, when you will likely be in a lower tax bracket. The third benefit is greater investment growth. Since you get to save what would otherwise be given to the government in taxes, this money also earns interest that compounds.

For employers. All the above benefits also apply to employees who are enrolled in a company-sponsored plan. The older an employee mix is, the more crucial having a company-sponsored plan is in retaining staff. Employees typically begin becoming interested in their early thirties or when they start a family. Few senior-level employees will work for a firm without a plan.

Plans for yourself. Self-employed individuals can select from the following financial vehicles. These do not require employees, although for all but regular IRAs, any employees would have to be included.

IRAs. If you have only a limited amount of money each year to invest, setting up an Individual Retirement Account (IRA) is the option to choose. You qualify as long as you are not an active participant in another tax-deferred retirement plan. At this writing you can invest up to $5,500 annually, but this amount will ultimately be pegged to inflation. You have until April 15 of the following year to make a yearly deposit. IRAs are widely available from banks and other financial institutions and are easy to set up. Sales and administration fees are a few tens of dollars yearly and are sometimes waived.

Because there are eleven types of IRAs at this writing, financial advice is recommended. For most individuals, however, a traditional IRA, described above, and a SEP-IRA, described below, are adequate.

The next step up from traditional IRAs are SEP-IRAs—Simplified Employee Pension Plans/Individual Retirement Accounts. (A freelancer can be considered to be his or her own employee.) They are similar to traditional IRAs except more money can be saved. They do, however, require a formal plan, although no additional tax reports have to be filed. At this writing, SEP-IRAs allow you to contribute up to 25 percent of eligible income, or an amount not exceeding $51,000 yearly. You have until April 15 of the following year to both set up a plan and make your yearly deposit. The major drawback of a SEP-IRA is that if you have employees you must also set up and contribute to employee accounts. SEP-IRAs are offered by most banks and financial institutions who take care of the paperwork. Setup costs are a few hundred dollars; administration fees are typically between $75 and $100 yearly per participant.

Keoghs. This is one more step up. Keoghs provide maximum savings potential, but here, too, any employees have to be included. In addition, a formal plan is required along with separate yearly tax reporting. The account must be set up before December 31 of the year in which it takes effect, but thereafter deposits can be made as late as when your tax return is filed.

Profit-sharing Keoghs. They allow flexibility in the amount and frequency of contributions. There is no minimum amount or required schedule. See your accountant for details.

Money-purchase Keoghs. They allow for a higher yearly total but require contributing a previously determined amount on a regular schedule. See your accountant for details.

Combination Keoghs. As the name implies, they permit combining flexible and fixed contributions. Because the only requirement is meeting the fixed percentage specified, most are set up around a low percentage that can be easily exceeded. See your accountant for details.

Defined-benefit Keoghs. They are in addition to the above. (The above are categorized as defined-contribution plans.) Defined-benefit Keoghs allow you to decide how much you want to receive as a future payout, then base your contributions on this goal. Although they require expensive legal and actuarial help to start and maintain, they also allow an individual, particularly a prosperous one nearing retirement, to squirrel away far more than the other Keoghs, potentially into the six figures.

Most banks and financial institutions offer one or all Keogh options. With the exception of Defined-benefit Keoghs (where costs can run into several thousands), costs to create and administer a Keogh are moderate, typically from $250 to $500 for set up; administration fees run from $100 to $200 yearly (per participant if it is a company plan).

Plans for employees. The following plans can be sponsored by a company and offered as an employment benefit.

401(k)s. This is the retirement plan of choice for many creative firms because it is the only one that does not require employers to contribute to employee accounts. Employers set up a 401(k) with a financial institution that offers master plans in which a firm can be included for nominal setup and annual fees. Employers can contribute or not to employee accounts as they choose either by matching deposits or depositing lump sums, including occasional profit-sharing bonuses. Employees do not have to participate, but those who choose to do so indicate when and how much to deduct and where to invest it among the options available. Employers have fiduciary responsibility to ensure that employee accounts are properly handled.

The total amount (employer and employee contributions) that can be saved in one year is based on a complex formula that relates higher-paid to lower-paid employee compensation. It could be as high as 25 percent of an employee's salary, although substantially lower in most creative firms. Only employee contributions are immediately vested—that is, the funds are theirs to keep when they leave the company. Having an employment period before an employer's contribution becomes vested discourages employee turnover, and it can provide additional discretionary funds through contributions made for employees who leave before meeting the vesting requirements. Employer contributions can be vested in two ways: "graded" vesting and "cliff" vesting. With graded vesting an employee is entitled to a portion of the employer contributions each year. After six years an employer's contributions become the employee's. With cliff vesting each employer's contribution becomes 100 percent vested after a set period of time, no more than three years later.

Most large financial institutions offer 401(k) plans, but it may take shopping around for one that will accept a firm with a small number of employees. Nonetheless, consider only reputable institutions that offer several well-established investment funds.

Setting up a 401(k) runs a couple thousand dollars; yearly fees are based on participants and the amount of money handled, typically less than $100 per employee annually, including administration, tax reporting, etc.

SIMPLE 401(k)s. The major differences with a regular 401(k) are that employers must also contribute to employee accounts and all contributions are immediately vested. (SIMPLE stands for Savings Incentive Match Plan for Employees.) These restrictions make them much less popular, but they are not as costly to set up and administer as regular 401(k)s for firms committed to making even small contributions to employee accounts.

SIMPLE IRAs. These are usually the plans of choice for firms of up to 100 employees that wish to make regular contributions to employee retirement accounts. There are no setup or administration fees for employers, and they have no fiduciary responsibility. At this writing, the amount that could have been deposited in an employee account yearly was $21,000; $10,500 from the employee, $10,500 from the employer, but not more than 3 percent of an employee's salary. All contributions are immediately vested.

SEP-IRAs. These previously described IRAs are mostly selected by freelancers and partners without employees. That's because they allow only employer contributions and all employees, including part-timers, must be covered. Contributions are also immediately vested.

Keoghs. They can be set up only by sole proprietorships, partnerships, and Limited Liability Companies (LLCs). The major distinction from a SEP-IRA is the amount that can be set aside yearly. At this writing it is up to 25 percent of employee compensation up to a maximum of $35,000. In addition, there is more employer flexibility—plans need enroll only those who work more than 1,000 hours a year, a provision that eliminates most part-timers. Administration is a little more time-consuming than with a SEP. Keoghs are selected mostly by firms with only occasional part-time employees, or firms with employees who typically leave the company within six years.

ESOPs. Employee Stock Ownership Plans set up to allow employees to purchase company stock can qualify as tax-advantaged retirement plans. There are, however, substantial statutory (ERISA) requirements regarding vesting, participation, and operating procedures. For these reasons, ESOPs are normally impractical for all but the largest creative companies. Check with your accountant.

Custom pension plans. They are seldom a viable option for small businesses. Fees for setup and administration in keeping with the rules of the Employee Retirement Income Security Act (ERISA) can run into the tens of thousands of dollars.

Paying the tax man

Despite all your newly acquired knowledge and strategies for reducing taxes, you will indeed be a rare and lucky person if you can legally avoid them altogether. So it is also important to the long-term success of your business to know how future income tax payments will differ from the automatic salary deductions and filing procedures you might be used to.

Quarterly income tax payments. When you are self-employed, you are expected to pay income taxes during the taxable year, just as you did when you worked for someone else. However, rather than automatic weekly or monthly payroll deductions, you are required to pay quarterly. The dates are April 15, June 15, September 15, and January 15th for the preceding three months. Payments are based on your salary of last year and remitted with Form 1040-ES, "Declaration of Estimated Tax for Individuals."

For example, if you paid $16,000 in federal income taxes last year, you will be expected to pay $4,000 every quarter for the first year after you start in business. At the end of the year, when your tax return is compiled, you will get a refund or remit more, as appropriate. Next year's estimated quarterly payments will be based on this year's salary, and so forth. Most states have similar requirements for state income taxes. By law, you must pay 90 percent of your annual federal tax bill in quarterly payments or you risk an underpayment penalty. In addition, you risk this penalty if you forget to file a quarterly payment. If you should file but lack the cash to pay, at the time this is written you would be assessed a penalty of .5 percent of the amount owed each month. There are some extenuating circumstances (loopholes) that your accountant may be able to use to avoid these penalties, but don't count on them. Be prepared to pay on time.

If you are incorporated, the quarterly payment procedure is similar, but the corporation will be required to submit the taxes "withheld" from your salary, based upon your annual earnings. You will then file your personal income tax return at the end of the year, just as you did when you worked for someone else.

If you have employees, income taxes must be withheld from their salaries, placed in escrow, and paid to the IRS (and most states) on a regular basis. How frequently is determined by the number of employees, but it could be as often as weekly. The penalty for not doing so is 100 percent of the amount owed, plus the actual taxes. (This subject is covered in detail under "Tax and bookkeeping necessities" in Chapter 17.)

Social security and self-employment tax payments. When you worked for someone else, your employer picked up part of your social security (FICA) tax payments; you paid the rest. Now, working for yourself, one way or another you will end up paying the whole thing. Like income tax payments, social security tax payments are due quarterly. If you do business as a sole proprietor or partnership, the FICA tax rate percentage and the amount of salary that is taxable stands at this writing at 15.3 percent of the first $113,700 of earnings, or $17,396. Half of the total FICA tax paid (50 percent) can later be deducted from your gross income when filing your tax return.

If you have incorporated, the corporation is expected to pay 7.65 percent of the first $113,700 of your earnings and you are also expected to pay 7.65 percent, a total of 15.3 percent or $17,396. All of the corporation's FICA tax payment can be deducted from income as a business expense. Despite the deductibility of some or all of your social security tax payments from federal income tax, chances are you will pay several thousand dollars more in social security taxes every year for the privilege of working for yourself. In addition, some cities and states impose a separate "self-employment" tax. Check with your accountant to see whether such a tax is levied in your area.

If you have employees, FICA taxes must be withheld from their salaries, placed in escrow, and paid to the IRS on a regular basis, just like income taxes. The same penalty for not doing so, 100 percent of the amount owed plus the actual taxes, also applies.

Sales taxes. There are thousands of regulations regarding the collection and payment of sales and use taxes. They vary by state, and sometimes by municipality, as well. Ask your accountant what collection and payment procedures you should follow.

Get advice. One of the reasons for having an accountant is the ability to pick up the phone and get tax advice to help you plan, or to keep you from making a mistake. You can also pick up the phone and call the IRS directly and anonymously. They have taxpayer assistance telephones in most major cities. Although these phones are often tied up, especially in the spring, persistence will pay off. While you are on the phone to the IRS, also ask them how to receive a copy of their "Small Business Tax Kit." (Many states have something comparable, as well.)

Pay on time. In this day of computers and automatic fund transfers, the IRS (and most state and municipal tax authorities) is no longer lenient or forgiving about late filing or late payments. They expect you to report on time, and they will cash your check with surprising speed. Penalties for late payments and bounced checks are stiff. However, if, you work with a good accountant, as suggested earlier, neither should be a problem. You may even get to discover how easy it is to get a filing and payment extension when you know the right procedure.

10. Protecting Your Financial Interests

This chapter is about self-preservation—how to make sure your business remains viable and financially lucrative for many, many years. It is also about how to keep your business success from exacting an unacceptably high personal toll, physically and psychologically.

Altruism is a wonderful trait and there is certainly not enough of it in daily life. But when it comes to business, any individual who puts the welfare of others before his or her own loses—each and every time. In the business world, smart individuals always look out for Number One, and the very smartest individuals always look out for Number One without appearing to do so.

When you work for someone else, much of this looking out for Number One is actually done for you. Of course, no one ever gave you a job you didn't deserve, a raise you didn't earn, or a promotion you didn't fight for. Nonetheless, the overall economic well-being of employees is a concern today in even the most callous of organizations. Altruism is not the reason; good business practice is. Now, your company has to adopt the same good business practices towards its most important employee—you. Because yours is a business that is constantly entering new markets with new products (every client and creative execution is different), risk must be minimized everywhere possible. There are several ways to do this. They include being as prepared as you can be for any business eventuality; keeping accurate, up-to-date records of your business activity; staying on top of accounts receivable; knowing how to bill and how to collect; steering clear of potential trouble-making situations; and guarding your empire with unremitting zealousness.

Preparing for the unexpected

Life for an entrepreneur is less predictable and contains more surprises than it does when you work for someone else. You are also much less protected from life's inconsistencies. So your first self-preservation concern is to be as prepared as possible for any eventuality.

Too little business. Here's the classic self-employment dilemma: when you're busy, you don't think about soliciting new work; yet if you don't solicit new work, you won't stay busy. Of course, the solution to the problem is to constantly keep your name in front of potential clients, and to solicit their work, regardless of your current state of busyness. But remembering to promote, whether you currently need to or not, is much easier said than done. It takes considerable diligence.

Typically, what happens to a new freelance is that either through initial promotion, industry friends, or business brought along from the previous employer, there is a period of initial success, maybe six months or a year. Then, ever so slowly the business begins to dry up. Income gets tight and discouragement sets in, maybe to the point of deciding to give up the independent life in favor of the more "secure" income of a regular job. Or perhaps years after you have established a prosperous, seemingly solid business, a key client declares bankruptcy, the economy suddenly sours, an important friend/contact leaves town, or the moon enters into some mysterious phase. Whatever the cause, the result is the same: you find out, too late, that your "prosperous" little company was too dependent upon too few clients.

To guard against the crippling effect of depending upon a few clients, you must, repeat must, continue to solicit new business through good times and bad. People change, businesses change, situations change. Your only protection is to be prepared for change. If you don't, one thing is for certain: Your business will have a short run. (Marketing ideas and techniques are in Section Three.)

Too much business. Is it possible? You bet it is. Too much business might not pose the immediate problems that too little business does, but it creates problems nonetheless. In fact, too much business today often leads directly to too little business tomorrow.

What happens is that you get overloaded, your creative output becomes mediocre, your service gets sloppy, and a good client never calls again—often without telling you why. Or you must turn away a potentially good client because you're booked, already working on a number of smaller, less lucrative jobs. Or you develop the arrogance of omnipotence, a fatal flaw for anyone involved in commercial creativity, no matter how talented. Or you destroy your health trying to keep ahead of your workload.

One solution to the problem of too much business is to add staff, but hiring is expensive and requires commitment, although it is certainly a long-term option you may wish to consider. But here, let's assume that for now you want to keep the status quo—either to remain working alone, or with your current employees; to have enough but not too much work. How do you go about it? How do you regulate demand?

Don't do what might seem logical at first. Don't cut back on contacting new clients and promoting your services. A continuous source of new clients is absolutely essential to your long-term success, regardless of present conditions. Instead, try establishing a stable of noncompetitive freelances to whom you can "farm out" your more routine work when necessary. Students, beginners, retirees, and professionals at home with children are ideal because they appreciate the work, don't charge much, are flexible, and can take direction easily. If you choose your help carefully, you can make even more money than doing all the work yourself. There will also be less effort, and your clients will never know the difference. A small ad in the local trade press will flood you with resumés of possible helpers. (See "The freelance option" in Chapter 17.)

Farming out your overload does call for a certain amount of project management, so you may wish to try another route to profitably controlling your business—start playing in a better league. Gradually increase your prices and simultaneously go after fewer, more sophisticated clients, the ones with larger, more lucrative projects. In other words, try to make the same money by working less hard and keeping fewer clients happier. If you are regularly overloaded with work now, chances are you both are underpriced and have adequately demonstrated your ability to work on more "upscale" projects.

Accident or illness. If your small company were publicly held, it would be considered a very, very poor investment risk. The reason is simply that most, perhaps all, of its resources and potential are tied up in a few individuals (perhaps even one). It would take nothing more serious than a short illness or a simple accident to constrict cash flow while expenses continued more or less unaffected. Setting aside your own feelings of omnipotence, would you invest in such a company without some guarantees that it could easily weather such downturns? Probably not. Do try to be equally objective about your company's vulnerability and set up ways to ensure that the effects of the inevitable illnesses or accidents will be minimal. After all, you are making more than just a financial commitment here; you are also investing a good chunk of your life.

The best protection your small company can have against short-term illness or minor accidents is money in the bank. When starting your business, your capital (liquid assets) should ideally equal about six months

of salary. Later, once established, your company's capital reserves should probably equal at least three months' gross income. This will provide minimum protection against both business downturns and your inability to work for a short time.

For even better protection, start your own short-term, self-insurance fund by opening a special savings account to which you contribute any earnings above a specified amount. Then draw your salary from the account anytime you are physically unable to work. For longer-term protection a comprehensive medical/disability/life insurance plan is critically important. (See "Buying insurance" in Chapter 4.) However, since insurance is very costly, you should also have a long-term goal to take on more and more of the insurance burden yourself.

Finally, and most important, protect your health. It is among your small company's most valuable assets, and the thing you, personally, should be most concerned about. Recognize the inherent hazards of the business, that many independent creatives burn out after only a few years. Working for yourself involves periods of frenetic activity, other periods of slothful inactivity, tremendous financial uncertainty, and the need to constantly expose your creativity to the insensitivity of others. Quite simply, this can be a prescription for medical disaster unless you're prepared to cope with it. Your method of coping has to be a personal decision based upon your own metabolism and life-style. There are, however, three ways that have been proven successful in reducing stress.

First, set aside regular free time—nights, weekends, and vacations— and guard it with religious zeal. Of course, the exigencies of business will occasionally require you to cut into your free time, but this should be the exception, not the rule.

Second, cultivate a variety of other interests to take your mind off business matters and force you away from a workaholic life style. For most people, long-term mental and physical health requires a diversity of interests and activities.

Third, exercise regularly—run, do aerobics, take up tennis, etc. Exercise not only has direct benefits in terms of physical health and fitness, it is also tremendously helpful in relieving mental stress. There is just no better way to keep from accumulating the daily frustrations that so often result in creative burnout.

Client disagreements. Providing creative services is very much a person-to-person business often as reliant on personal chemistry as on talent. Because so much subjectivity is involved in what you do, this personal chemistry can easily turn sour. When this happens, being the individual up against an organization puts you at a distinct disadvantage. The more clearly you explain in advance your method of operation and billing—the two areas in which misunderstandings often arise—the less the possibility of being challenged, and the better your chances to prevail if you are.

Before starting work for any client, always make sure you provide a written statement of what can be expected, when, and for approximately how much. This statement can be in the form of an estimate or proposal, a letter of agreement, a summary of how you work, or a purchase order request. How formal you make the statement, and what type of acceptance you require, depend in large measure upon the size of the job and your trust of the client. Make sure that every client, including good friends, has some written statement (see Chapter 8). And go out of your way to provide regular updates as a job progresses.

In addition, getting some portion of your estimated fee up-front, before starting work, can also be helpful in reducing later client disagreements; it gives the client an immediate financial stake in the job. As discussed under "Terms and conditions" in Chapter 7, the industry standard is one third of the job estimate.

Copyright violation. Under the United States Copyright Law (Public Law 94-553), you own the exclusive rights to every creative work you independently produce until you release those rights to someone else. If you are in an independent, contractual relationship, you probably own what you produce until you are paid for it. Thus, if a client uses your material without paying you, he or she probably has violated your copyright and you can sue for infringement. (Important qualification: if you are engaged in "an employment relationship"—i.e., you are either an employee or have privileges normally associated with employment— the copyright probably belongs to the employer.)

Regardless of your rights, however, your goal should be to do everything you can to stay out of court. It is very possible, even likely, that you can lose in court even when the law is on your side. Prevention being the best medicine, it is wise to include the following line on the cover of any creative submission: "© Copyright (year) (name)." This simple statement is businesslike, and it puts clients on notice that you are prepared to defend your copyright. Moreover, if you should have to sue for infringement, such notice will strengthen your case considerably. Formal registration of copyright with the Copyright Office is required only as a prerequisite for an infringement suit, or to strengthen your rights.

You can also use your copyright as leverage against slow-paying clients. A simple, tactful letter reminding the client that use of your material before payment constitutes violation of a federal statute can do wonders for speeding along a check. For obvious reasons, however, it should be used only as a last resort.

Keeping good records

Perhaps nothing separates a dilettante from a successful businessperson as clearly as his or her ability to keep good records. Not that one should put clerical skill ahead of creative skill, but the ability to keep track of time, income, and costs is nonetheless critical in maintaining client credibility, in justifying expenses to the IRS, and in providing accurate benchmarks of performance. (Note: the information below applies primarily to freelances and two- to three-person operations. For information on record keeping for larger shops, see Chapter 18.)

For client relations. After a job is completed, and long after some of its elements fade from memory, it is necessary to invoice the client. The only thing ensuring the accuracy of the invoice—the difference between fairness to all and "hosing" the client or yourself—is the completeness of your records. If you bill by the job, you will need to add whatever expenses were incurred to the amount previously agreed upon. If you bill by time, you will need to tally hours or days expended, as well as expenses. If you exceeded an estimate, you will need to tell why. To be unable to justify an invoice with corroborative detail on request is to provide an open invitation to suspicion, and eventual loss of clients.

The simplest way to ensure accurate records is to open a separate job jacket—a simple file folder—for every assignment you get. Number the jobs sequentially, and use the same number for material contained in other places such as a computer file, flat art file, etc. Collect in the jacket all the notes, information, and materials related to the job. Staple sheets to its inside front cover for recording the date and time of all travel and client meetings, every hour working on the job, and every expense that should be billed to it. Keep the jacket for several years after the job has been billed. It could prove invaluable in helping you to estimate a similar job in the future.

For the tax man. You should have a good accountant who has advised you on how to set up a checking account and bookkeeping system, and what constitutes legitimate business income and expenses. He or she should also advise you on the level of miscellaneous—i.e., nonchecking account—record keeping appropriate to your particular business. Most of the expenses you incur in the course of soliciting or doing business are deductible for federal (and sometimes state and municipal) tax purposes. Briefly, there should be an invoice to justify every check you write, and there should be "accurate and contemporaneous records" of every cash expenditure, including reimbursement of employee expenses. These records can be in the form of a receipt, or a "petty cash" notation, depending upon the amount and circumstance of the expense.

If your tax returns are audited, you will be expected to furnish a receipt for every cash expenditure over $50. For example, if you take a client out to lunch and pay for it with a credit card, a copy of the receipt should be in your file, annotated with information on the client, and what business was discussed. Likewise, if you pay cash for lunch, you should have an annotated restaurant receipt in the file. If the receipts are all there and properly annotated, and the total of your expenses does not appear to the examiner to be excessive in light of your income, chances are they will all be allowed. (If they are not documented, or appear to the examiner to be excessive, chances are some portion will be disallowed.)

For expenditures less than $50, receipts are always helpful, but not essential. In a few cases receipts are impossible to get, in many others inconvenient, especially under the pressures of doing business in a metropolitan area. For example you may park at meters that charge $1.00 per hour or more in quarters, or you may take a lot of short but expensive taxi trips. You may buy coffee and donuts for quick morning meetings or fill up your car at self-service gas stations. By and large the IRS realizes that expecting you to obtain receipts under these varied circumstances is unrealistic. What they ask for, instead, is a daily log.

The simplest, and best, daily log will be your appointment calendar—paper or electronic. By its very nature it requires daily attention. Before each day, record all of your appointments. At the end of each day record all of your cash expenses, most of which will be directly related to the appointments anyway. If you should be audited, having your daily expenses and activity together will present a convincing argument for their validity.

For yourself. Good records of your time, income, and costs also allow you to measure how your business is doing. By using these records to establish performance benchmarks, you get early warning of potential problems, indications of how to best apply your limited resources, even notice of when it is safe to expand or go on a spending spree.

For the simplest of performance benchmarks, first tally up your fixed expenses for a month, including a minimal salary for yourself. Divide this amount by four to get how much business you must average every week. Then at the end of each week enter in your daily appointment calendar how much business you actually did, billings minus variable expenses. This will give you a quick weekly fix on how well you are doing relative to your needs. Adjust your business-building efforts and unnecessary expenditures accordingly. At the end of each month enter the four-week total and the excess or shortage in a ledger. Keep a running total throughout the year and save the ledgers so you can compare the monthly totals from year to year. Although very simple, this process establishes both a financial benchmark, and a way to measure progress against it. Even better, of course, is a more elaborate system of your own devising matched to your particular procedures and needs. One word of caution, however: don't devise a system so elaborate you don't use it. The name of the game here is self-help. Whatever performance-measuring system you come up with must be simple enough so that it gets used every single week.

In addition, you should also have a way to keep track of where your business is coming from—what type, what industries, what clients. Otherwise, you'll have only the vaguest notion of whether too many of your business eggs are in one basket. Every month tally up what type of work you are doing, and for whom. As months pass, watch for trends. Then use these trends as indicators of where you should expand or contract your efforts.

At the end of each year do a complete financial analysis, an inventory of all your personal (and company) assets and liabilities. From this analysis, detail will emerge on the strength of your finances, as well as one very specific number—your net worth. Use the financial analysis to compare your current standing against those of previous years, and to chart your progress against your personal financial objectives.

Unless you've had financial planning experience, the first time around you'll probably need help in knowing what to count and how, and in setting up the analysis form. In future years, most of what you'll do is simply change numbers, so you can probably do the yearly analysis by yourself. For initial help, see your accountant, or buy a financial planning software package.

Staying on top of accounts receivable

Your accounts receivable balance is the total amount of the invoices you have outstanding—in other words, completed, billed work for which you have not been paid. This figure, and the age of the invoices that comprise it, are important indicators of how successful your collection practices and overall business are. Given the diversity of commercial creativity, generalization is somewhat more difficult than for other businesses, but there are three benchmarks that should be considered.

The one-month average balance. It is in your interest to have a moderate amount of money owed to you; think of it as something like money in the bank. If the amount—your accounts receivable balance— is too small, you have little or no cushion against the inevitable ups and downs of the business. On the other hand, if the balance is too big, you have too much of your money tied up in a nonproductive way.

What is the right amount to have owed to you, the appropriate accounts receivable balance? Successful freelances and shop principals report that the right figure is about one month's income. That is, if monthly income averages $10,000, an average of $10,000 is appropriate to carry as an accounts receivable balance. Freelances just getting started should expect to carry a balance on the low side of the average; those who have more experience or who run larger organizations should expect to carry a balance on the high side of the average, up to a month and a half or two month's income.

The 45-day collection average. To get a feel for how well your collection practices are working, how well you manage cash flow, look at how long it takes, on average, from the time you send an invoice until you receive a check. If your accounts receivable collections average around 45 days, you are doing fine; there's no need for a major change. If your collection average is approximately 60 days, you should be concerned and take long-range steps to lower it. If it is between 60 and 90 days, you have a serious problem that should command your attention soon. If it is over 90 days, financial disaster may be just over the horizon; statistics show that about 70 percent of all invoices over 120 days old are never paid. (See "Proper billing procedures" later in this chapter.)

An accounts receivable aging report. It is a good predictor of cash flow, and can be automated in accounting and bookkeeping software. The calculation goes like this: 1) total the dollar amount of receivables, divide by annual gross income, 3) multiply by 365. The result is accounts receivable days outstanding. Aim to keep the number under 60, and be concerned if it starts to grow.

Avoiding trouble-prone situations

Freelancing or running a creative shop exposes you to all the negative aspects of business life. Yet, unlike larger firms, you don't have the resources to address them. So knowing where the land mines are, and how to best avoid them, is especially important to your economic survival. In more businesslike terms, this means you must learn to assiduously avoid any and all situations where you can't win, even though right may be on your side. Here are some situations that history indicates you should be particularly wary of:

Don't do speculative work. Doing a project on speculation is nearly always a long-shot gamble. Given the subjectivity of creativity, there's no guarantee a client will like even a world-class effort. No commitment usually means no money. If it is a project where the client asks several creative individuals and firms to submit ideas and concepts, all things being equal you'll have no better than a 50/50 chance of landing the assignment or account. The odds get even longer if, as is often the case, the client has a favorite among those asked and is using the ideas submitted by others as a way of turning up the heat.

What if you aren't busy? Then isn't it worth the gamble? Again, probably not. When measured by the expectation of a reasonable return on investment (ROI), speculative work usually falls far short of such activities as contacting new clients and making sales calls. More important, doing speculative work leaves the products of your business (ideas) very vulnerable. An unscrupulous client may simply steal them. Copyright protection not withstanding, there really isn't much you can do if it happens.

Even honest clients sometimes steal ideas, although not on purpose. Let's say you present a concept that the client, for valid reasons, decides not to use. Then, some months or years later, you notice the same approach—your idea—in other client material. Wasn't it stolen? Not necessarily. Maybe the client remembered "this great idea," but didn't remember where it came from. Whether misuse is intentional or not, once an idea is shown it is tough to prove ownership later. Even if you can, the cost and trouble of doing so may outweigh the benefits, or cause you to offend a good and otherwise honest client.

Most other professionals—lawyers, accountants, engineers, etc.— don't provide services on trial. Clients make decisions based upon reputations and the quality of past work. So should ours. To do otherwise encourages clients to think of creativity as insubstantial activity— the quickly arrived at Big Idea—and de-emphasizes the importance of research, execution, and service. In the few cases where professionals do work on speculation— e.g., architects in a design competition—the competition is in a public forum and there are tightly drawn specifications. Moreover, the projects usually involve contracts worth many millions of dollars.

If speculative work is so bad, why then do so many agencies and large shops accept it? Actually, many don't, but we tend to hear about those that do, especially when they're in competition with us. For a large agency or shop, speculative work is usually a very small percentage of overall activity; it may help keep staff busy during slow periods (sometimes avoiding layoffs after an account loss), and the potential reward—often ongoing business worth millions—may make it an attractive gamble. In contrast, for most of us a speculative project is a significant percentage of our activity; if times are slow there are other, more productive ways to keep ourselves and staff busy; and the potential reward—usually a single assignment or a small campaign—makes it a very unattractive wager. Finally, the reason most small agencies, shops, and freelances accept speculative projects is that they just don't know any better. If they are your competition, hang in there and resist the pressure to compete at this level. Most likely they won't be around to be your competitors in the future. (See "Why we don't make speculative presentations" in Appendix 3.)

Work for immediate reward. Sooner or later you will be approached by a client who wants your services "on the come." That is, they want to defer most or all of your payment until they are in a better financial position. Usually the pitch is something like this: "Do this little job for us for free now, while we're poor, and we'll give you all our advertising work later, when we're rich."

Like speculative presentations, working on the come is a big gamble, one that seldom pays off. Promises of future work are difficult or impossible to put on paper, and when not on paper may as well be written on the wind. Priorities change, responsibilities change, people change, companies change, and every change makes even well-intentioned promises harder and harder to remember.

Equally risky is payment in company securities. We've all heard stories like the one about the creditor who never had to work again because he accepted the stock of a nearly bankrupt company right before it invented a universal technology. Unfortunately, for every one of those stories, there are dozens of unreported cases of individuals who accepted stock that later became worthless. If company securities are offered to you, think long and hard about your immediate and long-term financial needs. When you accept securities in lieu of money, you are in effect making a bet on the future, and like any bet it shouldn't be made unless you are prepared to lose.

In a similar vein, you may be offered a company's products or services in lieu of money. For example, let's say you prepare a new brochure for a Caribbean resort and are offered an opportunity to trade your time for a vacation there next winter, or you are offered an opportunity to barter your services for merchandising credits with a local computer retailer, or with a manufacturer for specific products. Such arrangements are great, provided you genuinely need the products or services offered, and you are able to obtain them for substantially less than just taking the money and purchasing retail. The caution is not to let client pressures or your emotions get in the way of a rational evaluation of your actual needs.

Turn the meter on after the first call. It is reasonable for a potential new client to expect you to make one brief, and free, presentation for the purposes of showing your work, and soliciting business. Under normal circumstances, it shouldn't take more than that to see whether you are qualified to take on an assignment. So after one presentation it is equally reasonable that you should charge for every additional call you make.

If you don't make one call normal procedure for presenting your work, you leave yourself quite vulnerable. You will occasionally get called by potential clients who will have you return several times to interview with various levels of management before finally deciding "not to do the job right now." You will run into unscrupulous clients who will pick your brains for hours before informing you that the company (never he or she) has decided, "to save money and do the job in-house." Or you will be used by window-shopping clients who will look at your work and pricing as a way to verify that their present arrangements are, after all, the right ones.

Of course, how strongly you wish to adhere to this "one-presentation, one-job" principle depends a lot upon the size of a potential assignment, the feelings about integrity you get on the interview, and the future opportunities the assignment may lead to. Nonetheless, your norm should be no more than one free, and brief, call per client. When dealing with repeat clients, the meter should be running on each and every call you make.

Put agreements in writing. This has been said before, but it cannot be said too many times. You should provide every client with a statement of your terms and conditions as they relate to a particular job. You may, or may not, also want to provide a client with a written estimate; you should expect a client to give you a signed purchase order or letter of agreement based on your terms or estimate.

Verbal agreements and handshakes are great as far as they go, but they don't go very far. When all the cards are down, you can't borrow against them at the bank, you can't use them as leverage in the client's accounts payable department, and you can't show them to the judge in court. So don't pass "go" until you have some type of signed agreement. You needn't feel shy about asking for a signed agreement either. It is a professional way of doing business, appreciated by other professionals. Be cautious of anyone who considers it otherwise.

Bill quickly and professionally. You can't expect a client to be scrupulous about adhering to your mutually-agreed-upon working arrangements unless you are scrupulous about them as well. In addition to reporting any problems or discrepancies as they occur, delivering work when promised, and charging what is expected, this also requires thorough, professional accounting and billing procedures.

Proper billing procedures

How much detail your invoices should include is a matter of personal taste modified by a particular client's desires. However, it is probably a good idea to include at least the following: a statement of billed work (e.g., so many hours at so many dollars per hour); a breakdown of all expenses incurred; a total of the amount owed (work + expenses); job delivery date; the purchase order number or other form of client authorization; your tax number; and your payment terms. Including all this (and more if appropriate) demonstrates your professionalism, and addresses most billing questions/concerns before they need to be raised. The larger the client organization and the more individuals who must sign off, the greater the need for detail.

The invoice style can be highly individualistic, as long as it is businesslike. Preprinted forms are not necessary. Indeed, they make a bill for professional services look a little too much like a bill for equipment, or auto repair. Best bet is probably to type your invoices cleanly on your own letterhead.

Send your invoices at the times agreed upon, and normally no later than a week or so after the job has been delivered. Prompt billing has several advantages. It helps your cash flow. It forces the client to approve the invoice when the complexities of the job are still fresh in his or her mind. Finally, it will raise any questions or disagreements while your memory of events is still fresh enough to provide satisfactory answers.

When sending a final invoice, a nice additional touch is to attach a short, personal thank you note. It takes some of the coldness out of what is otherwise a formal process, and it reinforces your honesty and sincerity.

Checks from clients who are set up to pay on a "Net 30" basis often don't reach their vendors for 45 days. Take no follow-up within that time, but if payment still hasn't been received after 50 or so days, call the person with whom you dealt and ask him or her (or secretary) to look into the problem. Don't be shy about this; it is the professional thing to do and it often unearths such problems as a disagreement, or the invoice simply getting lost. In the latter case, ask that your invoice be taken out of the normal processing cycle and be put through for immediate payment. If the client needs time to "look into the problem," or promises payment that is not quickly forthcoming, continue to call at least once a week. Don't be discouraged. Be friendly, but don't let them off the hook. Remember, the problem is theirs, not yours.

At 60 days after the first invoice was sent, and regardless of whether you have telephoned or not, send a second invoice clearly labeled: SECOND INVOICE. PAST DUE. DO NOT DUPLICATE.

At 90 days after the first invoice was sent, send a third invoice clearly labeled: PAST DUE. THIRD AND FINAL INVOICE. IMMEDIATE PAYMENT REQUESTED.

Turning up the collection heat

Success in any endeavor requires strength of resolve. In the business world a test of that strength occurs whenever others threaten your legitimate interests. It happens most often when others delay or refuse payment owed you. For example, let's say you have a client whom you billed three months ago, who hasn't paid, and now stops returning your calls. Payment was promised, but you suspect it will be a long time in coming, if it comes at all. Meanwhile, the client continues to operate, business as usual. What's the best way to pressure the client to pay, maintain your professionalism, and not tie up a lot of precious time? Here are some tips and effective debt-collection procedures:

Never play upon client sympathies or resort to gimmickry. Such personal appeals as, "I really need the money to pay my rent next week," stamping your invoices with cutesy empty-pocket cartoons, or faxing humorous past-due reminders, are demeaning to you and unprofessional. You should never act as though paying a legitimate invoice is in some way doing you a favor. Rather, it is meeting a legitimate obligation. Even when such tactics actually do get you your money faster, they affect your self-esteem, lower professionalism, and reduce your ability to charge what you are worth in the future. Professionals don't grovel after money legitimately owed to them.

Don't consider harassment, no matter how wronged you feel. There are laws against the use of defamation of character, abuse (verbal as well as physical), or illegal means to collect debts. In other words, forget calling your cousin the bouncer. Trying anything other than regular requests through normal business channels probably will backfire, and subject you to more liability than the debt is worth.

The basic necessities. Although collecting from deadbeat clients is never easy, it is easier when there is no question about their obligation—no ambiguities, misunderstandings, or loopholes. The stronger your position, the more incontrovertible your proof, the sooner you'll get paid. Also, before labeling any invoice a bad debt and trying to force payment, you should have made reasonable and businesslike attempts to collect. If you have missed any of the three steps summarized below, try to correct the mistake before proceeding. If it is obviously too late (for example, you have no signed commitment by the client), proceed, but recognize that your chances of being successful have been compromised; you stand a chance of being stiffed. Chalk this mistake up to experience, and resolve never to make the same one again.

You have a signed agreement. Whatever the form—an estimate or letter signed by both parties, a purchase order (PO), or some type of written contract—it is important that you have written proof that the client actually authorized the work and has not lived up to his or her end of the bargain. It is also important that the document indicate the delivery date and payment terms (e.g., "Net 30").

Three invoices have been sent. As noted above, you should make three requests for payment before pressuring the client to pay. There is, however, no need for more than three payment requests.

Follow-up phone calls have been made. Also as noted above, you should have been in personal contact with the client by telephone or in person.

Having done all this, if you sense a problem, or any invoice gets to be more than 120 days old, you must now be prepared to go the next step and attempt to force payment. Professionalism demands nothing less. In doing so, recognize right up front that you are about to enter the land of hardball business and that everything done henceforth will likely anger the client. It may get you some or all your money eventually, but chances are you will kiss the client goodbye in the process.

Your courtroom alternatives. Since we live in society framed by law, it would seem that any obvious case of nonpayment for goods or services should be expeditiously enforceable by the courts. Unfortunately, this is not the way things work. As any honest lawyer will be quick to tell you, with one exception (see below) courts should be the last place you go to encourage a client to pay up.

Any suit against another party that involves nonpayment will be heard in civil (not criminal) court. The presumption of the court will be that no law has been broken and there is no innocence or guilt; simply a disagreement between two parties. The court is the place where both sides of the dispute will be heard, and a judgment will be made to settle it. Although generally the law recognizes the right of a creditor to receive money due for services satisfactorily performed, proving satisfactory performance can be difficult in a field where services are subjectively evaluated.

If, for example, the defendant (your client) says what you delivered was unsatisfactory, how can you prove otherwise? What you know to be a clear-cut case of malfeasance may appear to the judge to be a case of honest disagreement. (Now you can see why a signed agreement detailing working terms and conditions is important in settling any disagreement, in or out of court.) Even more discouraging is that most civil courts are backlogged, especially in metropolitan areas. A wait of a year or two to get a case heard is not unusual. The defendant's lawyer knows that for you to go to court involves this wait, plus legal costs, plus considerable hassle—all with no guarantee of satisfaction. At best you may get all you are owed with interest and court costs, but also likely is that you will end up with nothing but several hundred dollars in legal fees after a frustrating year-long wait.

Finally, even winning a case in court does not guarantee payment. All it does is get a debt turned into a judgment. The client may appeal, causing more months of delay, or just plain refuse to pay, pleading hardship, for example. To obtain payment you must begin proceedings for the attachment of assets—more delay, lawyers' fees, and court costs.

When to use small claims court. The single bright spot in the legal system is small claims court. In small claims court your case is usually heard within a month or two, and no lawyer is necessary. Small claims courts are set up specifically to keep small financial disputes out of the regular court system, and to thereby reduce the cost and increase the speed of settlements. Their aim is to provide a simple system that eliminates legal delays and maneuvering, and thus make justice more easily attainable, especially to individuals and small companies. How each state goes about this, however, varies tremendously.

For example, the definition of small claims—the maximum amount that can be awarded in small claims court—varies from as low as $750 to as high as $10,000, with the average being about $2,000. Some states allow lawyers for both sides, some only for defendants; some allow no lawyers at all. Some states don't allow appeal, some do. Some states offer litigants clerical help and advice. Some states allow the plaintiff (you) to bring suit only in the jurisdiction of the defendant (your client); others allow the plaintiff a choice of his or her jurisdiction or that of the defendant. And so forth.

To find out what the small claims court procedures and limitations are in your state, contact the Clerk of Courts in your local municipality. Generally you can get a booklet that describes exactly what claims are eligible and what you must do to file suit. Regardless of what the procedures and limitations are, however, if your claim can qualify you will probably find that filing suit in small claims court is preferable to filing in regular court. Even if you are owed $2,000 and the small claims limit is $1,500, it is probably better to get an immediate, inexpensive trial for $1,500 than to incur the cost and time necessary to go for the full amount in regular court. Filing suit in small claims court usually involves nothing more than filling in a simple form. Court fees are normally about $25, and are returned as part of the judgment if you win. It takes just a few weeks to get to trial, and case preparation requires nothing more than telling your story to the judge and showing corroborative creative work, invoices, letters, etc.

The big advantage you have in small claims court as opposed to regular, civil court is that the deck is stacked in your favor. Individuals and small businesses are normally given the benefit of the doubt. The defendant (or his or her representative) must appear to defend the charges, a time-consuming and expensive procedure for many large organizations. In many cases, a defendant faced with a notice to appear in small claims court will find it less costly to settle than to appear. If the defendant fails to appear, a judgment is made automatically in your favor.

What about "alternative dispute resolution" (ADR)? Although probably not the answer when you've clearly been "stiffed" or wronged, ADR may be the way to go for honest disagreements. An example would be a client refusing to pay because they believe they have been overcharged for project alterations. Essentially, ADR is a process whereby both parties agree to sit down before a "neutral" (industry term) and try to settle their differences.

Mediation. This is a non-legal procedure and is the first and some-times only step necessary. It can be proposed by either party at the time of a dispute (i.e., without prior agreement) and the results are not binding. Yet, it can be nonetheless effective because a third party can often suggest compromises that allow the antagonists to save face and keep from dukeing-it-out in the courtroom. Indeed, the effectiveness of mediation is such that some judges now require it before agreeing to hear civil suits. Mediation works best when both parties believe the dispute is an honest disagreement and also recognize the high cost of involvement in a winner-take-all legal suit. The more each is willing to concede that things might not be one sided, the better the chances are that mediation will work.

Arbitration. This is a legal process that takes place outside the court-room. It requires that both parties consent in writing to submit the dispute to arbitration and abide by the neutral's (arbitrator's) decision. If so, the decision is as enforceable as any court judgment. Lawyers may represent the parties at arbitration hearings, but they are not crucial. Hearings are not as adversarial as court sessions, and the laws of evidence do not apply. Because of the consent needed from both parties, arbitration is usually only effective when it is agreed on before there's a problem. For creative work this means a clause included in a project's signed estimate, proposal, or letter of agreement. Otherwise, you can ask the client to agree to submit to arbitration, but it's a long-shot, especially if there is animosity between you.

Local collection agencies. Every metropolitan area has several compa-nies whose business is collecting bad debts for other companies. For a listing of the ones available in your area look under "Commercial collections" in the Yellow Pages. For a fee of up to 40 percent of the amount recovered, they will write several carefully worded letters, and may telephone the client as well. Although a local collection agency may work effectively for you, more likely they won't, or they just won't want to accept a single small collection as an assignment. Most specialize in volume work for local retailers, physicians, dentists, etc.

Dun & Bradstreet's Debt Collection Service. Probably the simplest, most economical, and effective way to prod recalcitrant clients into paying is to use Dun & Bradstreet's Debt Collection Service. They are effective because Dun & Bradstreet (D&B) is the principal compiler of credit histories on American businesses. Thus, a mere threat to report slow payments to D&B packs considerable punch in the business community. Most honest, solvent companies don't like to risk damaging their D&B credit rating over something as insubstantial as a late payment to a small vendor. Equally important, simply invoking the name of Dun & Bradstreet will prove to clients, honest and dishonest alike, that you are sophisticated enough to call in D&B to help collect when necessary.

D&B offers three services. For $25 they will send a single "demand" letter on your behalf; for $40 they will send up to three letters; and for $15 plus a contingency fee they will use a combination of letters and telephone calls to collect. These actions affect the client's D&B credit rating. Debt resolution typically takes several months, although sometimes it happens faster. More significant, even with all their efforts and market clout, Dun & Bradstreet only claims a success ratio of about 40 percent. Success to D&B means resolution; it doesn't necessarily mean getting all your money. Often, settlement is some percentage of the amount actually owed. To get in touch with Dun & Bradstreet, look them up in the business pages of any metropolitan area telephone directory. Their website is www.smallbusiness.dnb.com.

A collection case history. Here is a typical debt collection experience: A creative firm was hired to write, photograph, and design several items that would establish a new identity for a small and growing organization in the health care business. Before accepting the project, a credit check showed the client to have an exemplary payment record. For this reason, with an immediate need to get started, no money was obtained before the firm began work (a mistake). After weeks of meetings and creative development, during which several ideas were shown, the company asked to have the project shelved temporarily. At this point, an invoice for approximately $10,000 was rendered.

When the invoice was not promptly paid, the firm made follow-up telephone calls and sent duplicate invoices. Each time the company was contacted they promised payment, "Next month, as soon as we get our recent cash-flow problems sorted out." After several broken promises, the firm called upon Dun & Bradstreet to speed collection. Over the next three months, D&B wrote several letters to the company with much the same response—they were having temporary problems, but all bills would ultimately be paid. Not satisfied with this, D&B also made a personal visit to the company's comptroller a month later. It was now nearly a year since the first invoice was sent. In addition, D&B had shared with the creative company credit information they had obtained showing the organization had fallen seriously behind on its payments to all other vendors. In short, the problem was not payment discrimination; it was, indeed, lack of money. The client's comptroller was candid with D&B about his company's financial condition and offered two alternatives to resolve the outstanding invoice. One was immediate payment of 33 cents on the dollar as complete settlement, the other was delay until year end when, the comptroller hoped, additional revenue would enable the company to pay the invoice in full. This choice was presented to the creative firm by Dun & Bradstreet as the best they could do.

In the spirit of a small one in the hand being worth more than a large one in the bush, the creative firm opted for immediate payment. A week later a check was delivered to Dun & Bradstreet for $3,333. From this, they deducted their 25 percent fee, or $833, and sent along a check of $2,500 as full payment of the debt and settlement of the claim.

In addition to the three normal collection options listed above, there is still another tactic that may be possible. It only works in a few situations, and even these may vary from state to state. It is also a little more difficult now than in the past due to recent court rulings, but it is certainly worth knowing, and asking a lawyer about. The procedure, covered next, is attaching the assets of the client.

Attaching the assets of a deadbeat client

In those situations where it is possible, attaching the assets of a client may get you your money faster, and it may also sow a little havoc in the client's business—perfectly legal, and sweet revenge—not an insubstantial benefit all by itself. Generally, this collection tactic is appropriate to pursue if the client has signed a clear agreement that has not been disputed, and the job has been satisfactorily completed, billed, and delivered, but payment is long overdue. It helps to have received at least some money from the client, although this is not absolutely necessary. Receipt of a previous check for partial payment indicates acceptance of satisfactory performance and general agreement with the job's total cost. In addition, a cancelled check serves as a means to get the client's bank and bank account number, which you will try to attach. It appears on the back of the check as part of the cancellation data.

If the above description fits your situation, and the client ignores repeated attempts to collect on one or more job invoices, here's how to proceed, and what may happen.

Step 1: Call a lawyer. Attaching assets is not something you can do yourself. You need to work through the courts, which means hiring a lawyer. Call, explain the situation, say what you want accomplished. The lawyer may tell you it is possible, impossible, or risky (the possibility of a countersuit). If the former, move on to step 2.

Step 2: Make sure the client has money. If you have the client's bank account number (see above), your lawyer can call the bank to check on availability of funds. Usually the lawyer says the call is to ascertain whether a check in the amount of the unpaid bill will clear. Most banks will honor such inquiries, although they won't say how much money is actually in the account. (It is not necessary for a client to have sufficient money in the account, but there is little point in going after a client who is obviously insolvent.)

Step 3: Go to court for an attachment. Armed with all the facts— a signed agreement detailing the project and your terms, samples of the work completed, previous payment information, unpaid invoices, and the solvency of the client—your lawyer now draws up a complaint or petition asking for a court attachment of assets. You will be asked to file an affidavit that the facts presented to the court are true. Both the complaint and the affidavit are now filed with the Clerk of Courts. At a judicial hearing, usually requested for later the same day, your lawyer will ask for an immediate attachment of assets in the client's bank equal to the amount owed.

In considering the request, the judge looks at the facts, assesses their validity and relevance, and determines whether there is a reasonable likelihood that you would prevail if the case were to go to court to be decided. In addition, the judge considers whether there is a chance that the assets might be removed by the client if he or she knew what was going on. Usually, the judge makes one of three rulings: 1) allowing the petition; 2) denying the petition; or 3) notifying the client in an attempt to resolve the problem before ordering an attachment. If the judge should decide on the latter course of action, it can serve the same purpose of attachment—getting your money. Up to this point, the client has no idea what is taking place. Note that getting an attachment is never a sure thing. Much depends upon how strongly your lawyer makes a case for its necessity, how the judge is predisposed, and the local legal precedents.

Step 4: Serve the attachment. If the attachment is granted, your lawyer now hires the local sheriff to serve it on the bank, then on the client. The attachment orders the bank to freeze (reserve) an amount in the account equal to your bill. Any funds in excess of this amount are not affected, but the client cannot make withdrawals that will bring the balance below it. Any checks that will bring the account below the court-ordered balance will not be honored (they will bounce).

Step 5: Wait for a call. Even if the client has multiple bank accounts, having one under a court-ordered attachment is at best an embarrassment, at worst crippling. Thus, most likely you will get an irate call within hours of the client's notification. Whether you hear from the client directly, or from the client's lawyer, your response should be to refer all calls to your lawyer.

Step 6: Get resolution. The client will try to get the attachment lifted immediately. Of course, one way of doing this is to pay up. Another option is for the lawyers to negotiate for some immediate payment to get the attachment lifted, with a promise of the balance to follow shortly. A third option is for the client to go to court to get the attachment lifted.

The cost. Legal time for work such as this normally runs in the range of $200 per hour. Interviewing you, gathering documents, filing papers, and appearing in court can take a day of your lawyer's time. Court and sheriff's fees may run another couple hundred dollars. In other words, be prepared to spend a couple thousand dollars or more. It may, however, be possible to get a lawyer who will take your case on a contingency basis (payment as a percentage of the amount recovered). In any case, don't proceed until you have a clear understanding of the legal fees involved, and the relative chances of success.

The time to fight

Legal action to collect debts, like war, is a last resort to be invoked only when diplomacy fails. However, sometimes winning is impossible without at least the threat of a fight. Here are some times when it may be appropriate to make warlike gestures: when a client absolutely refuses to pay, or compromise; when any invoice is over 120 days old, and you have sent at least two unanswered follow-up invoices; when telephone calls and letters about your unpaid invoice go unanswered; when your material is used (published) before you receive payment; when a client seeks court protection under "Chapter 11"; when you receive only a fraction of what is owed, along with a vague promise for later payment; when a company suddenly moves to smaller, less opulent quarters, and all of its invoices "got lost"; and when a client's checks repeatedly bounce.

Whenever such events happen, you have several options. As explained above, the best alternative for claims under $2,000 (depending upon the state in which you live) is probably small claims court; for more than $2,000 and up to $10,000, Dun & Bradstreet's services; and for claims over $10,000, call a lawyer about the advisability of attaching client assets or filing suit in civil court.

In the latter case chances are that the first thing your lawyer will do is to send the client, by certified mail, what is called a "lawyer's letter." It officially states your grievance so later there can be no claim of ignorance, and it contains a diplomatically worded threat about the consequences of nonsettlement. It should also establish a deadline beyond which you will take action. To send such a letter, most lawyers charge a fee of around $100.

The client may respond in several ways. You hope that by showing that you intend to pursue the matter and have set a timetable for doing so, settlement will follow. After all, beyond this point, defense may start to run up legal fees. The client may offer to compromise, in which case you have to decide, in consultation with your lawyer, how strong your case would be if you went to court, and what the costs in cash flow, time, and aggravation would be. Sometimes settlement for a fraction of what is owed is the most financially practical, if not the most emotionally satisfying solution.

More likely, however, the client will decide to stall or fight, especially if the organization has an in-house legal staff, or lawyers on retainer. There is little or no cost or risk (they can always settle later) and it puts more pressure on you to drop your demands, or to compromise. The client may even file a countersuit as a way of indicating the seriousness of the intention to challenge your claim. If you don't reach a settlement, your next move is to consider going to court.

Before taking this step, get from your lawyer a reasonable estimate of the litigation time and cost, and any courtroom or alternative strategies. For example, rather than fighting for every penny, it may be wiser to try and settle out-of-court for 75 percent of what is owed, or perhaps the client will agree to binding arbitration, or your lawyer may agree to work on a contingency-fee basis. In this arrangement, if you lose, you pay only out-of-pocket expenses, but if you win the lawyer takes a percentage (often 30 to 40 percent).

A courtroom case history. There is almost infinite variety in the ways that action can be taken in the civil court system, depending upon the facts and the legal jurisdiction in which the case is filed. Only your lawyer can give you a good idea of what might happen should you decide to sue a client (or a client or supplier decides to sue you). But to give you a feeling for the process, here is an actual case history that's typical of litigation a freelance or creative shop might bring against a client.

The facts are these: A freelance was hired in September to write a short annual report. He obtained the assignment after an interview with the client company's manager of public relations to whom he presented a written estimate similar to the sample in Appendix 3. A second, brief interview with the company's chief financial officer (CFO) followed. The freelance received no money up front.

In October, after extensive interviewing, the freelance produced a first concept/draft which, "Didn't capture what made this year so significant," according to the CFO. On the second concept/draft the CFO said, "Better, but still not right." When the third try also did not satisfy the CFO, the freelance, sensing basic incompatibilities, suggested that perhaps it would be better, in the interests of cost-savings, to move the job in-house. The public relations manager decided to do the writing, and the parting was amiable.

In mid-November, the freelance sent a bill for $4,200 covering two thirds of his time, a concession he made because the job didn't satisfy the client. There was no response. After 60 days, a follow-up telephone call unearthed a problem—the CFO was incensed for having been billed at all. "We don't pay for unsatisfactory goods or services," he said. Further, he claimed to have never seen or approved the estimate provided the public relations manager. At this point, the freelance called his attorney.

A lawyer's letter explaining the obligation to pay for consultation and creative services, even if not totally satisfactory, was sent to the CFO around the first of December. Included was an offer to compromise. A reply from the client company's lawyers essentially restating the CFO's contention—no satisfaction, no pay—was received at the end of the year. Thus, five months after the assignment, a suit to collect the $4,200 was filed in civil court.

In July, the "discovery" phase of the process began. The client's lawyers requested from the freelance's lawyer copies of all documents pertinent to the case, and sent along a list of some thirty questions (interrogatories) which were to be answered. Some of the questions were quite detailed and obviously designed to harass the freelance—for example, "Provide a complete and detailed history of similar work done for other clients, and amounts billed." (Some such questions were deemed irrelevant by the freelance's lawyer, and not answered; some had to be answered.) An offer to settle the case for $1,000 was also made by the client's lawyer. It was refused.

By December, fifteen months after the assignment, the client's lawyers filed a motion to have the case dismissed—another harassment tactic. The freelance's lawyer felt it was important to have him available when the judge heard the motion, so both the lawyer and the freelance had to spend a morning in court. After the judge ruled in favor of the freelance (and chastised the client's lawyers for bringing the motion), the client's lawyers offered to settle for $2,500. This offer was also refused.

Early in the next year, the court set a trial date for September. In preparing for the case, the freelance's lawyer informed the client's lawyer that it was his intention to subpoena the company's president and chairman of the board, as well as the chief financial officer and public relations manager, to appear in court. This was possible because all four had been interviewed for the report, and were involved in determining the quality of the writing.

In June, the week before the subpoenas were to be issued, an offer to settle for $3,500 was made, and refused. Later that month, shortly after the subpoenas were issued, a check for the full amount of $4,200 was received and the case was dropped.

Who won? Only the lawyers. The client managed to defer payment for nearly two years, but ran up a thousand dollars or more in legal fees. The freelance got only what was legitimately owed him, paid over five hundred dollars in legal and court fees, and waited two years for his money.

In many ways this case is typical—the delays, the legal maneuvering, the harassment and attempts at intimidation, but in many other ways it is not, because of the strength of the freelance's case. There was no dispute over whether the work was done on time, on budget, or professionally. The only dispute was over the work's quality—a subjective issue in which the freelance could claim more expertise than the client. Also significant, a statement of terms and conditions had been provided and agreed to by an appropriate client executive. Most important, the involvement of four corporate executives made it in the interests of the client to settle out of court, especially when the amount was so relatively small.

The moral: to paraphrase Oscar Wilde, "A freelance cannot be too careful in the choice of whom he sues." Put another way, only pick fights when you have a good chance of winning, and make sure you raise the odds by getting agreement in advance on what services you are going to provide, when, and for how much. Even so, as the case above indicates, it is better to stay away from the courtroom unless your pride or a relatively large sum of money absolutely demands it.

The value of credit checks

Any discussion of payment problems has to include these two unfortunate facts: 1) the less power a creditor has, the lower they will be on a debtor's payment priority list; and 2) creative businesses have virtually no power. Unlike other, high-priority creditors, we can't threaten to turn off the lights, delay shipments, ruin credit, or repossess goods. Thus, we end up very vulnerable—among the last to be paid whenever a client has a financial problem. For these reasons we need to take special care to avoid being in a bad position when the inevitable does happen.

One way to reduce somewhat the odds of being stuck by a financially strapped client (or one with a bad payment history) is to do an up-front credit check. It is important, however, not to let a credit check give you a false sense of security. A credit check only shows past history; it doesn't guarantee a client's present or future financial stability or flexibility on financial disagreements.

When to do it. All inquiries about a new client you are pitching should be done beforehand. It is unprofessional to first solicit a client's business, then ask for credit references, or to later turn down an assignment based on poor credit history. If a client approaches you about doing an assignment, however, you should have no reservations about asking for credit references, or doing a credit check before accepting.

The do-it-yourself method. You can often get a good feel for a potential client's credit worthiness by asking around. In particular, inquire of printer friends. As similar-type vendors, they often provide the best indication of any organization's payment priorities. To more formally check out a potential client who calls you, ask for three credit references when getting the assignment detail. Having your own credit reference form will make this both easier and appear routine. ("We ask each of our new clients to fill out this form.") Your credit reference form should ask for the name, account number, and account person at the client's principal bank. In addition, it should also ask for the names of two other organizations that have provided credit, along with the name of a contact person. If appropriate, ask for at least one photographer or printer. Finally, make sure you call each nonbank reference to check on the client's average payment history and ascertain whether they have had any collection problems.

Dun & Bradstreet Business Information Reports. D&B is probably your best bet when looking for a comprehensive overview of an organization's credit history and financial status. The only drawback is that D&B reports may not be available for many smaller firms, or may be less than comprehensive on those that are privately held. Three types of reports are offered. For $62 they will provide what they refer to as a "credit evaluation" of a company; for $162 they will provide a comprehensive report including a graphic of risk indicators and all the key data in a company's D&B file. For more information on D&B Business Information Reports, visit their website: www.dnb.com.

Bankruptcy and debt adjustment terms

Despite what you do to minimize your risk, you'll probably be affected by someone filing for protection from creditors sooner or later. This process is carried out in federal court, and the type of protection requested is usually referred to by its chapter number in the United State's Bankruptcy Code. Here's what it all means:

Chapter 7. This is a straight bankruptcy petition. Filers certify that debts are far greater than their ability to pay them. In essence, they have asked the court to seize and dispose of all assets, to use the proceeds to pay off as much debt as possible, and to cancel ("discharge") what remains. A filing company will go out of business in its present form. Individuals who file will get a chance to start over.

Chapter 11. This is a petition from a company trying to avoid bankruptcy. It believes it has future potential but needs temporary relief from its creditors. The court appoints a trustee who reorganizes and runs the company, and uses its resources to adjust its debts. The anticipation is that the company will be turned back over to its owners once its debts have been satisfactorily addressed.

Chapter 13. This is sometimes known as "wage-earner bankruptcy." In some respects it is the personal equivalent of Chapter 11, a plan that allows an individual debtor to keep certain property as long as court-approved monthly payments are met. Because of income unreliability, it is seldom approved for self-employed persons.

Chapter 20. This is not a court-approved bankruptcy plan, although it is often referred to as such by lawyers. It is the process in which an individual files Chapter 7 bankruptcy, followed by Chapter 13. All debts that are not eligible to be discharged under Chapter 7 fall under Chapter 13.

What to do when a client files for court protection

Whether a client files for Chapter 7, Chapter 11, or even Chapter 13 court protection, chances are that a creditor (you) will collect only a small fraction of what is owed. Nonetheless, if you don't follow the proper procedure you may get nothing.

Filing proof-of-claim. You must file an official proof-of-claim form with the court in order to be eligible for any payment. You should submit copies of documents such as proposals, invoices, and receipts along with it. If the debtor has already listed you among the creditors in its filing, the court will automatically send you the proof-of-claim form. If you do not receive a form automatically, call the closest bankruptcy court and request one. (It will be listed under "Courts" in the U. S. Government pages of the phone book.) Do not delay. Deadlines for filing proofs-of-claim are strictly enforced. Wait too long and you will surely get nothing.

Chapter 7 proceedings. Proof-of-claim forms must normally be filed within ninety days of the first court-ordered meeting of major creditors (this probably won't include you). During this meeting, a trustee will be chosen. Thereafter, it's up to the trustee to quickly liquidate the debtor's assets and distribute any proceeds to creditors. The trustee, lawyers, and accountants are paid first. Then come secured creditors (e.g., mortgage holders). Unsecured creditors (that's you) share what's left over. When the money runs out, remaining debts are discharged or legally forgiven.

Chapter 11 proceedings. The deadline for filing proof-of-claim is set by the court. Once received, this is usually followed by an offer to negotiate the claim. A negotiated settlement can take the form of receiving only a percentage of what is owed, accepting payments over a long period, or both. If you don't agree to a negotiated settlement, the court may impose one.

Five debt-collection points to remember

You are bound to get stuck sooner or later. It is part of doing business. You must do everything possible to minimize how often it happens, but don't expect to avoid it, and don't take it personally.

Your everyday pricing must be high enough to accommodate an occasional bad debt. In other words, put a factor in every estimate to self-insure against the occasional loss.

Doing credit checks before taking on a client is always wise, but never a guarantee. All good credit shows is past payment performance; it does not necessarily indicate future payment performance.

The more money you get before starting an assignment, the less likely a client is to stick you after it is finished. If you should get stuck, the smaller the loss, the less it hurts.

Unless you operate on an accrual (versus cash) accounting system, bad debts are not tax-deductible. However, expenses in attempting collection, including the collection fee, are.

SECTION TWO
HIGHLIGHTS

- **The importance of price is overemphasized.** Price alone is seldom the determining factor in getting or losing a good job; it is only important to good clients in the context of the value received. Also, the way you price your services is not the most important factor in long-term success.

- **A viable business must know its costs and price each job accordingly.** An hourly fee that includes labor (salary) and overhead costs is the foundation. To arrive at realistic, fair, and consistent job prices, this fee is then multiplied by job hours, and expenses and profit are added.

- **Estimating correctly is mostly learned by trial and error.** You can shorten the learning curve by eliminating as much guesswork as possible. Ask the client lots of questions and break the job down into as many components as practical. Keep good records of your time and expenses. And build a file that you can refer to for future jobs.

- **It is better to provide "estimates" than "quotes."** While there are more profit opportunities with the latter, the risk is significantly greater. Creative work normally involves too much subjectivity and too many changes to be appropriate for firm quotes.

- **Reducing your tax burden is as important as getting an extra job or two.** You can't avoid taxation, but you can minimize it by understanding the system and adopting tax reduction strategies. The money you save can equal or exceed the profit from one or more assignments.

- **Avoid trouble-prone situations.** Put all agreements in writing, do credit checks when possible, avoid spec work, don't give anything away, keep detailed job and business records, address client concerns immediately, and follow up on past-due invoices.

- **Know your collection options.** Bad debts are nothing personal; they're simply a part of business life that must be dealt with as quickly and efficiently as possible. As a general rule, use small claims court whenever possible, use a collection agency for larger bad debts up to $10,000, and use civil courts for bad debts over $10,000.

Financial norms

Hourly labor rate $90–$200+, depending on talent and experience

Markups on products and services   25% on average

Standard payment terms   1/3 at inception; 1/3 in middle; 1/3 at end

Standard invoice terms   Net 30 (payment due in 30 days)

Average accounts receivable   One month's income

Average invoice paid   45 days or less

Average cost of estimating an assignment   1–2% of creative billing

Average billable time (labor utilization rate)   50–70%

Average bad debts (over several years)   Less than 1.5% of income

Cash flow cushion to maintain   3 months of average overhead

Bill for work-to-date   After one month of inactivity

SELLING
&
MARKETING

*"In the long run, men hit
only what they aim at."*

HENRY D. THOREAU

As creative individuals, it is only natural that many of us think that selling and marketing shouldn't be necessary to achieve recognition and financial success. After all, it is our talent that's really important.

Be that as it may, in today's competitive environment knowing how to market and sell your services is critically important. This is true regardless of how much talent you possess, or how much experience you've accumulated. If you don't promote your services, many potential clients will never know of them, or only the wrong types of clients will know of them, or you'll end up working mostly for clients without enough money or sophistication to reward your talent and experience. Whatever your background, developing better selling and marketing skills gives you the opportunity to work for better clients at higher pay.

Moreover, competition in the world of creative services is getting tougher every year. The days of relying upon reputation and word of mouth referrals, of business coming in "over the transom," are long gone for everyone. Today even the largest and most prestigious creative firms—agencies, design studios, etc.—promote their services aggressively. If you plan to compete effectively in the world of creative services, you must learn to do likewise.

Okay, so you agree it's necessary. But perhaps your acceptance is simply recognition of the inevitable. Perhaps your heart isn't in it. After all, as right-brain-type individuals, many of us tend to classify selling as noncreative, detailed, left-brain activity. It takes calling, writing, knocking on doors, waiting in lobbies, and pitching rude people. It also results in many disappointments. Then, too, most of us have no sales training. The few times we've tried selling, we probably went about it all wrong.

All these reasons, and more, for not wanting to sell are partly right, but they are also very much exaggerated. You can sell, and you can sell well. This section tells you how to go about it.

11. Going Where the Money Is

In its essence being creative for a living is nothing more than designing, writing, or programming for money, regardless of whether you are doing Great Art or commercial schlock. Of course, some projects are more creatively satisfying than others, but quality and satisfaction have little to do with economics.

Fortunately, because creativity does often affect commercial prosperity, there can be a correlation between quality and reward. Nonetheless, how much money you make is related more closely to the use of the material you produce than to its quality, or the time you put into its preparation. Creating often takes the same amount of time regardless of the style or use of the result.

Because of this economic truism, and because you are working primarily to make money, not to create Great Art, you should consider carefully the type of assignments around which you want to build your business. (If you have a problem with this statement, you have bought the wrong book.) Assuming you possess broad talent, specific experience is much less important in the long term than your motivation and the way you direct your business-building efforts.

The motivation for change

Beginning creative students are always given the same solid advice: start in areas you know best, then explore new areas of creativity as your experience and confidence grow. Building a stable business is no different. When starting a business or a new sales effort, your effort should be oriented around the same type of work you have already been handling successfully. For example, if you've been laying out ads at an agency, you should go after ad work from agencies. If you've been doing editorial illustration, look for assignments from periodicals. If your company has been doing public relations work, seek out more corporate PR departments or small, growing companies.

Going after the type of work your portfolio is strongest in, from organizations you are familiar with, will bring you the highest initial level of sales success. This success is important, perhaps critical, in helping you build confidence in your abilities, and in providing the cash flow necessary to stay alive and grow.

However, at some point you must stop focusing on the short-term and look at what types of business are best in the long-term. To build a solid, viable business you must step back and objectively assess what businesses you should be going after. Where does the money and enjoyment lie for you? You may find that what you are doing is not what you really want to do. If so, the chances of building a satisfying career are small. The nature of creativity is such that we are only good as long as we enjoy what we are doing. In other words, you may be setting yourself up for creative failure in the future. You may find that the type of work you are doing, while satisfying, is not in high demand. You may have concentrated in an area that pays less than others. Such cases result in continuous frustration, sometimes even commercial failure. Also, if you do only one type of work, or work with only one type of client, you leave yourself excessively vulnerable to the vagaries of the marketplace. Common sense says that variety is not only the spice of creative life but also an effective shield against economic instability.

Don't make the mistake of accepting the status quo just because it is familiar. If you aren't as happy, or secure, or making as much money as you'd like, chances are it is because you haven't taken the time to think through what you should be doing, versus what you are doing. Keep this in mind: creative talent and experience are not as important in getting new business as your motivation and selling skills. Moreover, the hardest part of making a change is deciding to do it.

The following chapters cover the steps and techniques necessary to obtain new business, but before getting to that, it is important to understand where the good business is, and where it isn't. Whether you are a graphic designer, website designer, illustrator, or writer, freelancing or running a multiperson shop, for practical purposes all work will come from one of three types of places—publications, agencies, or companies/organizations. Although it may occasionally be possible for some extraordinarily talented or lucky individuals to make a living by, say, publishing novels or doing fine art, most self-employed creative people must get business from one of these three sources in order to survive. Each source has different

kinds of assignments, and pay scales vary, often with no relationship to the talent or time involved. So it is important to know what's the best business to go after.

Your options follow, presented in order of increasing potential reward-per-effort. Use this guide to help you orient your business-building activity, keeping in mind that if you freelance you will probably want to do at least some work in each of the three areas for both creative variety and economic stability.

Publications—low pay, high prestige

Publications—newspapers, books, magazines, and newsletters—usually offer the least lucrative assignments. This is generally true whether the work is done directly, through a third party such as an agency, or for a company-sponsored house organ.

For writers, editorial rates are often less than half what similar efforts receive for promotional copy done for agencies or corporations. Art directors/designers, too, find that doing magazine page layouts nets up to 50 percent less than doing page layouts for ads or brochures. Illustrators get paid less on average for magazine and book art than for advertising or collateral art.

Overall, the reason for low pay probably has more to do with tradition than anything else. It is also tied to the prestige factor, the "value" of seeing one's name or artwork in widely circulated print, and to the fact that creating for publications is a buyer's market because many publication reporters and art directors freelance part-time for extra money, depressing the creative fee structure.

In addition, many publications want submissions on speculation, paying for what they actually like and use, not necessarily the work done. To add insult to injury, they often pay on publication, maybe months after the work is actually completed.

There are three bright spots in this otherwise depressing picture. The first is the ability of illustrators to get paid on the basis of reader exposure, and thus to be adequately rewarded. The second is the possibility of writers and illustrators selling only "one time rights" to their work, enabling it to be sold again, and again. The third is the freedom to work anywhere you like, including the top of a mountain. This business is done over the phone, by fax, or email; location doesn't usually matter. These considerations aside, as a general rule it is difficult to make an acceptable living by doing only publication work. You have to work extraordinarily hard, have very good connections, or have minimal overhead. Freelances in your area making over $50,000 annually doing publication work could probably be counted on your fingers without affecting your ability to hold a cup of coffee, and only the largest design and editorial companies specializing in publication work are as prosperous as their less specialized counterparts.

That said, you may want to solicit publication assignments along with other work. They can be interesting and look impressive in your portfolio. They can help establish your credentials within a certain market. Publication work done on speculation can also serve as "fill" work between other assignments. Such speculative work will be frustrating; it won't pay a lot, but it will keep you busy, and it will definitely polish your skills for other, more lucrative assignments.

Accept publication work for prestige and for variety, but if you're a freelance don't try to make a living off it unless you're very prolific and have very good connections. The same advice goes for most multiperson shops.

Agencies—what price creativity?

Perhaps the most logical place for many of us to look for business is advertising, public relations, and interactive agencies, or larger design firms or studios. These organizations are in the same business we're in: creativity. So they understand how we work, speak the same language. In fact, many of us have worked in agencies, so we understand their needs as well. Moreover, agencies are easy to find, nearly every one is a potential client, and the cyclical nature of their business makes it difficult for them to be fully staffed for periodic overloads. In short, they are a natural.

All this is probably the root of the problem. Perhaps because so many freelances and small studios do look for work from agencies, it has become too much of a buyer's market. We don't always get the respect or compensation we deserve. In fact, some agencies take grossly unfair advantage of outside talent and there always seem to be individuals willing to accept it. The result is a depression of working standards.

Ad agency assignments are often among the least remunerative. They are always looking for ways to cut costs, especially when it means being a hero to a client. One of the easiest ways is to underpay, or to delay payment to suppliers. Since agencies must mark up and pass along any outside charges, there's always strong pressure on suppliers to charge less.

Working arrangements can also be less than ideal. Typically, agencies don't call upon outsiders until they have discovered, too late, that they can't meet a deadline, so many jobs are of the panic variety. Also, agencies tend to keep the creatively exciting jobs in-house, and farm out the less stimulating work. Once a job is completed, agencies are reluctant to admit that an outsider, not their own staff, did the work.

For these reasons and more, agencies can be tough to deal with. Nonetheless, many of us have to rely on agencies for at least part of our work. For illustrators, those with largely broadcast experience, "pair of hands" talent, or others who work in a market dominated by agencies, agencies may account for most opportunities. With this in mind, here are some tips on developing better working relationships with them.

Be selective; all agencies are not equal. Some agencies are very professional in dealing with their suppliers; some are not. Ask around. Learn to discriminate. Have enough confidence to ask for what your talent is worth, and to turn down agencies that pay poorly, pay late, or make unrealistic demands. This may be difficult advice to take, but it is the only route to long-term success.

The best agencies to solicit are large design firms or studios. The assignments are bigger, the deadlines less severe, the pay better. Next in priority are public relations, interactive, and direct mail agencies.

When soliciting ad agencies, the ideal is usually a start-up formed by principals who used to work in a big agency. They need help, and they have the background to appreciate talent. They usually pay well because with minimal staff they are more likely to view your work in the context of a straight return on investment. The worst agencies are small local outfits. They usually have much more work than money or sophistication.

The best work to solicit is collateral, not ad or internet work. Collateral—brochures and booklets—is where most agencies are weakest, where they can most use help, where they are less likely to question your work. Collateral projects are also longer-term, with more flexible deadlines, and there is less price pressure.

Corporations and organizations—better pay, fewer hassles

The best money and the fewest hassles for both freelances and multi-person shops come from working directly for companies—the "corporate" market. The few exceptions to this are the fields of illustration, production work, and broadcast. Unfortunately, in these areas most assignments come from agencies; little comes from companies directly. For the rest of us, however, companies are probably the most lucrative place to concentrate our selling efforts, the best foundation upon which we can build a viable, long-term business. There are several reasons why.

Perhaps most important is the tremendous number and variety of companies. Regardless of our location, there are always many more companies than publications or agencies. Most need occasional creative help of some sort. Why shouldn't they purchase that help directly from you? You can offer lower prices than a large agency, along with direct creative contact and faster service, all without compromising quality. Competition is less intense when you deal with companies because of their number and variety, and the fact that many freelances are either unfamiliar with company opportunities or choose the easier route of pitching only publications and agencies. Whatever the reason, the result is more of a seller's market. So you are more likely to be appreciated and get paid what you are worth, on time.

Companies also have a much wider variety of assignments than either publications or agencies. Among the more common needs are: annual reports, product literature, ads, packaging, logos and identity programs, direct mail solicitations, multimedia, speeches, case history articles, press releases, instructional manuals, and websites. Such variety not only provides a good economic hedge; it also continuously sharpens your creativity.

As a rule, large companies provide the best long-term potential because of their relative sophistication and bigger budgets. As with most things in life, the best is usually the toughest to get. It can be difficult to determine whom to call upon in a large company (see "Whom you need to reach to get assignments" in Chapter 12), and once you find the right person(s) it can be a very tough sell. But the ultimate rewards are well worth the effort.

Smaller companies are easier to sell, there are more of them, and they offer greater variety of work. Their relative lack of sophistication often makes them appreciate creative help, so they are often the place to concentrate initially. Move up to the bigger assignments and budgets of larger companies as your confidence and experience grow.

There are also many opportunities with not-for-profit organizations. They don't pay as well as profit-making companies, but on balance they pay about as well as many publications and agencies, and they are usually easier to work with. They also provide experience, and help you build a portfolio that will be helpful in getting more lucrative company assignments.

The best and worst clients to work for

Although there are good and bad clients in every line of business, some have a much better track record of treating creative suppliers well than others. Sometimes this is due to tradition, sometimes it is linked to profitability, and sometimes it is the result of competitive intensity. Some businesses and industries also have more need for creative services. Whatever the reason, if you want to become prosperous and stay healthy, it is clearly better to concentrate your efforts in some places than in others. Long-term viability is strongly affected by the ability to seek out good businesses and clients, and recognize and turn down not-so-good ones.

Presented here is the consensus of hundreds of suppliers around North America on the relative merits of twelve common businesses or industries that contract for outside creative services. Although not intended to be all-inclusive, the businesses and industries listed are responsible for about 90 percent of all creativity purchased today on the open market. This list is presented for general guideline purposes, a way to help you determine relative odds for success and satisfaction. Within any given business area there are, of course, both great clients and rotten ones.

Most readers will have the opportunity to obtain work in several of the business areas listed. You have broad talents and work in metropolitan markets with a variety of options. Keeping in mind the creative and financial benefits of variety, it will probably make sense for you to concentrate on those areas that treat creative suppliers well, and leave those that don't to less-well-informed peers. Other readers, however, have limited choices. Experience or geography restrict where and for whom you work. Even when this is the case, it still helps to know the extent of a problem or opportunity. One that can be defined is usually one that can be at least partially addressed.

Each business type is rated by five criteria: 1) availability of work, the number and diversity of clients; 2) steadiness of work, its volume and consistency; 3) satisfaction, how enjoyable most assignments are; 4) pay, how compensation compares to similar work done in other businesses; and 5) an overall grade, a summary. The twelve areas are listed in order of increasing desirability—worst first, best last.

Retail—like to work hard for little money? Perhaps it is because retailing is a business of high volume, low margin. Perhaps it is because it is a business of fast turnaround, tight deadlines. Whatever the reason, creative individuals working for the retailing industry nearly unanimously report low wages, demanding clients, and scant satisfaction.

Advantages? Retailers are everywhere—big cities and small. Most use outside illustration, writing, advertising, and website help. The deadlines are demanding, but the work can be easy, once you know the formula, and often very steady, too.

Grades:
Availability: B+; Steadiness: B–; Satisfaction: D; Pay: E; Overall grade: D

Publishing—no money, but ah, the prestige. It's too bad you can't take prestige to the bank, because it seems to be the primary compensation provided by the publishers of books, magazines, e-zines, newspapers, and newsletters. You get your prose, illustration, or page layouts in widely circulated print. What you don't get is much money. Publication work is seldom steady and payment is often for what is actually used, not submitted. Moreover, assignments are sometimes on speculation.

Advantages? The opportunity to work anywhere and (sometimes) leisurely. There are many publishers buying creative services, too. Journalists and illustrators can also sell "one time rights" to their work, providing the opportunity for multiple sales. For certain specialized assignments such as "advertorials," or for "name contributors," compensation can be quite good.

Grades:
Availability: B; Steadiness: D; Satisfaction: B+; Pay: E; Overall grade: D+

Not-for-profits—a way to be charitable? In every community there are dozens of not-for-profit organizations with small staffs and big communication needs, so there's lots of work available. Not-for-profits sometimes also provide high visibility and contacts, and the satisfaction of contributing to society.

However, the not-so-pleasant aspects are usually even more significant: low-budget assignments, unrealistic creative demands, and the frustration of having to deal with nonprofessional staff.

Grades:
Availability: A; Steadiness: C; Satisfaction: C+; Pay: D; Overall grade: C–

Hospitality and recreation—big industry, mixed reviews. This is one of those business areas that can be either very good or very bad. Here are the comments, positive and negative. Availability is widespread—lots of hotels, resorts, restaurants, etc.—but most of the routine work is produced by specialized suppliers who seldom go outside for help. As for steadiness, low marks here: if you don't specialize in this business, it is either boom or bust. Creative satisfaction depends on job and client: for occasional jobs, very high, but more often, creating to a formula. It's the same with pay: high for the creative assignments, low for the formula assignments.

A bottom-line generalization: this is only a good business with the right (big and sophisticated) client.

Grades:
Availability: C; Steadiness: C; Satisfaction: C; Pay: C; Overall grade: C

Ad agencies—their problems become our problems. There are only a limited number of advertising agencies in even the largest metropolitan areas and there are lots of creative individuals calling upon them. This is a buyer's market. In addition, since many agencies (especially smaller ones) aren't well managed, direction may be unclear, time wasted, and payment late. Many agencies only farm out problem work to freelance writers, art directors, and web developers, which means unrealistic deadlines, hassles, and little creative stimulation.

On the positive side, if you are choosy about whom you work for, and under what conditions, assignments can be quite lucrative. Ad agencies are easy to contact and sell. Some (usually larger ones) are very professional. For specialized skills (broadcast art direction, writing humorous commercials, technical or medical illustration, etc.), pay can be high and assignments pleasant.

Grades:
Availability: C; Steadiness: C+; Satisfaction: B–; Pay: C; Overall grade: C+

PR and interactive agencies—a better overall record. Unlike advertising agencies, most public relations (PR) and interactive agencies don't have large staffs, so they tend to rely more on outside help. They are usually involved in project-type (versus campaign-type) work for which there is less deadline pressure. Because they usually hire brains and experience rather than just "a pair of hands," there's more respect for creative input, too.

On the other hand, they are harder to contact and, being smaller, there is relatively little volume in each. Also, there is less work for illustrators and art directors, although more for writers, graphic designers, and web developers. Although there are more assignments in these agencies, the best—in pay and satisfaction—still come from ad agencies.

Grades:

Availability: C; Steadiness: C+; Satisfaction: B–; Pay: B; Overall grade: C+

Design studios—our kind of agencies. The best type of "agency" to get assignments from is usually a graphic design studio/marketing communications firm. They have the best jobs—special projects or needs they aren't staffed to handle. They are easy to contact and sell to. They pay well because they are usually sufficiently profitable. There is little time wasted through bad direction or working hassles.

The major negative is simply that the number of graphic design studios is small, with only a few outside major metropolitan centers. Also, some don't want outsiders contributing to strategy or direction. "We've already decided what to do; you just execute it."

Grades:

Availability: D; Steadiness: B; Satisfaction: B–; Pay: B; Overall grade: B–

Health care—not always healthy for us. Health care is a fast-growing industry, encompassing everything from local hospitals to large corporations providing medical products and services. It is also one that has become increasingly marketing-oriented and, thus, is in need of creative help. The consensus is that local health care institutions (primarily hospitals) generally offer low pay and creative stimulation, but somewhat relaxed working conditions. This is probably a reflection of the need to tightly control costs, as well as the not-for-profit heritage of the industry.

On the other hand, national providers of health care products and services seem to pay well. They do, however, have a reputation for being somewhat less creatively sophisticated, although that seems to be changing. Due to the volatility of the industry and the way in which they get paid (government reimbursements, etc.), some also have a reputation for being poor credit risks.

Grades:
Availability: B+; Steadiness: B; Satisfaction: C–; Pay: B; Overall grade: B–

Real estate—it all depends on local market conditions. The efforts associated with the construction, buying, and leasing of commercial real estate generates a high demand for marketing material—positioning presentations, ads, brochures, illustrations, signs, CD-ROMs, and websites. The success of any given real estate venture is strongly affected by this material. Commercial real estate firms are located in every city, and few are large enough to have an in-house creative staff. Moreover, since marketing materials are usually a small expenditure in the overall scheme of things, pricing is seldom sensitive.

The only negative in this otherwise rosy picture is that commercial real estate is a very volatile industry, rising and falling with local economic conditions. When real estate is not selling, there is little or no work available.

Grades:
Availability: B+; Steadiness: E; Satisfaction: B; Pay: B; Overall grade: B–

Entrepreneurial firms—they need bad what we do good. Startup ventures in any industry are usually heavy users of outside creative services. Some types of industries—high technology, biotechnology, software, etc.—have a particularly high proportion of start-ups. Although volume and type of work varies with the industry and size of the business, most young, growing firms have a need for ads, brochures, corporate identity materials, and websites. Many are not yet large or sophisticated enough to employ an agency, or their needs outpace the limited capacity of their in-house staff. Lines of communication can be short and working procedures informal.

The downside of dealing with young, growing companies is their very smallness and lack of structure. Staffs can be unprofessional and have little idea of working procedures or pricing norms, and companies may be on shaky financial ground.

Grades:
Availability: B+; Steadiness: E; Satisfaction: B; Pay: B; Overall grade: B–

Direct marketers—if it sells, you get paid big. Direct marketers—clients who produce catalogs, mail packages, response ads, and web catalogs—are high on the list of lucrative opportunities for illustrators.

For graphic designers, web developers, and writers, they can be either among the best or the worst of opportunities. It all depends.

The reason for the creative schizophrenia is that this is a highly specialized business with relatively few clients and assignments. It is also tough to break in without a portfolio that demonstrates results. But once you have broken in, proven that you have the "touch" that can sell products, it can be among the most lucrative of business areas. Often the financial reward is directly proportionate to just how good you really are.

Grades:
Availability: D; Steadiness: B+; Satisfaction: B; Pay: A; Overall grade: B+

Financial services—the clients with the money. Financial institutions not only have money, but most are religious about paying on time, too. There are several banks and credit unions in every city and town, and all produce lots of communications material—from ads to counter literature to financial prospectuses to website changes. Moreover, larger institutions pay as well as any large company, and smaller ones pay as well as any small company, in any industry. For all these reasons, financial service institutions are usually the single best type of client organization to seek out.

The major negative is that the ability to do highly creative work is limited, especially for smaller organizations. It also seems important to match talent and pricing to organization; do not, for example, try to get big-city work from small-town institutions. And small credit unions may not be very sophisticated in their marketing. To be successful in this area, it is necessary to be somewhat conservative in style.

Grades:
Availability: A; Steadiness: B+; Satisfaction: B–; Pay: A; Overall grade: A–

Ten ways to evaluate any client. Good clients exist in all types of businesses. Listed below are ten criteria by which you can judge yours. To rate a client, give 10 points for each matching characteristic, 0 points if there is not a match. A good client:

1. Never calls asking you to do speculative work or adopt unprofessional procedures.

2. Has projects with well-defined objectives, budgets, and timetables.

3. Doesn't waste time in unproductive meetings, is organized, and provides complete information.

4. Provides adequate time to do good work—a week or more, depending on the job.

5. Demands great work — and can recognize it when he or she sees it.

6. Doesn't nitpick over details or style.

7. Is objective and consistent in comments and criticisms.

8. States as precisely as possible what is wrong, but never tells you how to fix it.

9. Is appreciative of your talent and effort, and doesn't begrudge you your financial reward.

10. Pays within 45 days.

Scoring. Clients scoring 90 or above are so valuable you will want to sell your spouse to keep them. A score of 70 or so indicates clients worth fighting with lifelong friends to keep. Scores of around 50 indicate clients who are definitely worth an occasional lunch. Refer clients who score below 30 to a competitor.

The inter(tra)net market

Whether for site development, maintenance, or both, the Inter(tra)net market for creative services firms has three segments. They reflect the fact that today most established clients, even the smallest, already have some Web presence.

Low-end market. Clients in this segment need nothing more than a simple presence (web brochure). They are typically unsophisticated and don't recognize the value of different media or creative strategies, or their website budgets are small. The competition is extensive to the point of overwhelming. It ranges from do-it-yourself software, to ISP freebies, to computer geeks, to less experienced designers, to internet developers using offshore talent. For these reasons the work is seldom adequately remunerative. The single good-business exception is when site development can be bundled with other client needs. Otherwise, this is a segment to studiously avoid.

Mid-market. Clients in this segment present the most opportunity. They need the experience, talent, and skills necessary to develop an effective, stylish, multipage, custom site. But they do not need the complexity associated with extensive database integration, high-security firewalls, or multinode Intranets. There are three distinct opportunity areas in this segment. Each occasionally involves working with corporate IT (information technology) personnel, or outside programmers.

One is site development for new business startups. The client could be a venture-funded organization, or a new division of a larger organization. In the former, site development often comes as part of a total package of services; in the latter it is a stand-alone project.

The second area is site revision and/or maintenance. The client already has an existing site but it needs updating. This might involve major modifications to a relatively simple site, or minor modifications to one with sophisticated programming.

The third area in the mid-market segment is developing a "look and feel" that will be implemented mostly by others. It can mean being selected by an interactive firm for style development, turning style sheets over to another firm for implementation, or helping client personnel with internal development. While this is as close as internet work comes to pure design, it also requires enough technical expertise to know what is economically and creatively feasible.

High-end market. Clients in this segment are the top of the internet food chain. They are the ones whose sites require extensive database integration, high-security firewalls, and multinode Intranets, among many other things. In short, needs that can only be efficiently addressed by dedicated firms with extensive experience and technological and staff resources. It is a market segment dominated by a few well-capitalized interactive firms and is largely inaccessible to others.

Contacting clients

Whichever market or markets you go after, making regular contact with prospective clients is essential to business success. There are essentially two ways to go about this: 1) you can do it yourself, or 2) you can hire somone else to do it for you. What follows next are two ways to do the latter—hiring talent reps and temp agencies. (Hiring full-time marketing help is covered in Chapter 17.) They are covered here because the rest of the chapters in this section cover the procedures for doing your own marketing.

Using a talent rep

Talent reps are self-employed individuals who solicit prospective clients on behalf of several freelances. They do this in return for some degree of representation exclusivity, and a percentage of any resulting sales. This arrangement has several advantages. It reduces, occasionally even eliminates, the need for personal sales involvement. Selling activity continues regardless of how busy you become. Reps can often get to places that are otherwise inaccessible—certain clients, or other geographic regions. Reps usually provide pricing, negotiating, and contract help, too. Best of all, there is little expense unless they actually deliver a check.

For illustrators and photographers. Representing these individuals is where reps work best. Clients looking for illustration and photography are strongly influenced by a unique style and a long list of credits. Client/freelance interaction and working arrangements are often immaterial, nearly always less important than in other creative disciplines. The client universe is relatively small and easily identified (mostly agencies and publications in large cities). Personal contacts and relationships are critical. Assignments are usually well defined and prices easily quoted. Because of all this, a good rep offers a freelance the potential of a steady flow of assignments. Nonetheless, with the exception of well-known individuals, assignments generated by reps are usually less than 50 percent of a freelance's workload. As for working relationships, as many freelances swear at reps, as swear by them.

For designers, art directors, and copywriters. At best, reps have had limited success selling the work of these individuals. Indeed, today few reps even try. The reasons are several. First, the client universe is much more diverse and hard to reach. Then, too, selling involves more prospecting, much less making the rounds of agencies and publishers. Also, the assignments are typically more complex, making it more difficult to quote schedules and prices. Finally, clients nearly always want to personally interact with the person doing the work.

Finding a talent rep. Those who have been through the selection process often comment that finding a rep can be best described as chasing many until one finally catches you. The hard fact is, most reps handle fewer than a dozen freelances, and there isn't much turnover. You must take the initiative in making the contacts. And you have to keep trying until you find Ms. or Mr. Right. If the relationship is to work, the decision has to be mutual—you have to select the right individual; she or he has to see the value in taking on your work. Although an old pro is usually considered preferable, an eager newcomer who has enthusiasm and understands your talent and its potential can also do a fine job.

Where to get rep names. Perhaps the best way to get a list of appropriate reps is to contact the Society of Photographers and Artists Representatives (SPAR) at www.spar.org. They publish a nationwide directory that lists their several hundred members, both geographically and by talent specialty. Another source is the section on reps in the book, *Artist's and Graphic Designer's Market.* It is updated yearly and can be ordered from F&W Publications, 1507 Dana Avenue, Cincinnati, OH 45207, (800) 289-0963 (www.f&wpublications. com). Don't forget to peruse source books to see who is representing whom. Individuals usually note the name of their rep on the ad.

A more personal way to find a rep is simply to ask around. Whom do peers know and recommend, and which have the best reputation for being active in the market(s) you want to go after? Call clients, too. Say you have become so busy you are now seriously thinking about taking on a rep, and ask if they have any suggestions. Do the same in meetings of the local creative club, Graphic Artists Guild, or Society of Illustrators.

Selection criteria. Ideally, you want to look for a rep who has these traits: an understanding of your type of talent, an interest in your professional and financial goals, a knowledge of current business practices, extensive contacts in the market you want to go after, and promotional skills, is good at dealing with people, and has tenacity (being pushy isn't a negative).

How to make contact. Write a simple, straightforward letter introducing yourself and stating that you are seeking representation. Enclose a brochure or autobiographical sketch, and a promotion sheet showing your style. (If you haven't yet prepared such a sheet, a couple of sample tearsheets, photocopies, or color prints will do.) It is better not to send disks (tough to look at), and never send original artwork. Enclosing a self-addressed envelope will give you a 50/50 chance of getting your material returned, but don't count on it.

Don't call for an appointment before sending a letter of introduction and samples. Most reps are far too busy to see every individual who calls. It is okay, however, to place a follow-up call a week or so after sending the introduction letter to see whether an appointment would be appropriate. If you want a rep and at first you don't succeed, keep trying. The rep market is very fluid. They come and they go. Individual situations change. Don't be reluctant to contact a rep once a year to ask if she or he would be interested in handling your work.

Working arrangements. All talent reps agree that when it comes to portfolios, less is more. They want just a few samples that are cleanly presented, attractively packaged, and oriented to their contacts. Specifically, this usually means no more than a dozen pieces that show your style and your problem-solving abilities. The best portfolios often have a 50/50 mix of actual samples, to show what has already been done for clients, and personal spec work, to show your ability to take on new types of assignment challenges.

Remember that the nature of the rep/talent relationship is fraught with the potential of misunderstanding. The parties have different expectations. A written agreement is necessary to keep misunderstandings to a minimum. More important, reps (technically "agents") have a legal right to act in behalf of their employers in stipulated areas, so a contract defining those areas is necessary for your legal protection. In short, never let anyone represent you without a written contract that defines the responsibilities of both parties.

To make sure everything necessary is covered, obtain the "Do it yourself rep kit" from SPAR. It costs about $55, and contains sample contracts as well as other helpful information. Also look at the contracts printed in one or more of the following books: *Pricing and Ethical Guidelines,* published by the Graphic Artists Guild (www.gag.org); *Business and Legal Forms for Illustrators,* published by Allworth Press (www.allworth. com); or *The Artist's Friendly Legal Guide,* published by North Light Books (www.artistsnetwork. com). Now draw up your own contract using this published material as a guide. Make sure it details the following: contract period (length and dates); each party's responsibilities in detail; exclusivity by geography, specialty, or both; who is responsible for what expenses; percentage of commissions paid; who will do billing and when the other party will be paid; who is responsible for the promotional budget and how much it will be; a termination clause; and commission due following termination and for how long (very important). Finally, get a lawyer to look over your contract. Most will review a contract and make minor suggestions and revisions for a modest fee ($150 to $250).

Fee guidelines. Most reps think of assignments coming through them as one of two types: a "new account" or a "house account." New accounts always include anything the rep brings in through her or his efforts or connections and anything from a dormant source that the rep reactivates, even if you made the initial contact. For this purpose, dormancy is usually considered as a year or longer. House accounts are usually anything from clients who have provided at least one other job in the last twelve months. They also include any accounts that have been specifically designated in the contract (for example, a client you've been pitching for years, but has not yet come through with an assignment). These definitions recognize that it is more difficult to get business from new than from existing clients. They also encourage the rep to spend more effort in finding new clients than in acting as an account representative to existing ones.

Assignment commission on new accounts is normally 25 to 30 percent of the creative fee when the client is local to the rep's area. For clients who are out of the rep's area, it is often 30 to 40 percent because these accounts are more expensive to obtain and require more servicing time. The commission on house accounts (local and out of town) is usually 10 percent of the creative fee.

Most reps insist on handling the billing, deducting their commission when the invoice is paid and passing on the rest. Regardless of who bills, reps are always paid when the receivable is collected, not before. If there's no collection, there's no fee.

Expenses are negotiable, depending mostly upon your reputation and salability. As a guideline, the rep usually covers all expenses related to obtaining and getting to and from appointments; you cover all expenses of maintaining the portfolio; promotional expenses—"showcase" ads, mailings, etc.—may be wholly your responsibility, or be split. (Many reps require you to make an initial investment for promotional samples and materials.)

Reviewing the relationship. Much rep/freelance dissatisfaction is caused by simple lack of communication. Reps are motivated by—work hardest for—individuals who take a very active interest in how their work is being marketed. Every few weeks ask where the portfolio has been shown and what client reactions were. Provide new ideas, direction, and leads. Every few months ask for a written summary of activity. If you do this, and the rep is good, you should see a steady stream of assignments after several months. If not, it is probably not in your best interest, or the rep's, to continue the relationship. Start looking for someone new.

Signing up with a temp agency

In any large metropolitan market today there are dozens, perhaps even hundreds, of temporary employment firms. Since many of these firms specialize in one or more industries, finding the right ones for you takes a little effort. Start by scouting the local Yellow Pages display ads to identify those firms that specialize in creative talent. Then look through the ads in the back of a local creative publication (e.g., *AdWeek*) to see which firms are actively and aggressively trying to place individuals within the communications industry.

Unlike a talent rep who represents only a few freelances, a temp firm keeps files on hundreds of different individuals, their experience and their style. Reps make regular rounds of a few steady clients (largely ad agencies and publishers) to drum up business for their small "stable"; temp firms are much less narrowly focused. Clients call looking for an individual to handle a specific project within certain time and cost parameters. The temp firm usually presents several individuals who qualify.

The more specific your talent or experience, the better. Temp firms get few clients looking for "generic" graphic design, web development, or writing help. Today, most clients are looking for highly specific abilities.

For example: "We need a designer with QuarkXPress skills and experience in health care collateral to fill in for a vacationing staffer." "We are looking for a Spanish-speaking direct response copywriter to translate a mailer for the Hispanic market." "We need someone fluent in Flash and JavaScript."

The temp firm typically determines what to charge based on its knowledge of the assignment, the client's budget, and a sense of market rates. Your pay will be determined largely by market pricing for the particular skill you use. For example, production work is always billed at a lower rate than concept and design work. As a rule of thumb, individuals who have very rigid rate structures don't get a lot of work from temp firms. You should have a range of ± 30 percent from your average hourly rate. Factors affecting what you can expect to make include length of the assignment (long-term assignments are usually at a lower hourly rate), the level of skill required, and the desirability of the assignment (you may agree to a lower rate for the opportunity to work at the hottest shop in town).

As you would expect, freelances usually get paid less working through a temp firm than if they had got their own projects or on-site assignments. On the other hand, they sometimes end up actually making as much money because they have no marketing costs. In addition, because temp firms pay you as an employee, they also pay the employer's share of FICA and Medicare taxes, which you pay when you freelance. (At the time of writing this amounts to a 7.65 percent bonus on whatever amount you bill.) And pay is often on a predetermined schedule, irrespective of when the client pays the agency.

The major drawbacks. If you accept a lot of temporary assignments, you may not be available when a good client calls. Your business may atrophy because you have no time to solicit business. On the other hand, registering with reputable temp firms costs you nothing, and you don't have to accept any assignment they come up with.

12. Preparing Your Sales Strategy

The very words, "sales strategy," are enough to strike fear into the heart of most creative individuals. Nonetheless, directing your selling efforts—a sales strategy—is the critical next step in ensuring that your business always has a supply of clients. So the emphasis here is on developing a plan that is both effective and easy to implement.

If you work for yourself, before undertaking a sales strategy it is first necessary to put yourself in the right frame of mind. It is important to stop thinking in personal terms—i.e., as a "freelance"—and to start thinking like the president of a small business. This subtle shift is important in establishing the right tone for your upcoming efforts. It helps you guard against falling into the trap of promoting yourself rather than your business capabilities. It also helps you focus on how your business can help solve the problems of other businesses.

If you run a multiperson organization, it is important to perceive yourself more as the president of a business organization that provides professional services, less as the leader of a creative boutique.

Devoting enough time

How much time you set aside for your sales efforts depends on whether you are just starting out or already well established. It also depends upon how big you want your business to be.

If you are just starting out, think of sales activity in this context: you should organize your business around a normal forty-hour workweek. Every hour not spent doing remunerative work should be spent selling yourself to new potential clients. If you have little or no business, expand your workweek as necessary.

If you are already well established, tailor your sales efforts to what you want your business to be. How important is it to grow, and to what

extent? How important is it to change where your business comes from?

How important is it to get new types of work? If you answer "very" to such questions, devote 30 to 50 percent of your normal workweek to such efforts, even if it means putting in extra hours. If you answer "moderately," devote 15 to 30 percent of your normal workweek, again putting in extra hours if necessary. If you answer "not very, but I want to maintain my competitiveness," devote at least 10 percent of your time.

If you freelance, regardless of how successful your business is or ultimately becomes, be diligent about averaging at least four hours or the equivalent of 10 percent of your workweek to sales. Don't make the mistake of waiting for a business downturn before taking the initiative. The later you wait, the longer it takes, the more you suffer. Regular sales efforts ensure that you are always in control, rather than having the inevitable business downtown dictate how, when, and where you must react.

If you run a multiperson organization, you should devote the equivalent of at least four hours a week to selling for every individual employed (including noncreative staff) for up to three individuals. For larger organizations, devote up to eight hours a week per individual. Consider a full-time sales rep when dollar volume reaches $500,000 or when your creative staff reaches four or more. (See "Hiring marketing help" in Chapter 17.)

Analyzing the product

Each of us is unique. That is, we were born with different talents, have lived different experiences, and have developed different skills. Some of this uniqueness is important to business, some isn't. The first thing in developing a selling strategy is to determine what's important.

For the freelancer. Sort out what it is about you that will interest potential clients, and what will not. Start by defining yourself. Do you consider yourself to be primarily an art director, or graphic designer? A copywriter, or writer? An illustrator, or fine artist doing illustration? A technical person doing web design or a designer with programming skills? Now think about what you are good at, which of your many creative talents are the strongest. For example, for an illustrator it might be the rendering of people, for a designer the ability to visualize complex ideas, for a writer the craft of writing for the ear rather than the eye. To this creative definition, now add your working strengths and business skills. For example, unusual speed, an obsession for getting details correct, or extensive experience in certain industries or kinds of work, such as telecommunications or greeting card concepts.

For the multiperson firm. Determine what about your organization is different, what might give you a competitive edge with certain clients— industry experience, style and staff talents, equipment/location/service attributes. In this process strive for objectivity. Don't exaggerate; there's no one to impress yet. Also, don't under-value your firm's talents; don't damn your future efforts with false modesty.

For all size businesses. Put your thoughts down on paper, trying to evaluate them through the eyes of a potential client. Remember that most clients don't actually buy creativity; they buy solutions to business (or communications) problems. What in your or your organization's background is significant? What isn't?

Finally, compose a single paragraph (no more) that accurately describes what broad benefits you can offer to an audience of potential clients. Think of it as a resumé summary, a classified ad for your company, or your "elevator speech." Later, when you call on clients, it forms the basis for your "value-added proposition."

Copywriter with outstanding track record in positioning new and existing products and services. Fifteen years' diversified agency and corporate experience. Outstanding record of creating sales. Top creative awards from ads and sales promotions. A fast, deadline-oriented pro.

Or

Full-service graphic design studio—packaging to web design. Client list of Fortune 500 and smaller companies. Ten years' experience in markets ranging from consumer expendables to financial services to artificial intelligence software. Conveniently located downtown.

This is the statement that will, at least for now, provide a foundation for your sales strategy.

Analyzing the market

In any business, understanding the needs of your market and meeting them with the right (unfortunately, not always the best) products is the formula that spells long-term success. Another key to prosperity is in finding clients with products to which creativity will add significant value. The more of this type of clients there are locally, the more prosperity. For such clients, the money invested in better creativity results directly in increased sales and more profits. As with any business activity, when clients see a good return on their investment (ROI), they become easier to sell to, have larger budgets, and hassle less.

One secret to success is to try to match your talents to what local clients are looking for. This takes knowing a bit about the local business community, especially if you live outside a major metropolitan area. But even in a large, diverse metropolitan area, some industries often predominate; others are noticeable by their absence. If, for example, you are a designer with strong package goods experience, Detroit wouldn't be as good a market as Cincinnati; if you lived in Detroit it might be better to diversify. Conversely, if your skill is technical writing, Detroit is better than Cincinnati; if you lived in Cincinnati, it would be good to develop some promotional writing experience.

The fifty-mile rule. For most creative firms, a realistic market is an area within fifty miles of the office. Those located in rural areas can sometimes be successful dealing with a market area twice as large. The reason is simply that travel time—to call on and service clients—is costly. If you absorb the cost in your overhead, distant clients become less profitable than local clients. On the other hand, if you charge the client for travel, you run the risk of overpricing yourself in their local market. There are exceptions, but generally the closer the client, the greater the profit. If you are a freelance or studio with unusual talent, style, reputation, or experience, it is possible to look productively beyond your local horizons at a national market. However, the individuals and companies that can do it are few and far between. Don't bet your business on it. If it happens, consider yourself blessed.

What about trying to develop long-distance electronic relationships? In this age of the internet, social media, mobile phone facetime, video-conferencing, and overnight delivery services they're surely possible. But for most good projects, clients expect to meet and discuss things in person (eye to eye), at least initially. Notable exceptions are illustration, certain editorial projects, and web projects and hosting where personal contact is not always necessary. When a freelance or firm has already worked for a client and is well respected, it is often also possible to move to another location and keep the business. Nonetheless, for most of us proximity to clients is crucial to obtaining the types of projects that are both stimulating and profitable. (Also see "Can you do it anywhere?" in Chapter 3.)

Addressing commoditization. Commoditization (or commodifica-tion) is when products appear so similar to customers that price, not features or benefits, becomes the deciding factor in purchasing. Although usually associated with consumer expendables (think bread, gasoline, or dry cleaning), it has become a threat in creative services as well. What was previously a small, insular, and esoteric industry has become large and commonplace. The good side is that client needs and appreciation for good work have risen. The bad side is that there's also more competition, clients are more demanding, and some previously arcane (and profitable) processes can now be handled by anyone with a computer. The growing and expanding threat of commoditization must be considered when set-ting a sales strategy. A firm's—whether single- or multiperson—strategy in addressing it can have a major impact on its future. Following are several ways to fight the trend toward commoditization.

Client perceptions. Personal impressions, especially first ones, often categorize a firm—it's either a commodity supplier or a value supplier. Clients who get a downscale feeling anticipate and will accept only low prices (call this the Walmart effect). Conversely, those who get an upscale feeling are much more likely to accept higher prices (the Neiman Marcus effect). Small firms needing to overcome a credibility or experience deficit should be particularly attentive to the perceptions they create. For instance, individuals calling on clients need to appear at least as professional, in demeanor and dress, as whomever they are calling upon.

Branding and positioning. Distinctly branded services are the least sus-ceptible to commoditization. Clients assume that better-known firms with a distinctive approach to their market are more reputable and produce higher-quality work. Therefore, they are willing to pay more. So as crucial as new business activity can be in scoring new clients and projects, of equal importance is brand building and positioning promotion. Regular promotional activity, which raises the level of awareness, affects both what a firm can charge its new clients and its pricing latitude with current clients.

Creating diversity. The more business options available the less susceptible to having to accept commoditized work. More options come from regular marketing. It also has the potential of creating excess demand, which enables more selectivity in whom one does business with or what conditions it will be accepted. Avoid the mistake of viewing marketing only in the context of generating immediate business, and cutting back or ceasing activity as soon as an objective has been achieved. Although doing so results in short-term savings, it can be false economy in the long run. When marketing results in more business than can be comfortably handled, it produces one of three desirable options: 1) selecting only the better projects or clients, 2) raising prices to restrict future demand without affecting income, or 3) expanding staff and facilities to handle the extra business.

Being considered a partner. Think of this as a relationship-building strategy. The promise of a partnering relationship, as opposed to merely handling a client's project, dramatically decreases the pressure for commodity pricing. That's because a well-established relationship makes it easier for a client to think of an outsider as a member of its team—that is, a "partner" with specialized expertise. How can a firm make a partnering relationship happen? There are many ways, most of which are too personal, numerous, and complex to cover here. A way to begin, though, is right up front at a new business pitch. Projecting an ability to understand clients' needs and work hand-in-hand with them should be equal to or exceed in importance what's in a portfolio.

Explaining costs. Think of this as the "no-free-lunch" response. However wishful clients' thinking might be, quality work doesn't come at fire-sale prices. As in most aspects of life, clients will pretty much get what they're willing to pay for. Whether it is you or one of your competitors, pricing is determined by labor costs. The more talented and experienced an individual or employees, the higher these costs will be. And vice versa. So rock-bottom pricing is only feasible when labor costs are low (less talent and experience). Further, less experience often leads to costly, misdirected efforts, not to mention less creative impact, less bang for the buck. Question to ask the client: how much more will settling for less end up costing?

Pushing back. When a client presents an unrealistic budget or aggressively challenges a realistic price, act very surprised. Comment that, unfortunately, the client's expectation is well below normal industry pricing. Point out that firms agreeing to work at that price would be inexperienced, or forced to cut corners, or count on later "changes" to boost billing. Then, whenever possible, illustrate how the difference the client will pay is very small in the larger context of effectiveness. Truthfully, however, this seldom works with bottom-feeding clients, but it often does with others. And even where it doesn't, it's empowering and conducive to self-esteem. So it's worth a try.

Short- and long-term objectives

The short-term goal of your sales efforts is to get business by showing your portfolio to prospective new clients. The long-term objective is to become so well known that getting new and better projects from new and better clients becomes ever easier. Selling effort is cumulative. That is, the more you do the easier it becomes and the more effective it is. So don't make the common mistake of slacking off once you have met your short-term objectives. If you do, you will not only lose the benefits of cumulative effort, you will also miss the opportunity to move your business to a higher level through better clients and work. Making your business as competitive and strong as possible will always require regular sales effort, regardless of how successful you become. There are two reasons for this.

First, the best business—longest assignments, highest pay—comes from clients who only require occasional help. The better the business, the less often it happens. Think of corporate branding projects, which happen only occasionally. Or even annual reports, which only happen once a year. In short, months, even years, may go by before some clients need help. But when the time does come, you'll want them to think of you first. Cultivating this type of business requires etching your name in their memory, and this can only be accomplished through efforts that are consistent and cumulative. You must build the necessary awareness in their minds. If you already enjoy it, you must make sure it isn't replaced by that of a more aggressive competitor.

Second, memories fade, people move, priorities shift, old companies go out of business, new companies start in business. In such a volatile environment, the only way you are assured of being known by every important client in your market is through continuous contact.

Setting your objectives

Having recognized the difference between short- and long-term business objectives, and having identified your strengths and the needs of the market, you can now determine how you should "position" your services—your actual objectives. Although it would be much easier to try to be all things to all potential clients, that's just plain ineffective. There are too many clients, too much competition, and too few hours in your day. Sales success requires that you apply your strengths selectively, that you position yourself through a sales strategy. The key to an effective strategy is reinforcing the perceptions of those being sold, not confronting them.

If you have a portfolio with brilliant concepts but lack experience, decide to make young, growing organizations a high priority by going after their websites, collateral materials, or trade show design. If you have years of corporate PR experience, go after large organizations for executive speech-writing, annual reports, or corporate capability brochures.

Also important is where you fit vis-à-vis the competition. Who are your competitors? Are they agencies, interactive designers, studios, freelancers? Are they strongest in creativity? Service? Price? Try to stake out a competitive niche that fits both a market need and your previously defined profile. Keep in mind that creative business comes about in two ways. Both have to be cultivated.

The best source of business is through reputation and referrals. Contrary to impressions, this doesn't just happen. It is usually the result of joining organizations, having work published, winning awards, and being well known by other businesspeople, suppliers, and creatives. The second best source of business is through your own, direct promotion. It involves the more difficult and costly (but often less time-consuming) process of preparing materials and making sales calls.

When setting your sales strategy you also have to be realistic in what you can offer. It has often been said that service companies only offer three things: quality, service, and price, as illustrated in the following diagram. Clients get to choose only two out of the three; they can't have all three. You choose which two make the most long-term sense for your business.

Writing down a sales stategy

Putting an actual sales strategy statement down on paper is necessary for two reasons. First, the discipline of writing will ensure that you take the process seriously. Second, you should have something to refer to, to measure progress as the year passes. The form is not important. Only you need to see it. What is important is what it motivates you to accomplish. Treat your sales strategy as a living statement, something that you modify and update every year to help you continue to grow your business. The following is a short but effective strategy statement:

(Year) Sales Strategy

To balance my workload to 50% electronic, 50% print. To reduce my dependence on ad agencies for web production work for their clients from 30 to 15 percent of workload. To more heavily merchandise recent print awards. To obtain at least two new, steady, and diverse clients.

Making networking a high priority

You can get new clients and assignments—implement your sales strategy—two ways: from referrals based on your reputation, and from direct sales efforts. The best of these is referrals. They take less effort, so they are more profitable. For this reason, the number one priority of your sales-generating efforts should be cultivating and enlarging what is already established—your reputation among acquaintances.

Introducing yourself. Make a formal announcement of your new business, or expansion or change of an existing one, to friends and followers on social media, such as Facebook and Twitter. Next, compile a list of everyone you know, even remotely, in the local business and creative community. Include personal friends; acquaintances; people you've worked with; printers, paper merchants, and other suppliers; former bosses; writers, designers, illustrators, photographers, and programmers. Ask non-competitive friends to share their lists of contacts. If you are a writer, call designers and illustrators; if a designer, call writers and illustrators; if an illustrator, call designers and writers. Don't be shy; this is what friends are for. A favor asked could also be a favor returned. Offer to exchange the names of your contacts, now and in the future.

Use the list to send out an announcement letter or mailer. (Don't use e-mail for this phase, even if e-mail addresses are available.) Later, use the list to send out occasional reminder letters or mailers. (See Chapter 13.) Don't ask for a response. For this type of mailing no response is appropriate. Of course, this also means you probably won't see any effect. If this causes you to question the effectiveness of the mailing, don't. There are other ways to get appointment leads. These mailings are simply to remind those who already know you that you are in business and prosperous. The effects will be long-term but no less significant. Make the list you've compiled the nucleus of a larger list that you build over the years. Add to it and use it several times a year for promotional efforts.

Face-to-face networking. Once you have contacted your present acquaintances, the next priority is to make new ones. One of the best ways is through networking, the fashionable term for old-fashioned contact-making that has always gone on at clubs and organizations. It is no secret why many salespeople (for magazines, paper, printing, etc.) play an active role in advertising and creative club functions. You may have decried the fact that it often seems that everyone at club functions has a promotional reason for being there. Now you are on the other side of the fence. It is shortsighted not to take advantage of this proven opportunity to meet people who can help build your business. When you freelance, there's another, more personal benefit as well. Freelancing is a lonely way to make a living, and you get little feedback from peers. Club functions can provide a much-needed social outlet, as well as an opportunity to find out what others are doing and get objective input on what you are doing.

However, the main reason for joining professional clubs is that every club activity provides more visibility and the potential for new contacts— the stuff of good referrals. The more you partake, the more you get. Don't overlook clubs that are outside the creative community, especially in smaller cities: from church and local civic groups to traditional Kiwanis-type business organizations to expensive city and country clubs with their own dining and athletic facilities. All are sources for contacts. In general, the more exclusive their membership the higher the level of contacts (and jobs) that result.

Now look for ways you can help yourself become more broadly recognized in your market's communications and business communities—ways to develop "top of the mind" awareness among potential clients. How you do this is limited only by your imagination. The mistake most individuals make is never trying. For example, don't just join clubs and organizations; volunteer for their committees and make it a long-term goal to become an officer. Most clubs have trouble getting good talent to volunteer. Anyone who works hard helping the organization will end up in a highly visible leadership role. Along the same lines, organizations with regular meetings are constantly on the lookout for program speakers. Talks on such subjects as "the five tests of a good website" or "how to be sure your ads are written to sell" are sure to draw a good audience at business organization meetings. Aside from the advantage of meeting socially with potential clients, the other benefits of being a speaker are future credibility and immediate publicity through the organization's promotional efforts. There's no cost to you other than time and preparation.

Online networking. It can't match the power of face-to-face contact in building new business relationships, but sites such as LinkedIn can allow an individual to leverage existing connections. For instance, it provides an easy way for one of your friends or previous clients to refer you to one of her or his contacts, a prospect. Or you can join and participate in one of the countless special-interest business groups. Many potential clients will also look at your posted profile (résumé) to check you out before agreeing to a presentation. And the summary section of your profiling page provides a place to describe your firm's capabilities in detail, including a list of clients. It's your elevator pitch. Not least of all, online networking requires little investment of time, and is largely effortless, leaving no reason not to take full advantage of it. Just make sure that its primary use is to connect with potential clients, not other creatives. (There's more on online networking in Chapter 13.)

Other opportunities. Teaching offers an ideal way to get better known and increase your credibility at the same time. It also provides a little extra income. To many potential clients, anyone who teaches is, by definition, an expert. Another way to increase your visibility is to continue to develop your own art. Having a one-person show at a local gallery or having your novel published says a lot about your creativity to potential clients, but don't assume they'll just hear about it. Make sure by sending opening night invitations or copies of the book. Writers should do occasional magazine articles as a way of demonstrating versatility and getting their names known. Both writers and designers can author "expert" articles for the business press. For example: "How to refresh your brand without losing its equity," "Putting 'active' into interactive websites," "Using humor effectively in speeches," and so on.

Enter award competitions. Yes, they are expensive, but if your work is accepted, the publicity is invaluable. Not only do you become an "award-winning" individual or shop, but hundreds, perhaps thousands, of other freelances and potential clients see your best work. Select the pieces you will enter carefully. Don't just enter local "hanging" shows; also consider the national award publications.

Why you shouldn't rely on referrals

As previously mentioned, referrals are usually the most cost-effective way to get new clients and business. Yet there is also a paradox. What is arguably the most cost-effective is also one of the major reasons for the lack of profitability and failure of creative businesses. How can this be? Both statements are correct. So let's look at why no firm should rely solely on them.

The most obvious and significant reason is the hit-or-miss nature of referrals. You can't count on them. This not only poses a cash flow concern (bills are regular even when income isn't), but it can also raise havoc with workflow and scheduling, the disruption of which increases both project and general overhead costs. In contrast, active marketing to produce new business provides more project consistency and raises profitability. Although it is possible to increase the referrals you get by high visibility and many contacts, you can never completely control how many come in or count on them. The only way you can control the amount and type of business you get is through your own direct sales efforts.

Another problem is that referrals typically bring in more of the same types of clients and projects. Since individual clients provide referrals to others at their own level or lower, and usually for familiar types of work, over time referral business tends to move down the desirability ladder. Moreover, doing the same types of projects for similar clients pigeonholes an individual or firm and negatively affects creative flexibility and growth. The only way to ensure good new clients and projects and to move up the ladder is with active marketing. In fact, it can increase referrals by acting as a reminder to past clients.

Referrals often result in less pricing and scheduling latitude, too. Referral clients tend to expect preferred treatment. Even if they don't, there's a tendency to make pricing and scheduling concessions in order to stay in the good graces of a referring client. Given this phenomenon, any savings gained by relying on referrals can easily disappear through lower profits.

For the above and many other reasons, a creative business should never be totally dependent on referrals. At best, it will lead to erratic workflow and reduced profitability while diminishing control over the business. At worst, it will lead to failure, either through too little work or because of cash flow problems.

Making sales calls

Chapter 13 covers promotional activity, a step that normally precedes calling on potential clients. When prospects have never heard you, they are much less likely to want to entertain a portfolio or sales presentation, a subject covered in Chapter 14. Before looking at promotions and presentations, however, it first helps to consider making direct sales contact.

Appointment letter. This is the closest thing to a universally appropriate way to directly solicit potential clients. Overall, it is probably the most cost-effective way, too. Letters (postal, not e-mail) work well, regardless of your experience or business volume. They are fast to prepare and inexpensive when used in small quantities. You can literally write a letter today and have a dozen personalized copies of it in the mail tomorrow. All it takes are contact names, a little time, and something under $2 each for envelope and stamp. A well-written letter on good stationery makes a strong, positive statement about your business sophistication. Personally addressed and stamped letters will get through where direct mailings and telemarketing alone can't penetrate. See Appendix 3 for a sample Appointment Letter.

Telephone follow-up. An introductory letter helps avoid the two biggest problems with telemarketing. One is that prospects who have never heard of you are less likely to take your phone call. The second is that it's more difficult for most of us to pick up the phone and make a solicitation call without this introduction. In addition, even when your call is not taken, chances are that the message in the appointment letter—your capabilities, experience, and availability—will make an impression that may produce results down the road.

Whom you need to contact to get assignments

Whether client contact is made first through direct solicitation, or after the promotional activity described in Chapter 13, it helps to know who in the business world is responsible for assigning creative work.

Ads. In larger companies, the Director of Advertising or the Creative Director; in smaller companies, the Advertising Manager or Director of Sales or Marketing; in agencies, the Creative Director, or Art Buyer.

Animation. In larger companies, the Director of Advertising, Creative Director, or IT (Information Technology) Director; in smaller companies, the Advertising Manager or Director of Sales or Marketing; in agencies, the Creative Director or Art Buyer.

Annual reports. In larger companies, the Director of Public Relations, the Chief Financial Officer (CFO) or Director of Design; in smaller companies, the Public Relations Manager, President or Chief Executive Officer (CEO); in design firms, the Creative Director or principal.

Books. At larger publishers, the Art Buyer; at smaller publishers, the Senior Art Director.

Brochures and sales literature (collateral). Same as for ads except in design firms, the Creative Director or principal.

Case history articles. In larger companies, the Director of Public Relations; in smaller companies, the Public Relations Manager or Marketing Communications Manager; at magazines, the Editor.

Commercials. In agencies, the Creative Director; in smaller companies, the President.

Corporate identities, logos, and branding. In larger companies, the Director of Design; in smaller companies, the Art Director or Manager of Marketing Communications.

Illustration. In agencies, the Creative Director or Art Buyer; in design firms, the Creative Director or principal; at magazines, the Art Director or Art Buyer.

Interface design. In larger companies, the Director of Advertising, Creative Director, or IT Director; in smaller companies, the Advertising Manager or Director of Sales or Marketing; in agencies, the Creative Director or Art Buyer.

Magazines. The Editor (writers), Art Director (designers), or Art Buyer (illustrators).

Manuals and instructional materials. In larger companies, the Manager of Technical Publications.

Newsletters, house organs, e-zines. In larger companies, the Editor or the Director of Employee Communication or Information; in smaller firms, the Manager of Public Relations or Marketing Communications.

Newspapers. The Editor (writers) or Art Director (designers/illustrators).

Packaging. In larger companies, the Director of Design; in smaller companies, the Art Director or Director of Sales and Marketing.

Production work. In larger companies, the Director of Design; in smaller companies, the Manager of Marketing Communications; in agencies, the Creative Director or Art Buyer; at magazines, the Art Director or Art Buyer.

Sales promotion. In larger companies, the Creative Director or Sales

Promotion Manager; in smaller companies, the Art Director or Sales Manager; in sales promotion agencies, the Creative Director.

Speechwriting. In larger companies, the Director of Public Relations or Director of Marketing Communications; in smaller companies the Public Relations Manager, Marketing Communications Manager, or President; in public relations firms, the Copy Chief (large) or principal (small).

Storyboards and comps. In larger companies, the Director of Design; in agencies the Creative Director or Art Buyer (large) or Creative Director (small); in design firms, the Creative Director or principal.

Trade shows/exhibits. In larger companies, the Director of Design or Exhibits Manager; in smaller companies, the Art Director, Exhibit Manager, or Sales Manager; in display houses, the Creative Director.

Website development (interactive). In larger companies, the Director of Advertising or the Creative Director; in smaller companies, the Advertising Manager or Director of Sales or Marketing, or President; in agencies, the Creative Director.

13. Which Promotions Work, Which Don't

Visibility is fundamental to the success of any business. Those who don't know about you can't become your customers. So the challenge is: what's the most effective way to promote your business? To start, you must learn to look at promotional activity not just as spending money, although it is that, but as a business-building investment that will, when done well, return more than it costs. It is something of a paradox that creative firms, both single- and multiperson, have historically done a poor job addressing their own promotional needs, even though a major portion of their business comes from helping clients with theirs. One reason is the "cobbler's shoes" syndrome—we have trouble finding time to do at no charge for ourselves what we do for money for others. Another is the artistic persona—for some of us there's something crass about self-promotion. It really shouldn't be necessary for those with real talent; real talent should create its own visibility. And because we are talented people, when we do attempt to increase our visibility, we usually focus on what we know best and enjoy most: the artistic and qualitative. We tend to give less significance to the quantitative dimension: what will be the most cost-effective?

A different perspective

However much responsibility clients give us and however conscientious we might be, when we work for someone else we avoid the toughest of promotional decisions—timing, budgeting, the mix of media, and, most important, the return on our time and money. The perspective is different when it's our own money we're spending and our own business that will be impacted. Results, or lack of them, take on a new level of significance, particularly when the economy is down. Not only is it tougher to come up with promotional money, but there is an even greater need for a good payoff.

There are other impediments as well. We may have a specialty that gives us little promotional experience. Or we might be skilled in consumer promotions for clients, whereas our own business requires promoting business-to-business services. Then too sometimes our own talent gets in the way. We procrastinate, attempting to come up with something uniquely impressive, when, in reality, something good today will probably be more effective than something great tomorrow. Whatever the problem, regular, well-thought-out promotion allows a firm to be in control of its own business. It is a necessary component of growth and stability. There are at least ten reasons:

1. It produces new business leads.

2. It makes selling easier.

3. It reduces selling costs.

4. It enhances credibility with existing clients.

5. It showcases activity that attracts desirable clients.

6. It allows a firm to introduce new or reposition current services.

7. It increases employee morale.

8. It attracts talented employees.

9. It encourages referrals.

10. It intimidates competition.

Two concerns

Although anything anytime can be beneficial, there are two conditions that can dilute much of the effectiveness of promotional activity. They need to be recognized and avoided to the greatest extent possible.

Doing only "reactive" promotions. The most common promotional mistake made, particularly by smaller firms with limited time and resources, is waiting for a pressing need. Client projects, especially the most desirable ones, often have long gestation periods. So even when promotions are successful in drumming up new business, it often takes months before they are paying off in much-needed revenue. (Also, see "1. Objective" below.) In addition, multiple efforts are often needed to penetrate clients' "threshold of awareness," the repetition necessary to get their attention and land their business. (Also, see "4. Frequency" and "Lower thresholds" below.)

Lack of planning. It is the other reason why promotions are often less effective than they need to be. Planning not only can avoid the necessity of reactive promotions, but also help make sure that what's produced is strategically and creatively sound, and appropriately timed. It is less likely to forget what has been planned and scheduled in advance. A little forethought is all it takes. If you already have a yearly business plan, include a promotional schedule. If you don't have a business plan, preparing one will make sure that your promotional activities are in synch with your overall goals.

Keep in mind that promotional activity—making clients aware of the benefits of working with you—is but one of the three elements of successful marketing. It follows positioning (deciding what markets to go after); it precedes selling (calling on clients and presenting your work). For promotion to be effective, the other two components must be considered and coordinated. A lack of attention to positioning, for instance, can lead to a great creative effort absent a compelling message. Likewise, generating leads will be of little benefit if follow-up is lackluster.

Without considering the other two aspects of marketing, you very well might end up shooting a promotional arrow that scores a bull's-eye on the wrong target. Or create a situation that damages your credibility.

Promotion must also be in synch with the realities and goals of your organization—its finances, personnel, management, and so forth.

Six elements of effectiveness

After recognizing the interrelationships among the three marketing components, the next step in promotional planning is understanding the six elements that determine success.

1. Objective. Although not mutually exclusive, effective promotions normally fall into one of two broad categories: a) those intended to generate leads, and b) those intended to generate market awareness. The right media and message for each are often different. Lead-generating activity is more short-term, labor-intensive, narrow in focus, and costly on a per-contact basis. It should, obviously, be the choice when there is an immediate need to generate new business. Examples are presentation solicitation letters and mailers. Awareness-building activity is more long-term, broader in focus, less labor-intensive, and less costly on a per-contact basis. It should be the choice when the need is to sustain a certain business level. Examples are quarterly mailings showing recent work and blogs. (See "Short- and long-term objectives" in Chapter 12.)

2. Differentiation. To state the obvious, the more distinctive your efforts, the more impact they'll have and more memorable they will be. Not as easily recognized, though, is that this goes for strategy as well as creativity. Will a promotion fit your long-term goals? Which markets are best targeted? What's the best way to reach them? When? What positioning strategy should be adopted? Which strengths (client benefits) should be emphasized? These are issues at least as important as the creative concept.

3. Integration. You no doubt know the importance of consistency in style and content in the work you prepare for others. It's no less important in the promotional material you prepare for yourself. Uniformity in appearance and message generates a multiplier effect. Truly effective promotions are integrated with other efforts, such as a follow-up call, and also build on what has gone before.

4. Frequency. However accomplished, the primary goal should be ensuring that potential clients have a continuous awareness of you and your abilities. The reason why: many clients need what you do only occasionally. Their memory is short-lived, and those they remember are the ones that recently contacted them. Spending precious promotional money on occasional big-splash creative efforts is nearly always less effective than spending the same amount on several smaller efforts done more frequently. Large promotions are satisfying, often win awards, and do get noticed. But the effect is typically short-lived.

5. Mix. Promotional activities can be categorized as either hard or soft. Hard activities are concerted efforts that require significant expenditures and carry specific expectations, such as running an ad. Soft activities are those that are less formal, usually passive, and primarily supplementary, such as networking. A well-thought-out promotional program has a mix of both hard and soft activities.

6. Cost-effectiveness. The focus of every promotional effort should not just be on what works, but on what works best. The challenge is to first define the objective, then to come up with a concept or campaign that will meet it at the lowest possible cost. Whenever possible, there should also be a means of measuring impact. Given adequate talent, doing a creatively exciting promotion isn't difficult. But doing one that's also both strategically sound and cost-efficient can be.

What's appropriate

Once again for emphasis: when promotional activity is well done, it doesn't cost money, it makes money. Good promotions are investments. With this in mind, here are investing guidelines.

How often? Regular activity of some sort is usually necessary to maintain awareness and generate a steady stream of new business leads. The right frequency depends on the media used (ads, direct mail, e-mail blasts, blogs), the mix of targeted prospects (how many old versus new), the extent of your reputation (how well known, and what for), and the purpose (awareness, or sales leads?). Whatever the conditions, the guideline to remember is this: enough so that prospects and clients never forget about you. At minimum, this would be several times a year. (Also, see "Lower thresholds" below.)

How much time? *Creative Business* newsletter surveys show that successful firms of all sizes—single-person to shops with dozens of employees—typically put between 10 and 20 percent of payroll hours into all business development (marketing) activities. (I recommend 20 percent.) Sales time—calling on prospective clients, showing the portfolio, and so on—accounts for most of this. Promotional activities alone—producing a mail campaign, writing a blog, updating a website—typically account for only several hours a month when averaged over a year.

How much to spend? Here, *CB* surveys show that successful firms spend an average of 15 to 20 percent of fee-based income (gross margin) on all business development activities. Again, most of this is directly sales-related—salaries, commissions, and expenses. Promotional expenses—developers' salaries, media, printing, postage, and so on—typically run from 3 to 5 percent of fee-based income when averaged over several years.

Today's environment

How often, how much time, and how much to spend on promotion has not changed recently. What has changed are the media available, and how each can be best utilized. This is driven by the seemingly ever-expanding effect of the internet. It has not only has opened up more options, but it has changed the impact of each medium and the way it is used.

Website centrality. Whatever way a prospect learns about you, today each has the opportunity to further check you out without you even knowing. And most will do so before calling or agreeing to entertain a presentation. I like to call this new reality "website centrality," an acknowledgment that websites have become hubs that affect everything else. Not only are content and style crucial in their own right, but websites also impact other promotional media and activities. For instance, the dynamic of new business pitches changes because most prospects have already viewed at least some of an individual's or firm's work.

More affordable. Another effect of the internet is that it is easier and less costly to reach client prospects. Two major drawbacks in the past, high preparation (e.g., printing) and media (e.g., mailing) costs, are largely nonexistent for over-the-internet promotions. Today, there's no longer any reason not to have a regular and effective promotional schedule.

Lower thresholds. The more promotion an individual or firm does, the more it overcomes its audience's awareness threshold. All factors being equal, a second promotion to the same audience usually outscores the first, the third outscores the second, the fourth outscores the third, and so on. Put another way, the effectiveness of increasing activity is usually geometric, not arithmetic. Lower costs allow more promotional activity.

Greater choices. The changes brought by the internet don't mean that traditional media and promotions are obsolete or even passé. Just as TV hasn't replaced radio and DVDs haven't replaced movie theaters, there is a place for both. New technology hasn't changed what needs to be done. It has merely expanded the options and opportunities for doing it. A particular example of the blending of recent technologies and traditional needs is the probable ongoing need for a printed piece to use as a presentation leave-behind. Or a small run of direct mailers targeted to a specific industry. Both can now be produced on-demand with in-house desktop printers.

A downside. The negative side of today's promotional landscape is the temptation, particularly among those with less experience, to equate what is now easy and inexpensive with what works best. Sometimes it is, but sometimes it isn't.

Traditional media options

Since traditional media is both somewhat out of favor and more expensive than new media, let's start by looking at its role in staying in front of prospective clients. The two principal forms are direct (postal) mailings and magazine ads.

Direct mail. This has long been the primary and preferred medium, and with good reason. From an effectiveness standpoint, mailed promotions have maximum flexibility because there are few size and format constraints. Mailers provide a good canvas on which to display work, and they offer easy readability for telling a story. A means for response, a reply card, can be included. From a cost-effectiveness standpoint, mailers can be precisely targeted; as long as there's a good mailing list, there's little waste circulation. Mailers can also be produced quickly and inexpensively today in small quantities, even in-house on office printers. Use of a mailing company (mail house) for distribution can provide customization options, and its postal permit allows mailing at bulk rates when quantities exceed several hundred pieces (two hundred in the U.S.).

The major limitation (shared with e-mail) is the need for a good contact list. Developing and maintaining a prospect and client database is crucial, not only for mailings but also for making cold calls and for keeping a history of contacts made. Compiling a database that has a few hundred names is something that even someone working alone can accomplish. If used for mailings several times a year (postal or e-mail) it should create more than enough awareness and interest in one's capabilities to provide a steady stream of inquiries. The nucleus of your prospect/contact database should be everyone you know in the local business and creative community. Do not limit it to just potential clients; also include friends and other business contacts. They are the source of referral business.

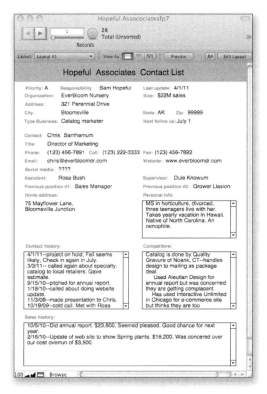

Be sure to include other creative service organizations and freelances to your database. Surprisingly, this is an opportunity often overlooked. For instance, if your talent is interface design you want to make sure that traditional design firms know of you. Likewise, if your talent is speechwriting, you want to make sure that advertising agencies have you, as the saying goes, "in their Rolodex." Some contacts may already have these capabilities, but they also occasionally need additional help or a fresh perspective. In addition, regular promotion will make you appear to be a more successful, formidable force in the local market. (Remember, sales success is based as much on perception as upon reality.) A database of clients and prospects not only provides a source of names for mailing (postal and e-mail) promotions, but also the account histories that are an important element in building long-lasting client relationships.

Postal mailing lists can also be rented for one-time use to reach specific market segments, such as marcom (marketing communications) managers in a certain industry. An internet search under "mailing lists for marketing" will turn up dozens of list brokers. Local list brokers can also be found under "Mailing Lists" in the local Yellow Pages. And local business organizations and regional magazines often rent their member/subscriber lists as well. The charge will likely be in the range of a $150 per thousand names with a minimum of a few hundred dollars.

Direct mail effectiveness. Mailers almost always get delivered to the addressee, not a small consideration when compared to their electronic counterparts (no deletes or spam filtering). When well designed and sent to the right individuals, the message, both visual and verbal, will almost certainly register. And the simple act of the addressee picking a mailer out of a stack of mail involves the tactile sense that's important in creating or reinforcing awareness, even if the mailer immediately goes into the wastebasket. (Also, see "E-mail effectiveness" below.) Response rates in mailers sent to solicit new business vary widely depending on circumstances, but normally run under 5 percent. Even in the age of electronic alternatives, postal direct mail is a very effective promotional medium for both appointment solicitation and general awareness. Whether or how much it is used is a personal choice with many considerations, but it should always be considered.

Advertising. Ads can produce a lot of exposure at a low per-reader cost, can make a firm appear more substantial than it might actually be, and, once prepared, can be rerun with little additional effort. But since the advertising of services needed only occasionally must be cumulative to be effective, it typically requires running a series (campaign) of insertions before the message sinks in enough to warrant the cost. Other factors that come into play in overcoming the awareness threshold are placement, consistency, and advertiser recognizability. Then, too, format restrictions limit how much can be communicated, and readership is limited to a publication's circulation, which seldom is as specific ("vertical") as desired.

Advertising effectiveness. Classified ads can be a cost-effective way to keep a firm's name in front of prospective clients, and they should be considered when well-targeted and inexpensive media are available. Display advertising, because of its higher cost in building and maintaining awareness, is seldom cost-effective unless a firm has $2 million or more in fee income, and a highly targeted publication is available. The key to making an advertising investment pay off is frequency. Ads typically have to run at least a half-dozen times in a monthly publication or twelve or more times in a weekly one to be cost-effective.

New media options

Online promotion has been around since the beginning of the internet. Although used by many firms over the years, it has often been selected more for its low-cost ease of preparation than for its effectiveness. This no longer needs to be the case; online promotion can now be effective as well. Today, there's wide acceptance by prospective clients who use it regularly in their own businesses. There's also less concern about spam, and broadband coverage is now universal. In short, online promotion does offer up many new opportunities. But let's also be clear: it is not the answer to a creative's prayers.

The major advantage of online promotion is its low cost, especially when combined with accountability. Every promotional medium, whether traditional or electronic, has waste. Addresses change, and some recipients ignore or trash anything they receive. But two things make online waste less of a concern. First, the cost of waste is a tiny fraction of what can be expected in traditional media, such as mailings or ads. For most readers, it will be so low as to be a nonissue. Second, viewer statistics are available to show just how much waste there actually is—for instance, how many e-mail messages have actually been opened, or "clicked through," for more information.

Except for certain formatting restrictions, an online PDF brochure can include everything that's in a printed one. Moreover, what's possible electronically isn't possible on paper: instant delivery, linking to other material and websites, and the inclusion of motion, sound, and video. Indeed, these capabilities, coupled with low production costs, provide temptations that can easily lead to gratuitous creativity and gimmickry. The attributes of electronic media open up totally new promotional avenues, varying from initial contact to relationship management to just keeping in touch. Some, like e-mail blasts, offer a new way to reach the same end: the promotion of a product. And some, like business networking, provide a means of making connections in more relaxed and informal contexts.

Websites. We'll start here because it is the oldest form of online promotion, albeit a largely passive one. As discussed previously (see "Website centrality" above), websites are crucial in that most prospects will visit one to check out a firm and its work. Additionally, a site can also provide the portal for entering a firm's social networking pages or blog, getting prospect contact information, or providing the means for client file transfer (FTP). Because of the growth in mobile devices, sites can now be accessed outside the normal business environment. The look, feel, and wire framing of a site are not only well beyond the scope here but should have minimal outside input anyway. A website needs to be a highly individualistic expression of what a firm wishes to communicate about its capabilities. Therefore, it must be self-directed. This said, the site needs to do nothing short of communicating the degree to which the firm embodies professionalism and business sophistication. Particular care should be taken not to go overboard on style or techniques that might indicate self-indulgence or more interest in craft than in conveying an ability to address clients' needs.

Website effectiveness. Although site-visit statistics (e.g., Google Analytics) are available and can be helpful in specific situations, such as tying page views to a specific promotion, most of the effect a site has on visitors will be largely unknown. This emphasizes the importance of the following: Websites should be designed to appeal to prospective clients, businesspeople, not one's peers. Keeping in mind the importance of the impressions it needs to create, make sure the site is quick to load, easy to navigate, and tells a firm's story concisely and convincingly.

E-mail promotions. Bulk e-mailing, the oldest form of active online promotion, has become increasingly accepted and effective. Anti-spam laws, filters, and opt-out links (required by law in the United States and Canada) have greatly diminished offensive messages. Moreover, many prospects and clients now use e-mail for some of their own promotions, which has provided it with a legitimacy previously lacking. Bulk messaging software and services also make mass transmissions easier and more effective, and they overcome the limitations of regular e-mailing software. Two types, standalone programs and web-based subscription services, are available. Pricing ranges from free to several hundred dollars, depending on feature sets and the number of messages sent monthly from subscription services. It is a good idea to check with your Internet service provider (ISP) first if messages are to be sent using standalone software. To control spam, many ISPs have limits on the number of messages they allow to be sent in a given period without special dispensation. Also, home-based firms might require a commercial versus a residential service contract to send bulk e-mails.

Much more than with postal mailings, the major limitation to bulk e-mailings is the address list. Unlike postal addresses, which are public record, e-mail addresses are private and thus more difficult to come by legitimately. Lists are available to purchase and are inexpensive, but they seldom are the targeted ones desired. Organizations that freely sell members' postal addresses rarely do the same for e-mail addresses. The upshot, at least for now, is that about the only way to get a good e-mail address list is to compile your own (opt-in) from clients and prospects who have contacted you. As for subject matter, anything that shows or summarizes what a firm has recently been up to is appropriate—new projects, clients, personnel, awards, activities, and the like. So is any information or tips recipients would find useful. A good strategy is sending press releases or other bulletins on news, supplemented quarterly by an "e-newsletter" or "zine" with interesting and informative material presented in a distinctive style. (Also see "Social networking" and "Blogs" below.)

E-mail effectiveness. Even when an e-mail list is composed of present or past clients, "open" or "click-through" statistics are often disappointing. Some messages are ignored, some are filtered out by ISPs and corporate firewalls, others are automatically routed to junk mail folders, and still others are opened but the recipient's e-mail software does not support reporting. Industry averages show that 10 to 20 percent of all bulk e-mail ends up in junk folders. For a list containing a mix of past and present clients and prospects, fewer than half will typically be reported as "opened," still fewer any "click-throughs." That there's little or no expense makes the cost-effectiveness of e-mailings high. But their transient nature and low penetration rate require frequency. An e-mailing at least once every other month is needed for impact.

Web listings. An internet search for "freelance job sites" will turn up a number of sites devoted to bringing together those looking for work with clients that have it. Registration is usually free, and the site generally collects a small commission (e.g., 10 percent) on payment. Other "directory" sites provide a place for firms to list and show their capabilities, usually for a fee. Potential clients do free searches to find firms that best meet their needs.

Web listing effectiveness. These sites appeal to bargain-seeking clients, typically with small projects. Those that feature bidding on projects show prices well below what is necessary to run a sustainable business. A possible exception is a directory site, which can be productive for illustrators and photographers where portfolio samples are 90 percent of selling. But for others, who must rely on a number of factors to land a client, listing sites are, at best, a supplemental medium that produces low-paid work. Free listing sites are worth about what they cost. Paid sites might be worth a try. But don't fall into the hope-springs-eternal trap of believing that suddenly there's an effortless, inexpensive way to find great clients. There isn't. And this isn't.

Keyword advertising. The short messages that appear next to the results of an internet search involving keywords (e.g., AdWords) are something of a hybrid. That is, they are not active in the sense of e-mail promotions, but they are not passive in the same way as a website. The viewer has self-selected through the search request, and there is interactivity by clicking through to the advertiser's site. The advertiser pays only for actual viewer impressions (not raw circulation), as well as for any click-throughs. Pricing is not set or arbitrary; it is determined by bidding based on the specificity of the keyword and the search criteria.

Keyword effectiveness. Creative Business newsletter subscribers report a mixed bag, based on local keyword pricing. As would be expected, cost-effectiveness is better in small markets than large. Also noted is that even where the cost per contact is small, the number of contacts and click-throughs adds up quickly. Keyword advertising is seldom as inexpensive as it first seems. Constant reporting does, however, make it possible to continuously evaluate its effectiveness. Use keyword advertising as long as doing so produces more in income than it costs, but be ready to stop as soon as it doesn't. There is no benefit otherwise because impact is not cumulative. Keyword advertising is not a medium for awareness building.

Online networking. Contacts—who you know and who knows you—have always played an important role in the promotional mix for service firms. As previously discussed in Chapter 12, today the traditional networking that occurs at business organizations and meetings has been greatly supplemented with the availability of online sites such as LinkedIn.com and Referrals.com. Although nothing beats traditional face-to-face contact, online networking provides ways to contact a larger group with similar business interests and to reconnect with former colleagues, college chums, and others who might put you on to new opportunities. And, of course, it is more convenient than traditional networking. Posting your personal profile (résumé) also allows a prospective client to find out more about your background and experiences. Prospective clients today are likely to first go to a firm's website to look at its portfolio and client list, then visit the networking site for the personal information that would be missing or inappropriate to include on the website.

Online networking effectiveness. The promotional opportunities are substantial, particularly for individuals and smaller firms with limited resources. An individual's profile and connections make easier the networking that has up to now been a time-consuming component of promotion. And, because online networking is largely free, there is little reason not to participate. The most common mistake is connecting with or only participating in groups that have a personal rather than a business interest. The second most common is not following up on the connection and referral possibilities available.

Social networking. This medium, dominated by Facebook, dramatically expanded promotional opportunities for many businesses, including for many clients. In consumer markets, for example, having social networking pages that customers follow is an inexpensive way to engage them with a brand's products, activities, and promotions. This not only builds loyalty but also—and more important—is a low-cost way to drive impulse purchasing of the consumables featured. For many B2B (business-to-business) organizations, the attraction is a more efficient and less expensive way to communicate with dealers, customers, and stakeholders on everything from announcements of price changes and sales promotions to reports of quarterly earnings. As transformative as this medium has been, its promotional benefits are limited for creative firms, especially smaller ones.

Social networking effectiveness. Although not promotion-critical, a Facebook page for your business (separate from your own personal profile page) is important nonetheless. It demonstrates familiarity with social media and can function as a mini website, communicating which projects and clients are current, highlighting recent awards and staff activities, and sharing information and contacts that could be helpful to client followers. There is a negative side, though. It is the tendency of social media to blur the distinction between real friends and business "friends." Posts of a personal nature that would be appealing to real friends—travel, interests, opinions, and so on—probably aren't to business "friends." Even when they might be, such posts can diminish professionalism. For reasons too numerous to discuss here, individuals' personal and business lives should be kept separate. The personal attractions of social networking sites should not be confused with their business attractions. Posts on a business social media site should be public and limited to items promotional in nature.

Micro-blogging. Services such as Twitter have even greater limitations for creative promotion. There is, of course, much less flexibility. Their attraction lies in the ability to pass along short comments or links to information of interest or helpful to followers. Tweeting things that would be of business interest can impress and build loyalty among followers that are current clients, as well as introduce a firm's business bona fides to new prospects.

Micro-blogging effectiveness. The downside, in addition to the time involved, is the potential for inappropriateness. Tweets should be about only topics with interest or information useful to clients—that is, business-related or economic subjects. This area is not a strength for many creatives. Messages that fail the appropriate test will likely be viewed as frivolous or annoying, and they can do more harm than good. Assuming that the time and appropriateness criteria can be met, micro-blogging can be an important addition, although not critical, to the long-term promotional mix.

Blogging. Blogs provide a forum for expressing individual viewpoints and for passing on information or showing work not necessarily related to normal business, or even business in general. Blogs can be powerful promotional tools because their essay format allows room for a firm principal or others to present insights into the firm's philosophy and communications skills that would not be otherwise apparent.

The most practical application of blogging is through postings on a website. A separate page on the site allows a firm's principal, or selected others, to comment at length on items that would be of interest to clients and prospects. These can include recent activities, cultural and business observations, approvals and criticisms of public ads and design, and helpful hints about things clients can do to improve the effectiveness of their communications programs.

Blogging effectiveness. Blogs can be a good way to address one of the most powerful promotional challenges—finding a way to engage, inform, and educate clients and prospects. But as beneficial as blogging can be in extending promotional effectiveness, the bar for doing it successfully is high. Preparation can be time-consuming and requires good writing skills, not to mention having engaging content. There is also the risk of being self-indulgent, controversial, or overtly promotional—three sure turnoffs. And blog entries have to appear regularly to sustain interest and keep from becoming stale. It is easier to start a blog than continue one. Like any editorial matter, blog postings have to be timely, interesting, and informative. Even more important, for better or worse they will expose personal and business philosophies and interests.

Preparing a yearly action plan

You are now ready to decide on a yearly promotional action plan to amplify the sales strategy previously determined in Chapter 12 with sales tactics. Keeping your sales strategy in mind, schedule the few promotional activities that make the most sense for you in the year ahead. Make sure each activity can be easily accomplished, and provide cost and expectation estimates. Place your action plan directly under your sales strategy statement. The result should look something like this:

(Year) Sales Strategy

To balance my workload to 50 percent electronic, 50 percent print. To reduce my dependence on ad agencies for web production work for their clients from 30 to 15 percent of workload. To more heavily merchandise recent print awards. To obtain at least two new, steady, and diverse clients.

(Year) Action Plan

January/December—Attend every meeting of my local business marketing association, volunteer for social committee assignments, become a dinner speaker on the value of integrated marketing for small companies.

January/December—Run a six-line classified ad under "Marketing Services" in *Madison County Business Journal* to develop new small-company clients.

    Cost: $2,000

    Expectation: 5 leads, 2 jobs with $6,000 income and ongoing potential

January/December—Develop and post on my website six blog posts on various marketing subjects.

    Cost: time only

    Expectation: awareness building

March—Do a 250-piece mailing to my contact list to showcase collateral services to new clients, sustain existing business. Follow up with telephone calls.

    Cost: $500

    Expectation: 4 leads, 1 job with $4,500 income and ongoing potential

July—Develop the creative for postal and e-mailing promotions on annual report/capability brochure strategies.

August—Buy Ad and PR club mailing lists for September postal mailing.

    Cost: $250

September—Do postal mailing to 500 prospects from Ad/PR club lists.

    Cost: $3,500

    Expectation: 5 leads, 1 job with $25,000 income and ongoing potential

October—Do e-mailing on annual report/capability brochure strategies to my contact list.

    Cost: time only

    Expectation: unknown

October—Develop creative for season's greetings card.

December—Send 150 season's greeting cards to contact list.

    Cost: $500

    Expectation: goodwill only

14. Making the All-important Sales Presentation

Your promotional activity has but one long-term objective: to get your or your company's name so well known among potential clients that they remember you every time they have a creative need. Because you provide a service whose quality is highly subjective, assuring this memorability usually requires personal acquaintance. Potential clients want to see your portfolio, check out your reliability, find out what you charge, and decide whether they would be comfortable working with you. If they like what they see, and you stay in touch, you'll get work.

Don't make the mistake of assuming that your portfolio is all that clients are interested in. When you call upon potential clients, less than half of the impression they get will be determined by the strength of your portfolio. More than half will be determined by how well you present yourself.

Handling inquiries

Inquiries from known companies. If you know the company, call to set up an appointment. The best time to call is midmorning or midafternoon. The best appointment time is early morning or early afternoon—the client will be more relaxed and receptive, there's less likelihood of cancellation or delay, and you'll have the rest of the day to work. Ask the prospective client if there is any particular type of work samples he or she would like you to bring.

Inquiries from unknown companies. Inquiries from companies you do not know may prove fruitless due to unrealistic budgets and/or deadlines. Qualify them before you waste time on an appointment. If it is unclear where they got your name, ask when you call to follow up. If the source is good—an experienced writer or designer friend, for example—simply make the appointment as described above. Even if you can't help the client at this time, you may in the future. If, however, the inquiry comes from a nonspecific source—a classified ad, or a vague referral ("I heard about you, and I need some work done")—check the prospect before going farther. You can do this over the phone by explaining briefly what types of work you do, who some of your clients are, and how much a typical job costs, or send a "thanks for your inquiry" letter, along with the same material you would leave behind after a sales call. (See "What to bring" later in this chapter.) Follow up the letter in about a week with a telephone call.

If asked what you would charge to do a certain type of job, be as candid as possible (see "How to cover pricing" later in this chapter). Don't dodge the question or give a conservative estimate. Indeed, estimate a little on the high side. It is in your best interest to determine right up front if the prospective client is serious, or just price shopping. Always be wary of any prospect who asks if you can handle a "rush" job without first having seen your portfolio.

What about "drop-offs"?

Some prospective clients (especially agencies when dealing with freelances) ask you to send or drop off samples of your work for review, rather than setting aside time for an interview. Although any review of your work is preferable to none, try to discourage it.

The main reason to discourage drop-offs is that the prospective client will relate to your work better and remember it longer if it is connected to a face and personality. Also, unless you are a complete social misfit, being there to explain it will greatly enhance the perceived quality of the work.

MAKING THE ALL-IMPORTANT SALES PRESENTATION

(Don't fall into the trap of thinking that your work is so good it will sell itself.) Finally, you run the risk of having your original samples damaged or lost unless you send copies, and then the impact of your portfolio suffers.

The best way to handle drop-off or sample requests is to say that as important as samples are in showing style and quality, more important is why you did what you did and how well it has worked for your clients. This takes personal explanation.

In many cases, this rationale will suffice. If it doesn't, a second choice is to direct the client to examples on your website. Otherwise, you'll have to decide whether to say "thanks, but no thanks." If the potential is large and the inconvenience/risk small, by all means go for it. But don't have unrealistic expectations.

The consensus is that very few good jobs come from leaving portfolios, unless one has a very impressive book of ad concepts and the client is a major agency. However, illustrators report some success because of the importance of style in their work.

The importance of impressions

Good assignments go to individuals whom clients like. Conversely, the less comfortable the client feels about the individual, the less the chances of providing good assignments, regardless of portfolio excellence or past experience. Most clients make assignment decisions without weighty consideration; they make their decisions quickly and emotionally, based upon personal impressions. Although we can't completely control who likes us and who doesn't, we can do a lot to create the positive impressions—initial and ongoing—that make clients comfortable. We can also avoid those things that experience shows are apt to create negative impressions. Here are some areas in which client impressions work either for or against us.

Impress them with your appearance. What you look like, what type of car you drive, and how you dress certainly don't affect your creativity, and shouldn't affect any potential client's evaluation of your work, but they do, especially on the first meeting.

Ideally, every client would like you to look and act as he or she does—to be a creative alter ego. Since this is obviously impossible, the best rule of thumb is to adopt more or less standard business dress. By and large, the better you're tailored and the neater you appear, the greater your chances of being considered for a good assignment from most organizations. Whenever possible, modify your garb slightly to match the client's style. For example, dress more conservatively when calling upon a banker than when calling

upon an agency creative director. Other nondress aspects of appearance—
your car, your hair style, your briefcase, even the pens and note pads you
use—should also create an impression of prosperity and professionalism.

Impress them with your promptness. Chances are the client's very
first impression will be whether or not you are on time. First impressions
are often the most important ones. Timeliness always creates a positive
impression; tardiness usually creates a negative impression, regardless of
the reason. Think of it this way. One of the major components of our business is an ability to meet deadlines. You can't afford to create an impression
among clients, however subtle, that you don't understand the importance
of time. Moreover, promptness demonstrates professional courtesy and
respect for the client's importance.

Given the difficulty of getting a cab, predicting traffic, or finding parking, you may wish to ask clients if you can schedule appointments within
a half-hour range—say, 10:00 to 10:30, as opposed to 10 o'clock. Just asking
will emphasize your concern about time and create a positive impression. If, however, it is only possible to set up an appointment at an exact
time, put some work or a magazine in your briefcase, leave early and sit
in your car or a nearby hotel lobby until the appointment time. It is better to waste time privately than to create the impression you are relaxed
about it publicly.

Impress them with your friendliness. By and large, ours is a very
personal business. An individual (the client) selects and commissions
another individual (you or your firm) to create an expensive, nonreturnable
product that will be subjectively reviewed and evaluated. In such a process,
the extent of the "personal chemistry" that exists between the client and
you is often of equal importance to the actual creative result. The more the
client likes you, the easier it will be to approve your creativity, and your
invoices. (Exceptions are illustration and journalism assignments where
personal chemistry, although it never hurts, is not as significant a factor.)

You can establish a personal relationship quickly with nearly any individual if you use "small talk" to discover areas of mutual interest, then
discuss them for several minutes. Discussing personal interests before
discussing business will put both you and the client at ease, and make
your future working relationship smoother.

Impress them with your confidence. To any new client you are an
unknown entity. Before giving you an assignment, the client must have
confidence in your ability to handle it. Personal mannerisms can belie the
very sense of confidence you are trying to achieve. Here are some things
clients are particularly apt to notice:

Strong handshake: a limp-wristed one conveys unsureness and apprehension. *Eye contact:* not looking someone directly in the eye communicates insincerity. *Definitive speech:* wishy-washy phrases like, "I think it is," or, "I guess so," create an impression of insecurity. *Control:* not taking the conversation/presentation initiative presents an appearance of lack of opinions and convictions. *False modesty:* secure, honest people aren't afraid to take credit for what they've accomplished. *Apologies:* too much concern or defensiveness, especially about pricing, is unprofessional. *Pleasantness:* self-confident people are usually flexible and easy to get along with.

Impress them with how much you know. One of the surest ways to impress a client is to know something about his or her business. The more knowledgeable you appear, the more positive the impression you'll make. In fact, often one of the first questions clients ask when meeting a potential supplier is, "How much do you know about us or our products?" Most creative individuals have to confess to knowing little or nothing, so any positive response will set you apart. Some basics to consider: What is the company's business, or agency's clients? How big are they (employees, factories/offices, sales/billings)? What are their products? How are products promoted or sold? What does their material look like, and how could you improve upon it?

To know this, and more, ask around. Look the company up on the internet. Better yet, call and ask for a copy of their annual report or sample product literature before you call on them. As well as providing information, the very process of asking will make a very positive impression and differentiate you from your creative competition.

Impress them by not trying too hard. You should deal on an informal and friendly peer basis with most clients. There is seldom any justification for client intimidation, real or perceived. Always keep in mind that you are a trained professional offering an honest service at good value. Don't try too hard to impress any client. Never put on airs or try to pass yourself off as something you aren't. There's simply no need. Chances are high that trying will backfire anyway, being viewed as unbecoming or unprofessional behavior.

As for your possible shortcomings—age, lack of specific experience, limited portfolio, high price, etc.—such concerns are nearly always less important than the way they are dealt with. First, don't call attention to any shortcomings. Unless the client notices them, they don't exist. If the client does notice and asks for an explanation, give a straightforward, honest answer designed to minimize concern. (Example: "While it is true I don't have any specific experience in the magnetic resonance imaging market, I learn fast. I think you can see from the quality and variety of my portfolio that I've done excellent work in unfamiliar situations before.")

Being relaxed, friendly, and informal—in other words, confident—will impress any good client far more than any artificial attempt at impression. Put another way, every potential client you call upon should think, "Your actions speak so loudly, I don't need to be impressed."

Preparing yourself for success

Once you've made appointments to show your portfolio, the next step is to prepare yourself to make them effective—to increase your potential for getting work.

Let's start absolutely fresh by forgetting everything you've ever heard or thought about selling. This is going to be exciting, fun, and different. You can be an excellent salesperson, regardless of your background. After all, the product is you. As your mother will undoubtedly attest, there has never been one more perfectly made, and selling a perfect product is easy. Moreover, becoming a good salesperson is something that's easily learned.

Selling is largely a matter of attitude. This is the very first thing you have to learn: positive attitude = positive results; negative attitude = negative results. Remember this; it is the foundation for everything else.

Confidence sets the stage. You must believe, absolutely, that you are good. Not necessarily the best in the world, just good; worth every penny of what you charge. If you have doubts about this, stop here and work at convincing yourself before you go any farther. Complete confidence in your own abilities is the crucial first step in selling yourself to others.

Enthusiasm creates the environment. You must also be enthusiastic about the work in your portfolio and applying your proven abilities to the prospective client's assignments. This is not the place to be laid back or indecisive. You can't expect a company to be excited about hiring you if you aren't excited about working for them. This doesn't mean you should be phony. It does mean you should come across as genuinely anticipating how you will solve the client's problems, and anxious to get on with the challenge. Enthusiasm makes clients feel good. Enthusiasm is convincing. Enthusiasm is contagious.

If you find it difficult to be enthusiastic because you are introverted or shy, work at it. Before you go on a sales call keep repeating to yourself how good you are and how much you want the work. Think of how bad the client's present material is, and how much you can improve it, how much more effective you can make it, how much better service you can provide, how much value the client will get for money spent.

Overcoming the fear of rejection

Although creative individuals exhibit all manner of personality traits, "sensitive" seems particularly high among them. If this describes you, it is a definite asset when it comes to creating, but it often turns against you when you present or defend your work. Fear of rejection can extract a heavy price if you aren't careful. Here is what to look out for, and some ways of fighting back.

Toughen your defenses. You can't be rejected unless you acquiesce. Others can refuse to see you, deny your abilities, and criticize your work, but it only becomes rejection when you view it that way. Rejection is a mental state, nothing more. Don't let the enemy be yourself. Be realistic about the world of commercial creativity. You have to be good, but you don't have to be perfect. It should be enough—for both personal satisfaction and financial prosperity—to please most clients most of the time. In every other talent-dependent occupation, getting it right most of the time is all that's expected. A superstar baseball player actually hits the ball less than 40 percent of the time. So why do you expect a perfect batting average?

Be more assertive. If you are an individual who's troubled by rejection, one reason may be that you're not as forward and assertive as you should be. For example, when trying to set up portfolio-showing appointments, you must be persistent. Nothing else—repeat, nothing else— works. If being persistent bothers you, think this way: you're doing potential clients a favor by offering to introduce them to a new, better source of creativity. Good clients seldom come easily. On average in the industry, it takes three to five calls before business changes hands.

Anyone who has been in business more than a few years has run into these or similar comments: "I wish I had known about you six months ago." "I'm glad you called; it's so hard finding reliable talent these days." One such comment—and the business that accompanies it—more than compensates for dozens of rebuffs and rejections.

Challenge negative input. Another reason many creative individuals are adversely affected by rejection is that they don't channel negative input in a way that is constructive. Instead, they accept it. As a professional, you have an obligation to yourself and the client to challenge any negative feedback. Never wimp-out and accept what is irrational or based on ignorance. When a client expresses general disapproval of a concept or proposal, ask for precise reasons. Then make sure you agree, or say why if you don't.

When you don't agree, first restate the client objections in your own words and try to offer some creative insight the client may be unaware of. Then, in a friendly and tactful way, question the wisdom of his or her approach. For example, "Let me play the devil's advocate here. If I were to take this approach, wouldn't it visually position the product very close to that of your major competitor? Is this wise?"

Many creative individuals are far too passive. Typical client comments are: "I never get a good rationale for what she does" and, "I get the distinct impression that whatever I say, he'll agree to it, even if he knows it's not necessarily in my best interest."

Remember, negative input is seldom personal. There are few absolutes in commercial creativity, only opinions. Your role in the process is to do your best, then argue persuasively and professionally why you believe it meets all the client's objectives. The client's role is to question, to challenge, to make absolutely sure that your approach is the best possible solution to the problem.

Don't seek to avoid criticism; it is part of the business. Instead, relish and challenge it as a process that keeps you sharp and makes each project better. When a client does turn down your best efforts, don't take it personally. It is seldom a reflection on your talent or abilities, usually just a statement that what you've done is not, in the client's opinion, appropriate.

Finally, when dealing with first-time clients, strive to be even more professional, even more forgiving of subjectivity and personal idiosyncrasies. Cultivating trust takes a long time, but it is always a harvest well worth the effort.

What to bring

The afternoon before or the morning of your appointment you may wish to reconfirm. There are two opinions on the wisdom of this. The first holds that calling to reconfirm saves you from showing up only to find that you've been stood up. The second is that calling first gives the prospective client an opportunity to rethink and cancel. Most creatives prefer to call first if they are busy; if not, just showing up seems to be worth the small risk of a wasted trip.

What to bring to a portfolio-showing appointment depends on the prospective client and the size of the potential assignment. As a general rule, most individuals bring too much and stay too long. In most cases you should be able to convincingly show your portfolio and discuss how you work in approximately thirty minutes.

Ten to twelve good samples per presentation is all you need. This is enough to show style, demonstrate versatility, draw out the client's interests, and allow you to make an interesting presentation; not so many as to confuse or bore the client. Another dozen or so samples should be kept in the back of the portfolio ready to be brought out, as necessary, to modify the presentation, or show more examples of a particular style or type of work.

The portfolio samples should be selected to match the interests of the potential client. A "standard" portfolio that is shown to all clients is never as effective as one that is custom-tailored for each showing. The first five or so of the samples should represent the type of work the client will be most interested in—similar to the type of assignment you hope to get, or work you have done for similar organizations. Add to these another five to seven samples of different types of work to show versatility.

The best way to show most printed samples is unmounted. Rigidly mounted and protected samples are only appropriate when the piece is delicate—original artwork, ad tearsheets, etc. Otherwise, samples should be handed to the client for examination as you discuss them. This provides an important sense of involvement by giving the client the opportunity to feel the paper, check the printing, and read the copy. Also, handing over the sample gives you a better opportunity to control the presentation and describe the piece on your terms, not to wait for client reaction. In short, it is far more effective and interactive than merely turning portfolio pages. Release prints and tapes (not outtakes) should be provided to show broadcast work.

Projection visuals, PowerPoint presentations, and laptop computer demonstrations are appropriate when presenting to a large audience; when the pitch includes methodology or process, as in ad or PR campaigns; when the interactivity of a website is being shown; or when the examples clearly require it, as in industrial or package design, or interactive or broadcast work.

Except in these instances, a good portfolio presentation does *not* typically require a "show" or technology demonstration. In fact, they may shift the focus away from you, your work, and personal service, and put it instead on the presentation. Formal presentations can easily wind up at cross purposes with the informality and flexibility needed for a convincing portfolio showing.

Don't necessarily include samples of your most creative, or best work. Heresy? Not at all. The best presentations are those that show the prospective client what he or she wants to see, not what you want to show. Most clients are more interested in work you have done for similar clients, or in meeting creative challenges similar to theirs, than they are in knock-out creativity. Appropriate good is much better than inappropriate best.

The case is not crucial. A mistake frequently made, especially among less experienced freelancers, is putting too much emphasis on the medium itself—the portfolio case. Actually, in many situations the best portfolio showing often requires no case at all; it is simply carrying samples in a good quality briefcase and handing them to the client as they are explained.

When a portfolio case is used, it should be compact and easy to present from. To the extent that it is unwieldy, or the samples in it are inaccessible, it defeats its purpose. Cases with bound pages of mounted samples also encourage standardized presentations. This does provide a crutch for those with limited presentation skills, but it is seldom as effective as a presentation around samples chosen specifically to appeal to a client's interests.

Put together a small package of materials to leave behind. Whenever making a client call, bring not only your portfolio but also a small package of leave-behind material. Include your business card, something on how you work and bill, a list of past clients or an assignment resumé, a list of awards (if impressive and of client interest), any brochures or other promotional materials on your firm, any samples or photocopies of work you wish to leave behind (always make sure they are clearly labeled as "style samples of [your company name]" in case they get separated later).

Thirty minutes is all it should take

Thirty minutes is about right for most portfolio presentations. This is long enough to say what is important, short enough to conserve the client's valuable time, and yours. The discipline of doing the presentation in half an hour will force you to be concise and businesslike.

When setting up a portfolio-showing appointment, promise the client it won't take a minute longer. Conversely, never willingly accept a portfolio appointment of less than half an hour. ("I'm sorry, but I'll need a full thirty minutes—no longer—to explain why I did what I did, my pricing, working procedures, etc.")

Think of the presentation in sections. To make it easier to do a presentation in half an hour, think of it as having three sections. The first, getting to know the client, should take about five minutes. The second, actually showing your work, should take twenty minutes or so. The last, closing the presentation, should occupy the remaining five minutes.

Start by developing personal chemistry. The bigger and better any potential job, the more likely it will be given to the individual the client feels most comfortable with. Even if you have some of the world's best work to show, your chances of getting a job are slim if a prospective client doesn't like you. So take the first five or so minutes of your presentation time to get to know the client. "Break the ice" by being friendly, asking about the client's business, and seeking things you may both have in common. Here are a few quick lessons in how to be more likable:

Use yourself as a conversation starter. When you are calling upon a client for the first time, you can often get a friendly conversation going by giving a positive and interesting response to a simple, "How are you, today?" greeting. ("Actually, right now I'm doing just great, but I had a little problem with my car earlier this morning." Or, "Well, I'm nice and cool now, thanks to your air conditioning. You should see how hot it has become outside.")

Look around. Another way of getting a friendly conversation started when you don't know the client is to get ideas from his or her work environment. When waiting in the reception area, look through any company literature for nuggets of information you can use. The more you appear to know about the company, the more impressed, and friendly, the client will be. ("When waiting in the lobby just now, I was looking through your annual report. Are you doing as well this year as last?") Similarly, when meeting in a client's office, look around at the pictures on the desk, the wall art, calendars, personal artifacts, and the way the office is decorated. They often provide a good indication of his or her interests. ("Are those pictures of your children?" or, "I love your Aztec rug. Did you get it in Mexico?")

Be prepared. When preparing for a concept presentation, you probably think quite a bit beforehand about what you'll say. Why not do the same when it comes to the important "ice breaking" conversation that often sets the stage for it? It serves to relax you, as well as enhancing your presentation. Take a minute and think about any similar interests you share with the client—a common friend, past business experience, interest in certain sports or cultural activities, a similar rush-hour commute. Then, when greeting the client, or setting up for the presentation, bring up your mutual interests in friendly conversation. ("By the way, what did you think of the Sonics game the other night?" "Did you manage to miss that big tie up on the Beltway this morning?")

Avoid controversial issues. As you probably suspect, politics, sex, religion, and hotly debated current events of the day all should be avoided in casual business conversation. Doing so doesn't imply that you have no convictions, just that business conversations are not the place to air them. There's a time and a place, and this isn't it. Even when the individual you're speaking with agrees with your point of view, discussing controversial issues is seldom appropriate. Often, the impression created is that you are an aggressive, opinionated person, not exactly the image you wish to project to someone whose business you want to cultivate.

Pay attention to body language—yours and theirs. Although how to "read" body language is much too complex to go into here, be attentive to the basic, easily recognizable signals every individual sends when engaged in conversation. On your part, you want to convey a relaxed, informal, nonthreatening sense of confidence. No good client is ever impressed by a vendor who is easily intimidated. Your confidence, or lack of it, is unmistakably communicated through your handshake, whether you look the client directly in the eye when speaking, how easily you handle questions on pricing, and your ability to be professional while also maintaining your sense of humor and overall amicability. On the client's part, smiles, informality, leading questions, nods of the head, and openly expressive hands are just a few of the ways he or she will signal friendliness.

Know when to make the transition between small talk and substantive discussion. Usually the client will signal when it is time to start talking business. When you see it, (a move towards your portfolio case, sitting down at the conference room table, etc.), take the hint. Unless you and the client have found an area of strong mutual interest, when there is no hint, segue into talking about the reason for your call within five minutes. ("Well, I know you're busy, so let me tell you a bit about our company." Or, "Now, the reason I wanted to see you was . . . ")

When showing samples, focus on problem/solution, not creative executions. Whether expressed or not, clients are seeking results, not creativity. Creativity shows; you don't have to talk about it. What you do have to talk about is how your creativity produces results. If you focus on your ability to understand problems and provide cost-effective solutions, not only will you make the client feel more comfortable; you will eliminate up front many of the pricing objections that would otherwise come up later.

Try to devote a couple of minutes or a little less to every major sample. (Unless, of course, the client wants to spend more time discussing it.) Your presentation goal is to show variety and capability. It will probably be easier for you to present each sample in a way that is relevant to client interests if you describe each in the same way.

Who the client was and why they called you. This is your chance to talk about your reputation, experience, speed, and skills in the context of fact, not braggadocio.

Your collaborators and what they contributed. By giving credit to the other team members or agencies involved, you will show your honesty and ability to work well in a team situation.

The problem your client faced and how you provided the solution. For example, "Acme's market research indicated the product was perceived as out-of-date. To give them the contemporary image they needed, we decided to . . . " By taking this approach, you demonstrate that you do applied, not off-the-wall creativity.

An indication of timing and budget. Without being too specific, indicate what cost and deadline concerns you met. Don't provide actual pricing information unless asked, and then say only, "I can't recall exactly, but I'll check and get back to you."

The results. Be as specific as you can—higher sales, wider recognition, etc. If you can't be specific, say something like, "I understand their sales people felt this was the most productive ad the company has yet run."

Any awards or industry recognition. Make this an afterthought, nothing more—an "Oh, by the way" comment that reinforces how good the work really is.

Although it helps to have a presentation structure to start with, you should also be flexible. Listen to what the client says, the questions asked. They are a sure giveaway to real interests and concerns. For example, if the client focuses on how you work, the production process, this probably reflects a desire to hire someone who can take charge. A client who asks what each job costs is very budget-conscious; one who doesn't is probably less so. Be prepared to listen and change your focus to what is of most interest.

End the presentation by describing how you work and bill. After you have shown the last sample, ask if there are any questions about your work or capabilities. If the client called you in because he or she had a specific project in mind, say something like, "Now, is there anything I can tell you regarding my capability to handle project X?"

If the portfolio showing was not for a specific project, a closing query will probably trigger a client question about price. (If asked sooner, say, "I'll cover that completely in a few minutes.")

Briefly, and without embarrassment or apology, describe how you charge. For example: "We charge $150 per hour for our time. What this means is that the design of an eight-page brochure normally runs from $6,000 to $10,000 depending upon complexity. Of course, we always give a specific estimate as soon as a job is clearly defined and before we start work."

Close the presentation by presenting the "leave-behind" materials previously prepared. For example, "Let me leave you with this package of materials that tells how we work and charge for our services. I'd also like to stay in touch. Can I add your name to my mailing list and give you a call every so often?"

How to cover pricing

Successful individuals are more concerned about how they and their portfolio are perceived than about pricing. More good jobs are lost to bad portfolio presentation than to high prices. (Rule of thumb: the best clients put effectiveness first, price second; the worst put price first, effectiveness second.) Regardless of the sophistication of the client or the size of the job, if you've shown great work and an ability to understand and solve communication problems, client concern about price will be greatly reduced. In some cases it will disappear entirely. In reality, most clients are not interested in price; they are actually interested in value — price in relationship to quality. Avoid discussing pricing until you have first shown how good your work is. Make it the last thing you talk about.

What do you do when a client asks about pricing up front? The best answer is that you will be in a better position to discuss it after he or she has seen your work, and/or after you have had an opportunity to learn more about the assignment. In other words, dodge the issue until you have had a chance to show why the quality of your work makes whatever you charge a bargain.

Be wary of price negotiation. When discussing your pricing with potential clients, be decisive and *never apologize.* You are a communications professional with years of experience at providing writing or art services at competitive prices with outstanding value. State clearly and positively how you estimate what a job will cost. Only ask what a client has to spend in the context of providing different estimates based on greater or lesser involvement or quality.

Your reputation will be considerably enhanced and your business will benefit in the long run if you establish the price, as opposed to just matching clients' budgets. You will lose some jobs this way, but you will also be surprised at how many budgets can be raised to meet a fair price from a quality-oriented vendor (you). In any event, whether your estimate comes in above or below the client's budget, the process puts you in charge and reinforces your professionalism. If you decide it is in your best interests to match a client budget that is below your estimate, always do it on an exceptional basis. Make it known what your normal price would be and why you are making an exception (the ability to combine it with a similar assignment, the desire for a certain type of work in your portfolio, etc.).

Never give the impression that you price to match budgets, that you charge "what the traffic will bear." Not only is this unprofessional, but it will forever mark you as someone who can always be beaten down on price. In turn, this is a magnet for cheap, unscrupulous clients.

How to respond to objections

Objection and/or rejection is a natural part of the selling process. It can't be avoided or eliminated, but it can be anticipated and minimized. You must never let it affect you.

When going in to show your portfolio, always remind yourself that it is the client's money being spent and the client's reputation on the line. If you get the assignment and the work you produce isn't good—the ad doesn't sell, the brochure doesn't explain, or the website doesn't motivate—the client pays, literally and figuratively. You don't.

Don't take offense when a potential client questions your style or abilities. He or she isn't judging you, only trying to determine whether it makes good business sense to hire you. It is his or her obligation to be skeptical and ask tough questions. Instead of being defensive, try to understand the concerns and turn them around. Below are some common objections and appropriate responses. Use them as guides to develop your own set of positive responses to questions you are commonly asked.

I like your work, but I'm not sure we can afford you. Answer: I'm actually inexpensive for work of this quality, and quality usually returns far more in (sales/impact) than the little extra it initially costs.

I like your work, but you don't have any (industry) experience. Answer: Actually, it's better that I don't. I'll bring a fresh perspective. Also, my demonstrated problem-solving ability and communications skills are more far more important than specific knowledge. I learn very quickly.

We'd like to try you first. Will you accept a job on speculation? Answer: As much as I'd like to, I can't. All I have to sell is time, and once it's gone, it can't be replaced. I believe my portfolio demonstrates my ability to do a good job for you.

Do you always work alone? (Often masks a concern about working with a single-person company.) Answer: I find I can give more creative and personal service this way. When necessary, I bring in people to help me out. I haven't missed a deadline yet.

We'd prefer a larger company with full-service capability. Answer: I provide full service, but I do it through assembling modular teams rather than relying on in-house staff. This way I can get the very best talent for each assignment, and you don't have to pay for a lot of overhead. I personally oversee everything, so you don't have to worry about your job being directed by an unknowledgeable account executive.

Why should I hire you, rather than a bigger firm? Answer: I'll give you better work, faster and cheaper. With me you get creativity without the overhead that adds to costs and without the layers that add delays and misunderstandings.

If a client decides not to hire you, at worst he or she has made a costly mistake. At best, you have eluded what might have turned out to be a bad situation. In either case, put it behind you and go on to your next appointment. You are good, and there many clients out there who can use your services. All it takes is a little time and effort to find them.

How to respond to competition

The amount and variety of competition is increasing. In the past, everyone more or less concentrated on the business mix best suited to their experience and talent. No more. Today, everyone goes after everything. Although this is partly driven by economics, much of it comes from the new role of computers as productivity and creativity "equalizers." Assignments that formerly could only be handled by those with certain levels of sophistication can now be easily attempted (albeit not always successfully) by just about anyone. Competing for assignments requires knowing how to respond to many different types of competitive challenges. Here are some ideas on how to handle the most common ones.

The "you're more expensive" situation. The objective here is to convince the client that price alone isn't important. What is important is value—price compared to the quality and effectiveness of what's produced. You provide the best value.

When the competition is lesser-quality talent. Your reaction: "I'm not surprised given our talent, experience, and service. We are, however, usually priced lower than others who do work of similar quality." Explain that with talent-dependent, subjectively evaluated creative work, purchasers usually get what they pay for. In other words, lower cost = lesser quality; higher cost = higher quality. Now explain the benefits of higher quality— easier working relationships, better service, and, most of all, creativity that is more productive in meeting the client's objectives. Finally, explain that when all the benefits of working with you are weighed against the (slight) cost difference, in the long run you will most likely be the least expensive alternative.

When your competition is similar-quality talent. Your reaction: "I'm very surprised. We are usually slightly less for work of comparable quality (especially when all the extras we include are considered). Can we go over the estimate to see what I can improve on?" Review the estimate with the client, explaining in detail the cost basis for each identifiable item or project phase. Ask whether the competitor's lower estimate includes everything yours does. If it didn't, either reduce your cost basis to provide a true "apples to apples" comparison, or indicate why you believe that what you've included in your estimate makes the value of the work greater than its cost. (Example: if you included art direction of photography and your competitor didn't, either eliminate it, or defend its necessity.) If the estimating basis is essentially the same, say that apparently your competitor(s) lowered prices during what must be a very slow period. Nonetheless, and without denigrating them, indicate that you still believe that you will be a better choice when your efficiency (ability to get it right the first time) and creative excellence (results) are fully considered.

When you think they want to use you, but need convincing. Your reaction: "Actually, our price is very reasonable for work of this quality, and this quality usually returns far more in (sales/impact) than the little extra it costs up front." Put the difference between the competitor's price and yours in a larger context. Show just how small a percentage of the total job costs the difference is, or show the difference in unit cost ("less than a dime a brochure"). Remind the client that risking the impact you could provide for savings so small might be false economy. Be inventive.

When you think they want to use you, but budget stands in the way. Your reaction: "In thinking more about your objectives, I believe I can come up with a way to give you what you want and still match (the competitor's) lower price." Go back to your office and do some thinking and figuring. Return with a plan that shows how both the objectives and lower price can be achieved by altering the job specifications. (Example: less client interviewing, using fewer photographs, less expensive paper stock, etc.)

When you're willing to cut price to meet the competition. Your reaction: "Because we would value the opportunity to broaden our experience in your field, we will be happy to meet any competitive price, even if it is below what we normally require to be profitable." In other words, cut your price, but make it an exception based on a legitimate business consideration, not just client pressure.

Price competition summary: Perception—how much the client thinks your work is worth—is far more important than the actual price.

Competing against larger shops. If you freelance or run a small shop, you must convince clients that smaller is better to compete against larger organizations. You must demonstrate that there are sound reasons to give up the "security blanket" larger organizations represent. If you grow, you may someday change your tune, but this is what to say today:

Each client is more important to us. The smaller the creative organization, the higher the percentage of "shop time" each job takes up, the more valuable the assignment becomes. The more that rides on satisfactory completion, the more incentive there is to please the client. "With us, your assignment is much more than just another job. It's a significant portion of our workload, and we'll treat it accordingly."

There's less creative interference. Talent is talent, regardless of the size of the organization providing it. The smaller organization's advantage is that there are fewer (or no) management layers between the client and those doing the work. If you are a principal, you have a direct financial stake in making sure the client is happy. "When you work with us there are no sales or account reps to filter and translate what you say. You communicate your needs and concerns directly to me/those doing the work."

Costs are lower. Matching quality for quality and service for service, a freelance or small shop can often bill 75 percent or less of what a large firm does and still be very profitable. This is especially true for smaller jobs because the high overhead burden of large firms often inflates these prices disproportionately. "Because our overhead is low, we are usually lower in price than our larger competitors. When our prices are comparable, we find that we provide higher quality service and creativity."

Large-shop competition summary: Why wouldn't a client rather be a big fish in a small pond?

Competing against freelances and small shops. The benefits a client gets from working with a large organization are the opposite of those afforded by working with a small one. When faced with smaller competition, play up the advantages of size and stability, and point out the disadvantages and risks of smallness.

More for the money. Employee specialization and procedures that are not possible in smaller firms allow each job to be handled in the most efficient way possible. This can mean more work for the same money, or higher quality. "With our procedures and economies of scale, we can provide better quality (service) for your budget. This is particularly important in reducing costs on larger, multifaceted jobs."

Greater resources equal greater comfort. The more people and procedures, the less chance of anything falling through the cracks. Your large investment in technology (computers, peripherals, and software) means there's virtually no situation that you can't handle both quickly and efficiently. "Given our staff and facilities, you can count on us to deliver, no matter what the challenge or problem. On time and on budget, too."

More business experience and creative variety. More employees give you more experience to draw upon when facing difficult or unusual problems and let you offer the client a variety of styles and creative ideas from which to choose. "No one can match us when it comes to communications experience and a variety of styles to choose from. If these are important to you, we're a logical choice."

A reputation to protect. Freelances and small shops come and go— here today, gone tomorrow. What makes you different is your size, stability, and longevity. Because of the artistic, subjective nature of creative work, these are important benefits to a client. Especially a client with a big job. "Creative talent is hardly rare. What is rare is a creative organization that's not only consistently excellent, but one that's stood the toughest test of all—pleasing hundreds of clients in hundreds of different situations."

Freelance and small-shop competition summary: Isn't yours the type of organization a smart client would feel most comfortable trusting an assignment to?

Competing against agencies. Larger advertising, public relations, interactive and direct mail agencies are set up to handle specialized, ongoing work. This results in procedures that make them ineffective and costly when it comes to work outside their expertise, small budget campaigns, or one-shot assignments.

For collateral and other work, position yourself as a specialist. Agencies often go after work—brochures, speeches, annual reports, corporate identity programs, etc.—that is peripheral to their major interest to demonstrate "full service" capability and to maintain control over all aspects of a client's communications. Some agencies also see this as easy additional profit. The best way to compete with them is to show the client that you, not the agency, are the expert in this field. For example, this is what to say to a client when your competition for a collateral (brochure) assignment is their advertising agency: "Collateral and advertising creativity are two related, but very different, disciplines. Brochures have to create a communications environment because they are viewed at a leisurely pace by a reader seeking information. Ads need only grab attention and make a single idea memorable. We do our thing best. They do their thing best."

For ads, PR, and web work, position yourself as the lower-cost alternative. Agencies are nothing more than a collection of creative talent surrounded by support staff (e.g., media), usually ensconced in a fancy office. The only thing most small clients need is the creative talent. Yet, the most junior (least expensive) creative talent usually ends up working on their account. How so? Despite agency promises (especially to autonomous groups within their major clients), they can't afford to lavish attention or expensive talent on small accounts. Overhead costs are just too high. Your USP (unique selling proposition—an agency term) is the ability to give small clients work that is more creative (senior talent), as well as faster and cheaper. "With our small organization you will actually be getting a higher level of talent than if you went with (agency). In addition, you'll work directly with the people doing the work. Of course, you will be a very big and important client to us."

For full-service work, position yourself as a "virtual agency." Although you should be careful not to promise what you can't deliver, it is often possible to satisfy a client's desire for full-service capability. You can do this by assembling teams of independent experts working under your direction and control. This arrangement can provide a client with higher-level talent at much lower cost. "We run a virtual shop. We assemble teams of outside experts as necessary to address the specific needs of our clients. You get better talent without paying for unused overhead."

Agency competition summary: You're the best bet whenever a client's need is either nontraditional agency work or occasional traditional assignments.

Competing against in-house groups. That going outside for creative services always costs much more than doing a job in-house is so widely believed it's a client tenet, an article of faith. Yet, when all costs are calculated—salaries, payroll taxes, employee benefits, expenses, equipment overhead, support overhead, profit requirements, and actual productivity—*Creative Business* surveys show that the actual differential on the creative portion of an assignment is usually about 15 percent. Except for the smallest of jobs, the creative portion is just a fraction of the total job costs. Thus, the incremental difference between going outside and doing a job in-house is seldom more than 5 to 10 percent of the total costs of the smallest brochure or ad, and can be less than 1 percent of the total costs on a major brochure or annual report.

Here's what the client can expect for that small additional difference: *Variety*—in-house staff seldom work on the same variety of assignments; they have less experience in solving a wide variety of creatively challenging problems. *Specialization*—when an organization needs special talent or experience, chances are they won't find it internally; in-house staff are nearly always generalists, or are specialists in one or two very specific areas. *Quality*—who they got is who they got, for better or worse; it may not be the best, or even qualified, talent. *Timing*—even a small assignment can cause havoc when an in-house staff is already overworked; going outside relieves the pressure, and it increases the chances that things will get done on time. *Objectivity*—fresh viewpoints and approaches are often critically needed; it is difficult for anyone working on the same challenges day after day to come up with them.

In-house competition summary: They'll pay out just a little more, but they get back a whole lot more.

When nothing you say will turn the tide. We all hope otherwise, but we can't expect to be successful in every single situation. Although "success ratios" are affected by many factors and vary widely, when there's strong competition, getting 50 percent of potential assignments is a realistic goal. If your success rate is higher, you are either very talented or facing weak competition. Perhaps you're being too competitive— giving away too much. If your success rate is lower, you could be having a string of bad luck, or you may need to sharpen your estimating pencil while also brushing up on how you communicate your benefits.

Whatever the case, whenever you lose a good job you probably end up somewhere between disturbed and devastated. Don't let losing one job affect your self-confidence. The client made a mistake. And who knows? Perhaps you eluded what might have been a bad situation. Put it behind you and apply what you learned to the next competitive challenge. Hope that client will be a little smarter. Remember, business success lies in your averages, never in any single project.

Following up the presentation

When you show your portfolio, in most cases you are planting seeds for the future. Continuing that analogy, most of the seeds you plant won't grow without additional attention. Don't make the mistake of believing that showing your portfolio is enough, that it is the end of the process. It should be just the beginning.

After showing your portfolio wait about two weeks, then send a thank-you note. Although it may seem more appropriate to send a thank-you note immediately, to do so is to waste an opportunity to make another impression on the client. It is much more effective to wait just long enough for the client to have forgotten about you, and then to refresh his or her memory. In other words, make the thank-you the equivalent of another sales call. Apologize for the tardiness, blame it on how busy you've been. Briefly summarize your capability and availability and reiterate that you want to stay in touch.

Add the client's name to your contact list and make sure that two or three times a year you send something—if not a promotional mailer, at the very least "hello" letters and Christmas cards. Keep in touch. If you do not, you have thrown away an opportunity for future business. Many assignments come from clients who were first "pitched" years earlier. Industry averages are that it takes two to three contacts to get most assignments, and three to five contacts are usually necessary before a client will switch business from one creative supplier to another.

If the client indicated a potential project in the future, mark the date on your calendar and call. Don't worry about being too aggressive; it will demonstrate spirit. Besides, chances are you are more sensitive about this than the client is.

If the portfolio presentation results in a request for a proposal, see Chapter 8 for style and ideas.

15. Working With Clients

Anyone who has been in the creative services business a while knows only too well that satisfying clients takes far more than great creativity. It takes an ability to understand what they really want. Too often, a "rough sketch" actually means a tight rendering; a projected "eight-page brochure" turns out to have more words than could fit in twice as many pages; "a couple of quick interviews" ends up taking a full two days. And so forth.

It's not that we're smart and clients aren't, or that most clients are difficult to deal with. It's just that we each see an assignment from somewhat different perspectives. Our world is pretty much oriented around creativity, and this is the way it should be. This is not the world inhabited by most clients. To them, creativity is only one aspect of communication, communication is only one aspect of marketing, and marketing is only one aspect of business.

Even clients with backgrounds similar to yours—agency creative directors or publication art buyers—take a much broader view. They have many concerns beyond creativity, not the least of which is constantly demonstrating to their bosses and clients that they produce bottom-line results. In fact, if bad work gets better results than good work (however unlikely), it is their obligation to choose the bad work, distasteful as that may be to you. Likewise, your obligation to your clients, whether agencies, publications or companies, is also to produce results—not always world-class creative efforts, just the results they are looking for.

When discussing any assignment, it is important that you adopt this business perspective and that the client also sense it: viewing creativity as nothing more, or less, than a means to an end; pleasing the client, not your own creative muse; doing the best you can within the time, cost, and strategy constraints given you; not doing the absolute best you can.

Starting with the Chemistry

Though it may not show, most new clients are uneasy about working with you, an untested entity. Even long-time, existing clients may be nervous if there's a lot riding on the assignment's successful completion. Remember, if you screw up, they take the blame; if you perform brilliantly, they get the credit. When the job is over, you walk away; they live with the results. Most clients, especially new ones, feel they have a lot more at stake than you do.

The very first step after accepting an assignment, therefore, is to make sure the client is absolutely comfortable with your work style. Some things that help make clients comfortable are: Be on time for appointments—in a buyer/seller relationship, the buyer can be late, but the seller should never be. Wear conservative business attire—it shows you are a business person, not a creative flake. Be informal and friendly—nice guys/gals are more trusted. Go over working procedures and scheduling—it shows you are methodical and organized. Talk about schedules and deadlines—it emphasizes how important they are to you. Ask if there are unusual procedures you should observe—it shows you think ahead. Treat the client's creative input as important—it will help later with approvals. Ask if there is anything specific you can do to make the assignment go smoother—it shows you care. Don't leave until both you and the client have a clear understanding of what happens next, and when.

Taking the initiative

What clients fear most from creative suppliers is misdirected or inappropriate creativity. This fear won't be stated, but it is present, especially with new clients. You can help lay it to rest by showing through preparation and action that the client's objectives are more important than your creative agenda.

Also not stated, but probably anticipated, is that the client wants you to take the initiative. The client has hired you to create; to give more direction than you take. Indeed, the more initiative you assume, the more you are worth; the less you take, the less you are worth. Of course, every client and every assignment is different, so just how much initiative to take varies. In general, keep in mind that it should be the client's obligation to define the budget, schedule, and objectives (results desired); it should be your obligation to determine how to best accomplish them.

The more any client wants to direct you, to be specific on what to do, the more insecurity he or she is showing. A high degree of client insecurity can indicate a simple personality fault, or a very rational reaction to your lack of preparation and initiative. While it is difficult to do much about the former, the latter is totally under your control. Saying "Tell me what to do" creates the worst impression. To create the best impression say, "Give me the facts, then relax. I'll handle the rest." Creating this impression is a combination of how well you are prepared, how you relate to the client's needs, and how aggressive you are in gathering the information needed.

When accepting an assignment, most individuals are not aggressive enough in finding out everything they need to know about the client's company, product/service, and competition/market. This not only results in inappropriate creative executions, but a person who does not take the initiative is often seen as someone who puts his or her own creative agenda above the client's needs.

Asking questions

Getting the information needed to produce work that's both strategically sound and creatively exciting depends on your ability to interview and ask the right questions. When done well, it ensures that you identify the essence of the problem or opportunity and reduces considerably the possibility of "lightweight" concepts or "errant creativity."

Just as important, good interviewing helps the client focus on actual, as opposed to apparent, needs. Many assignments have not been well thought out, or they've been inaccurately defined. By probing and questioning, you'll help (re)define and sharpen the project objectives, a process any smart client will greatly appreciate. Flushing out any uncertainties and inconsistencies now, rather than later through the trial-and-error of multiple concepts and meetings, is less costly to the client and certainly easier on you. The bigger and more creative the assignment, the more important it is to get good information up front.

The basics of information gathering. If you are working as part of a creative team (writer and designer), most information gathering should be conducted jointly. Although in many situations the writer takes the lead, it is also important that the designer contribute. Not to do so marks the designer as interested only in "art," not in solving the client's communications problem.

Ask the client to set aside sufficient time for an initial fact-gathering meeting. For large or complex assignments (branding, an ad campaign, a website) plan on up to an hour and a half; for smaller assignments (small print ad, radio spot, press release) plan on up to an hour. If the client claims he or she is too busy to set aside this much time, insist it is necessary to get quality work. Firmness impresses most clients; it sets you apart from the vast majority of other creative suppliers. Also insist that all individuals necessary for conceptual input be included. In particular, insist that decision makers attend. Their input now will save many revisions later, and if they leave the meeting impressed, approvals will be much easier as well. (For detailed input on large projects, additional meetings with specific individuals will probably be necessary).

Facts about the company/organization. The more you know about the company/organization and its culture, the better. Find out as much as you can in advance, then ask some "ice breaking" questions at the start of the first meeting. (For example: "How's business?" "How many facilities, people, and product lines do you now have?" "Is the company (still) growing, or (just) managing to keep ahead of today's economy?" "From your viewpoint, what kind of conditions do you see in the future?")

The more important your creative efforts are to the future of the company (a branding project, for example), the more critical it is to express this interest. Even if your assignment is of minor importance (a local ad, for example), taking an interest in the company, not just the assignment, will set you apart from others and often provide information that will be helpful in ensuring effective creativity.

Facts about the product/service. If communication is to be "salesmanship in print," you have to know enough about the product or service to "sell" it through what you'll be producing. For example: What is its history? Applications? Good features? Bad features? Pricing? User benefits? Potential? Competition? Is its market elastic (expandable) or inelastic (not expandable)?

Facts about the marketing/communications objectives. To do a good job, you'll need detail about the purpose of the piece you'll be working on. Is it intended to sell more products, or increase market awareness? Is there a window of opportunity? Can the objectives be quantified? How will success be determined? Who are the typical readers/viewers? What is their age, sex, economic condition, social stature? How typical is typical?

Facts about the conditions/preconceived notions. Finally, before starting work you'll need to know what limitations to be aware of. For example, what is the budget and schedule? What creative and media considerations have to be accommodated? What client style, tone, and personality considerations must be accommodated?

Be thorough. How you actually get the information you need is a matter of personal style and how well you know the client. For some clients it might come in a loosely structured, informal conversation. For others it might require a formally structured interview meeting. Whatever method you use, never hurry it or minimize its importance. Information gathering not only helps you; it also impresses clients and sets the stage for easier concept approval. Ask lots of questions, even when you already know the answers. And take lots of notes, even when you won't need to refer to them later. The process is as important as the information gathered.

If you need help organizing your thoughts, or want to impress the client with your thoroughness, use the Assignment Questionnaire in Appendix 3, or, using it as a guide, develop your own. Many agencies use similar forms to ensure the consistency of information gathered by their account executives. Doing likewise is just one more way you can demonstrate to your clients that you are equally thorough and professional.

Preparing concepts

At the end of the first fact-gathering meeting, continue taking the initiative by telling the client when you will have a concept (rough sketch or draft) to show. Unless it is a rush job requiring you to meet a specific deadline, you should control the timing of the concept presentation, not the client. If the client wants to see something sooner rather than later, insist that you need enough time to do a good job. Normal development time for small jobs is a week; average jobs two weeks; very large jobs three weeks. Rush jobs excluded, what you show is far more important than when you show it.

For most design and web projects. Prepare three different approaches, no more. Pick one to show as your recommendation as the best way to solve the client's communications problem/opportunity. The concept/approach you pick should be more fully developed; others can be just rough sketches. (Exception: for assignments involving developing logos, marks, branding programs, and packaging, it is probably better to show a progression of many concepts—see "Presenting concepts" below.)

How fully developed your "best" concept/idea should be is a judgment call, depending upon budget, timing, and client sophistication. Keep in mind, however, that even the most sophisticated clients often have trouble appreciating creative ideas and judging conceptual approaches. What seems perfectly clear to you may pass over their heads. Most designers assume far too much.

The closer to real you make your one "best" concept, the easier the appreciation, the faster the approval, the fewer the changes, the more the profit. Extra time and effort spent up front usually pay off. Always prepare the most comprehensive treatment you can afford. The ideal concept is full size and accurately rendered—a dummy book on the actual stock with several life-like spreads is always better than thumbnails; a real package better than a sketch; an ad concept placed in a magazine is better than one mounted on art board; and an on-screen simulation of a site is better than a sketch.

Artistically presented concepts may seem natural to you, but many clients interpret them as emphasizing art over communication. You may see preparing several concepts for client choice as providing valid alternatives, but many clients will interpret it as the lack of a clear point of view.

For most writing projects. The ideal is a full outline, polished heads and subheads, at least one page to show style, and a pagination dummy (if appropriate).

For most illustration projects. The ideal is even harder to define. It depends upon the background and talent of the art director or art buyer with whom you're dealing, and how much free rein you've been given. However, always err on the side of providing more than expected, not less.

For all projects. Whenever there's a choice of which material to render or copy to write, select what best shows or describes the client's product or service, not what presents the greatest creative challenge. In other words, select what the client is most interested in. It will provide a much better indicator of your success in addressing his or her needs.

Presenting concepts

You have landed a plum assignment from a good client. You are excited and creatively challenged. You work hard and come up with some "gang-buster" ideas. Then the client nitpicks every concept you present, or bastardizes it. Or rejects it. So, totally discouraged, your creative selfconfidence shattered, it is back to the computer for another try.

Ever happen to you? You would be very unusual if it didn't. Occasionally having even your best efforts summarily challenged is part of the business; it comes with the territory. With something as subjective as creativity, it's virtually impossible to please every client every time. Nonetheless, you should expect to get most of your important ideas and treatments accepted most of the time. If not, the cost is very high—to your pocketbook and to your self-esteem.

How many great concepts have been rejected because the creator presented them badly? We will never know, but we can guess it is a lot. There's simply no excuse for a bad presentation by persons trained in the communication arts. Good presentations are necessary in a creative business because they provide the reason and logic that's the only effective way to counter the subjectivity with which work is reviewed.

If you have a problem getting your concepts easily accepted, chances are it stems from one or both of two sources: 1) You may not be doing a good job convincing clients of your problem-solving abilities when getting assignments, so they're already predisposed to question your solutions (see "Taking the initiative" and "Asking questions" earlier in this chapter). 2) You may not be doing a good job showing clients how the ideas you've come up with actually solve their problems. Although there is no single, "best" way to show your concepts, there is a consensus about some things that will increase your odds of success.

Be as concerned about "selling" the concept, as the concept itself. Nothing is more important than getting your ideas accepted. No matter how great your ideas are, if clients cannot appreciate them, the ideas will never be executed, or they will only be executed after much exhausting effort and damaging modification. Moreover, whenever your ideas don't get accepted easily, your ego probably will be bruised, your creative energies sapped, and the profitability of your business reduced. Never fall into the trap of believing that good ideas sell themselves, that simply showing them is enough. It seldom happens this way. The more demanding the assignment or unusual the creative solution, the more selling becomes necessary. Even ideas that would otherwise be readily accepted can always be considerably enhanced by the way in which they're presented.

Insist on enough time. The first essential in getting creative ideas accepted is to insist on enough time to show and explain them properly. This means setting up, well in advance, a meeting of an hour or more for major projects, a half hour or so for smaller projects. Attendance at the presentation should be limited to the individual who gave the assignment and perhaps one other client representative, seldom any more. Larger meetings always degenerate into discussions of personal likes and dislikes and design by committee—concepts end up being compromised to death. Be firm about the need for a small meeting, and tell the client why. If, however, you are facing an insecure client who insists that "my boss" and others be present, suggest: "I really believe it would be better if we met alone first. That way there's no chance I'll show something you don't totally agree with." Such concern appeals to the client's self-interest.

Before presenting your work, remind yourself of these three important points:

- There are almost infinite ways to approach any creative problem, so you must explain why you did everything.

- What's perfectly obvious to you, a highly trained professional, is almost never obvious to even the most sophisticated client.

- The more you discuss and explain the creative process, the more value you add to the result—the concept.

Summarize the input you were given. By restating all the parameters and objectives the client provided, you clearly indicate that you understand the assignment and that the concept you are about to show was developed according to a well-thought-out plan, not some creative whim. Equally important, going over the input helps identify any possible misunderstandings before you show the work. This gives you the opportunity to modify your comments accordingly. Taking your time makes the presentation more significant.

Show one concept. For any given job, chances are that you develop and work through several ideas; you may even have been trained to produce three different conceptual approaches that are appropriate. Shouldn't you show all of them to the client, to provide a choice? Contrary to common habits and some client requests, probably not, at least initially.

Experience shows that for most assignments the best way to impress clients and enhance your working relationship is to start by selecting one concept as the approach that best addresses their problem. Then be prepared to present and defend it as your recommendation, "the best creative solution."

Presenting several concepts to a client at once, and letting him or her select among them, may seem to you a valid way of offering alternatives. Despite your intuition and schooling, however, experience shows that offering alternatives confuses many clients. Worse, it often leads them to "cherry pick"—to select elements from each of the concepts and ask that they all be combined in a new concept. It can also be perceived by clients as lack of strong conviction on your part.

Only if your "best" concept isn't accepted should you show a second, alternative concept, and only if that's not accepted should you show a third. The second and third concepts should be more conceptual, less polished. (Important exceptions: for some assignments, such as logo or package design work, it probably is better to show the evolution of an idea—all the roughs—that leads up to your recommendation.)

If, when giving out an assignment, a client specifically asks you to "bring back several approaches," say that you will, of course, develop several approaches, but you'd prefer to first show the one you believe best solves the problem. Then say, "After that, if necessary, I'll be happy to talk about some alternatives."

By taking this tack, you show that you have done your homework and have strong, professional convictions about what works and what doesn't. This dramatically increases the value and potential for acceptance of every concept you present.

Explain your approach in the context of the client's objectives. Explain everything you did as a way of addressing a stated client need. For example: "Because you said you needed maximum impact without spending a lot of money, I decided to . . . " "In order to create the fast, easy readability that's your goal, I chose to . . . "

This method of presentation not only serves to reinforce your belief in the correctness of your approach, but makes it seem logical to the client. It makes the concept much harder to criticize rationally. If you don't relate your creative approach to the client's objectives, you've set yourself up for criticism, even rejection. Be thorough and enthusiastic in your explanation. For a storyboard or illustration, describe what's going on. For an ad, read the headlines and body copy. For a brochure, walk the client through the pages by reading headlines and describing visuals. For a website, show the navigation and how it will be developed.

Stay in control. When you've finished describing the concept, hand it to the client, look him or her in the eye, and wait. Don't be embarrassed by a temporary silence; it won't last long and it will work for you by forcing the client to make a comment to which you can then respond. This keeps you in control of the presentation. Never ask if the client "likes" the concept. To do so is to issue an open invitation for criticism. Clients like everything unless they tell you otherwise.

If the client isn't sold on the concept and asks to see other approaches, now is the time to present an alternative concept, your second choice. Be honest, call it your second choice, but also state that since creativity is such a subjective field, it may be more what the client has in mind. When showing it, try to emphasize ways it addresses the client's criticisms of the first concept. If the second concept isn't acceptable, bring out your third alternative. Present it in the same manner as the second.

If none of your concepts is acceptable, get more detail on what the client has in mind and go back to your drawing board or computer. Make one more presentation, showing at most two new ideas. If these ideas are not acceptable, chances are strong that nothing ever will be. Resign the business.

Always be opinionated, but never be inflexible. Clients should expect you, as a professional, to have a strong point of view. When presenting ideas for the first time, you owe them nothing less than your absolute best effort. Having done this, you should then be prepared to willingly accept closer direction.

The mark of a true professional is the understanding that this work is, after all, commercial. The client must pay your bill as well as the production expenses, and ultimately has to live with the results, good or bad. Therefore, the client has the right to expect you to execute whatever he or she chooses. If you don't like what you are finally asked to do, either resign the business or (usually better) grit your teeth and smile all the way to the bank.

Getting new business from old clients

Working with new clients is important. These assignments provide new creative stimulation, as well as business diversity and the security that goes with it. On the other hand, work from current or former clients is also an important component of any creative company's business mix. The smaller the company, the more important is work from current or former clients. (Smaller firms get fewer jobs based on reputation, and they usually can't afford as much selling effort.) These jobs, where sales and learning expenses are lower, often produce profit that's up to 30 percent higher.

Assuming you have several clients (no one client should ever contribute more than 25 percent of yearly income), a good mix of existing to new client work is about 2 to 1 (66 percent) for freelances and midsize firms (up to twelve individuals). The larger the firm, the lower the ratio that is usually acceptable; some larger firms operate comfortably on an old-to-new client ratio as low as 1 to 2 (33 percent). There are, however, two stumbling blocks on this road to happiness, two reasons why a good mix is difficult to attain. We tend to take previous clients for granted, not to solicit them with the same zeal we do new ones. Also, clients tend to categorize us, to identify each of us only with a certain limited expertise or ability. Here are some suggestions for broadening your appeal.

You're only as good as what they *think* you can do. Simple notions, strong impressions, and isolated events are easy to remember; everything else is easy to forget. Perhaps it has to do with the limitations of the human brain, perhaps with the clutter and confusion of modern life. Whatever, it's the way things are. Like it or not, most clients will think of you for only one, or perhaps two, of the many things you're capable of doing. No more. Most likely you'll come to mind only when the client is looking for a particular type of talent or experience. If you want to be remembered for more and to be considered for other, different types of work, you have to work at breaking this mind-set. Another way of putting it: no matter how good and versatile you know you are, when it comes to getting work, you're no better than what clients think of you. You can't wait for them to wake up to your true talents. Unless you've been very aggressive in the past (unlikely), most of your clients just don't know all you can do.

You may need to get on a preferred vendors' list. Many large organizations have preferred vendors' lists for certain types of work. Unless your name is there, you probably won't be hired. Whenever you call upon large clients, ask if they have such a list and make sure your name is added to all the job categories you feel comfortable working in.

Mail samples. Whenever you complete a print job you're proud of, buy reprints from the publication or samples from the printer. Attach a short, personal note—"I thought you'd be interested in seeing this"—and mail one to every client who might not be aware of your ability in this area. For electronic jobs, do the same with screenshot printouts.

Pick up the phone and call. Say, for example, "I've been doing a lot of [type of work] lately and it occurred to me that this is one area in which we've never worked together. I'd love to come over and show you what I've been doing. Can we set up a time?"

Talk up your versatility when visiting. Always be on the lookout for ways to mention your versatility. For example, when a client asks, "How are you?" don't just say, "fine" or "busy." Be specific. Say, "Actually, I've been quite busy. I just finished a packaging assignment for ABC Corporation and I'm about to start on a series of product ads for the Smith and Smith Agency." Weave a mention of another assignment into casual conversations. For example, "You know, I've really been enjoying this project. Right before this, I was doing a complex branding program that involved . . . so the change of pace is just great." Or simply ask for more business. For example, "I was thinking this morning about how well this (type of work) project has gone. Do you also need occasional help on (other types of work)? If so, I'd love to take a crack at them."

Saying "Thank you"

Once upon a time it was accepted that suppliers did favors, bought gifts, and wined and dined those who gave them business. It was a way of saying "thank you," and not to do so was a sure way to stop getting business. Fortunately, those days are largely past. Today, many clients find gifts and expensive entertaining offensive, out of keeping with the times. Many large organizations (the very ones that pay best) have policies that forbid their employees from receiving favors or gifts that exceed $25 in value. In short, it is no longer necessary to "buy" business in order to be successful.

It should go without saying that if you are offered any type of kickback you should refuse. Accepting is not only unethical and unnecessary, but probably illegal. Likewise, it is probably best to stay away from any client who expects you to buy expensive meals, entertainment, and/or gifts. Chances are strong that clients who expect this type of catering are insecure and difficult to please anyway—in other words, not good investments. The more you spend treating clients, the less profit you make, too. Here is what is considered both appropriate and productive in today's business climate.

Breakfasts are the best meal settings for discussing business. They provide a pleasant, productive atmosphere in which to discuss assignments and treat the client at the same time. The client is fresh and not distracted, and while not exactly uncommon, meeting for breakfast is more of a treat. Your money goes a lot farther than at lunch, too.

Buying present clients lunch should be restricted to when you have a meeting immediately before or after noontime. Never schedule a lunch meeting if you can avoid it. In many cases, crowded conditions and the consumption of alcohol makes it unproductive. The more you discuss business, the less social and enjoyable it is for both you and the client.

Treat good clients to lunch between jobs. This ensures that no specific business will be discussed and it makes it a purely social occasion. It will also serve to keep you in the client's mind between jobs. Pick an occasion—Christmas, the coming of spring, etc.—and call the client well in advance with an invitation to celebrate.

Don't buy dinner, provide sporting/cultural event tickets, or send Christmas gifts except to exceptional clients. In most cases the cost is out of line with the potential. Clients used to such treatment won't be all that impressed by your (costly) efforts and probably do not expect them anyway.

When entertaining or sending gifts to exceptional clients, make what you do unique and genuinely appreciative. Demonstrate your sophistication by matching the client's specific interests: a favorite wine, or book by a favorite author; tickets to a particular cultural or sporting event; a lunch at a much-talked-about restaurant; a bouquet of favorite flowers. This is the only way to make what you do long-remembered and worth the money.

The single best, easiest, and least costly way to say "thank you." Write a personal note and attach it to the invoice you send at the job's completion. Make it short and sincere, on note paper or your personal (not business) stationery. For example:

> Jerry:
> *Thanks again for calling me on this.*
> *I really enjoyed working with you and getting to know (company/ product).*
> *I look forward to receiving samples (tearsheets) so I can add them to my portfolio.*
> *Stay in touch.*
> *Sally*

By attaching a personal thank-you note to the final invoice, you make what is necessarily a formal process much less so. The touch of friendliness it adds will also make it more difficult psychologically for the client to question minor invoice items. Plus, it should help remind you to bill promptly. (Bill every job on the schedule agreed upon with the client, but no later than ten days or so days after completion. Not only do you need the money, but many clients have a difficult time approving an invoice for work that is more than a month old.)

Finally, if you have not received tearsheets or samples after the work is published, use this as another opportunity to establish contact. Call and ask for samples and say again how much you enjoyed working together.

Ten ways to remember client names

Everyone likes to be personally recognized or remembered. There's just no better way to do it than by addressing an individual by his or her first name. "Good to see you, Joe" is a lot more powerful than a simple, "Hello." Saying, "You make a very good point, Anne," will disarm her criticism much better than if Anne's name isn't used. (Although first name familiarity is appropriate in most situations, there are times, such as a first meeting with older clients, when more formality is called for.) Remembering the names of individuals to whom you've just been introduced, or have met in the past, is a powerful business advantage. Addressing anyone by his or her name tells them they are important enough to be remembered, and encourages a personal and friendly working relationship. The problem is, it isn't easy to remember names. If you're typical, you probably recall faces quite well, but often draw a blank when it comes to recalling names. How can you remember the names of individuals introduced to you at an important client meeting? Or of those individuals you see only at occasional meetings? Here are ten proven techniques to sharpen your name-memorization skills:

Pay attention. When we meet someone, most of us are more concerned about what we're going to say, or how we look or act, than what the other person is saying. So, first learn to shift your mental focus—from yourself to them. This requires being relaxed and self-confident enough about yourself to be free to concentrate on what others are saying.

Repeat. Always repeat the person's first name when being introduced: "Glad to meet you, John." Doing this not only helps you fix the name in your memory, but it will impress them, as well. If you don't understand their name, ask them to repeat it: "I'm sorry, I'm afraid I didn't catch your first name."

Forget last names. Except in situations where you will continue to use them, don't try to remember last names when being introduced. It is too much to remember, and not necessary for conversation. Later, if necessary, you can always ask under the pretext of writing it down: "For my records, John, how do you spell your last name?"

Associate. Immediately upon hearing a name, identify its owner in your mind with something or someone else. For example, relate the name to that of an old boyfriend or girlfriend. or with something alliterative, such as, "The silk dress is Sally," or with something completely incongruous, such as, "The dark, fat, bald-headed guy has the Scandinavian name, Lars."

Swap business cards. Exchanging business cards during introductions slows down the pace, helping to make names more memorable. By glancing at them as they are handed to you, they also provide name reinforcement. If you leave them on the table or in your open notebook, you can surreptitiously glance at them during the meeting.

Write names in your notes. At the start of every meeting, while introductions are still fresh, write the names at the top of first page of your meeting notes. If you are meeting around a conference room table, put the names in seating order, person to the far left at the top. Don't be embarrassed or try to hide this. Having an attendee list in your notes is businesslike and professional.

Listen. If you miss someone's name, listen carefully to see whether someone else uses it in conversation. If so, as soon as the name is said concentrate on remembering it. If you are in a meeting, write it down in your notes. If the person's name is not used, and you must address him or her, say simply and without apology: "I'm sorry, but I'm afraid I missed your name." (Don't say, "I forgot your name.")

Refresh. Before going to a meeting with persons whom you've met previously, go over your notes. Try to recall a face for each and every name. This exercise much reduces the chances of being embarrassed by not remembering a name.

Take the initiative. Whenever there is someone at a gathering whom you haven't met and there are no introductions, introduce yourself: "Hello, I'm Charlie Creative. I don't believe we've met." Don't be shy about taking the initiative. It is in your interest to know who's who. Most individuals will welcome your introduction as a friendly gesture.

Practice. Contrary to popular belief, no one is born with an innate ability to remember names. Like all forms of memory, it is developed by practice. Those who do it well simply practice more than those who don't. Those who do it well have better client relationships, too.

SECTION THREE
HIGHLIGHTS

- **Talent is only tenuously connected with self-employment success.** No matter how talented you are, good marketing can bring you better clients, bigger assignments, more profit, and greater satisfaction.

- **All clients and assignments are not equal.** There are substantial quality and profit differences. Learn from history and go after those with a track record of providing stimulating assignments and adequate pay. Eschew most others.

- **Prepare a sales strategy that recognizes your strengths, fits local market needs, and meets long-term goals.** Market yourself as you would any other product. Determine the benefits you offer clients, then plan the most cost-effective way to promote them.

- **Selling is largely a matter of attitude.** Be prompt, friendly, confident, and well prepared. Most of all be yourself. Don't worry about rejection. You only need a few clients to do very, very well.

- **You are at least as important as your portfolio.** Only half of the impression a client gets is from your portiolio. The other half is personal. By and large, clients give business to individuals they like.

- **Periodically go after new business from old clients.** Your sales success will be greater, and the assignments are usually more profitable. Because existing clients are usually more tolerant, it is an ideal way to cut your teeth on new types of work.

- **When getting an assignment, take the initiative and ask lots of questions.** There is no such thing as a dumb question. Learning all you can about the client and the product will result in creative solutions that are strategically more sound, and will impress the client with your enthusiasm and throroughness.

- **When making an assignment presentation, explain and try to "sell" one concept first.** Show a second or third concept only if the first is not acceptable. Showing multiple concepts too early leads to "cherry picking," and marks you as an individual without a strong conviction of what's the most appropriate approach for the client.

Selling & marketing norms

Effective marketing radius	For most individuals/firms about 50 miles
Average postal mailing response rate	1–3%
Average e-mail response rate	.25 to .50%
Appropriate selling effort	10–20% of labor hours
When to consider a full-time sales rep	When you have four or more full-time employees
Average sales rep commission	15% of billings
Average total marketing costs	20% of yearly expenses
Average direct, nonlabor promotion costs	3% of yearly expenses
Talent rep commission	25–40% of assignment price
Right length of portfolio-presenting sales call	30 minutes
Average assignments backlog	2–4 weeks' worth of work
Comfortable ratio of existing to new clients' work	2 to 1
Average number of calls before business changes hands	3 to 5
Expected success in getting competitive jobs	50–75% of those bid

RUNNING A MULTIPERSON SHOP

"If anything can go wrong it will."

MURPHY'S LAW

"Murphy was an extreme optimist."

AMERICAN BUSINESS PROVERB

If you decide to grow a freelance business, what is the best way to go about it? What new procedures must be established? How do you hire the right help? What are the trade-offs of expansion? How much growth is possible? How big is appropriate? What should be avoided? What performance standards should you set?

If you already run a multiperson shop, how are you doing? Do you have happy, loyal, and productive employees? Are you a good manager? Do things run at maximum efficiency? Do you track key performance ratios? Are you making money? Are you creating equity in your business? Are you happy?

These are not insignificant challenges. Indeed, how many old, well-established creative firms do you know? Probably not many. For a creative services company to be around for a decade is significant. In most places, those that have been around for several decades can be counted on one hand without impairing the ability to hold a cup of coffee. Why? Many reasons, surely. Certainly one reason is the seemingly innate inability of many creative individuals to establish organizations with proper business procedures.

This section addresses that issue—what the principal(s) of a creative services organization should know and practice. It applies general small-business methods and procedures to the very specific needs of a small creative organization. It is written to help the freelance who wishes to expand and experienced individuals leaving another firm to set up their own, and to provide techniques, standards, and reality checks for an established business.

Additional information on managing is in "The Creative Business Guide to Running a Graphic Design Business" (Norton).

16. Creating a Viable Organization

The very foundation of a viable business in any industry is planning. Thus, the place to begin constructing, evaluating, or repairing a multiperson creative firm is with its business plan.

Planning for success

Creative Business surveys show that most start-up creative businesses fail within the first two years. The cause is usually a combination of too much reliance on a few well-known contacts for assignments, coupled with an inability to realistically predict long-term costs. As expenses and the need to find new clients and assignments rise, so does the failure rate. There is also a sharp spike in the failure curve about three years or so down the road. This is the time when the reality of constantly finding new ways to sustain and manage a long-term business often becomes overwhelming. It is when a business has to become serious, or else. Still another danger point comes a couple of years later. This is when the "prosperity trap" is often sprung. The firm overexpands and overcommits based upon nothing more than past success and the hope that it will all continue. Finally, firms face the constant danger of not staying on top of change. The more dynamic a market is, the more of a problem this becomes.

Of course, many factors contribute to the failure of a creative business, and not all of them are predictable or preventable. But certainly one predictable and preventable factor is lack of planning. Planning doesn't guarantee success, but it surely lays the groundwork for it. Conversely, lack of planning doesn't guarantee you will be blindsided, but it surely contributes. Most failed businesses lack good planning. Why, then, do we, perhaps more than any other type of business, resist it? In part because it strikes many of us as uncreative. Also because we just don't know how to go about it.

The first potential problem—your attitude toward planning—only you can address. You have to want to succeed in business, not just do creative work you get paid for. You must be willing to do whatever is necessary to make it happen. As "right-brain" people, we often tend to think of the more analytical aspects of business, such as planning, as "left-brain," non-stimulating activities. Yet in truth, mapping your future and then working to make sure it happens can be among the more stimulating and creative aspects of working for yourself.

If you are one who finds this difficult—i.e., you have trouble focusing on planning when creating is so much more fun—consider this: business skill is what makes more and better creativity possible. The better your business is run, the more satisfying the assignments you'll get, the less hard you'll have to work, and the more money you'll make. There is a direct correlation between how well a business is run and the creative satisfaction of its principals.

The second potential problem with business planning is that many of us forgo it simply because we don't think about it, or know how to go about it. Yet the planning process is neither mysterious nor difficult, and can be easily formalized into a working document that will guide successful growth—a business plan. Although the number of thick books on business planning in bookstores may suggest otherwise, this is not like learning nuclear science. Moreover, most of the information published isn't relevant. The books (and computer software) don't fit our specialized needs. The extensive research and lengthy documents they usually recommend are doubly dangerous—at once both wasteful of our time, and totally inappropriate. Plus, the very extent and complexity of what's recommended tends to scare many of us off.

Formalizing the planning process

Regardless of how ambitious your goals may be, planning a creative services business is just the simple and interesting process of assembling information, pondering it, and then preparing to organize your future activities based upon it. In fact, whether we define it as such or not, most of us already do considerable planning. For example, it happens in the shower when we think about how to get better clients. It happens while stuck in traffic when we consider how to allocate workflow among employees. It happens when we are paying bills and must decide which vendors to pay now and which to put off until cash flow improves. Whatever, these and similar activities are all valid forms of planning. They are typical of

the mental activity everyone in every business has to constantly engage in. As much as we might like it to be otherwise, no business is ever static. Business constantly changes, and this requires us constantly to consider how we will cope with change—planning.

But while we are all occasionally engaged in business planning, very few of us do it on a regular, formal basis—i.e., being organized and disciplined in our considerations, then committing them to paper. Therein lies the problem. Without discipline, organization, and recording, no plan is ever more than just an idea, ephemeral as a wisp of smoke.

Rule Number One. There should be a planning process. Devote time and effort at least once a year to future-think. This rule applies to all creative businesses regardless of size, location, or services offered. The only major difference between planning for a small rather than a large operation is the extent of the effort and its formality.

Rule Number Two. A plan is only as good as what it says on paper. It must be written down in some detail to be effective. The discipline of writing ensures that you will take the process and result seriously. In addition, it also provides benchmarks against which to measure progress and refine your ideas as time passes. A mistake too often made by creative firms is to do a written business plan only when it is required by the circumstances of asking for a loan or talking to a potential partner. Not only does this preparation pressure result in inefficiency and hasty planning, but what results does not benefit from a history of plan refinement.

The most important component of a business plan is the quality of thought that goes into it. Its effectiveness lies in how well it is able to match the unusual attributes of a company to its potential markets and customers. Good plans are not something quickly cobbled together. They are the result of serious thought focused on getting facts, setting goals, and preparing strategies. This process does not have to take a long time, especially for a two- or three-person operation, but it should be thorough. If you run a larger organization, you may want to spend a day off-site to brainstorm with key employees.

Start with the facts. Jot down everything important you can think about your business, present and future. For example: Where do most assignments come from? Who are the competition, and what are their strengths and weaknesses? What is the realistic potential compared to present activity? Is the business acceptably profitable? What problems and opportunities can you predict for the future?

Identify realistic goals. Facing the hard facts of reality, now consider practical options and alternatives for growth or greater prosperity. As tentative goals for next year, write down up to ten business changes/options with the greatest potential. Try to think in specific, quantifiable terms. For example: Expand the business base from five to seven dependable clients; reduce the work from a specific type of client or industry from 65 to 55 percent of revenue; increase the number of a certain type of assignment from ten to twelve yearly.

Rough-out strategies. Now set next to the goals thoughts on what it would take to make them come true. Weed out those that are obviously not feasible, settling on six or fewer that have a good chance of success. (Don't try to accomplish more; doing so will probably dilute your efforts.) For example: To expand your business base, plan to make a presentation to at least one potentially new client each week. To reduce dependence on one type of client or industry, plan to do six promotional mailings showcasing your broader capabilities. To increase a specific type of business, plan to seek out competitors' dissatisfied clients.

Now modify the above general considerations with those things that define your unique talent, style, experience, and client service.

What are your strengths; what distinguishes your talent? Example: If you're an illustrator, it may be the rendering of people; if a designer, the ability to visualize complex ideas; if a writer, writing for the ear rather than the eye; if a web designer, easy navigation. If you already have employees, it is the collective abilities of your staff.

What is the extent of your business skill and experience? Examples: unusual speed, convenience, an obsession for getting details correct, or experience in certain areas, such as high technology or the greeting card industry.

CREATING A VIABLE ORGANIZATION

Where does your unique combination of talent, business skill, and experience best fit? Example: If you are a writer with fifteen years of corporate PR experience, a good fit will probably be executive speech writing, annual reports, or corporate capability brochures. If your design firm has several employees with big-league packaging experience, an obvious fit is packaged goods clients. If you find your talents best fit your current mix of clients, your planning should probably concentrate on getting more of the same type of assignments. If not, you should probably concentrate on exploring new clients and areas of business.

What type of work would you like to do more of, and what is the competition? Example: If you are interested in the impact of technology and design, perhaps it might make sense to consider a greater emphasis on interactive media.

Finally, with all this as background, you are now ready to start writing a detailed one-year strategy—your business plan. (For style and format, see Appendix 2.)

Structuring considerations

An important element of a business plan is describing the way the company is structured. The relative merits of different legal structures— sole proprietorships, partnerships and corporations—are covered in detail in Appendix 1. Here we cover organization, the company's personnel structure. (Information on the administration of staff—hiring, paying, and firing—is in Chapter 17.)

Whether you have two employees or twenty, your company's personnel structure is critically important because of the very nature of your business. Providing creative services is a labor-intensive activity where most profit comes from the relative efficiency of employees. Regardless of the present or future size of your organization, the best way to be financially successful is to focus on staff efficiency. Having a clear, well-understood structure is the first step in this process. In such organizations, employees always know where they stand and what to expect, and principals delegate more easily and predictably.

The chain-of-command business model

A top-down, hierarchal model would come to the mind's eye of most of us if asked to visualize an organizational structure. It is the familiar, traditional approach in which organization charts look like pyramids. It is the default of organizational structuring. Consciously or not, and for better or for worse, it is the way most of us run our businesses: we (the boss) make decisions, others (employees) carry them out.

Where it works. The larger the organization and the more specialized the functions of its employees, the better a chain-of-command organization works, and vice versa. The perfect example is a manufacturer's assembly line where each employee carries out one prescribed operation. This model can also be appropriate in larger creative businesses where employees handle single project functions. For instance, agency copywriters or art directors who work within a creative department or account structure. Even in these situations, however, chain-of-command models need to reflect the times. In today's complex, information-driven economy, employees also need to be encouraged to contribute outside their specific job function. Doing so—empowering employees—increases enthusiasm and morale and provides an additional source of ideas as well.

For these reasons, many large creative firms today operate with a modified chain-of-command model. Firms organize the business into many units, within which the structure is relatively flat. This allows greater teamwork, while preserving the business' overall chain-of-command structure.

Where it doesn't work. Despite its widespread use, the chain-of-command model is seldom suitable for small to mid-size creative organizations. It is too rigid and doesn't work well where employees handle entire projects. It is particularly ineffective when combined with informal, laissez-faire management, the style of many creative firm principals. A chain-of-command structure and laissez-faire management combined produce the worst of both worlds—minimum potential for employee initiative, maximum potential for confusion—a square-peg management style within a round-hole organization. Where there are multiple owners, the situation can be even worse unless there are clear-cut and well-understood divisions of responsibility.

Generally, the broader the functions of employees and the more subjectively their work is evaluated, the less efficient the chain-of-command model is. This is especially true in small creative organizations where employee teamwork is crucial. Such firms typically require maximum employee empowerment, top to bottom.

The coaching business model

This model, also traditional, is a stylistic modification to the chain-of-command approach. It came out of the experiences of organizations seeking efficient ways to work with independent-minded, creative employees—

inventors, teachers, researchers, designers, planners, etc. It recognizes that true creativity can only be encouraged and directed, it can't be specified, ordered, or demanded. So how to encourage and direct most efficiently? The answer lies in a sports analogy: the coach and his or her team.

In the coaching business model, the coach (principal or supervisor) has overall responsibility for winning; the team, or "players" (employees), has specific performance responsibilities. There is no question about authority and who gets to set direction and strategy. But there is also recognition that the coach stays mostly on the sidelines and team members make most on-the-spot decisions. It works best when there are no more than 10 "players" to each "coach."

The role of coach. A coach organizes, strategizes, directs, motivates, and mentors in whatever ways to produce winning results. This usually requires having experiences and talents similar to those of the team members, recognizing that the talents of team members are often greater than those he or she possesses, and maintaining the respect of the team, because without it their performance will lag. Good coaching also requires a willingness to delegate, share knowledge and experience, and make unpopular decisions. In short, the role of coach is to lead by inspiration, example, and respect, not to direct because of authority or rank.

Picking the team. Good coaches pick team members based exclusively on how much strength and depth they add to the team. They don't hire those who duplicate existing talents and experiences, or just because they like them or their style. This is particularly important for creative businesses because variety of experience, talent, and style is a crucial factor in both problem-solving and attracting a mix of clients. Shop principals who suppress variety by hiring employees whose styles and backgrounds closely match their own unknowingly strangle their businesses. The more diverse the employees, the greater the opportunity to solve the challenges posed by a greater variety of clients. The less the chance of being adversely affected by fads and trends, too.

Working with the team. Teamwork requires that every team member be informed of, and perhaps participate in, most project (or account) stages—sales, strategy, budget, scheduling, etc. The greater the involvement, the more employees will feel a part of a team, the higher their satisfaction, the better the quality of their work, the happier the client.

Implementing a team environment may be as simple as providing more detail in staff meetings, calling for employee participation in new functions and activities, or delegating more. However implemented, the goal is the same: to get employees more interested in the big picture.

The coaching business model counteracts the tendency among creatives to focus on creativity-inspiring tasks to the exclusion of others; it shifts focus in a way that keeps projects on track and employees' feet planted firmly in business reality.

Fulfilling the promise. I recommend most principals of small to medium-size firms (up to 25 employees) follow the coaching model when running their businesses. It combines the familiarity of traditional structuring with the flexibility required to stimulate creatively talented employees. The distinction between it and the chain-of-command model is mostly in style. Policies, standards, job descriptions, and employee evaluations needn't change. But principals' attitudes, actions, and behavior should. (For more, see "Being a coach, not a boss" in Chapter 18.)

The associate business model

This model provides a way of organizing and running a project-based creative business that goes well beyond mere style. It involves both a different way of thinking about the business and a radical restructuring of its operations. In some ways it is an updated version of the historic guilds that were the very first commercial creative establishments.

Background. The traditional, chain-of-command employer/employee system assumes different level of abilities (management and labor), value added through experience, and more or less predictable market demand. It is a system designed around traditional product manufacturing and sales environments. In contrast, creative businesses are comprised of individuals with more or less comparable skills whose talents do not become appreciably more valuable with experience. In addition, in traditional project-based markets (e.g., design), demand is highly fluctuating.

For these reasons, a traditional management/labor structure, rewarding employees based on seniority and paying them the same in times of high or low activity, may not be appropriate. Even more of a concern is paying employees a regular salary when they are not busy, then paying them overtime or farming work out to freelancers in times of extreme activity.

A possible solution to these issues is adopting a system more in keeping with that used by other professional service organizations, such as consultants, lawyers, and accountants. It is the associate model and is based on employee profit-sharing. For principals it avoids many of the management issues that accompany having employees. For employees, it is a way to enjoy many benefits of self-employment without many risks.

Basics. In the associate model some senior employees are given the chance to become associates of the firm and work not for a salary, but for a percentage (commission) on each project for which they are given responsibility. In effect, they become project managers with a financial stake in individual projects. To clients, this arrangement is transparent: they deal with the firm no differently than they would deal with any other.

The associate model is based around three components: 1) the firm, which is the owner, and her or his facilities, 2) sales associates, who find new clients, handle account service, and oversee all jobs (they may also be principals in firms without professional sales help), and 3) creative associates, employees who are assigned responsibility for a project, including getting it done on time, on budget, and according to the firm's quality and client's specifications. The firm's legal structure (e.g., its status as a corporation) is not affected. The owner has full management responsibilities, including hiring, firing, and quality control. Associate employees are partners in individual projects, but not in the firm itself. For tax and benefit purposes, they are treated no differently than other employees.

Income distribution. Billable income for each project handled by associate employees is divided three ways. Fifteen percent goes to the sales associate. This is her or his "salary." She or he also gets the same percentage on any markup of outside services. Forty-five percent goes to the creative associate. This is her or his "salary." She or he also gets the same percentage on any markup of outside services. And 40 percent goes to the firm, to cover overhead and profit. The firm also gets the same percentage on any markup of outside services. These percentages are recommended as starting points based on the need to attract and hold valuable employees, and provide a fair return on a firm's investment in facilities and support. They may be modified as appropriate.

Obtaining and estimating projects. Working within the associate model requires a strong commitment to ongoing sales and marketing. Creative associates depend on sales associates (or a shop principal) to provide a steady stream of work, which is distributed based on talent and busyness. Because both the sales and creative associates have a stake in completing each project profitably, pricing and deciding what will or will not be provided is a joint exercise. A proposal is written, and a commitment made to the client only when both agree.

The attractions to employees. For creatives, the associate model combines the major benefits of self-employment—freedom and opportunity—without all the downsides of establishing their own businesses. For salespeople, it removes any earning cap.

Money. Employees have the potential of earning what they are worth, despite seniority or experience. Ambitious, talented ones can earn more than they could in any other employment relationship, possibly more than they could in their own businesses. A firm's size, reputation, and experience are important in the eyes of many clients, and the associate structure is transparent to them. So, an employee, working as an independent associate within a well-known firm, can work on projects that might be impossible to land as a freelancer.

Facilities. Office, computer, software, etc. are all provided, just as they would be for any regular employee. So, there's never a concern about keeping up with technology or paying the rent.

Support. Having full-time sales representation eliminates the biggest headache of freelancing—the constant need to find new clients and projects. It becomes possible to concentrate on creating, not worrying about where the work will come from. Likewise, clerical support eliminates paperwork concerns.

Lifestyle. Because compensation is directly tied to their output, associates are largely free to make their own working arrangements. This freedom within a structure is a particularly strong attraction to working parents or anyone who wants independence, but not the isolation of working alone.

The attractions to the firm. The associate model eliminates many financial and management concerns that accompany business growth.

Less cash-flow worry. Associate employees are paid their percentage of a project's billings only after the client pays. So, the only regular payroll expense is for draws against future commissions, support staff, and employees not working as associates. Thus, the cash-flow crunch that plagues many firms with a hefty professional payroll is minimized. The need to carry a substantial bank balance or line of credit is also reduced.

Less management worry. Associates are self-managed. They require no supervision, performance reviews, raises, or bonus calculations. They also assume management responsibility for each project they work on. This reduces regular management issues to support staff and employees not working as associates. It frees up principals to devote more time to business management and strategic issues.

Reduced turnover. Associates are not only well rewarded, but they play the major role in deciding what work to take, how to approach it creatively, and how much to charge. This level of involvement eliminates nearly all the reasons an associate might move to another organization (few would pay better, or offer more stimulation), as well as most of the reasons for considering setting up their own shop (many more risks with only marginally more opportunity).

Accumulation of equity. A creative firm's cash value (owner's equity) is largely dependent on how little of its activity would be lost with new owners. The more intimately involved the principal is in the business, the less value the business has. Even in small firms working on the associate model, principal(s) need not be involved with every project or client. So, it is less likely that many clients or projects will be lost with a change of ownership.

Downside. The associate model does not offer the immediate profit potential of the chain-of-command or coaching models. This is not the model for a principal who wishes to maximize profit, especially in the short-term. Indeed, it is possible that in some years principals may actually make less money than some of their associate employees.

Nonetheless, annual net margins up to 10 percent of sales are possible from the firm's business activities. Moreover, if the principals also work on some projects as associates (sales or creative) they can supplement what they take out of the firm in profit with their project commissions. Plus, the principals can also benefit from any buildup of equity.

In summary, the associate model is not one that's focused exclusively on business profitability. Rather, it is a balanced business model that combines reasonable short-term profits, a more collegial working environment, a low-stress management style, and the potential for equity buildup.

What is the right size?

All the above begs the question: what is the right size for your creative company? And the answer is: it all depends.

By most measures, creative services organizations are very small businesses. A handful of the very largest, multiple-location design firms have a few hundred employees. For example, at this writing, Landor Associates has a staff of around three hundred; Fitch, Inc. about two hundred fifty; Walter Dorwin Teague around two hundred. And some of the most respected names in the industry—Anspach Grossman Portugal, Chermayeff & Geismar, Massimo Vignelli, Primo Angeli, etc.— have only a few dozen employees. In many metropolitan areas, the largest design studio has a staff of fewer than fifty; and the majority have less than a dozen. Aside from the big names, most advertising and public relations agencies have only a dozen or two employees.

All this indicates that growth and size are not essential to either creative reputation or economic viability. It is, of course, unlikely that a freelance working off the kitchen table will ever be considered for a major corporate identity project. And the smaller a business is, generally the more vulnerable it is. But freelances and small-, mid-, and large-size shops alike all have a shot at success, profitability, and longevity.

Growth can be either good or bad. On one hand it may provide the route to larger clients, bigger assignments, and more money. On the other hand, it is equally likely to jeopardize creative output, increase overhead, and make life less enjoyable. In short, growth always impacts three key areas—product quality, profitability, and quality of life.

If there is a rule of thumb about growth it is this: creative businesses become vulnerable as soon as they exceed the interests and capabilities of the principals. So the question for the principal of any creative business—freelance or multiperson—comes down to what is right for you.

Evaluating new office or studio space

Growth usually implies moving to new space—now or later. When evaluating the costs and need for a move, you should not select any space that will not allow you to recoup the relocation expenses within a year through either new business or greater efficiency. The additional cost of yearly rent should be covered by at least an equal increase in yearly billings. Indeed, some firms believe that a 2 to 1 payback is more appropriate. When figuring payback, be careful to include all the expected one-time and ongoing costs of the move—redecorating, new furniture and equipment, utility relocation and fees, moving expenses, changes in parking and commuting costs, additional insurance, and changes in cleaning and maintenance services.

If you cannot justify the move on a financial or efficiency basis, it can only be considered as a speculative investment in the future. As with any investment, time will determine whether it was good or not, but try to protect yourself by taking a short-term lease, constantly monitoring your income, and being prepared to move back to less costly quarters. Even if your pre-move analysis shows that the location you have selected is eminently appropriate, don't forget that it is based on a projection of future activity, and business volume can drop as easily as increase. In other words, be conservative. Don't base your move to new, expensive quarters on a highly speculative projection of future income; it is risky enough to base a move upon what appears to be steady business. Economic downturns have provided dozens of examples of agencies, studios, and individuals who went belly up by overextending themselves based on overly optimistic revenue projections.

Another danger is the urge to move to unnecessarily "design-y," impressive, and expensive quarters. If so possessed, remember that the sophistication and style of your office or studio is likely to be far more important to you than to most clients. Suppressing the urge to prematurely emulate something you saw in *Architectural Digest* or *Communication Arts* magazines can be a constant and difficult battle, but it is one that's much too important to lose.

As a guideline to help you keep your feet on the ground, my experience is that a creative firm should budget around 6 percent of *predictable* revenues for office rent, including basic utilities and cleaning services. Keep in mind that rent is a fixed expense, payable on time each month regardless of fluctuating business volume.

How much space? More than most others, creative individuals cannot be happy and productive shoehorned into a corner or rattling around in a barnlike auditorium. Personal preferences, the type of work one does, layout (open space or individual cubicles), and building amenities all affect space requirements. Because of this, it is tough to generalize about what is necessary. It helps, however, if you begin by thinking about what has been called the "3Cs Formula" of space planning. First, work space must always be *cozy*, providing a feeling of home-away-from-home. Second, it must be *creative* in the sense of offering a stimulating environment. Third, the space must be *comfortable* in a way that enhances productivity.

The minimum two-person dedicated office (not shared with another firm) is usually about 250 square feet; the best size is around 400 square feet. Maximum size is about 600 square feet. Predicting space requirements for larger firms is more difficult. For example, as support staff and equipment (printers, copiers, etc.) are added, layout and placement become more critical. If the space is open (undivided), less is required per individual, but it must be more carefully configured or productivity can suffer. The need for common areas always grows geometrically with staff. One of the side benefits of computerization has been a decrease in space requirements for creative firms. Today there is much less need for space-gobbling flat files and drawing boards. As a general rule, my experience is that 3–5 person shops require about 900 square feet; 6–10 person shops 2,000 square feet or so. A good starting point is to multiply the number of employees by 200.

The **"executive-suite" possibility.** If you are still working alone, have one or two employees, or only need temporary space, a relatively hassle-free way to get it is to rent a turnkey office in an executive-suites building. As described in Chapter 4, "executive suites" is the term used to describe the rental arrangement where many separate small business offices are clustered around and share common facilities and services. Amenities vary, but usually include a good address, furniture, utilities, conference/meeting rooms, fax and copy machines, high-speed internet connection, and mailing, phone answering, secretarial, and cleaning services. The advantage is that by sharing facilities and services with other small businesses, it is possible to get good space quickly and obtain a wide variety of office support services economically.

On a square-foot comparison basis, executive-suite offices usually rent for a premium of up to 50 percent more than comparable "bare" office space. However, when pricing the alternatives, make sure you compare apples to apples. For example, if you rent a regular office and don't already have it, you'll need to buy furniture, and possibly a copy machine, items you can forgo in an executive suite. On the other hand, if you already have these items, the duplication may make an executive suite very expensive.

In an executive suite, utilities (except telephone) and cleaning services are normally included, while they may or may not be with traditional office space. Insurance coverage may be cheaper, too. Then, too, there's the intangible worth of the location (prestige and convenience), and of having a receptionist without the cost and inconvenience of hiring staff. The rental terms for executive suites are much more flexible than for regular offices, with shorter leases. So, if you are not sure where you'll be in six months, an executive suite is probably your best bet. Most can be rented on a month-to-month basis.

Other than the higher cost, the downside of executive suites is that they are usually "office functional" in appearance, often don't allow much creativity in decoration, and can be quite expensive if you have several employees. You will also have to share the common facilities with mostly noncreative tenants. In most complexes over half of the tenants are sales people of one type or another.

To find companies with executive suites for rent in your locale, look in the Yellow Pages under the category "Office and Desk Space Rental Services." Most metropolitan areas have dozens of listings.

Leasing commercial space

Negotiating a lease is a somewhat arcane activity, comfortable mostly to those who do it every day, like your prospective landlord, who happens to be sitting on the other side of the negotiating table. Typical commercial leases run from three to ten years, although shorter terms can sometimes be negotiated. Obviously, the longer the term, the lower the price, the greater the inflation protection, and the more stable your address. The price for all these benefits is financial commitment, and some cashflow risk. Speaking of risk, don't take lease obligations lightly. A lease is a legally binding contract usually backed up by more lawyers than you can afford to fight.

Follow two basic rules when negotiating any lease. The first, which you're probably already aware of, is that everything is negotiable. In practice this means that prices or terms, no matter how "firm," are always open for discussion. Every landlord must balance the financial drain of vacant space against the speed and ease with which the property can be rented. Most will readily give up something for an immediate commitment.

The second rule is to never take anything for granted, especially if you've driven a hard bargain, or come to a quick agreement. A lease is among the largest legal contracts most businesses sign. Not understanding all the terms, or accepting ambiguous language, can be a costly mistake that can haunt you for months or years to come.

Compare all the costs. To make a valid comparison between commercial properties, make sure it's really an "apples to apples" evaluation. Although things can get complicated with big-space, long-term leases, for most creative business there are only a few things that are truly significant.

How much room are you getting for your money? Start with the rent, usually expressed as the annual cost of a square foot of space (e.g., $15 a square foot means $15,000 a year for 1,000 square feet). Now take the space layout (floor plan) and plan working areas, furniture and equipment fit, and workflow patterns to determine how much space you'll find usable. There are at least a couple of inexpensive software programs that can help. Subtract any square footage (odd corners, etc.) that you can't use.

Next, find out how much of the square footage you'll be paying for has been apportioned to public areas—lobbies, bathrooms, and mechanical space. Called the "loss factor" by real estate people, it can be 15 percent or more, depending on the formula used to calculate it. Subtract this figure.

Now that you know how much usable work space you'll get, consider the services provided. Most office properties operate on what's called a "gross lease," an agreement that holds the landlord responsible for all building expenses, including taxes, insurance, maintenance, and repairs. Heating, ventilation, and air conditioning (HVAC) costs are usually included, but not always, and sometimes there's a surcharge for usage over a specific level. Even more important to consider is that commercial space seldom has twenty-four-hour, seven-day-a-week HVAC service. If you occasionally need to work nights and weekends to make deadlines, make sure that such service is possible, and that the lease specifies how much extra you'll be billed.

Can the rent go up? Look for what is usually referred to as an "escalation clause." It's a way landlords cover themselves against rising expenses. Some clauses are based on inflation (the Consumer Price Index), others are prorated on increases in taxes, heating, maintenance, and other costs.

Who pays for improvements? This is the area where landlords are usually most flexible, which also means it is where lease negotiation is most productive, the land of hard bargaining. Obviously, the longer the lease, the more willing the landlord will be to chip in. If you're thinking about a loft or converted warehouse space, improvements will probably be on you. By definition, older buildings are more costly to renovate, and the landlord seldom has on-site maintenance staff available to do any work.

On the other hand, space in most modern office buildings is relatively easy to reconfigure and redecorate, and there's usually on-site staff available to handle it. Most of these leases come with a renovation or "build-out" allowance. How much varies and is negotiable. Regardless of the age or condition of the building, you should press for the improvements you desire. When doing so, remember that you're much more likely to get the landlord to pick up the tab for something beyond a cosmetic coat of paint if it will enhance the space beyond your tenancy. A wiring upgrade for phone lines or computer networking may be agreed to in a flash. On the other hand, things you desire to help make a creative statement—unusual partitioning, designer colors, and decorator lighting, to name just three—probably won't be covered. They don't increase the value of the landlord's property. Moreover, they may even have to be removed or changed at some expense after you leave.

This brings up another point: any agreements about major renovations—yours or the landlord's—should be put in writing, preferably with detailed plans and sketches attached. Sometimes referred to as a "work-letter," the document should specify who owns the improvements. As illogical as it may sound, everything a tenant (you) attaches—light fixtures, work counters, bookshelves, cabinets, even window air conditioners—is usually considered property of the landlord. Make sure you specify in the lease which of your improvements you'll later be able to take with you and which you won't.

Check the terms. Is the space available the way you want it, today? If so, there's probably no problem. But what if there's remodeling to be done, or the current tenant has to move out, and there's a holdup? Don't take a chance on finding out the hard way. Make sure the lease clearly spells out what happens when the space is not available on the move-in date. This should take the form of a significant financial penalty or a reduction in the rent for several months. Be particularly wary of an arrangement to provide "equivalent space" unless it is contiguous. Otherwise, you'll suffer from double moving costs and dislocation disruption.

Will you be able to renew? Now is the time to make sure that you'll have first rights to the space when your lease expires. Also, agree on a renewal pricing formula, typically a percentage change that's tied to an inflationary or business cost index. If you don't have this protection, you may have to move at lease end. Even if allowed to stay, chances are you'll end up paying higher rates. While you are negotiating this clause, also check on how and when you must give your intent to renew. In some leases, a tenant must provide notification of intent to stay, in writing, several months in advance, or the lease automatically expires.

Who are your neighbors? Check to see what types of firms are allowed in the building. Although zoning laws usually protect you against totally incompatible neighbors, not always. What about the current occupants of contiguous space? Will their activities bother you, or vice versa? How long does their lease have to run?

Can you sublet? It is an understatement to say that ours is a volatile business. What if halfway through your lease you have to find a new location because you've run out of room? Even worse, what if business takes a downturn and you need to move to less expensive digs? What about easing the rent burden by sharing the space with another firm? It could be a problem unless there is a clear definition of what the landlord will and won't allow. The best you will probably be able to negotiate is having the right to sublease to new tenants that meet the same standards as others in the building. Keep in mind that the more freedom you have to sublet, the more your neighbors have as well.

How are you protected? Office buildings usually have one or more insurance policies that cover common areas against liability (e.g., one of your clients being injured in the lobby). In addition, most will insist on their tenants carrying commercial general liability (CGL) insurance to protect them against an accident in your office, or damage to other parts of the building (e.g., starting a fire). *Your insurance agent should review the landlord's policies to assess your risk, then provide protection that plugs any gaps.* Don't rely on a standard CGL policy alone. Disaster stories abound of businesses that were caught up in conflicting insurance claims after a major fire, flood, or earthquake.

Equally significant, what happens if the landlord goes bankrupt and the mortgage holder forecloses on the property? Your lease may suddenly be declared invalid. Don't take a chance on the goodwill of the new landlord to honor it. You can protect yourself by insisting that the lease contain a standard "recognition" or nondisturbance clause.

Purchasing commercial space

If you have the capital and can afford the risk, owning your own office or studio in an up-and-coming area can be an excellent investment. It may also have significant tax sheltering implications and lifestyle benefits. Although historically this has been an option mostly exercised by larger organizations acquiring distinctive, stand-alone buildings, it needn't be any longer. Today, office condominiums of varying sizes, locations, and prices, some organized around common facilities and amenities (similar to the executive-suite concept) are available. Residential condominiums can sometimes be utilized for small offices as well. (Caution: Check local zoning ordinances.)

It goes without saying that purchasing any real estate is a long-term investment not to be undertaken lightly. As many investors have discovered, property prices can fall as well as rise. Further, commercial real estate has a dynamic of its own, related but not tied to other economic indicators.

For these reasons, you may find that locating a property for sale today is easier than actually purchasing it. Most banks will want at least 20 percent down for a commercial property investment and the federal loan guarantees that often make residential properties affordable will probably not be available. In addition, the bank will probably want to see a healthy bank account, a well-prepared business plan, and a history of strong business growth. Also, chances are that you personally, not just your business, will be liable for the note. Everything you own will be put on the line. If you're willing and can convince a banker, purchasing rather than renting can provide your firm with substantial benefits: a stable address and rent (mortgage payments), elimination of the periodic lease negotiation hassle, and great latitude in selecting location, architecture, and decoration.

Even more important can be the financial effect of owning on your income. Here's how. You, personally, purchase commercial real estate. Then, rather than looking for a tenant, you lease it to your firm for going market rates, ideally at or near the same amount as your mortgage payments. When you do this, the rent payments are fully tax-deductible for your company, just as if made to another landlord. The rental income

CREATING A VIABLE ORGANIZATION

you personally receive is taxable, but all expenses—mortgage payments, utilities, maintenance, taxes—are deductible because it is investment property. (This arrangement is cleaner from an accounting standpoint if your company is incorporated, but incorporation isn't necessary.)

If planned right, the immediate result can be a wash—no change in company taxes, and your additional personal income will be offset by additional personal investment expenses. In the process, however, you are actually purchasing the real estate, paying down the mortgage, with before-tax company funds. You also get an immediate tax break through depreciating the property. Some of this will probably have to be paid back through capital-gains taxes when you sell, but not all.

Whether you purchase a building, office, or residential condominium, you will personally benefit from any appreciation in the value of the property over the years. Since it is difficult to build transferrable equity in any creative services business, many shop principals have discovered that a personal investment in real estate for their firm ultimately becomes a major portion of their future retirement package. (See "Can your business be sold someday?" in Chapter 19.)

17. Staffing the Organization

The most common mistake made in hiring any employee—first or hundredth—is doing it too soon. As a guideline, the need for another employee usually does not exist until you, or the affected employees, work up to 60 hours a week or turn work away. Hiring should not take place until the need is at least six months old. (This is sometimes referred to as the 60/6 rule.) Hiring an employee on nothing but the promise or anticipation of new business is very risky.

When an excessive workload is less than six months old or you see an opportunity that will require additional staff, first consider the three nonpermanent alternatives—freelances, temporary help, and interns. With nonpermanent help you may pay more in wages for a given amount of work, and you won't get the benefits of employee continuity and stability. On the other hand, you'll avoid a long-term commitment and its cash-flow risks. An additional benefit: You won't have any employer's costly payroll taxes and expenses to worry about.

The freelance option

Freelances are the simplest nonemployee option, one you're no doubt familiar with. What you may not be aware of is the risk you run if you don't go about it in the right way. The risk is in giving a freelance a large volume of work over an extended time—that is, when you hire him or her to help you out in lieu of hiring a regular employee.

To see why, let's look at a hypothetical situation: You've been offered a large, ongoing assignment, one too big to handle by yourself or with your current staff. Since you are not sure how long the assignment will last, you decide to take on a freelance rather than a permanent employee.

In this arrangement, you'll probably have to pay about twice as much per hour in wages, but you avoid a long-term commitment to the individual hired and you won't have to provide any employee benefits, such as health insurance. You won't have any employer's payroll headaches and expenses to worry about: withholding and escrowing payroll taxes, and paying employer FICA, worker's compensation, unemployment, or state taxes. (See "Tax and bookkeeping necessities" and "Paperwork necessities" later in this chapter.)

It is often a good deal for the freelance, too. There is no permanent commitment, and he or she gets paid much more than a regular employee (albeit less than an "outside" freelance). As an independent contractor, a freelance is also entitled to deduct all business-related expenses when computing taxes, such as traveling to your office. Freelances can also more easily qualify for business deductions for computers, autos, and home offices, and have more latitude in tax-favored retirement plans. (For more on this subject from an employee's perspective, see "Are you really self-employed?" in Chapter 5.)

So what's the problem? In this situation, chances are high that, if audited, both employer and freelance could be accused by the IRS and state revenue departments of avoiding taxes and be slapped with penalties and interest. The reason has to do with their interpretation—not yours—of who is self-employed and who is an employee.

Who is an employee? While you may believe that any individual with a temporary—i.e., nonpermanent—work assignment is a freelance, the IRS and state taxing authorities usually take a different view. Not surprisingly, their much narrower definition is designed to maximize taxable income and minimize tax avoidance and deductibility. State and federal governments are looking for more sources of revenue; small businesses that may "misclassify" their workers, to avoid taxes, have come under increasing scrutiny. Then, too, by the IRS's own estimates, approximately 40 percent of all unreported taxes are attributable to self-employed taxpayers, such as freelances, so any way of tightening collection and reporting procedures is beneficial to the government.

The IRS utilizes a twenty-part test to determine whether a worker is an employee (subject to more taxation), or an independent contractor (allowed more deductions). Basically, the test attempts to determine the extent to which a business directs and controls how, when, and where a worker performs his or her duties. If there is much direction and control, the worker is an employee; if little or none, he or she is self-employed. If you wonder what conclusions the IRS might reach if you were to be audited, call a local office and ask for Form SS-8, "Determination of Employee Work

Status." It provides four pages of questions that will give you a good insight. You may also return a completed copy to the IRS to get a determination. (Recommended only if you want their determination on file.)

In addition to the IRS criteria, many states now utilize a somewhat tougher standard, what has come to be called the "ABC Test," to determine when state unemployment taxes (and sometimes workers' compensation insurance) must be contributed by the employer. Any employer who cannot answer "yes" to these three questions is probably liable for state employee taxes:

Is the worker free from direction and control over his or her work performance?

Is some of the service performed outside the regular course or place of the employer's business?

Is the worker customarily engaged in an independent business?

How to avoid a problem. Whenever you hire freelance help, you should insist that they act and operate like independent business people. If they don't, don't take a chance; don't hire them. Granted, this eliminates from consideration much inexpensive talent, but it will help keep you from paying a much higher price in audits and possible penalties later on. The freelance should conduct his or her affairs under a business name (e.g., Jane Smith & Associates) and have all the normal attributes of a separate business—a business address, letterhead, and a business telephone. In addition, the more clients the freelance has, the better. (If your payment becomes a major percentage of his or her yearly income, chances are high the freelance will be considered an employee.)

Before hiring, ask for a written cost estimate, then issue a purchase order against it. State on the purchase order what is expected as precisely as possible, and give a termination date. Always make sure that the freelance submits an invoice, on business letterhead, for work done. Weekly invoicing is best. *If you issue checks without an invoice, the individual will almost certainly be considered an employee.* Also, be careful not to treat freelances as you would regular staff. For example, hours should be defined as "flexible"; they should have a minimum of direction, and if possible should work in different locations, including occasionally working on your assignment in their own offices. (Interrupting their work for you occasionally to take another assignment is even better.)

Finally, before making a commitment, inform your accountant of what you have in mind and seek his or her counsel.

The "temp" option

A way around the possible problem of hiring freelance help is to go through an employment agency. In this situation, the freelance will officially work for the agency, which handles all the tax deductions and reporting requirements. You pay a weekly fee based upon the qualification and experience of the individual(s) they provide. The employee typically gets 60 percent of the agency fee, the agency 40 percent.

Another possible benefit of hiring temporary employees is the opportunity to try out different individuals. If the workload continues and you find an individual you like, you can then make an offer of permanent employment. (Be sure first to check the employment agency's policies to avoid getting hit with an additional placement fee.)

The downside of using an employment agency is that it can cost up to double what you would pay an independent freelance with the same qualifications, and the selection of individuals is usually more limited and is more oriented to production (computer and software skills) than creativity.

Placing temporary help is the fastest growing segment of the employment industry. In every metropolitan area there are several agencies that specialize in providing communications professionals on a temporary basis.

The intern option

Interns are the least expensive way to obtain temporary help, one worth looking into if your need is not overwhelming. Here too, however, there are some things to keep in mind if you want to do it right.

Let's say you open the mail one day in early spring and find an impressive letter and resumé from a student at a prestigious school who offers to work for FREE this summer just for "the experience of working in a productive agency or studio." Maybe you've been thinking about getting someone to fill in for vacationing staff. Maybe the letter causes you to think about all those little things you never seem to have the time to get done. Sounds like a great opportunity. Or does it?

The business of applied creativity remains one that is largely untaught. Even the best institutions focus almost entirely on art, craft, and theory, leaving instruction in working procedures to the school of hard knocks. To get "real world" education, most institutions encourage students to seek out free or reduced-pay internships. Theoretically, both parties benefit. The student gets to learn firsthand how things actually get done—practice, not theory. The employer gets additional productivity—either free or well below the prevailing market rate.

Should you? Unfortunately, what should be a golden opportunity can be a disaster. The practice most often breaks down because of employer naivete or greed. Employers who look upon getting an intern primarily as a way of quickly obtaining cheap help are almost always disappointed. This attitude encourages poor performance. Also, and not insignificantly, it creates resentment by the intern, one of the young people who represent the very future of our industry, our best and brightest.

To ensure that providing an internship in your organization will be a winning situation, first carefully examine your motives. Don't do it unless you can answer an unqualified "yes" to each of the following three questions: Do you have or can you create a position with clearly defined responsibilities? Will you or someone you designate devote the time required to train, answer questions, and prepare evaluations? Will the value of the work performed be higher than the costs of intern training, work disruption, and additional bookkeeping?

Your options. Nearly all institutions with communications curricula have set up internship procedures. To find out what they are at a given school, call the Career Services or Placement Office, or the appropriate academic department (e.g., Graphic Design). Although there is no uniformity from institution to institution, there are some similarities.

Students are often available for credit-granting, part-time internships during the academic year. These are course-specific and seldom last longer than one semester, although often one intern can be replaced with another. Because they earn academic credit, these internships are usually controlled by individual professors who require evaluations of student performance. Interns receiving course credit do not normally expect to be paid. Some institutions also have similar full-time, for-credit "intern sponsorship" programs during summers and school breaks. Most full-time internships are informal. For employers seeking interns, typically the institution will provide a free listing medium, such as a bulletin board posting or a newsletter ad. Students then set up their own interviews. The school seldom grants academic credit, and because of this students normally expect to be paid.

Involve your employees. Do this first. If you don't solicit employee input, they may be uncooperative or feel threatened. (Typical reaction: "Does this mean I'll have to share my workstation?")

Choose carefully. There are many more students than there are intern positions. This is a buyer's market. Interview several individuals and select the one who has the best combination of experience, talent, and personality. Selection is especially important if the internship is a trial that may eventually lead to a permanent position.

Define responsibilities. The intern should know exactly what is expected and be comfortable with it, even if it is nothing more than being a "gofer." One person should be designated to answer questions and determine priorities. Set regular working hours and provide a spot where the intern will work.

Provide compensation. The only way to ensure productivity is to compensate interns in a meaningful way. It helps both you and them take their responsibilities seriously. Interns who work totally free are worth less than what they are paid—they cost heavily in terms of work disruption. Meaningful compensation does not necessarily mean cash. It may also mean course credit, or it may be a combination. The going rate for interns is from $10 to $15 per hour, depending on responsibilities and experience.

Defining a position

Although you should take it slow and never hire a permanent employee before it is absolutely necessary, you should also keep in mind that the most important resource any creative firm has is its talent. If you want to grow, chances are you'll have to offer your clients the dependable, consistent talent that usually only comes from having permanent employees. They give you more control and can allow your business to obtain the size that usually leads to larger clients, workload consistency, creative variety, and internal economies.

Your first employee is the first step down the path to growth, and it often leads to the second most common mistake: hiring without proper forethought. Like an unplanned pregnancy, it often just happens, and it changes one's life forever in the process. Having even one employee not only requires substantial bookkeeping, operational and tax changes, but it also requires you to become a manager for the first time.

The first step in becoming an effective manager, the kind who gets maximum benefit from an employee, is to think about what you want him or her to accomplish. Then put it down on paper—a job description. Every job should have a job description.

The goal is fourfold: First, a job description will help ensure that you advertise for, interview, and hire the right person. Neither you nor the prospective employee can afford to be unrealistic about the position and what is expected. Second, a detailed job description helps ensure that you get maximum productivity from the employee once hired. If you don't, you lose money. Third, preparing a job description is a test. You aren't ready to grow a viable creative organization until you can prove that you can handle the structural necessities. Fourth, a job description is the best defense against paying too much, especially long-term salary escalation. It sets a salary range, beyond which an employee can't progress without being promoted to a new position.

Good job descriptions describe necessary and desirable traits (education, experience, and personal attributes), detail primary and secondary responsibilities, provide a salary range, outline career potentials (possibility of creative and salary growth), and show whom the employee reports to. Typically most small to midsize creative services firms define three creative positions (e.g., junior designer, designer, and senior designer) and a couple of noncreative positions (e.g., receptionist/secretary, bookkeeper).

Defining personnel policies

In addition to a description for each type of job, it is important to have written procedures that cover those policies that affect all jobs. Commonly called "personnel policies," they go a long way toward ensuring that all employees are always treated equally. When every employee understands the company's personnel policies, and that they are fairly and uniformly administered, morale is vastly improved, as is overall efficiency. To be effective, personnel policies should also be observed by the principals.

Personnel policies in a small creative organization can usually be defined in one or two pages; in large creative organizations they often take the form of an employee handbook. Regardless of the size, organization, or detail required, they should encompass the following:

Working hours. Normal starting, quitting, lunch, and break times. If there is a provision for "flex time" or working off-site, it should be spelled out as well.

Overtime. The policy on payment for working extra hours, and how they are defined. The Federal Fair Labor Standards Act (FLSA) requires employers to pay employees one and a half times their regular pay for hours worked over forty in one week. However, "executives, administrators, professionals, and sales persons" (sometimes referred to as "exempt" positions) are not entitled by federal law to overtime pay. Most states follow FLSA guidelines with some variations. This means that you are probably not required by law to pay overtime to professional staff (graphic designers, sales reps, etc.), but you probably are required to pay it to clerical staff (receptionist, bookkeeper, etc.). Check with your accountant to be sure. Then determine your firm's policy based on the law and your budget and sense of fairness. Some firms provide compensatory time to professionals in lieu of money. Also, if overtime is paid, be sure to indicate what authorization (permission) is required.

Payroll schedule. How often employees are paid and expenses reimbursed. Professional staff are typically paid every four weeks, sometimes every two weeks, occasionally weekly. Office and administrative staff are usually paid either every other week or weekly. Employers like to pay less frequently because it reduces bookkeeping costs and cashflow pressure; employees often like to be paid as frequently as possible because it results in less budgeting pressure.

Salary reviews. How often an employee's performance is reviewed for salary adjustment (a raise). Typically, new employees are reviewed after six months, yearly thereafter.

Holidays. The days the company is closed in observance of national, local, and religious holidays. The average is eight—New Year's, President's Day, Memorial Day, July 4th, Labor Day, Thanksgiving, and Christmas, plus another local or "floating" holiday (e.g., the day after Christmas).

Vacations. How vacation time is accrued (example: one day a month, credited on the last day of the month), how much can be accrued (example: twenty-four days), any relationship to sick or personal days, and whether you pay for unused vacation time on employee termination (some states require it).

Paid sick and personal days. Days off granted each year for personal reasons (sickness, funerals, etc.). Are such days a subtraction from vacation time, or will the company grant whatever days are requested, subject to a supervisor's review and approval?

Leaves of absence. The policy toward employees who request unpaid leaves of absence for child care or to take a once-in-a-lifetime trip. Will their job be held open? If so, for how long? (Caution: Employees may be entitled to certain rights, especially for maternity or jury duty. Check with your accountant or lawyer before finalizing this policy.)

Benefits. Medical care, dental care, insurance, profit sharing, 401(k) plans, etc. (See "What about benefits?" later in this chapter.)

Miscellaneous. Will the company pay for social and professional association dues, attendance at dinner meetings, and entry fees for creative award competitions?

How to interview, whom to hire

Even with adequate forethought, whenever you hire another person you're putting a portion of your business at risk. The fewer the employees, the more crucial each is. In a two-person operation, one employee represents up to half a firm's talent resources. Even in larger organizations employees have a tremendous impact on the "look" of the creative product, and may become the primary contact with some clients.

Finding qualified applicants. This shouldn't be a problem for your first employee, a junior creative/production talent. Asking peers, contacting a local college, or running an ad in a local creative publication or club newsletter will usually bring enough resumés.

If you are looking for a high-level or specific talent to round out your staff, you'll want to be more selective and allow plenty of time. Talent searches often take several months. List your opening on industry websites (e.g., www.aiga.org) and advertise in creative publications (e.g., *How* magazine). An alternative to advertising in creative publications and sorting through the pile of resumés it will produce is to engage an employment agency ("headhunter"). Chances are you already know several who specialize in creative and advertising personnel. If not, check through the ads in *Advertising Age, AdWeek,* and *Graphic Design USA* for names. Be aware that the agency's fee, paid by you, is up to 35 percent of the employee's salary. Also, if you consider individuals from outside your immediate area (the situation in which headhunters are most effective), the employee may expect you to pay for relocation expenses, usually $10,000 and up.

When advertising, be careful not to give the appearance of discrimination. (Example: Don't advertise for a "young" person, or for applicants by sex.) Even though small businesses are exempted from many state and federal antidiscrimination laws, some do apply. Besides, it is wrong to discriminate in any fashion.

Whichever way you solicit resumés, require them, even from an individual whom you know well, who has a great "book," and will occupy a minor role in your organization. A resumé requires an individual to go on record. It is both a summary of skills and experience, and a fileable listing of important data such as education and references. For most small creative businesses a resumé also serves double duty as a job application. (Note: Some firms also require job applications—their own custom form—because they ensure that each employee provides similar information, making comparison easier.)

Reviewing resumés is the time-saving filter that limits your interviewing/portfolio reviews to fewer than a dozen of the most promising candidates. Although knowing how to look between the lines when reviewing resumés is an an important skill for most employers, it is less so for a creative business because of the importance of the portfolio review. Most principals use resumés simply to get an idea of training, experience, and general business sense before a portfolio review. (Some principals feel that given the importance of a portfolio review, it should take place before looking at resumés. Although appropriate in an ongoing effort to see what creative talent is currently available, a portfolio review can be excessively time-consuming when there is a need to fill a specific position quickly.)

Given the number of resumés you will receive from any listing, you'll probably want to separate them into three groups: 1) the best—the half dozen or so that warrant an interview/portfolio review; 2) the "maybes"—a half dozen or so others that are worth seeing if you can't get an employee from the first group; and 3) those that don't make the cut for the first two groups.

Special considerations when interviewing for your first employee. Because the fewer employees you have, the more you will be directly involved in their work, interviewing for your first employee is a little different than if you already had several. Here are four important things to look for:

Personal chemistry. Since you will be working very closely together, often in stressful (deadline) situations, how well you get along is much more important than raw talent.

Attention to detail. In a two- or three-person shop, the principal always remains heavily involved in conceptual development and creative direction. Therefore, you want help that is executional and detail-oriented, an individual who is at least as much a craftsperson as an artist.

Complementary skills. As natural as it may be to do so, do not hire a clone of yourself, creative or otherwise. The smaller the organization, the more important it is that each new employee bring additional capabilities to the business.

Growth potential. Hire the very best talent you can afford, then train and help the employee grow. Don't worry about whether or when he or she might leave. In most cases your business will benefit far more from a real talent who leaves to go on to bigger and better things than from a lesser light who sticks around, thankful for any job.

What to say when interviewing a candidate. The art of interviewing is to obtain specific information and valid impressions in a short space of time. Although always a challenge, it can be especially so among creative individuals who often are more oriented to visual than oral communication. Given this situation, it is up to you to take the lead, to explain the job and the company, and to ask questions revealing a candidate's personality, experiences, and attributes. A good interview takes at least half an hour, most take an hour, a few (mostly for higher-level positions) may take place several times and involve a lunch or two.

Begin by briefly explaining your company, its history, and what types of work you do. Show a few appropriate samples. Next, explain the position, the responsibilities, the salary, the chances for future growth, and who the employee will report to. Follow this with a brief summary of the company's personnel policies. Provide copies of the job description and personnel policies and a few samples.

Now get the candidate to talk about what makes him or her tick, personally and creatively. Usually the best way to do this is to ask leading and open-ended questions. For example: What type of work do you think you do best? What type of work do you think you do least well? What's the best job you've had, and why? Which ad campaigns (or graphic designers, or writers, or illustrators) do you like best, which do you like least? What are your greatest frustrations? What would you like to be doing twenty years from now? What are your interests outside of work? What interests you most about joining our organization?

Ask specific questions about relevant skills (example: software proficiency) and about anything on the resumé you would like explained further (example: a gap in employment history). In this process, be especially careful not ask questions that might imply discrimination. For example: When did you attend school? (age discrimination). Are you married? (sex discrimination). Who takes care of your children? (sex discrimination). Is there anything that might affect your work that we should know about?

(often used as code for finding out about handicaps). What does your spouse do for a living? (often used as code for whether the individual might need to relocate).

During the interviewing process let the candidate do most of the talking; you should do most of the the the listening. Don't be concerned about putting him or her on the spot; it's necessary to protect both your interests. After all, there's a lot at stake here for both parties.

What to look for when interviewing a candidate. The purpose of asking questions is to give you a good feel for the candidate's overall interests, character, and experience. In addition, you should look for these specific characteristics:

Business sense. The best employees are those who know that your company, and their job, depends not only on producing good work, but doing so in a way to produce a predictable profit.

A team player. As much as anything else, the success of a multiperson creative services firm requires teamwork. The larger the firm grows, the truer this becomes. An objective when hiring any employee—creative or administrative—should be how he or she strengthens your team. This not only includes bringing complementary skills (see below), but also the ability to interact positively with other team members. Introduce leading candidates to other staff members, allow them the opportunity to chat casually for a few minutes, then solicit their impressions before making a decision.

Adaptability. The job an employee is hired for quickly changes in most organizations, especially in a small organization or at a higher-level position. This is because circumstances are constantly changing, and because each individual brings to each position his or her own style and ambitions. The more flexibile, versatile, and easygoing the candidate is, the greater the chances that he or she will perform satisfactorily in a changing environment.

Complementary skills. It is worth repeating: do not hire clones of yourself. The future of a stable and growing creative services business lies in being able to offer a variety of clients a variety of styles, techniques, and solutions to problems. You want to offer as many choices as possible. Have a staff that can be a source of different creative and business perspectives. In short, hire employees who complement and enhance your capabilities, rather than duplicating them.

Enthusiastic references. Checking references is the last step, usually taken just before your make the candidate an offer. It is your protection, albeit imperfect, against hiring somebody else's problem. Call and personally talk not only to each reference provided (usually three), but also any appropriate employers and clients. (Caution: Do this only with the candidate's permission, as it may alert the world to the fact that he or she is looking for another job.) Given the reluctance of many references to say anything that might adversely affect an individual's employment possibilities, look for unqualified recommendations.

What to look for in a portfolio. No doubt you already have strong ideas about what type of style and experience you're looking for. Moreover, when evaluating any creative work, there is no right or wrong, only subjective opinions. Nonetheless, you should weigh your subjective evaluation—"I really like (don't like) this person's stuff"— against some more objective criteria. Also, it often helps to have a trusted friend or employee look at the one or two portfolios you like best, and compare impressions.

Problem-solving. Solving clients' communications problems is the very essence of a creative services business. The more the candidate talks about objectives and strategy and how his or her creativity addresses them, the better. Regardless of their samples, beware of candidates (especially younger ones) who demonstrate excessive concern about style and "integrity." They may be talented, but have trouble adapting to the compromising realities of the real world.

Variety. Simply put, the more the better.

Originality. Good commercial creativity, the type that pleases clients, requires coming up with original solutions. Adapting something already done in another situation, "cloning," is not only a demonstration of artistic ennui, but it is usually inappropriate, too.

Execution. As architect Mies van der Rohe put it, "God is in the details." So is client satisfaction, and much of your profit margin.

Potential. A portfolio is only an indication of what the individual has accomplished, not necessarily what he or she is capable of doing with proper training and experience. Does he or she show promise? It is usually cheaper and better to hire someone with lots of promise and enthusiasm than one with good samples, less initiative, and limited growth potential.

Informing the candidates. It is seldom appropriate to make a hiring decision on the spot. You should end every interview by informing the candidate when you will make a decision, giving yourself as much time as possible (two weeks is normal). If you are seriously interested in the candidate, say he or she is on the "short list" (no more) and that you would appreciate a call before another offer is accepted. If you are unable to make a decision within the time you've indicated, write each remaining candidate and say that you have decided to continue your search. Give a new date on which you expect to reach a decision.

Candidates who don't make the cut should be informed as soon as possible. This should always be done by letter, pleasant and short. Say that as impressive as his or her resumé and portfolio are, the candidate's experience and capabilities do not, in your opinion, match the requirements for the job. As much as you may be tempted, don't be more specific. A pleasant, timely letter informing them of your decision, more or less phrased in this way, and wishing them well in their continued search for a new career opportunity, is not only the proper thing to do, it is also your best defense against any later charge of hiring impropriety or discrimination.

Proceeding with caution

As described in Chapter 18, terminating an employee is one of the toughest jobs a manager faces. It is a task that nearly everyone finds difficult. It affects the morale of other employees, reduces shop productivity, and is fraught with potential legal problems.

One of the best defenses against hiring employees you may later have to terminate is to first hire them on a non-permanent basis. This gives you a chance to evaluate them under actual shop conditions and pressures.

One way to do this is to "shop" through the individuals working for temp agencies, as described earlier in this chapter. Some, not all, would welcome the opportunity to land a permanent position. Arrange to hire interested and qualified individuals for periods of two weeks to a month to test their skills and compatibility with your organization. When you find the right one, make an offer. Not only does this allow you time to evaluate an individual's talent and work style without making a commitment, but during this time all employee tax responsibilities are handled by the temp agency. It is, however, more expensive, because temps cost more than employees. Also, the agency may assess you a healthy fee if you hire one of their temps away, so be sure to check your obligations first.

Another way to increase the odds of getting the right individual is to hire the most qualified applicant for a short time first, with the understanding that the job may (or may not) turn into a permanent one. This may be acceptable to those anxious for employment, but the necessity of removing themselves from the job-search process without a commitment may make it impossible for others. In discussing this arrangement, be sure to avoid terms like "probationary" and "trial." That way, when the employment period ends you don't need to worry about providing a reason for not renewing the arrangement—the term simply ended. Wait a week or two and call the next person on your list. When hiring individuals on this basis, you are responsible for all tax obligations. To attempt to avoid them by classifying the employee as a freelance is very, very risky. (See "The freelance option" earlier in this chapter.)

How much to pay creative staff

The best way to find out about local pay practices is simply to ask around. While few employer friends and peers will (or should) tell you the specific salary of an individual, most will willingly share what going pay rates are. Another way to get information is to call an employment agency specializing in placing creative individuals in temporary positions. Without making any commitment, inquire what their weekly freelance rate is for the type of individual you seek. You should be prepared to pay from half to two-thirds of this amount.

A web search for "salary information" will provide several sites that provide representative wages by job title. A free source for graphic design salaries is www.designsalaries.com.

When assessing what you can afford, be sure to think beyond just covering salary cost. The industry rule of thumb is that each billable employee should contribute between three and four times his or her salary in income. This covers wages, benefits, company overhead (including nonbillable staff), downtime (employees average only 50 to 70 percent billable time), and profit. Viewed another way, a new employee whom you pay $25 per hour ($1,000 weekly, or $52,000 yearly) should have billable time worth at least $156,000 annually. If you can't reasonably project this in the near-term future, better stick with freelance or temporary help.

Even acknowledging that very low employee salaries can raise the principals' take in the short term, it is usually bad business practice. The talent, enthusiasm, and dedication of employees are the foundation of a viable creative services business. Pay employees too little and you only hurt yourself. This is not to suggest that you be Santa Claus, but that you think in terms of enlightened self-interest when setting employee wages. As one principal puts it, "Don't pay peanuts unless you want to hire monkeys." If you desire to build the best creative shop in your area, you should plan on paying above-average wages. (For information on giving raises, see "Evaluating employee performance" in Chapter 18.)

What about benefits?

The normal order of priority for creative employees is pay, followed by the opportunity to work on stimulating assignments, followed by insurance coverage, followed by the availability of a retirement plan.

Universal benefits. Most creative firms provide employees with two weeks of paid vacation, available on their anniversary date. Some, especially larger firms provide three and four weeks for long-term employees (typically after five and ten years). Eight paid holidays yearly is average. Most firms also provide free sick and personal days within an undefined, "reasonable" limit. (Employers are required by the Federal Family and Medical Leave Act to provide time off in some cases. If you dock a professional employee's pay for taking off a partial day, you may be violating local labor laws.) For professional staff (normally creative staff, sales reps, managers) benefits are usually just that, and can be granted, changed, or withdrawn at will. For certain nonprofessional staff (like clerical help) some benefits may be required by law. Check with your accountant or your state's Department of Labor.

Health insurance. The benefit most employees care about— whether they work in a small or large shop—is health insurance. If you are already affiliated with a health insurance group, it is probably possible to add new employees to this coverage. Although group health insurance costs vary considerably across the country, single-person premiums normally run from $300 to $500 monthly, family coverage from $750 to $1,250. *Creative Business* surveys show that most midsize and large shops (6+ persons) contribute something to the monthly premiums; a little less than half of all small ones (2–5 persons) contribute nothing. Of those contributing, 50 percent of the monthly premium is most common; a few pay 100 percent. If you currently work alone and aren't in a group plan, ask your insurance agent whether it is possible to set one up. Some group plans can be established with as few as two employees—you and one other person. (Also see "Buying Insurance" in Chapter 4.)

Other benefits. Discuss other possible benefits and costs with your insurance agent and accountant. Smaller firms may find that benefits are prohibitively expensive to set up, fund, and administer. It is important to inquire, however, because providing one or more benefits may be a way to attract better employees. Plus, it is important to know what additional business costs you might incur if your company continues to grow. (Keep in mind that cost increases due to growth are often more than offset by greater economies of scale.)

Other benefits to consider in addition to health insurance are disability insurance, life insurance, dental insurance, profit-sharing bonus plans, and retirement plans (see the following page). You should also recognize that employee attitudes often change when a creative firm's staff grows to half a dozen or more. The increasing inaccessibility of the principals, combined with the need for more formal operating procedures and the inevitability of job stresses, office politics, and career concerns, usually results in employees starting to think of themselves more like workers doing a job for pay, less like colleagues in an exciting place to work. Benefit plans—usually thought of by employees as a sharing of the wealth their labor helps create—are a way of redressing the perceived imbalance. Although much less true than in years past, without some package of fringe benefits it is difficult for a larger firm to compete for, attract, and hold the loyalty of the talented employees who are the foundation of any prosperous creative services business.

A major benefit small shops can offer—one that is more difficult the larger the organization becomes—is "work style." For younger individuals particularly, a relaxed working environment, combined with an opportunity to learn and do meaningful, exciting work, often more than compensates for the more traditional benefits offered by larger firms. Defining a relaxed, productive work style is highly subjective, but it often includes such elements as flexible hours, the ability to bring children (or pets) to work, free coffee and soft drinks, occasional group parties and outings, creative club memberships, health club privileges, and the like.

Company retirement ("pension") plans. The older and more senior an individual is, the more important a retirement plan benefit is to attract and hold him or her as an employee. Typically, individuals start becoming interested in their early thirties or when they start a family.

To qualify for tax deferral, company-sponsored retirement plans must be set up and administered according the guidelines of the Employee Retirement Income Security Act (ERISA). Plans can be totally employee-funded, totally company-funded, or funded by a combination of employee and company contributions. More than half of all multiperson creative shops provide some type of retirement plan. Among those with fewer than three employees, the percentage is about 30; among 3–9 person shops it is about 45 percent; for 9–12 person shops it is about 70 percent; it is almost universal among larger shops. Most plans are funded solely by employee contributions. The smaller the firm, the more likely this is to be true. Fewer than 10 percent of companies with under a dozen employees who have plans contribute to them; about 35 percent of those with more employees do.

Pretax contributions can be made solely by the employee through automatic payroll withholding, or on an occasional-deposit basis through the company. As an additional benefit, the company can make occasional discretionary contributions to employee accounts, or match their contributions on a percentage basis. How much an employee can contribute each year (or an employer can contribute to an employee's account) varies according to retirement plan type. Contributions vary widely, usually depending on profitability and the principal's feelings about the value of benefits. Most common is to tie contributions to a year-end, profit-sharing bonus—most of the bonus as a check, some as a contribution to the employee's retirement account. A few, usually larger, firms contribute a percentage of everything the employee contributes. Whatever the plan type, the company pays the setup costs; yearly administration costs can be covered by the employer, or charged proportionately to each participating employee's account.

As desirable as it may appear, never consider offering an employee retirement plan until your company has first achieved several years of operating stability and predictable profit. This is not a make-or-break business decision, whereas protecting the positive cash flow that guarantees the company's survival (and the employees' jobs) is.

Shop around before making a decision. Most large banks, insurance companies, brokerages, and financial services companies offer "canned" plans for small businesses that are appropriate for all but unusual situations. Check with your bank and ask your accountant for recommendations. Also talk to your insurance agent, because it is important that your company have special insurance adequate to cover it against any claims filed by employee investors unhappy with the performance or operation of the plan. (As a trustee of the plan, the employer is held to fiduciary standards.) This additional expense often runs hundreds of dollars yearly. All employer contributions, fees, administrative costs, and insurance are deductible as business expenses. (For information on types of retirement plans, see Chapter 9.)

Hiring marketing help

Until a shop grows to four or more creative individuals, a full-time salesperson is not normally practical. Sales responsibility is typically handled by shop principals or one of the senior staff. Although it is possible to have part-time, outside salespersons to ease this additional burden, it seldom seems to work well. One reason is that unlike other job functions that are more or less adaptable to flex-time, calling on clients and servicing accounts requires being available during most regular business hours.

The experience of most creative firms around the country is that a full-time sales or new business development person is necessary to support every four or five creative individuals on the payroll of a project-based organization. Put another way, the fifth, tenth, fifteenth, etc., individuals a design firm hires should probably be devoted full-time to sales activity.

This supports the rule of thumb that about 20 percent of a creative firm's total labor hours should be devoted to sales. Another rule of thumb is that a full-time salesperson is probably needed when fee income reaches $500,000, and for every additional $600,000 to $700,000 thereafter. This size requires a consistent flow of new assignments to ensure regular cash flow and good employee productivity. In addition, the greater the number of assignments, the more important it becomes to provide professional client contact and service. If a principal or senior creative individual has previously been selling, enjoys it, and is good at it, she or he may wish to continue. If so, however, the individual should sell full-time and give up most day-to-day creative activities.

Prehiring considerations. Many sales reps are hired for the wrong reason: principals want to avoid selling altogether. This leads to unrealistic expectations and disappointment. The truth is, selling can only be avoided by the principals of very large shops. Even with good representation, many sales have to be "closed" by the principals, and many clients still expect ongoing contact with "the person in charge."

There are two right reasons to hire a sales rep: 1) A sales rep can provide consistent, professional sales activity, month-in, month-out; having a rep to sell allows principals more time to do what they do best—creative management—by avoiding time-consuming "prospecting" activity.

Consider the rep's role. After reviewing your business plan, decide exactly what it is you want the rep to accomplish. Is it to go after the packaging market? Increase the number of branding projects you do? Get more upscale clients? Increase billings by 25 percent? Next, consider what type of working relationship you want. How much interaction do you want with clients, and how much will be the rep's responsibility? What are your present business practices, and how will they affect the rep's performance?

Prepare to be supportive. Success with a rep takes a commitment to teamwork—two of you working together toward mutually agreed upon goals. While a good sales rep has to be a self-starter, you must also be willing to provide input and support. Will you be totally candid and forthcoming in providing everything that's needed? A good rep will probably make your job more challenging by forcing you to think more about your business goals, strategy, and promotional tactics. Can you accept and act upon a rep's input even if when it is not what you want to hear?

Give authority as well as responsibility. The importance of a sales rep in determining the future of the business argues that he or she should have rank, title, prestige, and authority equal to senior creative staff. A rep also has to be given enough independence to be successful. Among other things this means a rep should have a strong say in pricing, delivery, and client satisfaction issues. Further, since most clients need to be reassured that everyone they deal with is important, it is also wise to give her or him an impressive title—Vice President of Marketing, or Director of New Business Development.

How to get applications. The best approach in recruiting is to put out the word that your firm is looking. Talk about your needs among peers at creative club and other meetings. Ask every printing salesperson you deal with for recommendations. Ask the same of paper salespeople. Advertise in the local business press (small community) or an industry medium such as *AdWeek* (larger metropolitan areas). When advertising, be clear about the nature of your business, and plan to run the ad several times. As with any employment ad, be careful not to discriminate. For example, don't indicate you prefer a person of a certain age or sex. Although you will probably get a pile of inappropriate resumés, it is better to sort through hundreds to get the right person than to have your choice limited. If you prefer not to advertise and sort through many resumés, engage an employment agency ("headhunter"), but be aware that the agency's fee, paid by you, is 30 percent or more of the rep's first-year earnings.

What type of person to look for. Shop principals who have been through the selection process find that the best sales reps are usually individuals who have previously been involved in some facet of creative work. Highest on their preferred list are graphic designers who, for a variety of reasons, now prefer to sell. Also prized are printing and paper salespeople who wish to be involved with a "more creative" product; they have previous sales experience, understand the business, and have client connections. Advertising agency account executives also make good sales reps, particularly when they want to get more heavily involved in promotional work. Consider former magazine space reps as well. Don't necessarily rule out those without creative or communications experience, however. Traditional salespeople often work out fine, especially in larger shops where they are one of several reps. Also worth noting, and not to encourage sexist or discriminatory behavior, is that women often make particularly good reps. Women seem to more easily grasp the idea of relationship selling—the ability to determine and relate to client needs. Relationship selling is usually the key to long-term business, especially with larger accounts.

Recognizing what's important. Unlike most of the creative staff, a rep is a very public employee. Everything a rep does affects your firm's image. Like it or not, she or he will "become" your company in the eyes of many clients. Clients may still consider your firm based on its creativity and past performance. In the future they will actually select it based, at least in part, on the promises made by the sales rep. By definition, good sales reps have a different set of skills and objectives than most of the creative staff. Don't hold it against them if they are a little different. They should be more polished, more aggressive, and have a certain nonchalance about rejection. When necessary, they should also become a client's in-house advocate. Most important, they should be more interested in the salability of the work than in its craftsmanship and quality. In today's buyer's market, where clients have so many choices, a good sales rep is the ideal complement to a good creative environment. Together, each enhances the other by making sure that all interests—quality and business, shop's and client's—are constantly addressed.

Working arrangement. One reason many shop principals are dissatisfied with the reps they hire is that they expect great performance but want to pay next to nothing. To allow adequate compensation without undue financial strain, creative companies who work on a project-to-project basis—design shops, interactive firms, editorial service companies, etc.—should consider compensating sales reps on a sales commission basis. A sales commission (versus a salary) provides a strong incentive for the rep to perform, while also reducing the firm's cash-flow exposure (no sales, no pay). In addition, when properly structured, a commission setup removes the artificial earnings ceiling that jeopardizes the very entrepreneurial spirit every good salesperson must possess to be effective.

Sales reps can work on a straight (total) commission or receive a small salary plus commission. Most reps on straight commission expect to have a draw arrangement—i.e., they can draw a small regular "salary" from an account that is periodically replenished by their commissions. If commissions don't equal the amount drawn and the rep is terminated, the firm loses the money paid to the rep. For this reason, you should balance draw accounts at least every six months.

A straight salary is usually only appropriate for creative firms with heavy account service needs—e.g., advertising and PR agencies. In such situations, the rep salary structure should be equal to that of senior creative talent.

Fees and commissions. On new-client work, sales rep commissions typically are between 10 and 15 percent of fee income, depending on whether there is also a small salary base (15 percent is most common for straight commission). On work from existing clients (so-called house accounts), slightly lower commissions (7 to 12 percent) are typical. Some firms pay reps the same commission for both new and house account work, but most feel that this does not provide a sufficient incentive for them to go after new clients. When a new rep brings along an account from a previous employer, 20 to 25 percent of fee income is typical for the first project, 15 percent thereafter. These higher percentages provide an incentive for a rep to try to "switch" clients and also recognize that sales expenses are lower. On markup (not fee) income, the rep typically gets 15 percent of the firm's markup (i.e., 15 percent of 25 percent). Commissions are paid to the rep, either directly or into a draw account, only after the client pays.

Keep in mind that when paid on a reasonable commission basis for work generated, how much money a rep takes home is immaterial.

Expenses. Everything is negotiable, but the following is more or less typical: The firm covers all advertising and promotion, portfolio expenses, office space, support services (telephone, photocopies, faxes, proposal preparation, etc.), taxis, and transportation (including auto mileage). When it comes to client lunches and entertainment, some firms pick up the tab, some don't. About the closest to a consensus on this issue is that they are often covered for experienced, productive reps, but seldom for new ones or those not performing up to sales goals or expectations.

Account service. Although a sales rep should be actively involved in account service, the rep's primary role is new business development. Therefore, the ratio of account service time to new business prospecting time should seldom rise above 30 percent. Conversely, because a happy client often becomes a repeat client, for most types of assignments, account service probably shouldn't fall below about 20 percent.

Hiring a bookkeeper

Just as most good creative people share certain common characteristics, so do most good bookkeepers. She or he is typically rather conservative, absolutely dependable, religiously punctual, oriented around the small details of life, and not prone to making intuitive decisions. Solid, analytical substance, not intangibles like style and taste, is what is important. In short, a good bookkeeper has the type of personality not normally found around most creative organizations. This is exactly why you need her or him.

The full-time, freelance bookkeeper. The type of bookkeeper for one- to five-person shops, the full-time freelance bookkeeper services several clients seen as regularly as needed: one day every other week, one day a week, twice a week, whatever. This is a professional who has the proven skills and flexibility to serve the needs of a wide range of clients. For every business that needs a full-time bookkeeper, there are dozens who can use a freelance person on a regular basis. Don't let the word "freelance" deter you. Unlike some freelances in our business, freelance bookkeepers are nearly always stable, rooted individuals who have built strong and loyal followings in their areas. Once you find the right person, you can rest easy knowing that even if you are only on a once-a-month schedule, she or he will show up on time, as predictable as Halley's Comet, to keep your books in order.

The full-time, in-house bookkeeper. A full-time, in-house person who combines bookkeeping with other office functions is usually required for shops with six to a dozen employees. Hiring a full-time, in-house bookkeeper should be done much more carefully than hiring creative staff. Not only do you know less about this function than about creativity, or even management, but the risk, should you hire the wrong person, is much greater.

Finding the right person. If you want to do it right, the best time to hire a bookkeeper is right after the close of your fiscal year and before you have a mess to clean up. However, if you do have a problem, or very sudden business growth, the sooner the better. In actuality, bookkeepers are first called in to most creative shops to clean up backlogs, sort out problems, or because of a transition (e.g., taking on a partner). Then, the benefits being apparent, she or he stays on. Remember, however, that just as in the business of creativity, a client who waits until the problem is large or the need urgent always pays more.

Advertising. Probably won't be effective in finding a full-time, freelance bookkeeper; probably will be for a full-time, in-house bookkeeper. Ask your accountant for help in reviewing resumés or interviewing.

Contacts. Something of a hit-or-miss method. A bookkeeper perfectly suited to other types of businesses may or may not be for yours; one experienced with other PR firms, ad agencies, or design shops would be a strong candidate. (Conflict-of-interest caution: Never consider a freelance bookkeeper who also works for a direct competitor.)

Temporary employment agencies. A good way to try out potential full-time bookkeepers. When you find one you like, make an offer. Contact agencies that specialize in accounting personnel.

Your accountant. Probably your best source. Accountants are in the best position by far to evaluate two important characteristics needed in a book-keeper: quality of work and an ability to interact with an accountant. Your accountant probably should not take over your bookkeeping. In nearly all cases this will end up costing you more, and it will deprive you of an additional source of independent financial advice. Also, an independent bookkeeper can act as a go-between for you and your accountant, trans-lating "accountant-speak" into English. If you have trouble appreciating much more than the bottom line, having a bookkeeper trusted by both you and your accountant is a big advantage. Whether you are looking for a full-time freelance or in-house bookkeeper, ask your accountant for recommendations and for help in reviewing resumés and interviewing. The few hundred dollars it costs will be well worth it.

However you find candidates and make a decision, make sure you get and check at least three references. Then go with your gut feeling. Chemistry is almost as important as qualifications. Finally, don't make the potentially fatal mistake of leaving your bookkeeper without any supervision.

How much to pay. As with an accountant (see Chapter 3), consider a bookkeeper an investment in business growth that will save more than it costs. Don't scrimp. The pay range for experienced full-time freelance bookkeepers runs from $30 to $45 per hour. The high end of the scale is for major metropolitan markets; the low end for rural areas. Anyone who charges less than $20 an hour is probably too inexperienced to be helpful. Of course, the total cost depends upon the amount of work done and your financial acumen. Two-person shops may require one day of bookkeeping a week; three- to four-person shops may need eight to twelve days a month.

The range for experienced full-time, in-house bookkeepers is $40,000 to $50,000 annually. For an exclusive, part-time individual, prorate the pay accordingly. In some cases, bookkeepers also double as receptionists. Although this appears very cost effective, be cautious: the two jobs are quite different. If you do decide to combine functions, hire the individual for her or his bookkeeping, not receptionist, qualifications. The high end of the pay scale is for metropolitan markets, or where there are other duties; the low end is for rural areas.

Employer tax and bookkeeping requirements

Becoming an employer requires changing a freelancer's accounting and bookkeeping. So, an accountant needs to be involved. If you don't have one (not just a tax preparer, preferably a CPA), you aren't ready to hire an employee, either part- or full-time. Most of what you need to know is also in IRS Circular E, "Employer's Tax Guide," downloadable from www.irs.gov/business. Similar information is available from state Departments of Revenue.

Employer Identification Number (EIN). You may already have one from opening a business checking account. If not, you'll have to get one. (Ask your accountant to handle it.) It will be used to identify your business on all payroll and income tax returns, state and local included.

Employee Allowance Certificate. Commonly referred to as IRS Form W-4, each employee must fill one out to specify marital status, and how many dependents he or she wants to claim for tax withholding. The form must be retained by the employer.

Employment Eligibility Verification. This is IRS Form I-9. It must be filled out by every employee certifying that he or she is eligible to work in the U.S. The form must be retained by the employer.

Payroll taxes. Income taxes must be withheld as required for the dependents the employee has claimed on his or her "Employee Allowance Certificate." A percentage of the employee wages up to a certain amount must also be withheld for Social Security (FICA) and Medicare taxes, and these amounts must be matched by the employer. If there are state or local income taxes (there are in most areas), they must be withheld, too. The mandated withholding must be sent to the proper authorities within a specified time. Failure can subject the employer to penalties as high as 100 percent more than what's due.

Unemployment taxes. With a few exceptions, employers are required to pay a small federal and substantial state unemployment tax. Although rates vary from state to state, the total unemployment tax, federal and state, is usually only a few hundred dollars a year.

Worker's Compensation Insurance. This is state-administered insurance that covers on-the-job disabling injuries. In some states it is required of all employers, in others only of those with more than a few employees. It is normally purchased from a private insurance company. What is required and how much it will cost is state and occupationally based. Your insurance agent can provide information on your state's requirements.

Payroll processing services. You could handle payroll processing yourself—issue employee checks, withhold taxes, and send taxes to the authorities—but it is unwise for all but very large firms to do so. Even a firm with two employees—you and one other—is better off leaving this to a payroll processing service. It is safer and doesn't cost much. Ask your accountant for a recommendation, and visit the websites of four popular ones: www.paycheck.com, www.adp.com, www.paycycle.com, and www.wellsfargo.com/biz/payroll.

A payroll service deducts the appropriate amount from your firm's checking account on a regular basis. It then issues employee checks based on the schedule you've arranged, withholding the appropriate taxes and sending them on to the proper authorities. Every quarter the service provides the IRS with the required quarterly summary of payroll and taxes withheld. At year end it provides the employer with a record of each employee's pay and taxes, and sends each a W-2 form before the January 31st IRS deadline.

Charges for this service vary depending on the number of employees and the payroll frequency. For the latter reason it is better to pay less often (every two weeks or once a month) than more often (every week). Typical yearly payroll processing service charges for a couple employees range from $300 to $400.

Employee noncompete agreements

Perhaps the final consideration when hiring an employee is whether to ask him or her to sign a noncompete agreement. Can you prohibit an employee who later leaves from taking your clients along? Or penalize vendors if they decide to work independently with your clients? In summary, the answer is a much-qualified "yes."

First, any legal contract is only as effective as it is specific. That is to say, if it is detailed and limited in scope, it will probably be tight enough to enforce. If it is not detailed, is broad in scope or unreasonable, it probably will not be. For example, a noncompete contract prohibiting an employee from "doing graphic design for clients within the banking industry for six months after termination" would probably not be enforceable because it could easily deprive an individual of his or her basic right to earn a living. However, another contract, one that prohibits a departing employee from "working for three months for any banking firm that has been a client of (company) within the past six months," is probably specific enough to enforce.

It is also important to be realistic about noncompete contracts. Although enforceable if well written, doing so can be time-consuming, disruptive, and expensive. The outcome can be anything from a simple "cease and desist" court injunction to monetary damages to a countersuit. It is also highly likely that any enforcement action will anger the very clients you are trying to save, like shooting off your foot in the process of drawing your gun. Attempts at enforcement often send a negative, "sour grapes" signal to other clients.

So what's the benefit? Mostly intimidation. Noncompete contracts put employees and vendors on notice that you take your business seriously and will fight for it if necessary. But like most confrontations, the ones you win are usually those you don't actually fight.

The best way for shops to protect their business is for principals and sales representatives constantly to demonstrate to clients that meeting their needs takes a combination of strategy, creativity, service, and experience. In other words, it is much more than the creativity and skills brought to projects by a single individual or outside vendor, no matter how talented they may be. The solution to most potential problems lies in addressing the underlying causes—typically employee discontent, or the principals and sales reps not taking an active enough role in servicing the business.

18. Managing a Creative Organization

Running a large organization is not a matter of simply expanding a small one. Different skills are called for, not the least of which is personnel management. It is a skill that comes naturally to some and with great difficulty to others. When you hire your first employee, you take on a significant new responsibility: you are now a boss, too. Although the art of personnel management is a large and constantly evolving subject, the most important aspects, at least as they relate to employees of a creative organization, are covered in this chapter.

To set the stage for understanding personnel management, first recognize that the secret to managing creative personnel is to hire the right individuals in the first place. This means selecting individuals who are pleasant and easy to work with, as well as talented. In addition, try to avoid these three common mistakes.

No matter how much you may like an individual you hire, never forget that he or she is different in one basic way: you have a large stake in the future of your business; the employee's is limited. Don't expect any employee to put into the business the same degree of dedication, hard work, and attention to detail that you may have come to consider normal.

Learn and practice the fine art of delegating and letting go. Don't "micromanage" or insist that everything be done your way. As the old saying goes, "Everyone rides a horse differently." Define what needs to be done, then let the employee decide how to best accomplish it. Productive employees are those with freedom, including the freedom to learn from making occasional mistakes.

Recognize that the other side of hiring is the unpleasant task of occasionally laying off or firing. If you've been careful in your business analysis and hiring procedures it may never be necessary to terminate an employee. If and when it is necessary, however, you must do it. Procrastination in letting employees go is very costly. The sooner you correct an unproductive situation, the healthier your business will become and the more money you will make.

Being a coach, not a boss

The step from working productively alone to working productively with staff is among the most difficult for any creative person to take. For most of us, our whole professional life has been focused on the highly individualistic expressing of our talent, and very few of us have had any significant management training. Becoming a good manager is not only a difficult step, but usually a very big one as well.

Nevertheless, once you become the principal of a multiperson shop, just being creative is seldom enough. From then on you usually must also direct and encourage—manage—the creative output of others. To do this well necessitates striking a balance that not only ensures that the work meets your standards and a client's needs, but is also both stimulating and rewarding for the employees.

The reason for considering employee satisfaction is not altruism, noble as that may be. Rather, it is the pragmatic realization that in fields where the "product" is usually a more or less novel solution to a problem, the care and feeding of the problem solvers (your employees) is just plain good business. Just being a traditional boss, telling employees what to do and when to do it, is almost never the most effective way to manage creative individuals.

In large organizations the management of creative people—inventors, researchers, designers, planners, etc.—has long been considered an especially challenging situation, and many resources have been devoted to figuring out how to do it right. By and large the conclusion is that the most productive management model is similar to that of a coach and team or mentor and performers, as previously discussed in Chaplter 16. In this arrangement, the coach has overall responsibility; the team has specific performance responsibility. There is no question about authority and who gets to call the shots, but there is also ample recognition of the importance of both unique individual talent and teamwork. Think, then, of yourself as coach and of your employees, one or many, as your team. Here are several suggestions on how to make the situation work:

Be open and friendly, but not too familiar. Good working relationships are critical if a team is to function efficiently and profitably. Certainly the concept of "me" versus "them" is inappropriate in any creative services organization. Nonetheless, it is tough to make decisions when doing so may adversely affect a close friend. So, employees should never become close friends. The best rule to follow regarding your relationship with your employees is always to be open and friendly and to take a genuine interest in their lives. At the same time, however, do not socialize with them outside the office or studio on a regular basis. Never confide in an employee about your personal life, and never discuss other employees or business details not commonly known to everyone.

Don't try to clone yourself. Variety in experience, expertise, and style is perhaps the most important strength in an organization whose product is creative problem-solving. Yet many shop principals suppress variety by rewarding employee habits, patterns, and styles that closely match their own. Although working as a team certainly requires a common direction, cohesion, and continuity, it should never go over the line into duplicating your idiosyncrasies, stylistic or otherwise. You may, consciously or unconsciously, want to perpetuate your style because you believe that it is what has made the business successful. While there may be truth in this, future success and growth is far more likely to come from variety rather than conformity. Indeed, the larger a creative services business becomes, the more diverse the styles required to meet its more diverse client base. The more stylistic variety offered by a creative services firm, the stronger its resistance to being adversely affected by fads and trends.

Involve employees as much as possible. Assignments must be done on time, on budget, and to your quality standards, but it is also important to encourage the creativity of the employees; to give them their "head." As a general rule, the more you involve employees in all the various stages of projects—sales, strategy, budget, and scheduling, as well as creativity—the greater the sense of satisfaction they feel, the harder they will work, the more valuable they will become. With this in mind, try to match assignments to employee talent, experience, and interests. When giving an assignment, provide context and strategy as well as budget and creative parameters. To the extent possible, also try to involve them in client meetings and in budgeting and scheduling activities.

Remember, you are ultimately responsible. Creative people tend to focus on the big picture and be uncomfortable with details. When they have little at stake, most creative employees focus on doing creatively inspired work and give inadequate thought to strategy, schedule, budget, and profitability. Although this can be minimized by getting them involved, accept that a certain amount of it is inherent in a normally structured creative organization. (For an alternative see "An organization of true associates" in Chapter 16.) Thus, you must continually provide the focus that keeps assignments on track and employees' feet firmly planted in reality.

Be a strong coach, a "benevolent dictator." Good creative managers are role models. They willingly share their knowledge and experience; they inspire employees through their actions, and they expect employees to grow and eventually seek greater opportunities. They keep the hours they expect employees to keep, they don't ask employees to do work they wouldn't do, and they aren't paranoid about employee loyalty. They recognize that you reap what you sow. Managing by intimidation is seldom effective, but neither is being a pussycat. Never forget that the business is yours, so you have the ultimate responsibility for what should and should not be done. Like the best coaches, the best managers solicit suggestions and comments from their employees, then they decide what course of action to take. Once they make a decision, they stick with it.

The fine art of delegating

Much of what is covered above comes under the broad heading of "delegation"—deciding which tasks and how much responsibility should be assigned to employees. It is one of the more difficult management challenges facing any supervisor, and is especially so in a field where the product is affected by employees' talents and personal creativity. Nonetheless, the better you are at delegating, the more productive your shop will be, and the more you should enjoy your role as principal and creative director.

Unfortunately, many principals today lack significant experience in delegating. In times past, the apprentice system in many design studios and ad agencies gave senior staff—the individuals most likely to start their own shops—considerable experience directing the activities of junior staff (their assistants). In the computer age the need for assistants has been practically eliminated, and with it so has delegation. Today there is less client-invisible (management) trial and error, but more client-visible (creative) trial and error. This exacerbates many principals' fear of loss of control. Although one result of delegating certainly is less control, it should not be a problem if adequate systems and procedures are in place. These checks and balances are explained in Chapter 19 (see "Project management" and "Creative direction, shop management, and communication") and are an essential first step in delegation.

Recognizing the "entrepreneur's disease." A universal problem for entrepreneurial companies, whether small service firms or growing manufacturers, is too much personal involvement of the founders. Sometimes this results only in inefficiency and reduced profitability, sometimes in outright business failure. The disease is particularly virulent among creative services companies because our product—creative work—involves a high degree of personal, artistic expression. A company's reputation is often built upon the creativity of one or two individuals and the way in which they meet the needs of their clients. It seems both logical and practical not to tamper with this success formula. Many creative services firms even carry the names of their principals, who feel a psychological imperative not to become too detached ("My personal reputation is on the line"). These considerations are valid, but consider three other factors as well.

Common sense tells us that the larger an organization grows, the more time consuming and difficult personal involvement becomes. Whether running a big organization or small, you have only one head and two arms, and there are only twenty-four hours in a day. The opportunities of an organization are theoretically infinite, but your physical and mental capacity is definitely finite.

Too much personal involvement, whether by trying to clone yourself when hiring, or by attempting to micromanage employees, reduces the variety of a shop's product, creativity. In turn, this reduces its market potential. Too much involvement in daily creative and operating procedures also limits the time you have for developing new business strategies.

When you are too closely associated with all aspects of a business, its market value is substantially reduced. As covered later in Chapter 19 (see "Can your business be sold someday?"), even under the best of circumstances it is very difficult to accumulate financial equity (market value) in a creative services business. When one or two individuals do everything, it is nearly impossible.

What and when to delegate. Standard management texts say that employers should give employees all the responsibility they can handle. Then add a little more. In other words, keep delegating tasks until they say "stop," or they screw up. The idea is that the more an employee is challenged, the more motivation and productivity result. The cost of an employee occasionally dropping the ball is more than offset by a surge in overall productivity. Will this approach work for a creative services firm? Yes, with reservations.

Very few principals give their employees enough responsibility. This is sometimes due to workload ("As soon as we slow down, I'll sit down and delegate some of my responsibilities"), sometimes ignorance ("It never occurred to me"), sometimes selfishness ("Why give up the fun stuff?"), sometimes ego ("They couldn't handle what I do"), sometimes fear ("Why should I train them how to run their own businesses?"). Whatever the reason, most principals are actively involved in many activities they don't need to be. The result is that they end up working harder than necessary, and their employees end up less challenged, motivated, and productive than they should be.

Most creative and all executional tasks can be delegated, as can most project management, most marketing and client contact, and most routine office management. How much delegation is practical within your organization depends upon the quality of your employees. This is directly related to how well you picked them and how much you pay them. When asked how he managed to build Ogilvy and Mather into one of the world's premier advertising organizations, David Ogilvy commented, "I always look to hire people who are better than I am." Added to this, he would probably agree, "And give them all the responsibility they deserve."

What and when not to delegate. Unless your organization grows quite large (in which case almost everything can be delegated), some things must remain your responsibility. Only you should determine your overall structural, financial, strategic, and creative direction. You must establish and monitor operating procedures. On the daily operational level, you must control hiring, firing, and evaluating employees; workflow planning and scheduling; marketing strategy and direction; accounts payable and accounts receivable; and all deposits and withdrawals. Since these often time-consuming responsibilities can't be delegated, when pressure builds up it is important to delegate those responsibilities that can.

How to go about delegating. When asking employees to take on responsibilities you previously handled, always inform them that doing so is a result of their increased skill and maturity, and the confidence it inspires in you. Indicate that it is the route to salary growth, but make no promises unless the new responsibilities are significant enough to warrant an overdue raise or promotion. Make sure you also tell them exactly what is required and when, and provide plenty of time for phasing new duties into their other responsibilities. Finally, make sure you give them the authority necessary; inform other employees of the change if appropriate. (The chief complaint of employees being handed a new responsibility is that it often comes without the means or authority to accomplish it.) If your organization is big enough, it is usually a good idea to record the change so that you don't forget and continue to handle the responsibility, or hand it over to someone else. (The second most common complaint of employees handed a new responsibility is that it is ultimately forgotten.) Keep a notebook or computer record with assignments and responsibilities, and record it in the organization's planning book or chart (see "Four record-keeping aids" in Chapter 19). If the responsibility is significant, it should also be added to the employee's job description.

The ultimate delegation test. If you had to work for yourself, how enjoyable and productive would you rate the experience? Do all your employees feel the same way?

Setting shop standards and procedures

Because a creative services business relies on the innovation of its employees, even if you were so inclined it wouldn't make sense to try to run it autocratically like a highly structured retail store, or a manufacturing plant. A minimum of structure and a relaxed, informal management style—again, the team-leader concept—is far more practical. Since chances are this is what you are comfortable with anyway, so far there is no problem.

Don't go overboard. Relaxed and informal shouldn't mean chaotic. Whether defined or not, every business operates around certain procedures (even lack of them becomes a procedure). Undefined procedures evolve and develop based on personal idiosyncrasies and individual convenience, not overall efficiency and the financial interests of the business.

Recognizing this, most larger agencies and design firms develop procedures manuals. These specify in varying degrees of detail how the organization is to operate and how the work is to be shown to clients. In other words, they prescribe standards. In firms with fewer than six employees, the principal is usually involved enough in daily activities to monitor and control them, and too many procedures may stifle employee freedom and creativity. It is usually enough for the principal to inform each new employee how things are to be done, and to make sure that they actually are. In firms with more than six employees, however, the relative inaccessibility of the principal and the reliance on management layers usually dictates the need for a more formal arrangement—the procedures manual.

Whether passed on orally or written down and codified, the firm's standards and procedures should be defined and controlled by the principal in no uncertain terms. Doing so should not hamper true creativity, although prima-donna employees may think it does. It reflects the reality that you are engaged in business, not just art. Attention to productivity and quality control actually makes employees' life easier by removing many uncertainties. More important, it helps minimize internal inefficiencies and mistakes, provides clients with an assurance that work will always be dependably excellent, and builds marketplace reputation and goodwill that result in more jobs, lower marketing costs, and the possibility of bankable equity. If any employee ever questions the need, ask: "Have you ever heard of a successful business that didn't have consistent and dependable products and services?"

The proper way to think of standards and procedures is as a supplement to job descriptions, personnel policies, and record keeping. (See "Defining a position" and "Defining personnel policies" in Chapter 17, and "Devising a flexible, expandable system" in Chapter 19.) Here are just a few of the things normally covered:

Letter and correspondence (style and formats), visitor greeting and hospitality (offering coffee, etc.), the telephone greeting (never just "hello"), staff meeting schedule and format (Monday morning, everyone to review what he or she is doing), vendors and suppliers (free choice or are some preferred?), purchase orders, approvals, and documentation of purchases, the creative review process (what, when, who), use of cabs and delivery services (when to avoid them), how concepts are prepared for presentation (full- or half-size, dummies, or storyboards?), how work is to be presented to clients (first go over assignment objectives, etc.), when time sheets are submitted (end of every day), invoicing schedule (1/3, 1/3, 1/3?), who backs up whom (is everyone backstopped, principal included?).

Only you can decide what is important for your employees to understand and handle consistently, day-in, day-out. Don't turn into a self-defeating control freak. Also, don't make the mistake of waiting until you become unprofitable, or a long-term client ditches you, before waking up to the importance of setting standards and procedures.

The forty-hour norm. An agency or studio where high pressure and a constant need to work nights and weekends are normal is one with bad management. Principals who brag about how long and hard their employees work are just exposing this weakness. Those who look at the hours an employee keeps, rather than how much he or she accomplishes, are focusing on the trees and missing the forest. When your staff constantly works under pressure and puts in long hours, the creative emphasis shifts from quality to quantity (getting it done). Details slip through the cracks and errors in judgment become common. In a well-managed shop, standards are oriented around a normal, forty-hour, 9-to-5 workweek that is occasionally exceeded as dictated by workflow variability.

Stimulating creative productivity

One of the benefits of a shop with proper standards and procedures is that it creates a well-functioning team of individuals, each sure of his or her responsibilities. In turn, this teamwork provides your clients with excellent custom products at attractive prices. The more creatively stimulated your team is, the better the process works.

Contrary to popular wisdom, creative ideas seldom come in a flash of inspiration, nor do they usually come from staring at a blank piece of paper or computer screen. More often than not, they come out of a process usually referred to as "blue-skying," or "brainstorming." One of the advantages of larger creative organizations is that the number of brainstorming opportunities increases exponentially with the size and diversity of staff.

Although by its very nature brainstorming is an uninhibited process, uninhibited doesn't mean totally unstructured, another popular misperception. As many shop principals ultimately discover, good brainstorming sessions seldom just happen. They are encouraged and planned. If you know a few techniques, combined with a little practice, most can be improved upon.

There is nothing wrong with creative individuals working alone, but teaming up to bat around ideas nearly always results in stronger, more original concepts. Not only are more ideas generated, but the process helps refine them as well. Likewise, although two writers or two designers teamed up are preferable to going it alone, the best results are obtained when two simpatico individuals with complementary talents and experiences are involved—typically a writer and art director/designer. In this tried and true approach used by ad agencies for generations, each participant brings to the table his or her unique viewpoint and creative training. Yet because of a common world view, their approaches clash only in productive ways.

To borrow from the metaphor approach (see page 341), good brainstorming techniques are the fertile soil usually required for ideas to blossom. Here are some techniques you can share with your creative team to help them grow good ideas:

The "time-based" approach. In this classic brainstorming technique undivided attention is focused on a problem for a limited period of time—usually an hour or two. In a variation on the same technique, a goal is set—say, twenty-five ideas in an hour. The team is secluded with paper and pencil. They get comfortable and clear their minds. Absolutely no phone calls, interruptions, or distractions are allowed. The pressure is now on to come up with as many ideas as possible: no idea is off limits, no thought too outrageous. To get started, sometimes it helps to try categorizing thoughts, perhaps by first thinking of every possible benefit a client's product has, and the most outrageous way it could be visualized or described. Everything is written down. Quantity, not quality, is what counts. Refinement can come later.

The "what if" approach. The team comes up with a dozen or so off-the-wall "what if" questions about the assignment. Then it works through each of them, refining and developing the best one or two as concepts. For example, to develop a marketing campaign that will help a retailer enter a specific market, the team may ask: "What if we took the promotion budget and used it to give gifts to the first hundred customers? Would it produce more or less customer awareness and store traffic (the client's objectives) than running ads?" "What if we had only half the budget? What would we do then?" This approach forces the team to consider a range of hypothetical perspectives and solutions that probably aren't a part of their normal thinking. Even if none of the ideas that result is accepted, the results make a very strong statement to the client that you are not creative thinkers who take the easy way out.

The "big challenge" approach. The team deliberately exaggerates the problem, making it more difficult than it really is. This forces them to address it from a different, higher-intensity perspective. Here's how it works: Let's say your firm is asked to come up with a sales meeting theme that will put a good face on a somewhat disappointing year. To help the creative team focus more aggressively on the problem, they consider what they would do if the client company was actually fighting for survival. Chances are, the ideas they come up with will be powerful. Then they ask: Are these ideas equally appropriate? Could they be modified or toned down slightly to make them appropriate? Whether what they come up with is suitable as is, or needs further refinement, the very process of exaggerating the problem helps avoid weak concepts. Remember, most clients would rather see concepts that are too strong, giving them the option of watering them down, than the other way around.

The "wrong way" approach. To do wrong-way brainstorming, team members initially forget thinking about "good" ideas and concentrate instead on what would actually exacerbate the client's problem—what would make things worse. Let's say the team is trying to produce an e-mail blast about a client's improving, but still somewhat poor, service. They start by asking: "How bad could bad really be? How could the client absolutely infuriate every single customer who walks through his door? How could he ensure that no first-time customer would ever buy from him a second time?" Now, once the worst of the worst is defined, the team begins thinking positively. They often find that they are suddenly able to come to grips with and build some ideas around how relatively good the client's service really is. For example, they may develop a comic, self-deprecating campaign that candidly admits the mistakes of the past and details the improvements under way.

The **"role playing" approach.** When searching for the best way to grab and hold the interest of a potential buyer or user of a product (customer), it often helps to try putting yourself in his or her shoes; not only to help produce ideas that are more relevant but also to avoid concepts that are too esoteric for the client to accept. Suppose, for instance, the assignment is to revamp an engineering organization's instructional and technical literature. The team may be confident they know how to attack the problem from a graphic or editorial standpoint, but have they also considered all the user's concerns? For example: What is an engineering reader most and least interested in (it affects the graphic treatment)? How is it referred to (use affects layout and writing style)? Where is the material stored (it affects the appropriateness of size)? Think. If you were the user, how would you write, design, or illustrate the material? The same, or differently? Going through this exercise might not only give the team a new perspective, but also helps anticipate any possible client concerns.

The **"metaphor" approach.** A metaphor is a word or phrase that symbolizes something other than its literal meaning. Metaphors can be very effective as a brainstorming tool because they provide a relatively simple means to come up with concepts that are easy to understand and memorable. For instance, you've been asked for a theme and graphics for a client's national sales meeting to be held in late winter at a southern resort. Visualizing the sales force metaphorically as a baseball team, the creative team might come up with: "Spring Training for Next Year's Champs." The graphics of the meeting could then be easily developed around a baseball motif with subthemes relating to training, teamwork, management, etc. Concepts that can tie into and build upon any well-known cultural phenomenon are usually very popular with literal-minded clients, and are easily remembered by customers as well.

The **"word association" approach.** In this approach, instead of trying right off the bat to generate concrete ideas, the team first generates a list of key associative words or phrases. Later, these are used as the nucleus around which to form more detailed concepts. If, for example, the assignment is to come up with a new identity program or positioning statement for a growing insurance company, the team might start by thinking of the key attribute of a good insurer—say, solidness. They think of as many appropriately synonymous word for "solid" as possible: "stable," "dependable," "durable," etc. With a thesaurus they increase the list, using each new word to lead to others in a constantly expanding expression of the feeling they are after (e.g., "solid" leads to "substantial" . . . leads to "permanent" . . . leads to "enduring" . . . leads to "perpetual," etc.). Finally, armed with every possible English descriptor for the concept of solidity, all but ten of the most appropriate are tossed out. Phrases or statements are combined, modified, and built from these until they produce just the right expression for the positioning statement or graphic treatment.

The "hunter" approach. To use this approach, derived from maintaining a "swipe file," the team scans websites and the pages of newspapers, magazines, and literature (or maybe even watches TV and movies) in search of random ideas that might have a bearing on the creative challenge. They shouldn't make the mistake of restricting themselves only to such industry sources as show annuals. The more places they look, the wider their vision, the more they'll discover. Aside from a variety of sources, the key to making this approach work is to remember that there is no such thing as an original idea, only original expressions of an idea. (This tenet is the foundation of copyright laws.) Don't be concerned by plagiarism at this point. For now, every idea is fair game. For every three similar ideas that show promise, the team should conceptualize one original execution that combines or utilizes elements of all of three. Working this way provides a source of "idea starters," and also ensures that what is produced will be unique.

Criticizing creativity

Working together effectively with employees is a necessary component in the success of every principal. It requires the ability to acknowledge (you may have forgotten) what makes creative individuals somewhat different from the rest of the population. Although stereotypes are inappropriate and there is certainly great personal variety among creative people and their talents and behavior, they do tend to share certain common characteristics. (Question to ponder: Are these common characteristics caused by the creative environment, or does the creative environment cause these common characteristics?)

Perhaps most important, creative individuals need more attention than do other types of employees. Given the lonely, highly personal, and psychologically risky nature of doing creative work, even long-term veterans need occasional input on what they have produced and overall reinforcement on how well they are doing. Secondly, most creative individuals tend to be shyer, more introspective and sensitive, than others. This means that the very individuals who need attention most are the ones least likely to ask for it, or take offense most easily if it is not what they want to hear. Finally, remember that anyone who asks for a critique or review of what they have done is probably seeking only affirmation. As British author W. Somerset Maugham once said, "People ask you for criticism, but they want only praise."

Critiquing employee creativity is, therefore, a potential minefield. It can't be avoided, at least not if you are going to maintain standards, but negotiating it can be very dangerous. Learning the art of navigation can pay big returns in raising morale, creativity, and productivity. Here are a few tips on how to make sure your criticism of employee creativity is viewed as constructive.

Don't be quick to judge. "Gut reactions" are fine when discussing options or approaches—"blue-skying"—but are nearly always inappropriate for criticizing developed, thought-through ideas or concepts. If the critique turns out to be positive, the offhand way in which it is given will make it less meaningful and appreciated. If it's a negative criticism, it will demean an honest effort and probably demoralize the creator as well.

Example: An employee catches you in the hallway, and asks for your quick opinion of a concept.

Response: For a promising idea: "You seem to be heading in the right direction." For a less-than-promising idea: "It looks like it still needs a little work." Either way, quickly follow up with: "But this is much too important for such a quick reaction. Let's sit down and go over it later. How about my office at 4:00 this afternoon?"

Do it in private. When two individuals work one-on-one in a team situation, there's little need to be concerned about tact and diplomacy, but when three or more people are together, the situation changes, especially when a boss/employee relationship exists. In such situations, constructive criticism is almost impossible. Never criticize an employee's work in public.

Example: You are in a meeting and you are asked for your opinion of a concept you have strong reservations about.

Response: "I'm not really sure. I think I'd like some time to think about it." Then, addressing the creator, "Why don't you and I get together later this afternoon after I've had time to organize my thoughts a bit."

Be a good listener. A willingness to listen to another's point of view is crucial to effective criticism. If you don't give the other person the opportunity to defend what he or she has done, you create resentment or rejection of your opinion out of hand. You may also miss a compelling reason to change your mind. Simply asking a creator to describe an approach will force him or her to reexamine its validity.

Example: An employee brings to your office concepts that are not what you wanted to see.

Response: "I think I understand what you're trying to say here, but it doesn't come through as clearly as I expected. Explain to me (again) what your overall approach (objective) is and why (specific examples) were incorporated."

Be businesslike. In creativity there are few if any absolute rights and wrongs, only endless expressions of taste. Commenting that you don't like something is never a valid criticism. The only valid criticisms relate to how the work meets the objectives of the client or assignment.

Example: You are asked what you think of a particular approach or idea.

Response: "Actually, it doesn't reflect my personal taste, but that's not important. What is important is that it meets all the objectives the client laid out for it. Therefore, it is a good concept."

Present an alternative. A criticism without an alternative is a critical comment, nothing else. Be careful about criticizing unless you can also suggest another approach. If you can't think of anything on the spot, either give yourself some thinking time (no more than twenty-four hours) or withdraw your criticism. When you do have an alternative, never present it by saying, "I think you should . . . " Use the much more positive and subtle, "What do you think about trying . . . ?"

Example: You are asked by an employee what you would do differently.

Response: "I'm not sure, but I know I'm uncomfortable. Give me a little time to think about it. Let's get back together first thing this afternoon and brainstorm a bit."

Evaluating employee performance

Good employee performance evaluations come about through a two-step process—a process as important for shops with one employee as it is for those with dozens. The first evaluation actually occurs, usually subconsciously, in the course of everyday interaction as the cumulative result of the impressions you form when talking to an employee and observing his or her working style and creative output. These are the primary source materials for evaluating any employee and require no special knowledge or skill to interpret. There is, after all, nothing more valid than what your eyes see, day-in, day-out. Because you are the boss, there are no more valid impressions than those you form.

As important as these impressions are, however, they are formed from many small, often insignificant, events. They are seldom modified by larger, longer-term considerations. They are also very subjective and don't necessarily relate to an employee's job description. Finally, they provide no record of employee growth or accomplishment (or lack of it) to refer back to later. For all these reasons and more, mere impressions by themselves do not provide a balanced evaluation of any employee's performance. A second, more analytical, step is called for.

The second step of the evaluation process should be a formal performance review when you consider, in writing, how an employee is doing against job criteria you've previously established. Later, sit down with the employee and go over your evaluation. This discussion should involve recommendations for change or improvement, the possibilities for career advancement and creative growth, and last but hardly least, what salary adjustment, if any, will be forthcoming. When the review is over, summarize it and put a write-up in the employee's file.

Obviously, this level of evaluation requires a little forethought and a good deal more comment than an occasional "Keep up the good work." Therein lies the problem. Because they require time, and because most of us are not practiced at managerial counseling, we often put off review sessions, sometimes indefinitely, or we attempt them but in the wrong way. Nonetheless, experts all agree that regular performance reviews are among the most important tools any manager has, especially in a service organization—more important even than creative critiques. In addition, performance reviews are usually eagerly anticipated by good employees as a regular means of assessing where they stand relative to peers and their own career ambitions.

Who, when, and where. The individual conducting the review should be the one who determines the employee's salary. In most small firms this is the principal. In some larger ones it may be the creative director, subject to approval by the principal. In mid-size shops where the individual reports to a manager (e.g., senior designer) but the principal determines employees' salaries, both the manager and principal should take part. In such instances, the manager should conduct the evaluation with the principal present to lend support and discuss salary in the context of what the shop can afford.

Reviews should be conducted annually for most employees. If you establish the first week of the employee's anniversary month as the time for a review each year, any salary adjustment can be made effective at the beginning of the next month, and if you have several employees their reviews won't all come together. New hires should be reviewed after six months on the job, and again on their first anniversary. Employees performing poorly should be reviewed every six months until things improve or you decide to sack them. (See "Letting employees go" later in this chapter.)

The best environment for a review is where there will be no interruptions, both parties can relax, and you won't be observed or overheard by other employees. This usually argues against doing it on premises, especially behind the ominous "closed door." The location that usually works best is a good restaurant over lunch. Choose a place that is quiet and affords privacy. The better the restaurant, the more important the employee will feel. Be careful to treat all employees equally. If you don't always go to the same place, select restaurants of comparable quality.

Being prepared. There are few things worse for an employee's morale than a boss who schedules a performance review, then shows up inadequately prepared to discuss past performance, future opportunities, and salary. No matter how busy you are, take time before the review to reflect on the employee's past performance, prepare specific suggestions for improvement, and consider the appropriateness of his or her salary. Do your homework. Rehearse what you will say.

Avoid cancelling or postponing a review session unless there's a bona fide emergency. Otherwise, you'll send a signal to the employee that other things are more important to you than his or her career.

Never forget that a performance review is a very important event to an employee. It is the rare opportunity to get the boss's ear and complete attention, to get to know you better, make requests, clear the air, and discuss creative and financial potential. Because of this, and the inherent need for recognition we all have, the hour or two you spend on a review may be among the most important hours of the month to the employee.

Define the position first. An employee's performance should always be related as objectively as possible to the requirements of the position. It should not be related to your personal whims, idiosyncrasies, likes, or dislikes. To do a good performance review, therefore, you need a formal job description to refer to. (See "Defining a position" in Chapter 17.)

Doing the evaluation. Second in importance to relating an employee's performance to the job description is organizing your observations and recommendations before the session. The best way to do this is to use an evaluation form similar to the one reproduced in Appendix 3.

An employee-evaluation form assures that there is consistency from

review to review and also from employee to employee. Not only does this make the job much easier, especially if you do several reviews a year, but it helps protect you from any later charges of arbitrary decision-making or favoritism.

A week or so before meeting with the employee, sit down and prepare the performance review using the evaluation form as a guide. First consider how well the employee meets the specific criteria established for the position. Next, evaluate how he or she stacks up by more general criteria—personality, attendance, initiative, organization, self-control, and ability to communicate. Then add your subjective comments. Finally, set goals you would like to see the employee meet before the next review.

To help ensure that you keep focused during the review session, you may want to jot down a few notes about things you want to be sure to cover. It is also helpful to give the employee a blank evaluation form a week before the review session and ask for a self-evaluation. (You'll be surprised at how honest most are.) This not only gives you a good idea of what the employee thinks, but demonstrates how fair you try to be. You may even want to provide a copy of your evaluations the night before the review as a way of keeping the next day's discussion on track.

Set the stage. Don't start a review session by jumping right into the subject. Devote the first ten minutes or so to making the employee comfortable by discussing topics of his or her interest outside the workplace. The less you know the employee, the more important it is to humanize the occasion and develop a comfort level that will allow productive discussion later. If you have a generally positive evaluation to discuss, segue into it by indicating what a pleasure it is to get away to share good news. If the evaluation is not generally positive, indicate that you wanted to get away so you could talk one-on-one about the future without being interrupted.

Minimize personality. You do not have to like someone for him or her to be a good employee. An individual's personality and life-style are only important to the extent that they affect work or the ability to relate to clients and other employees. The only valid review criteria are those that relate to job performance.

Be positive. Think of a review session as a way to help an employee improve his or her career and by so doing, improve your company's profitability. This approach requires you to zero in on ways to do things better, with only enough criticism to demonstrate why change is beneficial.

Solicit input. Although you should direct the conversation, the review should be a discussion, not a lecture. To keep the employee from becoming defensive, go over the self-evaluation and ask for input on your observations. Keep the emphasis on ways you can work together to improve what is not yet quite perfect.

Be specific. Vague comments, criticisms, suggestions, and objectives are subject to misinterpretation. What you've observed and what you recommend must be clearly understood—one reason for using numerical ratings on the evaluation form. Never criticize actions or behavior patterns without being prepared to say exactly how you would rather things be handled.

Reprimand separately. By and large, an evaluation session is not the time to reprimand an employee. This should be a time of constructive dialogue, even if it involves strong criticism of performance. Reprimands should be specific to an individual event and should be dealt with as close as possible to the time they occur.

Give raises carefully and consistently. All your comments and suggestions should lead to what is the employee's bottom line: what effect, if any, will your evaluation have on salary? Salary adjustment is the major interest of most employees at a performance review.

At the beginning of the year, before doing any performance reviews, you should decide how much additional money your company can put into salary increases based on the stability of your business, prospects for the coming year, past profitability, capitalization (cushion), and the total dollar amount of the increases and schedule when they will take effect. This is time-consuming and risky, but it is nonetheless a crucial decision-making process. The result should be one of three possibilities:

1) No money: no raises. 2) Very little money: inflation-only adjustments for qualifying employees. 3) Profitability that can support rewarding employees: inflation-plus-performance raises for qualifying employees.

No matter how prosperous the firm may be, do not succumb to the temptation, or employee pressure, to give raises based on seniority or on keeping up with inflation. (One of the few benefits of inflation is that it allows businesses to reduce the salaries of nonperforming employees.) Also, never give an employee a raise that will put him or her above the salary range for the job. If an employee deserves more, give a promotion to a new position with a new salary range; if the employee is doing good work but has reached the salary limit for that job and doesn't rate a promotion, provide an inflation-only raise and adjust the salary range of the job to accommodate inflation escalation. (See the "Salary Adjustment Compilation" form in Appendix 3 for specifics on calculating raises.)

If you have no money for raises, be candid about it when discussing the employee's performance. Indicate that this condition affects everyone (yourself included) and that when times change you will reevaluate salaries. Be sure that the employee understands that the lack of a raise is not an indication of substandard performance. Tell good employees you hope to be able to make it up to them in the future and that you hope they can afford to stay with you until things improve. Be careful not to make the mistake of giving some employees a salary increase while telling others that there is no money for raises. This is a managerial wimp-out, and it can land you in big trouble if you are caught because changing the employment ground rules from individual to individual is clearly discriminatory. You can (indeed, should) amply reward some employees while giving others nothing, but it must be done on the basis of fairness.

Finally, recognize that even if your shop provides a great working atmosphere, it is difficult to keep good employees without giving them an occasional raise. *Creative Business* has found that two years is about the limit of patience for talented employees unless times are really tough, or they have reached the top of what they can earn in the marketplace. Not only do even the most dedicated, loyal, and patient employees need to provide for rising material needs, but they also occasionally need a monetary vote of appreciation.

Set goals. End the review by mutually agreeing on specific ways in which job performance (and career growth) can be enhanced. Note these goals on the evaluation form so they get special notice at the next review.

Work with nonperformers. When you have employees who are lazy or otherwise performing well below their capabilities, you can deny them raises and hope they shape up or quit, or you can fire them, or you can try to make them productive. Unless you clearly have a loser on your hands, the latter is always the least expensive choice. As busy as you may be, "saving" an employee can be one of the most cost-effective things you can do as a manager.

First, attempt to pinpoint the root of the problem. For example, the employee may be sloppy, or slow, or always late, or difficult for other employees to work with. Note the problem and see whether there is an obvious solution. For example, move the employee's workspace to reduce personality conflicts, or adjust work hours to accommodate a commuting or day care schedule that conflicts. If you have an idea for a solution, ask the employee if he or she thinks this will help. Try to get him or her to make a commitment to take specific actions by a specific date.

Make notes of any agreement and put them in the employee's file. If you suspect that even a second chance may prove to be one too many, type up a formal summary of the agreement, and ask the employee to sign it. Schedule another evaluation meeting to go over the employee's progress in a couple of months. If you see improvement at that time, keep working with him or her. If you don't, start laying the groundwork for termination (see below).

Keep a file. Make notes of any significant points brought up during the review. Attach them to your copy of the evaluation form, along with the employee's self-evaluation. Keep everything in an employee file folder.

Letting employees go

Laying off employees because of business downturns or firing employees who don't fit in is one of the toughest challenges faced by the manager of a creative services firm. Nonetheless, you will be either lucky or foolish if it isn't necessary to dismiss one of your employees sometime.

The best action is prevention. The problem often begins at the time of hiring. Most principals are more comfortable making gut decisions than time-consuming reviews of applicant qualifications and compatibility ("Her book is great, let's hire her"). Quick, love-at-first-sight hiring decisions sometimes result in a mismatch that leads to minimum productivity, maximum frustration, and ultimate divorce. (See the relevant sections in Chapter 17.)

Regular conversations, staff meetings, creative critiques, and individual performance reviews can provide the early warning signals that are sometimes all it takes to identify and correct a situation long before it deteriorates beyond the point of no return. Unless an employee is insubordinate or incompetent, it is usually less expensive to try to bring him or her along than to resort to the replacement alternative. (See "Work with nonperformers" on the previous page.)

The best way to fire employees. There are three things that are important when terminating someone: making it easy for yourself, making it easy for the employee, and protecting yourself against any later charges of employer misconduct or discrimination. If you carefully follow the procedure outlined here, all three should be covered.

As indicated previously (see "Evaluating employee performance" earlier), periodic one-on-one appraisals are the foundation of personnel management. They tell each employee how well he or she is meeting both general expectations and specific job requirements. They provide the basis upon which the employer can make well-reasoned salary adjustments, and they give the employee a sense of his or her future potential within the organization. It is in this latter sense that performance reviews are crucial if the employee ultimately must be terminated.

Today, firing at will can be very dangerous. In most situations, you should not fire an employee without first giving at least one, and preferably several, uncomplimentary written performance reviews. The last review should state clearly that unless improvement is made by a certain date, termination is an option. Ask the employee to sign this evaluation and put a copy in his or her file. Giving the employee ample warning of potential termination and the reasons why is not only the ethical thing to do; if you don't, you may leave yourself open to charges of arbitrary and discriminatory behavior, even a wrongful-dismissal lawsuit.

The only common exception to the above is when you have recently hired an employee and it is quickly obvious that you have made a costly mistake. Although still somewhat risky, it is probably better to rectify the situation as soon as possible. Write a generous separation check of several weeks' salary depending upon the position the employee occupied and the amount of personal dislocation involved in joining your firm. This is expensive, but it should reduce the chances that the employee will file suit against you for breach of promise. If the employee is upset or acts litigious, consult a lawyer.

The actual lowering of the ax should occur in a way that is not obvious to nor overheard by other employees. Do it late in the day and near the end of the week so the individual has the evening or weekend to think things over. Don't do it around the employee's birthday, or before national or religious holidays.

In stating the reasons for your action, be candid and unemotional. Cite the functions not performed satisfactorily and express appreciation for the employee's other contributions. Indicate concern that the employment didn't work out, but don't apologize. Say that as difficult as a situation like this always is, it is probably for the best because it will allow the employee to find a position he or she is much better suited for. Keep your cool even if the employee gets angry. Never trade recriminations. Don't change your mind even if the employee promises change or pleads with you. If the employee has a grievance or makes threats, call in a witness, take notes, and consult a lawyer.

It is very important that you be honest throughout this process. To lie about the reason for the firing or to agree to cover it up by providing a good reference or certifying to the unemployment insurance office that the employee was laid off can land you in trouble. As sympathetic as you may be to the employee's plight, play it straight. There's too much at stake to do otherwise.

Many principals feel that asking the employee to leave at the end of the day lessens any potentially negative effects on shop morale. Others feel that such a quick dismissal appears draconian and allow a short grace period. Either way, help avoid potentially embarrassing situations by such considerations as permitting the employee to retrieve personal belongings after hours or on the weekend.

The best way to lay off employees. Your objective should be to avoid surprise at all costs. It is not only unethical to suddenly remove the security of an individual's regular paycheck, but the speculation that precedes a layoff can have a tremendously negative effect on shop morale and productivity. Employees who are kept in the dark and sense through reduced workflow that their jobs may be in jeopardy are always less motivated and productive than informed employees. The rumors about what might happen are usually much worse than the reality of what actually does happen. If you have regular, informative staff meetings and involve your employees in account management, they will already have a good sense of the extent of and reason for the slowdown, as well as future prospects with current clients. What they don't know and what you must provide is a best guess of what other potentials you see and how long you can sustain the present level of activity without reducing staff.

Assuming that your firm has followed rational salary practices (billings are three or more times total payroll) and that you maintain an appropriate salary reserve (three months of payroll in liquid form), you must consider reducing payroll expenses if your income drops to 2.5 times payroll for more than a month and a half. (See Chapter 17 for more on these subjects.) If your ratios are lower, you should probably take action sooner.

It is very risky to follow anything other than a "last enlisted, first cashiered" policy. To keep a more productive short-term employee while letting go an unproductive longer-term one looks suspiciously like an excuse for firing. This can by construed by the employee as discrimination ("Why me, not him?"), and it may also raise the suspicions of the unemployment insurance office and your insurance carrier. (Benefits for individuals laid off are usually greater than for those fired, or terminated "with cause.")

How much notice, severance, or help to provide. It should be possible to give potential layoff candidates several weeks' warning. Tell them that you hope it will not be necessary, but that it is only fair that you inform them of the possibility as far in advance as possible. Set a termination date (most personnel experts think the end of the month is best) that will be reviewed two weeks before the time comes. If the workflow doesn't pick up by then, the date indicated will be their last. Offer to let them take company time within reason to go on interviews, and provide job-hunting suggestions, contacts, and references. Severance pay should include payment for unused vacation days and two weeks pay for junior employees, several weeks for senior employees.

For fired employees it is, of course, tougher to be generous. You should pay for two weeks or more of notice given even if the employee doesn't work during that time, and unused vacation time. In addition, be magnanimous. Recognize that even though the employee didn't work out in your organization, there is a fit for him or her someplace. Offer your help in finding a new position. If the employee accepts, make a serious effort by putting the word out to industry contacts and peers. When asked why he or she is available, simply indicate that things didn't work out for you, and that the individual has many qualities that could be beneficial to someone else.

Company benefits are normally paid up through the end of the last month in which the employee works. Chances are your company is not obligated to continue any benefits to a terminated employee, but he or she may be eligible to continue purchasing health insurance at your group rates (COBRA benefits). Since state laws vary and federal regulations are constantly being reviewed, it is best to check with your accountant to be sure.

The best way to avoid a post-separation hangover. If, after the fact, you end up having second thoughts about whether it was really necessary to reduce staff, just remember that if you don't do it when called for, you may lose your reputation, good clients, even your business. That would mean pink slips for even more employees. Never treat staff reductions casually, but don't agonize excessively, either.

Most laid-off employees land a new position, especially if they are assisted in their job search. Freelancing—full- or part-time—is always a possibility; most have this option if they so desire. As for fired employees, you may actually have done them a favor. It is very doubtful whether staying on in a situation where the personal chemistry is bad, or where talents and skills don't match job requirements, is in the long-term interests of any employee. Being fired is usually a shock, but it is the type of shock that often forces the soul-searching that enables an individual to go on to bigger and better things.

Finally, whenever you let employees go, don't ignore the ones who remain. You can be sure that rumors are circulating, and that they all have questions they may be reluctant to ask. Call a staff meeting as soon as possible and explain what happened and why. Be honest and straightforward. The staff may not understand or agree with your actions. No matter. The purpose is not to get their approval. The purpose is to tell them that they are among the chosen who remain, and to assure them that, at least for now, their jobs are secure.

19. Operational and Profitability Issues

L arge or small, well established or brand new, there are two major management challenges for a creative services business. The first—personnel—is covered in the preceding chapter. In this chapter we cover the second—procedures and results.

Setting up and maintaining the right systems and procedures is the operational side of the business. It is the more quantitative (versus qualitative) aspect of management, the one concerned with establishing routines. Although it involves fewer day-to-day decisions and is therefore less dynamic, it is no less important to success. Not only is establishing the right systems critical, but they must be constantly reviewed and tweaked to maintain their effectiveness.

The importance of time tracking

Time—watching it, allocating it, manipulating it, recording it, billing it—is the keystone to profit. Without clocks none of us would have much of a business. Yet despite the importance of time, *Creative Business* surveys show that most employees who get paid for forty hours average only twenty-five to thirty billable hours. Disturbing? Actually, not as much as it may at first seem. The very nature of a service business requires that a portion of work time be devoted to nonbillable activity. For you, this includes planning, marketing, and administration tasks. Your employees' time is always less than 100 percent billable due to time off, work scheduling inefficiencies, and time-reporting errors.

The causes of low billable hours. The major cause of low billable hours is, of course, lack of work. You can't work more productively when there is nothing to work on. The second most common cause is estimating errors. You may have locked yourself into a price on a job that involves many more work hours than you anticipated. In both cases the solutions—more marketing activity and better estimating procedures—should be readily apparent. They are easily addressable, although how successfully is quite another matter. (These subjects are covered in Sections Two and Three.)

Here, we address the third most common reason for low billable hours—inadequate time-tracking and record-keeping procedures. Accurate means of recording all job details and costs—specifications and expenses as well as labor time—are critically important for maximizing job profitability, providing backup detail for questioning clients, and compiling performance benchmarks to improve future estimating.

Debunking some myths. Perhaps nothing identifies a successful shop principal quite as clearly as his or her organizational and recordkeeping abilities. Being highly organized is not the antithesis of creativity that some misguided souls believe. In fact, my experience indicates that it is usually just the opposite: the more organized you are, the more quality time you have for creativity and creative direction, and the more the shop's portfolio reflects it. Contrary to popular myth, long pressure-filled days are not an inherent component of the creative services business either. Pressure and work hours are primarily dictated by client mix and personal style, not by industry traditions. Daily stress and pressures can be changed by finding different clients and adopting different procedures—a management challenge.

Of course, how you choose to handle your work life is highly personal. When you worked alone it was primarily you that was affected by whether you were relaxed or frenetic, systematic, or chaotic. Whatever proved best for you was best. When you have employees, however, your personal style sets the pace and tone of the organization, its "culture." Is your personal style conducive to encouraging a culture that thrives on efficiency? If not, change should be a priority. For example, you may be able to work at an absolutely frantic pace well into each evening and still avoid errors and sloppy workmanship. But can your employees also do so? You may find hard work and long hours exhilarating because you own the business and have a direct stake in its success. But do you really believe that your employees share the same interest and dedication?

Three record-keeping requirements

Efficiency. In a service business time is money, and inefficiency wastes time. The first necessity of a record-keeping system is that it make the business substantially more efficient. Whatever forms and methods are employed must be simple and easy to work with. Procedures that are too complex or labor-intensive discourage use. Even the best designed system will fail if you and your employees don't want to utilize it.

Flexibility. As any organization changes and grows, traffic management—keeping track of all aspects of all jobs all the time—becomes increasingly problematic. A good system provides control at any level of activity while remaining routine to employees and invisible to clients. As an analogy, think of air-traffic-control systems: always understandable and dependable to airline employees, always reassuring and invisible to customers.

Completeness. If you ever get audited by the "authorities" (e.g., to see whether you have collected appropriate sales taxes), you will quickly understand this requirement. Thorough and complete records provide the only answers that are acceptable to federal and state officialdom. Occasionally you will need to justify an invoice item to a skeptical client, too. It will be nearly impossible—and your credibility will suffer—if you lack detailed time and expense records. Finally, for your own planning purposes, complete financial records of every job—all in- and out-of-house expenses—provide the only means to evaluate and improve on the accuracy of estimates. Taken together, a file of past jobs provides an invaluable historical database.

Four record-keeping aids

Notes. The more successful and busier you become, the tougher it is to remember all your ideas and client requests, which don't necessarily respect time and place. ("What was it the client asked me to take care of during that long lunch at La Grande Cuisine?") Get in the habit of, as soon as convenient while the memory is still perfect, recording your thoughts on your smartphone, tablet, or laptop.

A "to do" list. This management staple is as old as writing itself, probably because it is so simple and effective. At the end of each day compile a list by order of importance (either on paper or electronically) of the dozen or so most pressing things waiting to be done. Then, begin each morning by consulting it and scheduling your work day accordingly.

An appointment calendar/daily log. We all need a way to remember appointments, the primary function of a desk calendar or its electronic equivalent. If your organization has more than three employees, you will probably want to keep your own, and encourage key employees to do likewise. For smaller organizations, one all-employee appointment calendar may be more efficient, and it can also serve as a place to record nonbillable and petty-cash expenses.

Planning book or chart. Shops larger than a couple of individuals require some means to schedule and track the progress of jobs in-house. The goal is to find or develop a system that keeps things moving smoothly and efficiently and prevents mistakes and missed deadlines. Before the age of computers a planning book or schedule chart commonly available from office supply stores handled this. The most elaborate ones use a set of color-coded cards that are moved along as a job progresses. Less elaborate ones rely upon writing in each daily change. Today, you can still choose to use this type of visual system, or you can opt for software that handles it along with other job-tracking functions.

Devising a flexible, expandable system

Differences in work style and client mix require that the design of record-keeping forms and procedures be customized to your business. Nonetheless, it is possible to describe a system that can be adapted to any creative firm. The one explained here was created by the principals of a two-person firm that later grew to have annual billings of over $3 million. Although refined over the years, even in this computer age the basic structure has remained the same. Because it provides traffic control with a minimum of employee involvement, it is a prototype for firms of all sizes.

Project/production manager. Upon receipt of a new job, a project or production manager is assigned to be responsible for it; to oversee all aspects of the job—scheduling, creativity, production, and paperwork.

Job number. The project/production manager takes a number (e.g., 003-14—job number three in 2014) from a sequential list maintained in a master book (Job Log) and records the client's and his or her own name. This job number will be used on all future correspondence, purchase orders, invoices, and forms to assure proper recording.

Job card. The project/production manager next prepares this form to put the job officially into the shop's workflow. It contains all relevant job information—job number and name, client and purchase order number, size, colors, due date, production and billing schedule, etc. The number of copies varies depending upon the size of the shop and its record-keeping needs. In the simplest system only one copy is prepared, and it is stapled to the job folder that resides with the project/production manager. If job tracking is a separate function, another copy is sent to the person responsible. Still other copies can be sent to shop principals, other staff, and the bookkeeper as a way of informing them of work they will later be involved with.

Time sheets. These are the most important forms in any system. All billable employees (but not support staff) are required to compile them daily and submit them at least weekly. Each employee's sheet assigns the hours of his or her workday, either by billable job or nonbillable (house) account. Half-hour recording is the norm. In small firms time sheets are normally submitted to the principal, in large firms to clerical or bookkeeping staff, so that billable time can be transferred to each job's time and expense compilation form. Nonbillable (house account) time is recorded separately on the payroll productivity sheet (see below).

Getting time sheets accurately filled out and submitted promptly is one of the major management challenges for any creative services business, large or small. Indeed, one of the appeals of time-management software is the ability to automate this function. However it is accomplished, shop principals must realize the critical role time recording plays in profitability, and all employees must be made to recognize that their future employment depends upon doing it diligently. In addition, time sheets provide a running record of how long it takes each employee to accomplish given tasks, invaluable information for future estimating and performance evaluations.

Job time and expense compilation. This form is prepared at the time a job is opened. Time and expenses are transcribed into appropriate form columns. When the job is completed, employee time is totaled and multiplied by the appropriate billing rate(s). Expenses are totaled and multiplied by the appropriate markup. Other costs, such as sales tax and a possible profit factor, are also totaled. Finally, the total job costs are determined and the project/production manager determines what is to be billed. (If the project/production manager is not a principal, the form usually requires approval first.)

Job folder. Even in this electronic age, a "real" job folder (jacket) is still the universal means of assembling in one place all of a given job's records and paperwork. The only difference between the past and today is that the folder often contains electronic printouts as well as the usual paperwork. Job folders should be kept seven years for tax-audit purposes and to help in estimating work in the future.

Payroll productivity sheet. This form, although not part of the tracking procedure for a job, is nonetheless an important component of operations profitability. It is compiled from data submitted on daily time sheets and held in confidence by the shop's principal. Columns are provided to record each employee's daily billable and nonbillable hours. Each week the percentage of billable and nonbillable hours for each is calculated and the income contributed is compared to the cost of salary and benefits. The percentage of billable and nonbillable hours for the organization and the comparison of total income generation to total salary and benefit costs is normally computed monthly.

Electronic shortcuts. Given the relative complexity of even the simple system described and diagramed below and the difficulty many creative individuals have with record keeping (especially time recording), can some or all of this be circumvented with computer software? The answer is yes, but don't expect miracles. There is no magic bullet, no way of escaping what are, after all, fundamental and important management tasks. The most sophisticated software still requires intelligent human interaction (as computer dweebs love to remind us, "garbage in, garbage out"). Also, the detailed, sometimes extraneous data even simple programs can provide is only as good as your desire to utilize it. The programs are expensive, too—several thousand dollars.

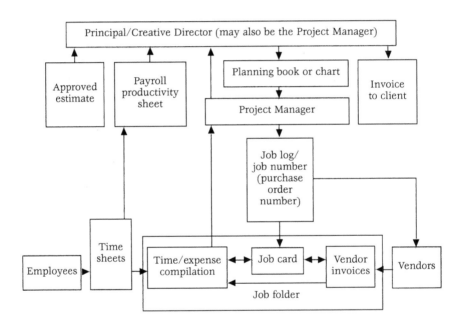

The needs and idiosyncrasies of every creative business and its principals are different; before making a software selection obtain demo disks. Then compare and evaluate them. In doing so, keep in mind the caveats and time- and job-tracking guidelines previously described.

Project management

In shops with fewer than three employees, ensuring that jobs get channeled productively through their various stages should be the responsibility of the principal. Although it helps to delegate as much as possible, there are too few jobs, too much riding on them, and too much overlap with other management responsibilities not to be intimately involved. The principal manages every project.

In larger shops, however, the situation is reversed. It is impossible to be involved in daily job monitoring without short-changing more important responsibilities. Recognizing this, running a large shop's production functions has traditionally been assigned to a production manager who handles scheduling and job-tracking details. Today, in the age of electronically assisted creativity and production, this arrangement needs to be modified. The need for production assistance is decreasing, while the need for creative direction is increasing. For this we can credit ever more powerful computers and software.

The proliferation of software offering formats, templates, and stock solutions has de-emphasized problem-solving, innovation, and originality. At the same time, the ability to prepare art, set type, size and retouch photos, and color correct when working out a design minimizes the need for other individuals to handle or coordinate all these formerly sequential and separate functions. One person often does it all, although how well is increasingly problematical. In today's world, more work is done in fewer places by fewer individuals needing more supervision.

One of the ways to address this sea change is with the radically different "associate" structure described in Chapter 16 (see "The associate business model"). Another, less radical way is by structuring a traffic management system that gives responsibility for every job—scheduling through to production—to a single individual, a project/production manager.

Whether an associate or the traditional employer/employee structure is used, however, every shop with more than three employees should be organized in a way that gives primary responsibility for every job to one individual. In today's electronic workplace, this arrangement is not only more flexible and efficient, it also results in more product (creative) variety, and an increase in marketing strength. (For reasons why, see "The fine art of delegating" in Chapter 18.) In addition, this arrangement provides more job satisfaction and helps reduce expensive employee turnover.

Creative direction, shop management, and communication

There is, of course, a large potential downside with decentralized project management. When more responsibility is placed in fewer hands, the results of a screw-up can be both less visible and more devastating. For this reason, every shop with more than three individuals should have a designated creative director, an experienced individual who is assigned the responsibility of setting and enforcing job standards. Whether this individual is the principal or an employee is not important, although he or she should have a significant role in performance evaluations. What is important is that the creative director take an activist role in educating employees and in prescribing, monitoring, and approving their output, including every assignment.

Another potential downside is that the agency or studio environment can be easily neglected. In a traditional organization, the production manager is often responsible for such tasks as general housekeeping and maintenance of supplies and equipment. In the absence of a production manager someone must be assigned these tasks to ensure that the shop doesn't slip into clutter, inefficiency, and chaos. In the associate or project-management system, that someone should be a designated studio or agency manager, with the responsibility for all non-job-specific or noncreative functions. These typically include everything from ensuring that working standards and procedures are maintained to monitoring and ordering materials to arranging for cleaning services.

Finally, because in a decentralized project-management system each employee operates more or less autonomously, more frequent and structured communications are required. Employees need not only the morale boost that comes from group reinforcement of what they are doing but also ways to share tips and discoveries. These objectives can be met with a weekly staff meeting, perhaps supplemented by publishing occasional status reports and memos that report items of interest to all (e.g., the discovery of a new freelance talent).

In summary, a decentralized project-management system is the most efficient structure for today and the foreseeable future. There are three keys to making it work: 1) a creative director who has total responsibility for the quality of the product; 2) a studio or agency manager who has total responsibility for the quality of the working environment; and 3) regular employee communications.

Managing paperwork

Despite the recurring science fiction of an eventual electronic, paperless office, paperwork is unavoidable, and will probably remain so during our lifetimes. Like oil in machinery, the function of paperwork in business is to keep everything moving smoothly. Also like oil, if paperwork doesn't get distributed on time or to the right places, things quickly break down. You need a technique to keep this from happening, especially as your responsibilities increase. The technique utilized by some principals is to prioritize into one of five categories every single piece of paper—mail, e-mail, memos, requests, phone messages, etc.—as it crosses their desk. Here are the categories and how to handle each:

Category 1—action. This is for everything you must act upon. Write a "received on" date on the top of the item. Then put it in an "Action" bin or basket. Unless quick response is called for (e.g., telephone or e-mail messages), make sure that it is acted on within one week. Set aside appropriate time each day—first thing in the morning or last thing in the evening usually works best—to go over items that are due for decisions.

Category 2—pass on. This is for everything you send to others for action. Do so by writing the name of the person(s) on top, what you wish them to do, and whether you wish to be informed of the outcome. Put it in a "For Others" bin or basket whose contents are distributed daily by yourself or an assistant.

Category 3—reading. This is for everything you should read, but not necessarily act upon—the "FYI" category. Date these items and put them in a "For Reading" bin or basket. Try to get to everything in it every week or two. Most shop principals find that the best time for getting caught up on reading is nights and weekends.

Category 4—file. This is for everything that has been noted and should be kept. Place these items in a separate "File" bin or basket, the contents of which are filed every several days. If someone else does the filing and it is not obvious where the item should go, be sure to indicate by writing instructions.

Category 5—toss. This is for everything that you can quickly judge has no business value. Put it in the "round file" immediately. Don't waste time reading it out of curiosity. Your time is valuable and should not be wasted.

Managing time

There's a cliché that the more creatively talented an individual is, the less likely he or she is to be concerned with mundane daily concerns, such as an awareness of time and its importance. This would mean that as your organization grows and acquires more talent, time management will become more difficult. Fortunately, it is a premise that is largely false. Growth is not a problem if you are prepared.

There is little evidence that your employees (or you) are substantially different from the population as a whole in regard to appreciation of time. The cliché may have some validity at the artistic genius level (don't all geniuses live in a different world?), but it has little or none at the talent level most of us deal with day-to-day. The time-oblivious "artistic persona" that some individuals (ourselves sometimes included) adopt is mostly just a means of promoting a self-serving differentness, a way to stand out from the crowd. Although it is true that managing an organization of creative individuals does require somewhat different techniques (see "Being a coach, not a boss" in Chapter 18), being lax about time is not one of them. As stated at the beginning of this chapter, time in all its permutations is the very heart of our business. Here are two ways to help make sure that time is properly utilized:

Keep everyone busy. One of the distinguishing features of any service business is inconsistency. Work tends to come in spurts, which in turn often leads to the "panic busy" or "nothing to do" cycles that most of us have experienced. This problem is very costly. During the busy phases, we typically make less profit (overtime and other charges that can not be billed to the client), we jeopardize quality, and we stress employees. During the not-busy periods, we pay for salaries, benefits, and overhead not covered by billable income.

Believe it or not, these cycles can be largely controlled by an aggressive, well-directed, and consistent marketing program. Doing so requires only an interest in and commitment to marketing by the shop principal, and devoting 20 percent of yearly expenses to marketing (commissions, expenses, and materials), an expenditure that should pay a return of many times this investment. Unless you are one of the fortunate few, it is unlikely that you will be able to break the costly cycle of being either too busy or not busy enough unless you make this commitment. (For more on how to go about it, see Section Three.)

Even with a strong commitment to marketing, however, some workload variability is to be expected. To keep up employee morale, give the problem some forethought, and have tasks waiting to be tackled. These can include general updating and housekeeping, such as installing new software or software training, or reorganizing files, or the time can be used for "blue-skying" promotional ideas, or working on new promotional literature. Employees should never be idle, even after periods of intense work pressure. Whenever an employee is on the premises, he or she should be productively occupied, or you promote bad work habits. If an employee deserves "comp" time for working long, uncompensated hours, it should be time off the job, not relaxation on it.

Control meetings. Management consultants have long identified how meetings grow geometrically with the size of an organization, and they all caution managers to watch and try to control them. Many meetings are not necessary or are badly run. They are often nothing more than a time-wasting stage for posturing and role-playing. To keep meetings from getting out of control, any formal gathering of three or more employees should be authorized by the shop's principal or creative director. Every meeting should have a leader, an agenda, and a time limit. Although this rule may smack of excessive control when first announced, it is usually accepted and always very effective.

Regular staff meetings (covered in "Creative direction, shop management, and communication" earlier in this chapter) are important in shops with three or more employees. To be efficient, however, they should follow certain rules: the meeting should be at the same time every week (preferably early Monday morning); all employees should be required to attend; the meeting should be run by the shop principal (or the creative director in larger shops) around an agenda, not be a freewheeling discussion; everyone should give a status report with the emphasis on problems or items of interest or concern to others; and the whole thing should be over in an hour and a half at most. In shops with more than a dozen employees, it is more productive to have two or more staff meetings, organized around primary activities or jobs.

Cash flow and financial management

There's an old business cliché that cash flow—when money comes in and how long it stays around—is more important than profitability. Although not necessarily true, it does emphasize its importance. While every type of business has to be concerned about cash flow, it can be of particular importance to a creative business. There's an inherent unevenness in client demand, and there's no inventory to sell off to even things out when business slows down.

Three reports. There are three reports that summarize the financial position of a firm—income, balance sheet, and cash flow. Data for all three can be compiled in bookkeeping software programs.

The income statement shows cash inflow and outflow during a given period, and is typically compiled at the end of each month. It shows profitability for that period and provides comparison data (e.g., month-to-month).

The balance sheet shows a firm's assets and liabilities (what it owns and what it owes) at any given time. Its "bottom line" is the firm's net worth.

The cash flow report is a means of forecasting when income and expenses will occur. It is to businesses what a budget is to individuals. The greater a firm's obligations, the more variable its income, the less its liquidity, the more important forecasting becomes. Cash flow is the only one of the three financial reports that does not merely show history. By providing "look ahead" data it not only supplements the other two, it also adds another dimension.

However small or large, most firms will get an immediate benefit from watching their cash flow. It can save a firm money by pointing out ways to spend more efficiently and minimize the need for borrowing. Equally important, the cash flow report can help avoid financial worry and the embarrassment that accompanies coming up short and delaying bill paying.

A cash flow report can be as complex as the best accounting brains can make it. One can be set up using a spreadsheet or specialized bookkeeping programs. For most readers, however, something simple, as described here, is good enough.

Timeframe. Do your cash flow forecasting for three months, starting at the first of each month. Predicting the upcoming three months, a fiscal quarter, is important for making sure occasional expenses (e.g., quarterly tax payments) are included. The three-month timeframe also helps you see the big picture and note any developing trends. Except for losing a client, cash flow problems are rarely sudden or isolated events, they usually occur with increasing frequency over time.

To start, enter your firm's actual cash balance from the month ending. In each succeeding month, the beginning cash balance will be the last balance from the one preceding it.

The "dummy ledger" method. This is the simplest way for most creative firms to predict cash flow. It is something akin to keeping an alternate set of books. Set up, in whatever bookkeeping software your firm uses (e.g., QuickBooks), a typical ledger sheet, calling it "projected cash flow." Although your firm's actual ledger could be used for this purpose by extending it beyond the current date with prospective transactions, it is safer to keep speculation out of a firm's official books.

After entering the firm's current cash balance, enter by date each expected transaction for the next three months. The firm's actual ledger for the previous three months will provide a good guide to typical cash inflow and outflow, especially for recurring expenses.

Some of the dummy ledger's projected transactions, such as payroll expenses, can be accurately predicted. Some others, such as accounts receivable payments, will be educated guesses. And still others, such as income from projects not yet in-house but with a high probability, will be speculative. Whatever the case, enter them all. Doing so will provide a running balance of projected cash on hand on any given date. This allows you to predict upcoming "wet" and "dry" periods well in advance. The format is also easy to update with transaction information from the firm's actual ledger. After set-up, update and enter any new transactions as information becomes available, but at least every two weeks.

Reading the numbers. However they're prepared, the accuracy of cash flow forecasts is dependent on the data entered. And, like weather forecasts, the farther out in time and the more speculative the data, the greater the error margin. Nonetheless, when carefully prepared and kept up to date, a cash flow report can provide an indication of a brewing problem while there is still plenty of time to address it.

The report can also indicate when it will be safe for a principal to take an additional personal disbursement, the feasibility of employee bonuses, or when to schedule paying certain bills. Of course, a cash flow forecast is only as good as the data that's been entered. It must be comprised of honest best guesses. Otherwise, especially when excessively optimistic, cash flow reports can be more harmful than useful. For highly speculative predictions made far in advance, erring should be on the side of underestimating potential cash income and overestimating potential cash outflow.

Most important, anything that's revealed in the process must be addressed by modifying procedures, obligations, and activities, never by adjusting the entries or numbers to fit your desires.

Growth danger signs

To maintain, or increase, profitability and security as size changes, keep your eye on these key indicators.

Liquidity. Divide short-term assets (mostly receivables) by short term liabilities (mostly payables). Try to keep this number (the Quick Ratio or Liquidity Index) constant, ideally from 1.0 to 1.5.

Billed time. Compare it month-to-month from employee time sheets. Most firms average 50 percent to 75 percent. The higher the percentage, the better. Be concerned if it starts to slip.

Income per employee. Divide monthly $ (billed time only) by number of employees. Allowing for seasonal variations, be concerned if the long-term trend is down, not up.

Number and size of clients. Getting more work from fewer clients can be risky, especially if one or two account for most of the increase. It is best to keep the income from any one client to less than a quarter of your total, and to have no more than half of your income in the hands of two clients.

Salary and profitability norms

Now we're getting to the bottom line.

It's tough to say how well you and your firm should be doing or how much money you should be making. It is possible, however, to indicate some norms, how well others with a given level of talent, experience, responsibility, and investment are doing. You can then make your own comparisons and draw your own conclusions.

Viability. The best way to put how well you are doing in the proper perspective is first to define the lower limit of viability. Theoretically, there is no lower limit—you can choose to work for as little as you like, including starving for the opportunity to stay creatively active. Practically, however, the lower limit of viability is usually defined by the need to reach and sustain a critical mass. Without it you don't have a business; you have a hobby, and you can't count on staying in business.

In this equation money isn't the only thing to consider. There may be other circumstances that affect your situation (you may have a two-income family and cost of living may be particularly low in your area). Nonetheless, from a purely practical perspective, if you are an experienced professional running a multiperson firm, you should not put yourself in a position of risking so much for any less than what you could command as salary working for someone else. Given all the risks, including the lack of financial security, it probably doesn't make sense to be in business unless you can make at least this much.

Fees. Because of limited billable time and high business expenses today (notably the cost of computerization and health insurance premiums), it is very tough for a multiperson creative business to grow and not charge over $100 an hour. Most shops charge from $100 to $175 per hour, with $135 the average. There is little significant regional variation, but in rural areas average fees tend to be about 25 percent less than in metropolitan areas. Nonetheless, many of the costs of doing business remain the same and average billable hours are often less. In fields or geographic areas where $100 per hour might be inappropriate, it is extraordinarily difficult to build a business that has long-term viability.

Most shops today don't share their fee structure with clients unless asked, and some never do. The larger the shop, the less likely it is to do so. In compiling fee information, *Creative Business* has seen an interesting and major difference between the hourly fees used for estimating and those actually charged. The larger the shop (the more employees), the more likely it is that the actual hourly fee (the number of hours a job takes divided by its billing) is less than the hourly fee used for estimating. In many cases the actual hourly fee ends up 10 to 20 percent less.

Productivity per employee. The goal of every principal should be to have every employee engaged in billable activity all the time. Despite this, and the fact that most employees don't have many nonbillable responsibilities, *Creative Business* surveys show that the percentage of billable time for a typical employee is only slightly greater on average than that of a typical freelance. We have found that most shops oscillate between being extremely busy and having little or no work. The result, even when all overtime is factored in, is that the average yearly billable time of most employees is only around 50 percent of potential. Larger, better managed shops seem to do better on average: billable time per employee averages 65 percent. This increase appears to be the result of both more consistent marketing and longer employee tenure (less downtime for new employee training).

Employee turnover. Many firms with fewer than a dozen employees have a rather discouraging 15 percent turnover of creative staff each year. The younger the average age of the staff (and the lower their salaries), the more turnover there usually is. Since turnover and retraining are major causes of low employee productivity, any reasonable measures to reduce them—investing in better working conditions, offering more fringe benefits, paying better salaries, providing profit-sharing incentives—usually pay back more than they cost. This takes planning and management sophistication because the investment costs are always up front and very visible, while the productivity benefits are always long-term and less visible.

Income related to number of employees. An oft-used formula states that approximately a third of the yearly income of a creative services company should be allocated for labor, a third for general overhead expenses, and a third for miscellaneous expenses, financing costs, capital expenditures, and profit. Although never more than a general guideline, in today's environment the proper ratio for labor is probably more like 40 percent, and this figure can be useful in computing roughly how much income a shop should have given the number of its employees. Multiply the total creative payroll of the firm by 3.5 (include principals but not clerical staff). For example, if your annual creative staff payroll is $200,000, the income of your firm should be around $700,000. With normal expenses, this level of income should ensure adequate compensation and return on investment for the principals. Another measure is that total yearly income divided by total employees (noncreative staff included) should be over $120,000.

Compensation of principals. In looking at the compensation of the principals of creative services companies, *Creative Business* found the following averages in 2013.

For shops with a total staff of one to five, including principals (income up to $650,000), compensation range (salary and profit) was from $65,000 to $125,000, with the median $90,000. For shops with a total staff of five to ten (gross up to $1,000,000), compensation range was from $85,000 to $140,000, with the median $120,000. For shops with ten to twenty employees (gross up to $2,500,000), the compensation range was from $80,000 to $210,000, with the median $160,000. Median compensation for principals of shops with a staff of over twenty was upward of $180,000.

These figures compare favorably with the average compensation received by the principals of other types of small business. There is, however, one significant difference: in most other businesses the principals are also building business equity (goodwill and capital) that has market value. In other words, in addition to their yearly compensation they can also look forward to cash when they eventually sell the company. As discussed below, however, this is probably an unrealistic expectation for principals of most creative services companies. Thus, when viewed in the context of total compensation, principals of creative firms fare less well than other entrepreneurs with comparable responsibilities.

Profit norms. For sole proprietorships, partnerships, and "S" corporations, profitability and salary are synonymous. For principals of privately held "C" corporations, however, there is another success measurement—operating profit—or what is left after all expenses, including the principals' salaries, are paid.

In "C" corporations, the more the principals take out in salary compensation, the lower the firm's profit, and vice versa. In creative services firms there is often little incentive to show increased profit because the traditional reason—accumulating equity in the business—is of little relevance, and doing so may raise taxes. Thus, traditional performance measurements—net profit, profit as a percentage of sales, return on equity, etc.—are usually inappropriate.

For advertising and PR agencies, or any firm desiring to increase its net worth, profit is a good indicator. Among service businesses as a class, profit margins as a percent of sales in the range of 5 to 10 percent are currently considered good. In *Creative Business*'s experience, most creative services firms are currently earning between 3 and 6 percent.

Can your business be sold someday?

In every industry, individuals who have built a successful company from the ground up normally anticipate that their reward will be only partly in year-to-year salary. They also expect to sell their company in the future for a price that reflects its accumulated inventory, facilities, and reputation, or business goodwill. This so-called back-end compensation is often considered not only as an additional reward for business-building acumen but as a way to fund retirement as well. Although many factors affect the reality of this expectation, by and large most successful companies do acquire market value. That is, they can be sold some time, at some price, to a willing buyer.

In the creative services industry the situation is not quite as straightforward. Unlike other types of companies, we seldom invest in facilities, have no inventory and relatively few hard assets, and our products are intangible, ephemeral ideas. Despite this, marketing communications and interactive agencies do often manage to find new owners, although sale prices can be lower than for other businesses with similar sales volume. Agencies engage in highly visible activity, usually have ongoing contracts that can be easily valued, and while their product may be creativity, it is based on collective (i.e., replaceable) talent, not the inspirations of one or two irreplaceable individuals.

Unfortunately, for most design and small communications firms the situation is less positive. As many principals have eventually found out to their surprise, most have little market value. The major reason is that the firm's income is usually directly related to (or perceived to be related to) the creative talent of the principal(s), a situation often exacerbated by the personal involvement of the principal(s) in all activities. It is clear to any potential buyer that without the principal(s) there would be little business to count on, little of market value. (In business school terms, the firms have failed to "institutionalize" their businesses.) This situation is the reasons why principals should at least consider structuring businesses around a group of associates (see "The associate business model" in Chapter 16). Although this system also has its drawbacks, mainly lower

year-to-year salary potential, it does provide an expectation of building salable business equity.

Valuation basics. There are two factors that determine what any business is worth. One is the physical property it owns, or its net asset value. The other is any value beyond what it actually owns, or its intangible asset value. Each is separately calculated, then added together. While the total figure is always somewhat subjective and sale prices are always negotiated, an accurate market value will allow a buyer to earn a reasonable salary, service any debt incurred, and earn an acceptable return on invested capital (ROI).

Net asset value. This is how much money the owner(s) would receive if everything were sold off or cashed in. It is determined by adding up cash on hand, accounts receivable, savings, and the market value of computers, peripherals, desks, chairs, and so forth. Subtracted from this figure are accounts payable, debt, leases, and other financial commitments. (Any real estate owned is generally considered and negotiated separately from the business transaction.) Net asset value is the foundation of valuation because the worth of a firm (although not necessarily its market value) can never be lower than this figure. It can be easily calculated without professional help.

Intangible asset value. This is sometimes referred to as the value of "goodwill" and usually needs a professional valuator to help determine. In accounting terms, it is any value that is not otherwise attributable (that is, any factors that make the business more desirable, and thus worth more). Included in this category is its value as a going concern, firm recognition and reputation, and so forth. Since creative firms don't have inventories or machinery, most of any potential worth lies here. Note, however, that in determining worth, client relationships are generally considered to have *no* intangible asset value for small- to medium-size firms. This is because there's no telling how long clients will stick around. Their only value is in the current income they produce. Indeed, "good" clients that provide a substantial portion of a firm's income can decrease its market value because of the negative impact that would be produced should they leave.

There are several ways to assess intangible asset value, but the one often used for small- to mid-size creative firms is computed from what's termed the sellers' discretionary earnings (SDE). It is all the cash that's available for owners to take out of the business annually—salary, bonuses, dividends, financial perks, and other disbursements. This figure is then multiplied by a risk-adjusted number between 1 and 3 assigned by an experienced valuator based on transactional information and on an analysis of affecting conditions and metrics. As an example, a multiplier of 2.10 would mean that a firm with SDE calculated to be $200,000 would have an intangible asset value of $420,000. The previously determined net asset value would then be added to this figure.

In assigning an SDE multiplier, valuators typically look at several of a firm's operational conditions. As examples, these would include the type of business (firms with clients that are contractually obligated, such as agencies, are normally assigned higher multipliers than those that don't, such as design firms); the role of principals (how much of business income is directly tied to their personal relationships?); the number and strength of competitive firms (is there much competition or little?); staff talent and loyalty (will they stick around if ownership changes?); and so on.

There are also several metrics that affect the SDE multiplier. They are indicators of how well the business has been run. As examples, these would include the cash reserve—what's been available to address unexpected situations such as sudden client loss (the current cash reserve increases a firm's net asset value); the accounts receivable average—the shorter it is, the better the clients probably are; the billable time (utilization rate)— a low percentage usually indicates overstaffing or undermarketing; and the percentage of income from the largest clients—too much from too few clients makes future SDE risky to predict.

The market value. Now for the reality check: creative firms with fewer than five individuals typically have little market value. Sales volume and profits are usually too low to interest potential buyers, the business is often closely associated with the owner(s), there are few if any hard assets, and a narrow client base makes the firm susceptible should one or two people depart. So the price and risk of purchasing are high relative to the alternative of a prospect growing his or her own firm or investing elsewhere. Put in economic terms, the opportunity cost is too high.

This is mentioned here not only to avoid unrealistic expectations, but also to alert owners of younger firms to the need to grow it to a saleable size if selling out is the ultimate goal. Or if this is not their intent, to build a business profitable enough over the years that there is little need to look for an eventual sale. Even when a conventional sale is neither feasible nor desirable, treating the business like it were available to purchase is still a good strategy though. It will make most firms more profitable, as well as easier and more enjoyable to manage.

Your best possibility. While nothing above precludes attracting an outside buyer, when small-firm ownership changes do occur they are most often a transition to an employee, a partner, or merger with another firm. Someone within an organization already knows how the firm operates, so there is less possibility of internal disruption or client defections. An inside sale also eliminates the need to deal with a broker or pay a sales commission, and financing might be easier to arrange.

When the buyer is a co-owner, transferring ownership share to a partner can be simple and straightforward, assuming, that is, that there are a predetermined valuation formula and an established procedure for selling shares to other owners. Also important, sometimes crucially so, is whether there is a way to fund a buyout, such as with key person insurance. If none of this exists, at best there will be difficult negotiations, at worst a disagreeable standoff.

When there is disagreement over the value of the business, and therefore each owner's share of it, two separate valuations should be obtained along with an agreement to accept the average of the two. Each valuation should be done by a valuator selected by one of the parties. The average then becomes the figure used to begin price negotiation. (Without a buy-sell agreement's mandate, valuation becomes only an asking price, as would be the case when selling to an outsider.) When an agreement can't be reached on a price for the selling owner's share, or financing can't be arranged, he or she has the choice of either staying on or forcing the dissolution of the firm.

For single-person firms, the insider route is to sell to an employee. Because of the money involved, and the possible effect on other employees, a plan needs to be put into motion long in advance. In some situations, it should be more than a year out. Without being specific about timing, approach a senior employee who is entrepreneurial, business oriented, and ideally possesses financial resources. Say you are considering moving on and would like to know if she or he would be interested in taking over. Indicate what it will probably take financially (market value). If interest is expressed, start increasing her or his involvement in business affairs. When you are satisfied with the progress, offer a written "right of first refusal." Then, at least six months ahead of your target date, announce your intentions, open up your books completely, negotiate terms, and ask for a commitment. Offering a right of first refusal is no guarantee of a future sale, but it does have benefits. For you, it increases your chances of selling to an employee, and it helps with orderly succession planning. For the employee, it is an immediate morale booster as well as a way to provide the opportunity for future job security and income growth. When you can't find an employee interested or eligible, list the business with a broker.

Listing with a business broker. Through their contacts, brokers (sometimes called business intermediaries) provide a way to reach a large number of potential buyers anonymously. They can also help prepare a firm for sale by providing value assessments and ensuring that a sale price is realistic. And they screen and qualify buyers, minimizing having to deal with "tire-kickers." Listing is normally free. Brokers get paid by commission when a business is sold. Their commission is typically around 10 percent, sometimes with a minimum fee.

SECTION FOUR
HIGHLIGHTS

- **The key to success in any service business is good employees.** Profitability is directly tied to their quality. Set up a structure—job descriptions, career ladder, profit sharing, associate status, etc.—that rewards incentive and talent and encourages employees to stay with you.

- **The most common mistake in hiring is doing it too soon; the second most common mistake is hiring clones.** Use the 60/6 rule to evaluate a real need—you (or other employees) working up to sixty hours a week for six months or more. When you hire, look for complementary, not similar talents and skills. A variety of experience, expertise, and styles is important in a business whose product is creative problem solving.

- **Be more of a coach than a boss.** Good creative managers set shop standards, then lead mostly by inspiration, never by fear or intimidation. They delegate, practice constructive criticism, and don't micromanage.

- **Set up good record-keeping procedures.** Sloppy time tracking and bad record-keeping are among the major causes of low billable hours. Low billable hours are the cause of low profitability. Every shop with more than three employees should be organized in a way that gives primary responsibility for every job to one individual.

- **Know when and how to lay off or fire an employee.** As unpleasant as it may be, sometimes it must be done if your company is to remain profitable. Unless done right, it can cost you dearly.

- **Watch your cash flow.** In the short term, it can be more important than profitability.

- **Be aware of growth danger signs.** They are: declining liquidity, billed time, income per employee, and number and size of clients.

- **Be realistic about the market value of your business.** Unless you are careful to build long-term equity by "institutionalizing" your business, it is probably worth nothing more than the liquidation value of its hard assets.

Multiperson shop norms

Pay/Benefits (excluding sales/AE personnel)*	60% of expenses
Marketing (including sales/AE personnel)	20% of expenses
General overhead	14% of expenses
Facilities expenses	6% of expenses
When to consider layoffs	When income is less than 2.5x payroll for more than a month
Length of time to keep most records	7 years
Bookkeeping time	About two hours per week per employee
Space requirements	200 sq. ft. per employee
Work backlog	2–4 weeks
Principals' average compensation**	Less than $650M sales—$90M
	$650M to $1MM sales—$120M
	$1MM to $2.5MM sales—$160M
	More than $2.5MM sales—$180M+

*Includes disbursement (profit) to principals/shareowners.
**Median based on *Creative Business* surveys conducted in 2013.

APPENDICES

Note: You can download the sample forms in the Appendices for your own use from the Creative Business *website,*
www.creativebusiness.com/bizbook.html

APPENDIX 1.
Partnerships, Corporations, LLCs, and LLPs

As noted in Chapter 3, there are four basic forms of business structure: sole proprietorship, partnership, corporation, and limited liability companies (LLCs) and partnerships (LLPs).

If you are the only principal of your company and have not incorporated, by definition you run a sole proprietorship. No formal structure is required. However, if you are thinking about taking on a partner or incorporating your company, read what follows first. It provides in-depth assessment of the benefits and liabilities of each. Note, however, that this is intended only to provide enough information to enable you to seek more through your accountant or an attorney. It applies general procedures and benefits to the very specific needs of an individual or firm providing creative services.

If you have already taken on a partner or incorporated, read this to alert you to potential concerns and opportunities you may not be fully aware of.

Partnerships

What better arrangement than this? Two or more individuals with complementary talents, maybe friends, decide to pool resources and efforts and enter business together. Everyone should benefit. The high costs of overhead—rent, computers, copiers, etc.—will be shared, there will be someone else to bounce ideas off, a small organization will suddenly appear larger and more stable to clients, and two or more heads are better than one when looking at new business opportunities. Fewer expenses, more business, more money, more fun! What a deal. Or is it?

You may already know the answer. Too often the arrangement that absolutely glitters in January is somewhat tarnished by June and self-destructs by December.

But your situation is different. After all, your new partners are lifelong friends. Perhaps you have extraordinarily compatible personalities, or strongly complementary talents. What happens to others can't possibly happen to you. Maybe you are right. There is always the exception to the rule. However, it is far more likely that you are temporarily blinded by the very human and understandable desire to make your business more efficient and your business life a little more pleasant at the same time. In this situation, as in so many others in life, emotion becomes a much stronger force than logic.

Some sobering facts. Most partnerships break up (over 90 percent), and many break up acrimoniously. The reasons are quite simple. There are few situations in life that equal the continuous, daily stresses of running a business.

First, business activity occupies from 40 to 80 + hours every week, week in, week out; probably far more time than you spend in any other activity, including relaxing with friends and loved ones. This means there's not only a lot more time for pressures to build, but there's a lot less opportunity to dissipate them in shared enjoyment.

Business activity also directly affects prosperity and the life-style it buys. It strongly influences one's sense of self-esteem, as well as much of the world's perception of an individual. Both financially and personally, business is important activity. This makes it a minefield of psychological tensions. One of the leading causes of the high marital divorce rate is financial pressure. Not only are the pressures greater between business partners, but they come unaccompanied by any of the good stuff—sex, fun times, children, and vacations. Is it any wonder, then, that the business divorce rate should be even higher?

Then, too, entering a partnership brings with it a new set of responsibilities that many of us don't think about until maybe it's too late. Partners not only share business opportunities and profits; they also share debts and obligations, business and sometimes personal. Partners' bad business judgments become yours to live with. You have to honor partners' commitments, even if you were not a party to making them. Likewise, you could become codefendant in a suit based upon partners' actions.

A partnership is also an inherently unstable organization, which makes it more difficult to get credit or a bank loan. If a partner dies, other partners are left holding the bag with the deceased partner's debts, or perhaps fighting the partner's heirs. In fact, in some states a partnership is automatically dissolved if one of the partners gets a divorce. For these reasons and many, many more that any lawyer can document, partnerships can be risky business arrangements. This is not to say, however, you should never enter into a mutually beneficial business relationship with others. It is simply to caution you to take the time to do it right.

What a partnership is. In many sections of the country (but not all), no registration is necessary to establish a partnership. In such situations, whenever two or more sole proprietors (unincorporated individuals in business) jointly conduct activity under a common name or identity, they can be considered partners. For example, a common telephone listing, letterhead, or business cards can legally establish a partnership. The partners' names do not have to be part of the company name, nor does there have to be a written partnership agreement.

Furthermore, anyone doing business with a partnership can hold all principals equally responsible for its activities and obligations. There is also no legal distinction or separation between the personal assets of the partners and their collective business assets.

Economic advantages. In business as in life, two can live almost as cheaply as one, especially in these days of high capital equipment costs.

Capital advantages. Inadequate capitalization—not having enough money in the bank to cover unanticipated expenses—is one of the principal reasons for failure of creative businesses. Another bank account to draw upon often solves the problem.

Cash flow advantages. One or more additional contributors reduce substantially the possibility of a business running out of cash while waiting for slow-paying clients to cough up.

Skills and companionship advantages. What you lack in talent or experience, well-selected partners can contribute, and vice versa. Partners also provide a sounding board for ideas and help avoid isolation and loneliness, other common reasons for business failure.

Growth advantages. More economies, capital, cash flow, skills, and companionship provide an environment that makes growing a business easier and more fun. Also, clients are usually more comfortable working with a several-person organization than with an individual.

Simplicity advantages. For individuals with growth in mind, setting up a partnership is much less complicated and expensive than setting up a multiperson corporation. Nothing more by way of registration is usually required for a partnership than for a sole proprietorship.

Tax advantages. Partnerships offer the benefits of a multiperson structure without the tax obligations of corporations. (Bookkeeping may or may not be less complicated.) Profits and losses are simply spread among the partners according to the partnership agreement, or proportionately in the absence of one. The partners then pay individual taxes on their share. (In the event of a loss, however, the amount a partner can claim is limited.)

Choosing the partners. Everyone who has ever been in a partnership says the same thing: the way one individual complements another should be the single, overriding consideration in choosing a partner. Moreover, complements refers at least as much, perhaps more, to business skills and creative talents as it does to personalities. Indeed, many partnerships have survived when the principals ceased liking each other, but few survive a mismatch of talent, style, or experience.

Complementary strengths. Look for a partner with talents you don't have—writing, design, or programming—or one with experience you don't have—in a certain industry, running a large organization, or handling sales and marketing. Set up your partnership around co-equal, carefully defined roles that do not overlap. Trust your partner to do what he or she does best, expect him or her to trust you to do what you do best. This way you not only avoid many destructive personal conflicts, you also get the true value-added benefit of the association.

Common objectives. Although talents and work experiences should be dissimilar, business objectives and philosophy should not be. Agree on the basics: the type of business you'll build, what types of clients you'll go after, what you wish to ultimately accomplish. Then put it in writing—a business plan—so there are no misunderstandings.

Personal compatibility. Do not—repeat, do not—choose someone only because you'd like to work with him or her (friend or lover). There's no surer way to ultimately break up both a relationship and a business. However, once the two criteria above—complementary strengths and common objectives—have been met, also look carefully at how compatible your personal styles are, how well you get along. You are about to enter into the most personal relationship two or more individuals can have without sharing a pillow at night.

Setting up a partnership. Because of the personal risk involved, never enter into a partnership without knowing and trusting the other individuals involved. More important, regardless of how well you do know and trust your partners, always get the personal advice and counsel of a lawyer.

Limiting your partnership exposure is possible, but it requires legal advice. A partnership can take many forms. For example, in a limited partnership one partner can have unlimited liability, while the others have no risk beyond their specific contributions. Likewise, joint-venture agreements are possible between individuals who agree to share responsibilities and returns in a certain fashion.

If other partners believe that legally binding agreements aren't necessary between friends, insist they are, secure in the knowledge that you are the wisest member of the partnership. If potential partners find an agreement offensive or balk at signing it, forget the partnership. On the other hand, if you find your partners agreeable to or insisting on such a document, be thankful you are about to go into business with people as smart as you.

An important component of the agreement should be partnership insurance, a combination of words spelling out what happens in the case of death or disability of a partner, and life and disability insurance policies. The latter will ensure that each partner's portion of the business is automatically paid off with a specified lump sum. An optional addition (recommended) can also provide protection from suits arising from the actions of partners. You can expect a good lawyer to charge several hundred dollars for a partnership agreement, depending on its complexity and the number of partners.

Partnership alternatives. A partnership should not be confused with an arrangement in which two or more colleagues get together and incorporate an organization in which each owns shares. An incorporated or limited liability (LLC) company can be identified by its name—i.e., Jones & Jones, Inc. (or Ltd., LLC, or Corp.). Without such public identification (e.g., Jones & Associates, or Jones & Jones), a company is assumed to be a sole proprietorship or a partnership, and is not afforded the legal protections of a corporation, or limited liability company.

A partnership also should not be confused with a working relationship in which individuals share space, facilities, and costs but work independently and don't do business under a common name. If two individuals jointly pitch a client, even two who work out of a common office, a partnership does not exist unless they represent themselves as being in business together. In other words, if both individuals clearly represent separate companies, as evidenced by different company names, business cards, and billing procedures, they operate independently in the eyes of the law and there is no partnership liability.

Obviously, the advantage of this method of operation is avoiding the risks of a partnership, while still being able to share some expenses and working arrangements. There is a downside, though. Income can't go into one account and expenses be paid from it, with all parties sharing proportionately in what remains. Your slow periods can't be offset by a partner's busy periods and vice versa. Each of the individuals in this loose association must remain responsible for his or her own assets and liabilities.

Facilities and materials that are shared must also be the responsibility of one individual who charges rent as a way of apportioning costs. Although these payments are tax-deductible business expenses to individuals paying, they are taxable income to the individual receiving them. (They can be offset, however, by the expenses incurred.) Finally, a team arrangement won't help gain entry to those clients who want to do business with a single, larger organization. From a client's perspective, dealing with individuals in a team is little different from dealing with individual freelancers who are not affiliated.

If you wish to work with others on a specific, large project only, the best way to do so is to form a joint venture or limited liability partnership (LLP) (see below). Although legally a partnership, an agreement can be drawn (a necessary safeguard) that limits an individual's or company's responsibilities to the single project and activity.

The five ingredients of partnership success. Don't consider a partnership unless these conditions exist:

1. There is a clear business (not emotional) reason; a mutual benefit achievable no better way.
2. The partners share a well-defined business strategy and long-term objectives.
3. The partners have different, complementary creative talents and business skills.
4. The partners have separate, clearly defined responsibilities that do not overlap.
5. The partners have compatible personalities and operating styles.

The ten essentials of a partnership agreement. If you form a partnership, draw up an agreement that covers these issues:

1. The name and purpose (the business) and the date of its effectiveness and termination.
2. The capital—money, services, supplies, or equipment—contributed by each partner.
3. How much time each partner will devote and what his or her specific functions will be.
4. How profits/losses are to be shared (usually related to capital and time devoted to the business).
5. The salaries, or rights to withdraw capital, allowed each partner and the schedule for doing so.
6. The authority of each partner—making commitments, hiring/firing employees, signing checks.

7. Who has primary responsibility for accounting and the preparation of financial documents.

8. Terms for terminating the partnership equitably.

9. How the assets or liabilities of the partnership will be distributed upon dissolution.

10. A provision for continuing the business upon the death or incapacity of a partner.

Incorporation

Forming a corporation with one or more partners, as opposed to entering into a partnership, makes it possible to have a shared-responsibility business arrangement without risk beyond the investment of the partners. In addition, because the operations of the corporation and the ownership of its assets are spelled out, dissolving or later changing the structure (as in a business divorce) are relatively straightforward. The major disadvantage of setting up a corporation is cost and additional taxes and bookkeeping. Before laying out the procedures, costs, and benefits of incorporation, it is first appropriate to consider when and why, or why not, it may make good sense for your business. Consider the following three issues:

To what extent does your business involve financial liability? For some individuals, doing business results in significant personal exposure; for some, virtually none. If you're in the former category, incorporation is essential. If not, it may be an expense that is not necessary. For example, if you're a designer who runs up large printing bills, relying upon prompt client payment to cover them, not to incorporate to limit your personal responsibility would be foolish. On the other hand, if you're billing mostly for time, incorporating to protect yourself from financial risk is not necessary. (Incorporation does not protect an individual against prosecution for any criminal activity or negligence of his or her company.)

What are the benefits and how do they weigh against the cost of incorporation—initial and ongoing? Some clients consider incorporated companies to be more reliable. Corporations get additional tax breaks, are less likely to have their records scrutinized by the IRS, and sometimes qualify for corporate discounts from suppliers. These benefits can directly add several hundred dollars yearly to the bottom line, but, like all good things in life, they come at a price. In most states, the one-time cost of incorporation, using a local lawyer, will run about $1,000, or you can do most of it yourself for less, say $250 or so, but you'll have to follow instructions carefully, and spend some time. More significant are such ongoing costs as corporate taxes (average $250 yearly for a small company) and increased bookkeeping and accounting costs (average $250 yearly for a small company).

Will continuity of life for your business be an asset or a liability? Most corporations are chartered for perpetual existence or for a very long period of time. The death, disability, or withdrawal of a shareowner, even one owning 100 percent of the shares, does not terminate it. This is a benefit if you wish to build up the value of a company, either through investments or business goodwill, and sell it at some time in the future. On the other hand, corporate obligations (primarily taxes) continue to accrue regardless of the existence of the original shareholder(s). In a worst-case scenario, the sole shareholder dies and his or her heirs find out years later they have inherited a whopping corporate tax bill that is continuing to grow.

Specific corporate advantages. The main advantages of incorporating are:

1. Individual financial liability is limited to the amount of money invested.

2. Corporate financial records are required to be separate from personal financial records, so there is less likelihood of problems arising from the mixing of personal and company income and expenses.

3. Because a corporation is perceived as being in business for the long term, a company so identified is often viewed by clients as being more substantial and stable.

4. Employee medical/dental/disability insurance premiums, as well as reimbursement for uncovered medical expenses and drugs, are tax-deductible business expenses ("C" corporations only). To qualify, the benefit must be offered to all employees (not just the officers), and a Medical Reimbursement Plan must be adopted by the board of directors.

5. Employee child care costs can be tax-deductible business expenses if set up as a corporate benefit available to all employees. (See your accountant for details.)

6. The employer portion (50 percent) of the federal social security tax (FICA) is a tax-deductible business expense.

7. Employee premiums for group term life insurance on policies up to $50,000 are tax-deductible expenses.

8. Business expenses—gifts, travel, entertainment, etc.—are much less likely to be questioned by the IRS.

9. Out-of-pocket, reimbursable expenses of employees, even if they are also the corporation's shareowners, are subject to less scrutiny by the IRS than are those reported by sole proprietors.

10. There is less likelihood of the IRS conducting an audit looking for unreported, taxable income. By IRS estimates, sole proprietors account for most unreported income.

11. Corporate directors are entitled to at least one tax-deductible trip a year to attend the firm's annual business meeting. The meeting can be scheduled at any domestic location, including expensive distant resorts in high season. At least four hours of each day must be devoted to business contemplation or discussion.

12. Reasonable expenses (e.g., meals and travel) incurred in conjunction with occasional board of directors meetings are tax-deductible business expenses.

13. A shareowner may borrow up to $10,000 from his or her corporation at no interest for several years. No tax is due on this disbursement, but it must be formally structured as a loan. (See your accountant for details.)

14. Commercial loans for such items as automobiles, computers, and office furniture never look to the IRS like personal loans, as they may when made to an individual. This can be important, since only the interest on commercial loans is currently tax deductible.

15. Because there is a procedure for transferring shares, changing ownership of the corporation, or a portion of it, can be easily arranged.

16. Additional shares of stock in the corporation can be issued and sold if necessary to raise expansion capital.

17. Clients do not have to provide 1099s to the IRS on payments they make to incorporated freelances, agencies, and studios. Although the income must still be reported, there is no IRS record, as there is with payments made to sole proprietors or partnerships.

Specific corporate disadvantages. The main disadvantages to incorporating are:

1. Unless your organization is involved in activities specifically involving financial risk and liability—purchasing expensive printing, doing product design, etc.—incorporating is appropriate only if the long-term tax savings outweigh the initial and ongoing costs.

2. Although the needs of every company and its owners are different,

the costs of incorporation often outweigh the financial (not liability) benefits unless net taxable income averages more than $50,000.

3. A corporation must prepare and file separate federal and state tax returns, an additional accounting cost that typically runs a couple hundred dollars.

4. A regular "C" corporation (but not an "S" corporation) must pay federal (and usually state) income tax on its profits. A corporation may reduce these taxes by minimizing profits through such means as giving high salaries and fringe benefits to its officers (see below). If it never shows a profit, however, its legitimacy may be questioned by the IRS.

5. Shareowner/employees of a "C" corporation (but not an "S" corporation) run the risk of double taxation—once on the corporation's profits, again if they take out the profits as stock dividends. Although this can be minimized by paying high salaries and fringe benefits to increase expenses and reduce profits (see above), it is difficult to avoid totally if the corporation becomes very profitable.

6. A corporation must file a report and pay a licensing fee (sometimes called a franchising tax) annually to the state in which it is chartered. Costs vary, from as little as $5 annually to more than $300.

7. A corporation must be registered and pay taxes and fees in every state in which it has an office. Foreign (out-of-state) corporate taxes and fees average about $250 per state. If a foreign corporation is found to be operating illegally, it may be required to pay substantial penalties and discontinue doing business in that state. In addition, shareholders, directors, or officers may be open to personal liability.

8. Corporate status does not limit personal financial liability in situations where a creditor insists upon a personal guarantee before lending money or extending credit. Personal guarantees (cosigning) have now become standard procedure for most institutions lending to small corporations.

9. Because a corporation has a life separate from that of its founders and/or shareowners, it will continue to accrue obligations, regardless of their future activity. A forgotten corporation can run up a sizeable tax bill in a short period. It is important, therefore, that arrangements are made to disincorporate the organization when the corporate structure is no longer useful.

10. An advantage of the corporate structure in other industries—the ability to build financial equity and valuable goodwill with the ultimate objective of selling the corporation—is limited in creative firms due to

the personal nature of the business. Incorporated or not, it is very difficult to accumulate transferrable market value in a creative business.

11. Owners of a "C" corporation must be careful not to define the business of the corporation as performing arts or consulting. To do so may classify it as a personal service corporation, which, in turn, may subject it to higher tax rates and restrictive rules. (See your accountant for details.)

12. Corporations must withhold social security tax for all employees; sole proprietors do not have to do so for any of their children (under 18) whom they employ. This reduces the benefits of hiring your children for income-shifting purposes.

How to go about it. If you decide to incorporate, whether it is better to hire a lawyer or do it yourself is a source of much debate. With a lawyer you probably can be assured that everything will be done the way it should be, and it will take much less of your time. On the other hand, it is possible to incorporate yourself if you're careful. And by so doing you can save several hundred dollars. Everything below applies to either route.

Although deciding whether to seek the services of a lawyer is a personal decision, seeking accounting advice should not be. Setting up a corporation has many long-term business and personal ramifications. You need an accountant familiar with your financial history and goals. Up-front accounting advice is a relatively small (a few hundred dollars), tax-deductible expense that will save many times its cost in reduced organizational expenses, taxes, and legal fees.

Be informed. The very first thing you must know about incorporation is that the procedures, structures, and fees vary from state to state. Therefore, being knowledgeable requires a little education. Fortunately, the state in which a company is incorporated doesn't affect its legal or federal tax status or limit its right to do business in other states. A little knowledge also can be economically beneficial. Generally, it is best to incorporate in the state in which you plan to do business. The reasons are twofold. 1) You avoid the necessity of filing extra forms and paying higher taxes as a foreign (out-of-state) corporation. 2) If the services of a lawyer are required in the future, he or she will be familiar with relevant corporate law. If you are chartered out of state, the lawyer probably will have to call in additional (expensive) counsel.

To get information on in-state incorporation, contact the Secretary of State, Corporation Division, in your state capital. Pamphlets, usually free, sometimes for a nominal charge, explain the regulations and procedure.

You may find that setting up a corporation in your state involves requirements, such as having several incorporators, directors, and officers, that make it expensive, difficult, or impossible for you. In such cases, it will pay you to examine the alternative—incorporating in a neighboring state, or in one of the two tax haven states, Delaware or Nevada. If so, write for information or look them up on the web. (Two useful addresses: Delaware Secretary of State, Dover, DE 19901; Nevada Secretary of State, Carson City, NV 89701.) If you choose to incorporate in a state where your business does not have an address, you will need a local registered agent to give you one, forward your corporate mail, and deal with local authorities. For this, the charge is from $75 to $150 annually. Most will also set up the corporation for fees of about $200. You can get a list of registered agents from the state's Secretary of State, or look under the category of registered agents in the state over the internet.

Reserve a name. The state in which you plan to incorporate must clear the name you choose for your corporation. This avoids duplication and possible public deception. The name normally must include one of the following words: corporation, incorporated, or limited, or any of their abbreviations. Given the great number of corporations in any state, and the similarity of many names, it is best to prepare a list of five or so alternatives and have them checked before going any further. Checking and reserving names is normally done by the Corporation Division of the Secretary of States office for a fee of $5 to $25. Write or call them for information. Names can be reserved from 30 days to one year, depending upon the state.

Obtain an Employer Identification Number (EIN). Sometimes called a Federal ID number (FID), this is how the IRS keeps track of company taxpayers, much as it uses social security numbers for tracking individual taxpayers. A new EIN registering the corporation must be obtained whether or not you already have one. Banks will not open a corporate account without a corporate EIN. The easiest way to obtain an EIN is over the phone through the IRSs TELE-TIN (telephone taxpayer identification number) service. Call your regional IRS service center (the same place you send your tax forms each year) and ask for the telephone number for the TELE-TIN service, or take the traditional route by filling out IRS Form SS-4 and sending it to your region's IRS service center. This should take about four weeks.

File a Certificate of Incorporation. This is the procedure by which you actually apply to the state for corporate status. Every state has slightly different procedures, but most are straightforward and involve filling out a single, albeit lengthy, form. Once the designated state official certifies that the certificate of incorporation contains the required information and has been properly executed, that your activities will be legal, and that the name has not been registered by another corporation, your corporation's charter is issued.

When you fill out the paperwork, you have to make many decisions, but the following are particularly important. First is the number of shares of stock and their distribution. It probably is in your interest to authorize relatively few shares: 200–500 are enough to give a small corporation flexibility, but not so many as to subject it to unnecessary taxes. (Many states charge a filing fee and yearly taxes based upon the number of shares.) Don't issue all the shares. Keep 25 to 50 percent of them within the corporation (unissued) as a reserve for the future. This will allow you to issue shares later (to take on partners or to give to your children) without amending the corporate charter. A majority of the shares issued should be in your name. If you are already in business and are transferring assets from a sole proprietorship into the corporation (desks, computers, telephones, etc.), make sure at least 80 percent of the shares issued are in your name. If they are not, you may be taxed on the value of the assets you transfer. (If you are setting up a corporation with several co-equal participants, follow the recommendation of your accountant.)

Finally, make the corporate charter as broad as possible. It is better to charter "for any legal business," than "for internet communication services" or "graphic design." In the former case you probably can use the corporation to enter other businesses in the future if opportunities present themselves. In the latter cases, you probably can't.

Get a corporate kit. A corporate kit, which you can obtain from any legal stationer for $50 or less, contains a couple dozen stock certificates (each can be assigned a value of many shares), a bylaws form, a corporate seal (if required in your state), and a looseleaf booklet to keep shareowner records and the minutes of director meetings.

Write the bylaws and hold an organizational meeting. Bylaws are the rules under which a corporation operates. The bylaws form supplied in the corporate kit tells you what must be specified. Typically: offices, board of directors, officers, shareowners, shareowner meetings, and such general matters as fiscal year, who can sign checks, etc. The organizational meeting can be as formal or as informal as you like—including a family meeting after dinner—but minutes of the meeting should be recorded and an official notice sent to the state that all its requirements have been met. In fact, in some states a corporation isn't legal until a report of the organizational meeting has been filed.

Decide on "S" or "C" status. Immediately after incorporating, decide whether your new corporation will adopt the Subchapter "S" form for tax-paying purposes. If you choose Subchapter "S" status, you must inform the IRS no later than the fifteenth day of the third month of the corporation's life. There are no exceptions. If you do not choose to do so, or simply forget to file, your organization will automatically be classified as a Subchapter "C" corporation.

The distinction between Subchapter "S" and Subchapter "C" corporations is simple but has significant tax implications. In "S" corporations, all corporate profits are taxed at personal tax rates. There is no possibility of a separate tax on corporate profits. Protection from personal liability is the same as with a "C" corporation. In essence, an "S" corporation treats you as a sole proprietorship in terms of income, but as a corporation in terms of liability protection. There are some eligibility restrictions for forming an "S" corporation, but they are not normally a problem for a small firm.

Most freelances and many principals of small creative companies choose the "S" status. It can be especially beneficial when you start out because it allows the corporations losses to offset other income, including that of a wage-earning spouse. It is also simpler, and permits taking out all the corporations profits each year without worrying about profit buildup or double taxation. Many larger organizations opt for the Subchapter "C" status because it offers a growing firm additional tax advantages and ways to build financial equity.

Whichever form you choose initially, you should ask your accountant to review it periodically. Changing business priorities often make a corporate status change beneficial. It is relatively easy to elect and to terminate a Subchapter "S" status, but there is normally a five-year waiting period between terminating and reelecting Subchapter "S" status.

"S" corporation advantages. The advantages of an "S" corporation are:

1. Corporate losses can usually be used to offset (tax-shelter) personal income received from other sources. With "C" corporations, any losses can only be carried forward to offset future corporate profits.

2. There are no salary limitations ("C" corporations salaries, which are tax-deductible expenses, cannot exceed reasonable compensation). This could be important for the principals of highly profitable organizations.

3. There is no chance of double taxation. Income is taxed at personal tax rates. In "C" corporations, profits are taxed once at the corporate level and again if distributed as dividends to shareowners.

4. Since there is little buildup of corporate profit, future liquidation is simple.

"C" corporation advantages. The advantages of a "C" corporation are:

1. All medical and disability insurance premiums can be tax-deductible business expenses.
2. Premiums on up to $50,000 of life insurance are tax-deductible business expenses.
3. Shareholders are permitted to borrow from corporate pension plans.
4. It is possible to build equity in the corporation, which may give it value for future sale.
5. You can have an unlimited number of shareholders ("S" corporations are limited to 35). If you wish to sell stock in the future, or provide it to employees, it may pay to charter as a "C" corporation.
6. Some states only recognize "C" corporation status. When this is the case, having an "S" corporation for federal tax purposes may cause problems.

Corporate pitfalls. As explained previously, incorporation is a business strategy best undertaken only when it has long-term legal, financial, and marketing benefits. Equally important, a company must take care not to operate in any way that could invalidate its new corporate status. The founders of many small corporations have found out too late that their actions, or lack of them, destroyed the corporate protection and advantages they thought they had. To have and maintain corporate benefits, the corporation must operate as such at all times. In short, simply chartering a corporation does not automatically confer corporate benefits.

A typical problem is that at some future time the IRS disallows a tax benefit on the grounds that the organization is sham corporation—that is, one set up not for legitimate business purposes but only for illegitimate tax avoidance—or, in the process of litigation affected by corporate status, the other party's lawyers claim that individual shareowners should be held personally liable for the corporation's actions because it isn't legitimate—a process often referred to as "piercing the corporate veil."

In these cases the "proof" is usually that the records and activities of the corporation are either not in keeping with the law or with common, everyday business practices. When such a case is made and upheld by the courts, the corporation loses. The moral is: Be sure to run your incorporated business as one.

Running a corporation properly requires, but is not necessarily limited to: ensuring that the corporate identification (incorporated, limited, corporation, or their abbreviations) always appears as part of the company name; holding and documenting regular shareholder and board of director meetings; keeping appropriate corporate records; abiding by the corporate bylaws, keeping personal and corporate affairs separate (not "commingling" them); never treating corporate property as personal possessions; paying annual state fees; filing state and federal corporate returns; and paying tax obligations on time.

Limited liability companies and partnerships

Limited liability companies (LLCs). This legal structure is becoming increasingly popular. Many small firms today go this route because it offers financial liability protection equal to "C" or "S" corporations in most cases, but is less costly to set up. Perhaps more important, reporting obligations, fees, and taxes are usually considerably less. The major drawback is that LLC case law is not as highly developed as corporate case law. Although this is usually not significant for smaller firms working within a state, it can be for larger firms with more legal exposure, especially out of state.

Whether an LLC is a viable alternative to incorporation can only be answered by viewing a firm's activities, potential liabilities, and where it does business. Check with your accountant about the procedures and cost for establishing an LLC within your state, and the extent of protection that it will provide.

Limited liability partnerships (LLPs). This is often a preferable option to a general partnership for sole proprietors and existing partnerships who wish to share ownership. LLPs are governed by state laws that vary, but some generalizations can be made. They are similar to general partnerships in that they provide flexibility in structuring and management. There are also specific tax advantages that can make them preferable for estate planning purposes, especially when other family members are involved as partners. Most important is the limitation of liability they offer to all but one individual: the general partner. All others, the limited partners, have no financial liability beyond that of their investment, so sharing ownership poses no great financial risk for them. The general partner does incur all the business risks, but he or she has no liability for nonbusiness actions of the limited partners.

LLPs have to be formally registered and adhere to the specific laws of the state in which they are registered. This usually requires attorney and registration fees, and some additional ongoing reporting expenses. There may also be restrictions on operating procedures. For firms that are not incorporated or LLCs, and, for tax or other reasons, prefer not to become one, LLPs can be a good means of ownership sharing.

APPENDIX 2.
Sample Business
Plans

Basic internal plan

Business Plan
Independent Associates
December 31, 0000

Overall objective: Strengthen the business and my financial independence, now and in the future

1. *Reorient the business mix.* Reduce dependence on agency overflow work and small retailer ads; get more collateral and website updating projects from mid-size corporate clients.

   a) Build a corporate mailing/contact list with 25 new names and e-mail addresses each month; at least 250 by year-end.

   b) Write as many introductory letters as often as necessary to average at least one corporate portfolio showing each week.

   c) Join BPAA and local Ad & Sales Club to meet and network with corporate personnel.

   d) Develop, post, and publicize a "communications insights" blog on my website.

Expect that agency overflow and retailer projects, 75% of volume presently, will drop to 60% by mid-year and 40% by year end (corporate work will be 60%).

2. *Grow net income from $70,000 to $85,000.*

   a) Raise current billing rate of $110 per hour to $125 for all new clients.

   b) Improve billing practices to ensure that all time is billed.

Expect 20% ($17,000) of yearly net income by April 30, 40% ($34,000) by June 30; 75% ($63,750) by September 30. Monthly billable efficiency should be at least 50% by mid-year, and 55% by year-end.

3. *Establish a retirement/long-term savings plan.*

   a) Talk to my accountant about diverting income into a tax-advantaged savings plan so as to allow retirement by age 60.

Expect the plan to be set up, and to begin making contributions by June 30.

Formal business plan

A Plan for
the Growth of
Dedicated Associates

Prepard for:
Arnold Moneytree
Citizens Trust Company
Big Sky, Montana

Dedicated Associates, Inc.
1784 Big Sky Blvd.
Big Sky, Montana 00000
(000) 000-0000
January 00, 0000

Formal business plan, continued

Summary

Dedicated Associates, Inc. provides graphic design and marketing communications services.

The firm has six full-time employees in addition to the full-time participation of its two principals.

Gross income in 0000 was $0,000,000.

The Company is a Montana corporation chartered in October, 0000, and has been operating without interruption since. Fifty-one percent of the Company's outstanding stock is held by Sally J. Dedicated; 49% by Joseph H. Dedicated.

This plan outlines the business activities, projections, and opportunities for Dedicated Associates, and details the need for additional capital in 0000 to finance growth.

Principals

Dedicated Associates was founded by Mr. and Ms. Dedicated shortly after their marriage in 0000. Their objective was to utilize the skills they had developed in New York City to found a stable business offering Montana companies and organizations the same high-level design and marketing communication services traditionally associated only with larger metropolitan areas.

Prior to founding Dedicated Associates, Ms. Dedicated was a Senior Account Executive and Group Vice President at Dernbach, Dones & Dale advertising, where she worked primarily on the advertising campaigns of Freedom Equity Fund, Big Pit Copper Products, and Machismo Trucks. She began her career as a writer in the Chicago advertising agencies of Hand, Triangle & Gelding. In her ten years at that firm she worked on a variety of client communications problems. She is a graduate of Oxford University.

Mr. Dedicated was a Senior Designer and Vice President of Imperious Design where he worked with such clients as National Accounting Machines, Regional Airlines, Analog Computers, and Gamble and Doctor. Before joining Imperious Design he worked for nearly ten years in various design capacities for several well-known New York graphic design firms. He is a graduate of the Montana Academy of Design.

(2)

Facilities and Staff

Dedicated Associates occupies 2,600 square feet of office space in the Cattleman's Bank Building. The space is leased through March 0000, and is adequate for the growth projected.

The firm owns miscellaneous office furniture and equipment valued at approximately $00,000, including several Macintosh Computers, software, and peripheral devices with current market value of over $00,000. All equipment is appropriate for the growth projected, but will need to be supplemented.

Dedicated's staff consists of eight individuals with a variety of appropriate talents, experiences, and functions. No additional staffing is projected in the short-term.

Freelance talent—writers, illustrators, and photographers—is also contracted as business volume requires.

Services Provided

Dedicated Associate's business is offering graphic design and marketing communications services. We consult on and conceive, design, and produce corporate identity (branding) programs, Internet sites, trade show exhibits, packaging, signs, booklets, annual reports, and print advertising.

We are among the top five firms in Montana providing these services, and have clients throughout the region, including the State of Montana. We are the recipients of many state and national awards for excellence. We also enjoy a reputation as being an innovation leader, and have received national recognition for some of our operating procedures.

Several of the services we offer to our clients, such as printing, direct mailing, and sophisticated software programming, are contracted out to specialty suppliers.

(3)

The Market

The traditional market for graphic design and marketing communications services has been expanding for decades as more organizations have recognized the necessity of having well-designed and persuasive communications in today's business environment. This expansion has been considerably accelerated in the past decade by the expansion of new, computer-driven technologies, especially the Internet.

The overall growth of the market, and particularly the growth made possible by computer-driven technologies, has enabled our firm to prosper in Montana. The "New York" quality we can bring to our clients at Montana prices simply would not have been possible a decade ago.

Now the continued development of technology makes it possible for us to enter a new, dynamic, and profitable market segment.

Opportunity

Our new opportunity is providing one-stop, full-capability Internet (Web) site preparation and hosting for the Big Sky market.

There is no other firm offering this capability; the closest competitor is in Helena, nearly 100 miles away. By providing it, we will be able to offer local convenience when helping clients assess their needs, local service addressing any problems that arise, and the quality control that comes only from local site preparation and hosting. We anticipate success in marketing this service to the many smaller firms needing Internet site preparation and hosting that have recently located in the Big Sky area.

Our projections indicate that we can handle this expansion with no increase in facilities or staff, and only a moderate and manageable increase in equipment.

As the financial projections indicate, we believe this opportunity will be a highly profitable market extension. We also believe it is a natural and timely one. We are unique in having a combination of staff, equipment, experience, and clients that will allow us to establish a primary position in a still-developing technology before there is serious competition in our market.

(4)

Financial Need

To supplement our present Internet site preparation capabilities with hosting services it will be necessary to obtain a more powerful computer server, high speed and high capacity telecom lines, and additional software programs. The total outlay is approximately $00,000 as outlined below:

Software	
(type and description here)	$ 000
High speed/high capacity telecom lines	
(type and description here)	$ 000
Computer server	
(model number and description here)	00,000
Total	$ 00,000

We wish to finance the purchase of this capability with a five-year loan.

(5)

Formal business plan, continued

Additional Profit Projection

The additional profit projection upon which the loan is requested is:

Monthly income	
Present (12-month, 0000 average)	$00,000
Additional Web site preparation	
0 new sites at $00,000 each	0,000
New Web site hosting	
00 clients at $000 each	0,000
Projected future income	$00,000

Monthly expenses	
Present labor (December 0000)	$ 0,000
Present overhead (12-month, 2006 average)	0,000
Loan payment and interest***	000
Projected costs	$00,000
Projected future profit	$ 0,000
Profit as a percent of additional sales	00%

Following pages provide further detail on the financial condition of Dedicated Associates.

Corporate and the owners' individual tax returns are attached, along with an Annual Statement of Financial Condition, prepared by Barney & Smith, CPAs.

***Assumes a five-year note for $00,000 @ x.x% interest.

(6)

P&L Statement
December 31st, 0000

Revenues

Gross Sales	$1,076,343
Less Pass-Through Income (Printing, Media etc.)	—$ 260,000
Non-Sale Revenues (Interest, etc.)	$ 780
Other	$ 1,444
Agency Gross Income (AGI or Net Revenue)	$ 818,567

Operating Expenses

Salaries/Benefits	$ 502,000
Payroll Taxes	$ 30,068
Insurance	$ 3,050
Professional Services (Legal/Accounting, etc.)	$ 5,200
Facilities, Utilities, Maintenance, RE Taxes	$ 60,000
Equipment Leasing, Repairs, & Maintenance	$ 61,000
Telephone, Internet & Communications	$ 7,500
Office Supplies, Shipping & Postage	$ 9,000
Depreciation & Amortization	$ 43,000
Promotion (Materials, Advertising, etc.)	$ 18,000
Travel & Entertainment	$ 7,200
Donations	$ 1,000
Pension Contributions	$ 10,200
Other	$ 1,455
Total Operating Expense	$ 758,673

Net Profit Before Corporate Taxes	$ 59,894

(7)

Balance Sheet
December 31, 0000

Assets—Short-Term or Current

Checking Account	$ 60,031
Savings/Investments	$ 6,434
Accounts Receivable	$139,048
Loans Receivable	$ 2,214
Work Completed But Not Billed	$ 38,345
Tax Escrow	$ 19,961
Prepaid Expenses	$ 23,294
Total Short-Term	$289,327

Assets—Long Term or Fixed

Equipment & Facilities (Fair Market Value)	$ 33,765
Less Accumulated Depreciation	—$ 28,612
Total Long-Term	$ 5,153

Total Assets	$294,480

Liabilities—Short-Term or Current

Accounts Payable	$ 120,837
Not-Yet Billed Payables	$ 21,000
Salaries Due	$ 62,750
Taxes due	$ 30,103
Loan/Lease Payments Due Within One Year	$ 12,200
Total Short-Term	$246,890

Liabilities—Long-Term

Loan/Lease Obligations Beyond One Year	$ 9,700
Total Long-Term	$ 9,700

Total Liabilities (Debt)	$256,590
Owner's Equity	$ 37,890
Total Liabilities & Owner's Equity	$294,480

(8)

(Tax returns and other financial information should be attached here as appropriate.)

APPENDIX 3.
Samples and
Forms

Biographical sketch

(print on letterhead)

Biographical Sketch
Joseph J. Freelance

Joseph J. Freelance is a principal in the firm of Freelance Associates, a Bozeman, Montana graphic design firm that specializes in corporate communications projects. Representative clients of Freelance Associates include: (name), (name), (name), (name), (name), and (name). Projects include advertisements, annual reports, company brochures, product sales literature, package design, Web-site design, and corporate identification.

Prior to founding Freelance Associates in 1993, Mr. Freelance was Senior Art Director at Big Sky Advertising where he worked primarily on the (name) and (name) accounts. Previously, Mr. Freelance worked for the Billings, Montana, advertising agency of Blank/Blank/Blank, as well as several smaller agencies. Corporate experience includes five years as graphic designer on the staff of Big Pit Copper, Incorporated.

Mr. Freelance's marketing communications experience covers a range from consumer expendables to financial services, with particularly strong expertise in natural resources.

Mr. Freelance's work has been cited for excellence by the following: Advertising Club of Bozeman (Bozie Awards); Montana Society of Advertising Arts (Monty Awards); The Greater Bozeman Chamber of Commerce (Booster Recognition); and Montana Roadways and Business Montana magazines.

Mr. Freelance is a 1987 graduate of the Inspired Institute of Design, Cuthank, Montana, where he is also currently Adjunct Professor of Advertising Art.

He is married, has two children and resides in suburban Deep Glen, Montana.

Working description

How We Work Together

Thank you for your consideration. We know that working with an organization such as ours for the first time often prompts a few questions. Sometimes more than a few concerns, too. How successful will we be in interpreting your needs? How can we do it most *effectively*? How can we do it most *efficiently*? How much will it cost?

Our Charges
Like all service organizations our invoices are based on the time we invest in a project. Currently we bill our time at $000 per hour, about 10% under what other firms of our quality and experience charge. Project costs range from a low of a couple thousand dollars up to tens of thousands, depending on our clients' needs and budgets. We always provide a detailed proposal and estimate for approval before starting. We adhere to our estimates unless project specifications change.

Laying The Foundation
The first thing we do after being assigned a project is schedule information-gathering meetings between our creative team and your key staff. We are interested not only in scheduling, budget and job specifications, but also in your preferences, target audience, and objectives. And, of course, we will want to know all the user features and benefits of the product.

Although this process is somewhat time-consuming (we don't like meetings any more than you do), it is also crucially important. It will help you sharpen your focus and objectives, and it will help us ensure that what we produce is not only creatively excellent, but strategically targeted.

Developing The Right Ideas
Despite popular misconceptions, good creative work doesn't often come in a flash of inspiration; usually it comes from lots of trial and error. This is why we also need to take the time to consider several approaches (concepts), work them through, try them out. Then revise them. In addition, there are usually some practical and functional ends we need to tie up before submitting our ideas—subcontractor availability, printing estimates, scheduling requirements, etc.

All this, plus the need to schedule our workflow in a businesslike fashion, means that we normally ask for up to two weeks, depending on the job's complexity, before we submit our rough approaches (concepts) for your review. Of course, if you have a rush project or deadline pressure we adjust our workflow and timing accordingly.

It is our experience that it is best if we first present our rough concepts to your project manager and just one or two others. This ensures that we all stay focused on the problem and are not distracted by too many personal opinions. Our rough concepts consist of (describe what is normally shown). They are adequate to convey what we believe is the best approach to take, taking into consideration your budget, schedule, objectives, and preferences. On the other hand, they are not so well-developed as to have wasted time and effort if we need a course correction.

After presenting, we'll ask for comments. The more objective and specific you can be, the better we will be able to respond. Comments are our input for revising the rough concepts into a finished one. Revision normally takes us about a week, and we schedule a second presentation shortly thereafter.

From the input at this second presentation meeting further minor refinements are made as necessary. We also finalize the production timetable, and the scheduling of additional services such as (photography) (illustration).

Ensuring Your Satisfaction
We recommend the finished (layout) (copy) (illustration) be routed to the appropriate decision makers for fact and detail checking only, reserving stylistic and subjective decisions to your project manager. To avoid costly confusion, it is also important that all communication with us come from the project manager.

During the course of the project we keep your project manager informed of our progress. Activities that will affect the schedule or budget are identified in writing. Our goal is to keep your project moving ahead quickly, smoothly, and cost-effectively, to make sure that we'll produce even better results than you hired us for.

Sincerely,

(name)
Principal, (firm)

Bill of rights statement

A Bill Of Rights
For Creative Suppliers and Their Clients

Consultation. Except in unusual circumstances, a creative firm should make one free, introductory visit to a prospective client. Subsequent calls should be part of a billable assignment, unless both parties agree otherwise.

Speculative work. Client organizations should not ask for work to be done "on speculation"—i.e., to have the assignment contingent on approval of the work. Speculative work is subject to widespread abuse, increases prices, and is otherwise unprofessional.

Estimates and proposals. When sufficient information is provided, creative firms should be expected to prepare a written estimate or proposal of a project schedule, costs, and terms and conditions. When sufficient detailed information is not provided, it is the obligation of the creative firm to say so. If information is unavailable, pricing should be based on an hourly rate with frequent reviews of time expended. No project should be started without a signed acceptance of the estimate or proposal, or a purchase order authorization.

Billing. The client organization should expect that the price on an estimate or proposal, plus additional expenses and taxes, will be the invoiced price unless otherwise appended, verbally or in writing, before invoicing.

Confidentiality. The client organization should expect that any information or material provided will be treated confidentially, and that all reasonable efforts will be taken to safeguard it. If requested, the creative firm should willingly sign a nondisclosure agreement.

Conflict of interest. Creative firms engaged in advertising and public relations should not have two clients who are directly competitive. It is acceptable for firms engaged in other types of projects to work with competitive clients, but usually not simultaneously. Where there is concern about conflict of interest, it is the responsibility of the creative firm to ask the first client if it is permissible to also accept the work of a competitor.

Working arrangements. Unless otherwise stipulated, every project should be considered as comprising two equal sections: 1) product specifics, market, objectives, and budget are the responsibility of the client; 2) conceptual approaches, creativity, management, and production expertise are the responsibility of the creative firm.

Submissions. It should be the responsibility of the creative firm to provide what, in its professional opinion, is the best solution to the client's problem or opportunity. Similarly, it should be its responsibility to follow the objectives, input, criticisms, and comments of the client closely.

Ownership. Unless otherwise indicated (often the case for illustration and photography), the output of the creative firm becomes, after payment, the property of the client organization. However, all preparatory materials (sketches, unaccepted concepts, computer disks, films, plates, etc.) remain the property of the creative firm.

Nonuse. In accordance with accepted professional services practice, the client organization is financially obligated for work done, whether or not it is utilized. In the event of dissatisfaction, the creative firm should resign at the earliest possible date and make an effort to find another firm to continue. The creative firm should only invoice for the time actually spent, not the amount of the original assignment estimate.

Mission statement

Goosefeather Design
Ten Business Principles

1 The goal of our company is to provide the highest possible quality creative services. We will do this at the most competitive prices possible, consistent with our quality and profit standards.

2 Our business will be run in a manner that allows us to make a fair profit. We believe that doing so strengthens our company and allows us to provide the additional resources that create added value for our clients.

3 We will strive to cultivate relationships with clients who need and can appreciate the additional impact that work of our quality creates for their organizations, products, and services.

4 We recognize that each of our clients can obtain similar services from other suppliers. We will constantly strive not merely to meet, but to exceed, the expectations of each of our clients.

5 We will measure the effectiveness of the services we provide not only by our own standards, but also by how well they meet the specific objectives of our clients.

6 We believe in open, ethical, and nondiscriminatory business practices. We will treat each of our vendors, clients, and employees in a respectful, fair, and above-board manner.

7 We acknowledge that our business is built on the collective talents of our employees. We pledge to be an equal opportunity employer that provides above average wages and benefits and a pleasant working environment.

8 We expect each of our employees to dress and act in a business-like manner, to treat others with respect, to be loyal to the best interests of the company, and to constantly strive for self-improvement.

9 We commit ourselves to keeping up with the business techniques and technologies that will allow us to provide better services for our clients, and better working conditions for our employees.

10 We commit ourselves to encouraging innovation and new ideas, styles, and approaches in order to maintain our competitive edge. We willingly accept the risks that come with this.

Professional design rationale

How (Your Firm) Defines Value-Oriented Design

Graphic design often involves activities and results whose effectiveness can't be easily quantified and measured.

Yet, in today's economic climate every organization must look for ways to economize. Our firm is sometimes asked to explain the ways in which we provide more value in addressing our clients' problems and opportunities.

So let us share a few thoughts about our value-oriented touchstones, and what they mean.

COMMUNICATION

Value-oriented design is not about style or fashion, as important as they are. First and foremost, it is about effectively communicating one or more of a client's strategic messages, which it is our business to craft.

How much more value do well-thought-out and easily-communicated visual messages have? Frankly, we can't quantify the answer. But we do know that the difference between the success or failure of a client's message is often in the details and execution of its design.

We live in a world that is over-communicated, and where media are excessively cluttered. Design must not only be strategically focused and visually arresting to combat this reality, but also perfectly suited to the media that will carry it. We develop everything with these three points in mind.

There's also another aspect to producing successful materials: how easily we work together with our clients. Thorough information-gathering procedures minimize their time, and help us to get things right the first time.

IMAGE

Value-oriented design is about image building as well. Over time, all products and organiza-

tions develop personalities, just as individuals do. Positive personalities, evident in well-known images and brands, are often among the most valuable properties any organization possesses.

In today's world, not to reinforce positive ones, or to strengthen weak ones, is to leave a positioning vacuum soon filled by competitors. Constant attentiveness to image and brand building is one of the ways smaller organizations get bigger, and bigger organizations stay on top.

Creating and maintaining strong visual identities and brands is our focus. Our years of experience tells us that it is far too important today to trust to chance, or a low bidder.

CURRENCY

The design business is constantly changing. The tools we use—computers and software—are evermore powerful. The media we employ—electronic and print—are forever evolving. This makes our expertise [and size, experience, etc.] increasingly more relevant.

It provides still another aspect of our value-oriented design process: the ability to adapt recent technologies and media changes to our clients' specific needs. This, not to mention the ability to look over the horizon and stay ahead of developing curves.

In short, by investing to keep ahead of technology and media changes we're able to provide more solutions, options, and ideas to further our clients' objectives.

WORTH

As important as technology and its tools are, however, in our business they don't actually solve problems. Only people do. (We're reminded of a saying

ascribed to the composer, Duke Ellington: "It is not the piano that makes great music; it is the person sitting at the piano.")

This means that, as with any type of professional service, most of what you contract for with a design firm is individuals' time. In turn, this means that most differences in their pricing are usually a direct reflection of the level of depth and breadth of talent that will be brought to bear.

Much design time is executional in nature—i.e., it involves "working things out." And unlike some other businesses, there are few economies of scale or shortcuts that can be taken advantage of. The process does not vary greatly from person to person, or often even firm to firm. So while it is perhaps a cliché to say so, with design services you'll pretty much get what you pay for.

The cost of employing highly-qualified, experienced, and talented professionals often does result in higher up front costs, but it usually also results in lower costs over time.

We hope you will let us prove it on your next project.

Professional copy rationale

Why Professional Copy Is More Than Worth The Cost

Nothing is more versatile and effective in informing, persuading, and motivating than the printed (or digitized) word. As in the past and into the foreseeable future, effective visual communication not only requires eye-arresting design and graphics (layout), it requires well-crafted words (copy). Anything less wastes money—it provides only half the bang for the buck.

Today, new technologies and media make generating copy easier than ever. But progress can come at a high price for those not careful. Because of the ease, and because we live in a world where the emphasis is on speed and visuals, many of us tend to overlook and minimize the importance of well-crafted words.

Next time you're tempted to cut costs or save time by giving short shrift to copy development, consider the following.

ORGANIZATIONAL BENEFITS

An organization opting for outside, professional writing help can look forward to several benefits seldom obtained when writing is handled internally.

No strain on resources. Good writing is labor intensive and time-consuming. There are no shortcuts. Developing copy internally often requires assigning the task to an employee who either gives it low priority, or whose regular work suffers in the process.

Tighter control. It's always easier to assign tough deadlines, be honestly critical, and make changes to work done outside than to work that was done in-house. There are no personal sensitivities, office politics, or organizational bureaucracies to consider.

True objectivity. It is difficult, if not impossible, to uncover unique characteristics and write

objectively about things that are familiar. Only an outsider will be impartial, feel free to probe, ask dumb questions, and play the devil's advocate—all necessary to the development of powerful, persuasive copy.

More relevant experience. It isn't necessary to have intimate knowledge of a product or service to write knowledgeably about it. A good, smart writer can learn more than enough in a few meetings. Much more important is that an outsider will bring a freshness and perspective to an assignment that can only come from the diverse experience of having met a variety of communication challenges in the past.

Better results. Everyone can write. Some can even write well. But few can write as well—as quickly and persuasively—as a professional who makes his or her living at it. Practice does, indeed, make (close to) perfect. So why settle for second best on your materials?

DESIGN BENEFITS

The best materials are always developed by a team—designer and writer working together in harmony. There are also some very practical working benefits in addition to the enhanced creativity that ensues from such a partnership.

Fact gathering. Writing about a product or service usually requires more interviews, facts, and detail than does design. When a writer is involved early on and shares information, it eliminates the need for some designer/client meetings, saving both time and cost.

Organization and outlining. For most copy-heavy print projects (brochures, annual reports, etc.) it is difficult to do good design without first having a copy structure. An outline of

the story to be told, including headlines and major breaks, makes designing easier and enhances any layout.

Detail checking. By training, writers are sensitive to different details than designers. Having a pair of eyes looking for bad copy breaks, inappropriate captions, and dropped heads reduces the possibility of embarrassing errors.

THE VALUE EFFECT

Except for the smallest of jobs, creative fees are always a small fraction of total costs. The incremental difference between having professional, outside writing or not will typically only increase costs from 5% to 10% on a small brochure or ad, or less than 1% on a large capability brochure, annual report, or multi-page Web site. And the difference between a good writer and a mediocre one is even less.

As for a cost comparison of in-house versus outside writing, when the true costs of internal preparation—salaries, overhead, lost productivity, etc.—are added up, outside writing nearly always costs less, not more.

In summary, professional writing is an extraordinarily small investment with a potentially big payoff in increased efficiency and effectiveness.

Professional illustration rationale

Illustration estimating worksheet

Appointment letter

(print on letterhead)

(date)

(name)
(title)
(company)
(address)
(city, state, zip)

Dear Mr (Ms) _____:

As you're no doubt aware, today (graphic design/editorial/advertising/public relations/Internet development services) can have a crucial effect on success. There are lots of suppliers available, but few that can combine creative talent with the reliability and strategic thinking that organizations like (client name) require.

This is why I would like to introduce you to a new source—(your company) (me).

Although (our) (my) name may be new to you, (I) (we) have over _____ years experience in fields ranging from _____, to _____, to _____. (Our/my specialty is_____.) Recent clients have included:_____, _____, _____, _____, and _____ for projects ranging from _____ to _____ _____.

Now, I would like to introduce (our) (my) services to (client name), and show you some of the ways (we) (I) have been able to increase the (marketing) (communications) effectiveness of similar organizations.

I'll call next (Thursday) to see if a short meeting would be appropriate at this time.

Sincerely,

(your name)
Principal

Referral letter

(print on letterhead)

January 15, 0000

Ms Rachel Referral
Director of Marketing
Appreciative Manufacturing
96 Satisfaction Street
Any City, XX, 12345

Dear Rachel:

Thanks again for the opportunity of working with you, (name), and all the staff on the new Widget rebranding. I hope you are still as happy with the result as we are.

As I'm sure you've experienced, finding qualified suppliers with reasonable prices who are comfortable to work with can be difficult, especially in a field like (rebranding, design, interactive, advertising, PR). This is why referrals from our past clients have become a major source of (name of firm's) future clients.

Could you help us help others by taking a minute or two to think of acquaintences who could also benefit from our services? I'd like to give them a call to introduce what we do.

I'll give you a call next week to see if you can think of anyone we should call on.

Many thanks in advance,

(your name)
(principal)

No spec rationale

Why We Don't Make Speculative Presentations

The main product of our business is ideas—creative solutions to the communications problems and opportunities facing our many clients. And good ideas—creativity—can be tough to define, or agree upon. One person's passion is often another's poison. So it's no wonder that potential clients often ask us to take a project on speculation. That is, to try out our creative product in much the same way they may try out other types of products before purchasing.

Unfortunately, we must turn down such projects. This will explain why doing so actually makes us a better, more stable and reliable supplier for you to do business with.

It lets us keep our prices low

We make money mostly by selling our time. Unlike businesses that sell products, we can't take time back and resell it. Thus, the less time we actually sell, the more we have to charge for it. So we attempt to hold our prices down by keeping constantly busy.

We also have substantial fixed overhead costs—computers, peripherals, software, etc. So the higher the percentage of our time that is productive (billable), the more we can spread these costs, and the less each individual client gets charged for them.

In addition, the only way we can recover our overhead costs is through what we charge our clients. If we accepted speculative projects, the overhead for these non-billable hours would have to be added to the factor we already charge our regular, paying clients. We don't think this would be fair.

We want to give you only our best

We are very proud of our track record of helping many different clients with many different challenges. In doing so, we have come to understand the crucial components in producing outstanding creativity.

First, outstanding creative work requires good, complete input from our clients. It takes time and effort that's tough for them to justify unless they are committed to awarding an assignment. Yet without it, we can't show how good we really are. Or our best effort may be misdirected; a great shot that hits the wrong target.

Equally important, great creativity requires enthusiasm. We need to be excited enough to pour all our energy into a project. Frankly, that's impossible without knowing whether we will be chosen to go all the way, or even get paid.

And, finally, developing creativity is very labor intensive. Although we wish it were otherwise, it seldom comes in a flash of inspiration. Rather, it usually requires research and thinking time, then the working through of many different ideas and approaches. This makes it difficult or impossible to do good work in a compressed time frame.

Speculative projects, whether done by us or some other firm, usually require cutting every creative corner. That's hardly in your best interests, or ours.

We're a small firm, in business to stay

We hope our small size is what attracted you to us. It has lots of business advantages.

Because we are small, you get to deal directly with those actually doing your work; there are no "middle-men" to muck things up. It also means we're more flexible, able to turn things around faster. We can offer better, more personal service, too. And because our overhead is lower than the big guys, so are our prices. In a business like creativity, size is seldom an advantage.

All these are reasons why we have been so successful. It may also be why you called us.

Another reason for our success is that we are good business people. We know that a small business like ours (probably yours, too) has to watch costs carefully and can't afford to give much away. If we weren't careful—if we did give away our time—it is likely we wouldn't be here next time you called, which means you'd have start all over again bringing someone else up to speed learning your business. We doubt you'd want that, and we know we wouldn't. We believe we should both be looking to build a long-term, mutually-productive and cost-efficient business relationship.

Truth is, small organizations like ours can seldom afford to accept speculative projects. If you find one that will, be skeptical. They may be desperate.

As for larger organizations and agencies, yes they can afford to do speculative projects, and often do. But that's the very point. If they do have the volume and staff that makes it a small risk for them, they're probably too big to give you the personal service and outstanding creativity you're searching for.

We hope you'll give us the opportunity sometime soon to prove just how good we really are. In the meantime, look carefully at our portfolio. The work we have done for many other clients with many other challenges speaks volumes about our abilities.

Retainer agreement

Retainer Agreement

This will constitute an agreement between (client) and (creative firm) for (graphic design/writing/public relations consulting/advertising/Internet-based) services for the period (date) to (date).

During this period, (creative firm) agrees to devote up to (number) hours per month on work to be determined by (client). It will normally be performed at the offices of (creative firm), but occasionally may take place at other locations as required. Priority and scheduling will be at the discretion of (client), but acknowledge the need to work within previously established schedules and processes of (creative firm). Work will normally occur between the hours of 9 to 5 on weekdays.

Payment for these services will be to (creative firm) at the rate of $0,000 per month and will be made for the month following no later than the 30th day of each month that this agreement is in force. No invoice will be submitted by (creative firm).

In the event fewer hours are used during a one month period, unused hours may be carried forward to the following month. Any hours unused at the end of the second month will be forfeited without compensation.

Work in excess of (hours) per month will be at the rate of $000 per hour and will be billed separately. Any expenses exclusive of normal overhead are not included in this agreement and will be invoiced separately at cost. Examples of such expenses are: delivery services, travel beyond 25 miles from (creative firm) or (client) facilities, and meals when traveling. All invoices will be payable within 30 days (net 30). Invoices paid after 30 days will be subject to interest at 1.5% per month.

All materials furnished by (client) will remain the property of (client) and will be returned upon request, or not more than 10 days from the termination of this agreement.

The results of any and all work performed under this agreement, including original creative work (with the exception of _____), will become the property of the (client). (Client) may use this material in any way deemed appropriate.

All materials developed by (creative firm) for production purposes, including but not limited to computer formats, files and code, will remain the property of (creative firm).

This agreement may be terminated on 30 days' written notice by either (creative firm) or (client). In event of termination, (creative firm) shall make a reasonable attempt to finish work in progress.

(Insert more paragraphs here with other terms and conditions as may be appropriate.)

(Signed)	(Signed)
(Name)	(Name)
(Title)	(Title)
(Creative firm)	(Client company)
(Date)	(Date)

Pricing rationale

Client background information

Creative brief questionnaire

Creative Brief Questionnaire

Date: Client:
Project: Job #:
In Attendance:

• *The objectives:* 1)

          2)

• *The target audience:*

• *The features:*

• *Customer/user benefits:*

• *Support for benefit claims:*

• *The competition:*

• *Considerations/preferences/limitations:*

• *Distribution considerations:*

• *The single most important point:*

Questionnaire instruction

Assignment Questionnaire Instructions

This form, supplemented with additional material as necessary, can help ensure that you always get the basic creative and positioning information needed when starting an assignment. Here are examples of the types of questions to ask when using it:

Project objectives. What is the purpose of the project? Examples: raise market awareness by 25%, sell 2,000 widgets, educate existing customers, enthuse salespeople, upgrade the company image, meet a legal requirement, build company loyalty or esprit de corps. *A creative approach should be developed around a primary and secondary objective only; no creative vehicle can be expected to accomplish more.*

Target audience. Who are the readers/viewers/customers? Determine sex, age, job titles, social/economic conditions, employment, geographic concentration. Are they already knowledgeable about the product, or not? What motivates them?

Product description. What are its features? Ask about specifications, components, manufacture, delivery, other marketing efforts. How is it used in everyday application? What is it that's different, unusual, or unique?

Customer (user) benefits. How will he or she be better off? Does it save time, effort, money? If so, how much? How relatively important is this to the customer? What are the trade-offs (example: higher quality usually means higher price)? Determine all benefits, but rank them—concentrate on the one or two strongest. Be as objective and specific as possible.

Additional notes and other considerations:

Support for benefits claims. Ask for proof of benefits: test data, focus group reports, user testimonials. Accept only facts, not opinions, only specifics, not generalizations. If possible, get information that is quantified.

Competition. What similar products/services are available and how good are they? Get names, specifications, prices, good and bad features. Insist on objectivity, not opinions.

Creative considerations. What limitations or constraints do you have? For example: budget, schedule, size, paper, use of color, number of photographs/illustrations, corporate standards, personal likes/dislikes. Where will complementary creativity (writing/design/illustration/photography) come from?

Distribution. Where will the ad run, the brochure be distributed, the mailer mailed? How does the distribution affect budget, creative time, use of color, and mechanical requirements?

Most important point. Most communications leave only one overall impression. Ask the client: "If you could choose only one thing the reader/viewer would remember, what would it be?" *Make this the primary focus for your creative concept.*

Estimating worksheet

Project budgeting form

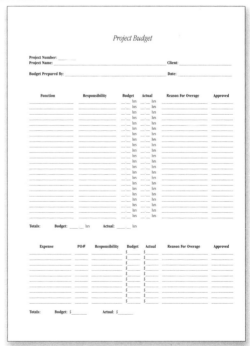

Creative review checklist

Creative Review Checklist

Date _____
Client _____
Project _____
Job # _____
Creative Team _____

Client Objectives

Primary objective: _____
_____
_____

Is addressed by: _____
_____
_____

Product/Service

☐ Is central to creative concept.
☐ Is correctly shown/explained.
☐ Its benefits/features (uniqueness) are properly emphasized.
☐ The way it is shown reinforces established positioning and customer perceptions.
☐ Logos/trademarks/names/intellectual property are treated correctly.
☐ Other products/services could not be easily substituted within this creative concept.

Secondary objective: _____
_____
_____

Is addressed by: _____
_____
_____

Creative Approach

☐ Is unique/unusual to the product/service.
☐ Is attention getting.
☐ Fits tone/style of the product/service.
☐ Fits tone/style of the client organization.
☐ Complements other media efforts.
☐ Addresses primary interests of readers/viewers.
☐ Has inherent interest or story appeal; is not merely decorative or explanatory.
☐ Directs readers/viewers attention to what's most important about the product/service.
☐ Is memorable.
☐ Is believable.
☐ Is persuasive.
☐ Appears stylish and contemporary.
☐ Encourages further action by readers/viewers.
☐ Provides means for contacting/next step.
☐ Has staying power (is not quickly outdated).

Other Considerations

_____
_____
_____
_____
_____
_____
_____
_____
_____
_____
_____

Evaluation

☐ Okay as is.

☐ Needs further refinement.

Shop Standards

☐ Can be produced within time and budget constraints.
☐ Presentation materials are organized and professional.
☐ Presentation has been gone over/rehearsed.

Comments _____
_____
_____
_____

Time sheet

DAILY TIME SHEET

Name: _____

Date: _____

	Job/Account	Client	Task	Posted		Job/Account	Client	Task	Posted
8:15					1:15				
8:30					1:30				
8:45					1:45				
9:00					2:00				
9:15					2:15				
9:30					2:30				
9:45					2:45				
10:00					3:00				
10:15					3:15				
10:30					3:30				
10:45					3:45				
11:00					4:00				
11:15					4:15				
11:30					4:30				
11:45					4:45				
12:00					5:00				
12:15									
12:30									
12:45									
1:00									

BEFORE/AFTER HOURS

Start	Finish	Job/Account	Client	Task	Posted

EXPENSES

Job/Account	Client	Item/$	Posted

Enter all productive time daily by job or account number, including in-home activity. For periods of no activity, enter 0000. Round up for activities taking less than 15 minutes. Do not assign more than one job/account number to each 15 minute segment. Entries in the first 30 minutes of each day, and the period from noon to 1:00 are not necessary unless you are productively occupied during those periods. Any time before 8:00 and after 5:00 should be recorded as before or after hours time in minimal increments of a half hour.

Business trend calculator

Five-Year Trend Tracker

Business	Last year	±*	Year -2	±*	Year -3	±*	Year -4	±*	Year -5
Billable efficiency	____%	__	____%	__	____%	__	____%	__	____%
Quick ratio	____	__	____	__	____	__	____	__	____
Income per employee	$____	__	$____	__	$____	__	$____	__	$____
Percentage of business from one client	____%	__	____%	__	____%	__	____%	__	____%
Average billing rate	$____	__	$____	__	$____	__	$____	__	$____
Debt-to-assets ratio	____	__	____	__	____	__	____	__	____
Agency Gross Income	$____	__	$____	__	$____	__	$____	__	$____
Profitability	$____	__	$____	__	$____	__	$____	__	$____
Equity	$____	__	$____	__	$____	__	$____	__	$____

Personal									
Weekly work hours	____	__	____	__	____	__	____	__	____
Yearly days off	____	__	____	__	____	__	____	__	____
Nest eggs	$____	__	$____	__	$____	__	$____	__	$____
Net worth	$____	__	$____	__	$____	__	$____	__	$____

*Increase/decrease from previous year.

Trend calculator instructions

Calculating Trend Indicators

Business

Billable efficiency (sometimes referred to as "utilization rate"). Divide the actual (not estimated) billed hours by total payroll hours (all employees). The acceptable range for creative services companies is 50% to 75%.

Quick ratio (sometimes referred to as "liquid ratio"). Divide short-term assets (receivables) by short-term liabilities (payables). Because assets and liabilities can fluctuate, averaging is best. The acceptable range for creative services companies (liquidity) is 1.25 to 2.0.

Income per employee. Divide AGI (see below) by total number of employees, including principals. (For part-time employees use fractions; single-person firms divide by 1.) The figure for most firms operating in a metropolitan market should be at least $120,000 yearly or $10,000 monthly.

Percentage of business from one client. Divide total income by number of clients in the same reporting period. 25% or more from one client is risky. Generally, the lower the percentage the better.

Average billing rate. Divide AGI (see below) by total billed hours. There is no "right" rate, but *Creative Business* surveys show that at least $90 an hour is needed to cover expenses and make a small profit. Most firms charge considerably much more.

Debt-to-assets ratio. Divide company assets (including accounts receivable) by its debt (including accounts payable). The figure should be in the range of .20 to .50.

Agency Gross Income (AGI). Subtract any pass-through expenses from total receipts. (Common examples: printing bills that were marked up, net media bills.) What remains—

AGI—is primarily creative fees and markup income, discretionary or spendable revenue.

Profitability. For these purposes (only) include the value of all disbursements to owners/shareowners—salaries, bonuses, monetary benefits (e.g., company car)—as well as any retained earnings. (Traditional profit measures—e.g., return on equity—are usually inappropriate for privately-held companies because how much the owners take out in salary and benefits affect firm profitability.)

Equity. In the absence of professional valuations, only Net Asset Value (NAV) should be calculated. The worth of a company's reputation ("good will") is not only subjective, but it might not have any dollar value because it might not transfer to a new owner. NAV is determined by adding all tangible assets and subtracting all tangible liabilities. Principals of small firms should take care to keep company and personal assets separate.

Personal

Weekly work hours. Estimate the weekly average.

Yearly days off. Count the total taken.

Nest eggs. Add up the total amount of tax-advantaged retirement plans (IRAs, 401ks, etc.)

Net worth. Add all personal assets (value of home and auto, money in bank, retirement funds, etc.) then subtract all personal liabilities (mortgages, loans, etc.).

Goodbye to abusive client letter

(print on letterhead)

(date)

Ms. U. R. Difficult
Vice President of Marketing
Toxic Industries
1234 Any Street
Pernicious, XY 00000

Dear U. R.:

Thank you again for meeting with me to have a frank discussion about the issues that have stood in the way of a mutually-beneficial relationship on the (name) project. The following will summarize the five procedural changes I believe are necessary to put the project back on track, and the alternative should they not be possible.

- To avoid any confusion on direction, all future communication must be solely between you and I, except when you are traveling.
- To keep the project from falling further behind when you are traveling, there must be one person I can call who has full decision-making authority.
- To avoid future misdirection, internal conflicts on direction or changes must be resolved before they reach me.
- Any additional failure to meet the schedule will result in rescheduling, as Optimist will no longer able to continue on the original schedule.
- Future invoices must be paid within the business standard of 30 to 45 days.

I hope you will be able to agree to these changes so that the (name) project can move forward. If so, I will prepare a new schedule and pricing.

Should you not be able to make these changes, Optimist Creative will bow out of the project, leaving you free to work with another firm. In doing so, we will turn over all work completed to date, which will provide as little disruption as possible. We will invoice you for $00,000, approximately 50% of our estimate, and less than half of the time we have thus far put on the (name) project.

Please let me know your decision at your earliest convenience.

Sincerely,

I. M. Fedup
Principle
Optimist Creative Limited

Simple estimate

(print on letterhead)

ESTIMATE

To:	Mr. George Carleton President Carleton Electrical Contractors, Inc. 825 Third Avenue Portland, OR 97202
Date:	(date)
For:	Writing services, 8-page sales brochure. Includes: Up to two 2-hour interview meetings; outline draft; rough draft; final draft; all reasonable expenses.
Cost:	$3,000. (30 hours @ $100 per hour.) This figure is an estimate, not a quote. It is based on the information provided, and may be inappropriate if additional information is forthcoming, or specifications change. It is valid for 60 days.
Terms:	One third ($1,000) invoiced immediately; two thirds ($2,000) invoiced at delivery of final draft. All invoices are Net 30. Interest charged after 30 days.
Our tax#:	03-378280

Thank you for the opportunity to submit this estimate. I look forward to working with you.

Jonathan Swift
Principal

Proposal letter

(print on letterhead)

(date)

Mr. William Prospect
Vice President, Sales
Breakthrough Medical Products
198 Swansea Drive
Dayton, OH 45427

Dear Bill:

This letter will constitute an agreement for Squeamish Graphics to develop a single-page magazine advertisement and a Web page announcing the introduction of the CleanSlice Ligament Cutter. Placement of the ad in appropriate magazines and implementation of the Web page on Breakthrough's Web site will be handled by Breakthrough.

Schedule: The project will include the following on approximately the dates indicated:

July 1—Fact gathering meeting with your staff and appropriate personnel from the product development group.

July 10—Presentation of our ideas and conceptual approaches for review and input.

July 18—Presentation of final ad and Web-page layouts.

July 19/August 1—Photography, artwork preparation, copywriting, electronic file development, and coding.

August 1/8—Approval routing at Breakthrough.

August 8/15—Final modifications and changes by Breakthrough.

August 15—Electronic files sent to Breakthrough's multimedia department for Web implementation.

more . . .

Proposal letter, continued

September 1—Ad films sent to appropriate magazines by Squeamish from a list supplied by Breakthrough.

Fees: The following is an estimate of our fees for this project based on the information you've provided. Please note that if conditions or the schedule changes, the actual price may be higher or lower. We will, however, keep you informed of any change which exceeds 10 percent of the estimate.

Phase I—Research and concept development	$1,750
Phase II—Photography, copywriting, and artwork	$3,250
Phase III—Art direction, typography, and layouts	$2,500
Phase IV—Electronic file and films	$1,600

Expenses: Out-of-pocket expenses will be billed at a 25 percent mark up, which covers our handling costs. Such items normally include deliveries, service bureau charges, and long-distance phone calls.

We estimate total expenses for this project will be: $ _250_

Estimated project cost: $9,350

Ownership. All original photographic film, including transparencies and negatives, remain the property of the photographer selected. All preparation materials, including original artwork and electronic files and printing films, remain the property of Squeamish Graphics. All ideas and concepts not used remain the property of Squeamish Graphics and may be used in the future as they deem appropriate.

Terms: Approximately one-third of this estimate ($3,000) to be billed upon acceptance; approximately one-third ($3,000) upon acceptance of final layouts; the balance upon completion of the project. If any phase of the project is delayed for longer than 60 days, we will bill for work completed.

All invoices are net, payable within 30 days of receipt. Interest of 1.5 percent per month may be charged on past-due accounts.

As I have previously indicated, I believe my firm's experience handling similar projects provides Squeamish Graphics with the expertise necessary to do an outstanding job for Breakthrough.

more . . .

If this proposal meets with your approval, please indicate by signing and returning one copy to me. A purchase order should be initiated as soon as possible.

If you have any questions, please call.

Thanks for the opportunity to submit this proposal. I'm looking forward to working with you.

Sincerely,

I. M. Squeamish
Principal

Detailed proposal

A PROPOSAL
TO PRODUCE A
CAPABILITY BROCHURE
FOR SECURITY FINANCIAL SERVICES

Prepared for
Sally D. Client
Director of Marketing Support
(date)

CONTENTS

2

ASSIGNMENT BACKGROUND

Security Financial Services, a division of Security National Bank, provides personal investment counseling and special banking services for individuals whose net worth exceeds one million dollars. The division was founded in 1995 to provide both a broader range of custom products and services and more personal attention to high-deposit customers. Security was the first bank in South Florida to provide this service. Since that time, all banks in Security's market area have offered similar programs and most have promoted them aggressively.

To date, the three-hundred-plus customers of the division have been acquired solely through referrals by officers of the bank's fifteen retail outlets. There has been no advertising and there is no literature to explain the division's products and services, or how they differ from that offered by other, competitive banks.

3

ASSIGNMENT OBJECTIVES

1) To broadly support a marketing campaign that will seek to double Security Financial Service's customer base within the next twelve months.

2) To fulfill the estimated 3,000 literature requests that will result from Security's "Talk to a Specialist" advertising campaign due to begin in December 2002 and run through April 2002. The material produced must key off the ad that will be producing the requests.

3) To provide literature that introduces the full range of the division's many services to its existing customers who may know of only one Security service.

4) To help educate and motivate all bank personnel about the "state of the art" nature of the products and services provided by Security Financial Services.

PRODUCTION AND SCHEDULING REQUIREMENTS

To design, write, and oversee production of a brochure that explains the immediate and long-term benefits of using Security Financial Services to handle a wealthy individual's financial and estate planning.

The brochure produced can be up to 20 pages (16 text plus cover) and utilize full color. Quantity will be 25,000. There are no restrictions on style, but it is desired that the brochure focus on the higher quality personal service provided by Security.

Due to the lack of any literature at present, and the formal announcement of the division's marketing campaign at a sales meeting starting on November 12, the brochure must be delivered by November 10, 2002.

4

Detailed proposal, continued

SAVANT ASSOCIATES' EXPERIENCE

Savant Associates is a Miami firm specializing in communications and graphic design services for businesses throughout the southeast. Our firm was founded in 1989 by John J. Creative and Sarah S. Smart who combined over twenty years of corporate communications experience. Previously Mr. Creative was Vice President and Creative Director for Outstanding Advertising of Fort Lauderdale; Ms Smart was Vice President of Marketing and Strategic Planning for Swamp Land Development Corporation of Hialeah.

Since its founding in 1989, Savant Associates has built an impressive reputation for producing materials and programs that are strongly market-focused, yet are also tasteful and contemporary.

We have worked for small firms and large, startups and those well established. Some of our more prominent clients have been: Cuba Libre Airlines... Belle Glade Jai Alai Fronton... Delectable Ugly Fruit... Barely An Island Bahamas Spa & Resort... and HelpingHand Medical Centers. Projects have included advertisements, brochures, sales literature, package design, store displays Web-page design, and corporate identity programs.

Our extensive financial services experience includes working with South Florida Savings & Loan, Coral Gables Municipal Savings Bank, and Retirement Funds Investments. (See pages 13 and 14 for examples.) Assignments for these and other institutions have included the production of annual reports, product sales literature, and identity and signage programs. We are not currently working for any other financial services institution.

Savant Associates currently has a staff of ten who encompass a wide range of design and marketing skills. If we are granted this assignment, strategic planning and account service will be handled by company principal Sarah S. Smart; creative development and project management will be handled by company principal John J. Creative.

5

SAVANT ASSOCIATES' APPROACH

Phase I — Information Gathering

First Meeting

The Savant Associates account team of Sarah S. Smart and John J. Creative will meet with Security Financial Services to clarify objectives, identify subjective preferences, discuss possible thematic approaches, and uncover potential marketing problems.

In addition to Sally Client, we suggest this meeting include Laurie Jameson, Vice President of Marketing; Craig Heritage, Group Vice President; Vicki Montenegro, Account Supervisor, Florida; and any other bank personnel who can contribute to the overview of opportunities, concerns and potential problems.

In addition, we suggest that representatives of Bamboozle & Bamboozle provide a briefing of their "Talk to a Specialist" advertising campaign strategy, creative approach, and fulfillment requirements.

We also suggest that any previously developed materials or information on the division and its competition be made available to us.

Second Meeting

Based upon the overview obtained in the first meeting, John J. Creative will interview Sally Client during the second meeting to gather the specific detail and information needed to write and art direct the brochure.

Schedule

To assure meeting your deadline of having brochures for the sales meeting on November 12, we suggest that the first meeting be scheduled the week of September 7. The second meeting should happen a week or so later, ideally during the week of September 14.

6

Phase II — Idea Development

Concepts

Based on the input from the two meetings with your staff, Savant Associates will develop up to three conceptual, or rough, approaches to the brochure. A cover treatment and one spread from one of these approaches, our recommendation, will be rendered in full size, in color, along with a quarter-size dummy (mock up) of the entire brochure. Also developed will be an outline of the copy.

Third meeting

At this meeting we will present our approaches to Sally Client and Craig Heritage. Input from this meeting will be used to set the final direction for the brochure.

Schedule

We anticipate that the third meeting (conceptual presentation) will take place approximately two weeks after the second (detailed input), ideally the week of September 28.

Phase III — Development and Approval

Photography

We will select the photographer and supervise the taking of photographs. We will ask Security to help us in making arrangements and providing technical supervision during each photographic session.

Writing

We will develop copy in keeping with the direction provided at the third meeting and submit drafts to Sally Client for approval.

Design

We will execute the design approved at the third meeting and will coordinate and integrate the copy when it is approved. We will set type and prepare electronic (printing) artwork for the approval of Sally Client.

Schedule

We anticipate that first copy draft will be completed approximately one week after the third meeting, ideally the week of October 5. Final draft will be completed approximately one week later, ideally the week of October 12.

We anticipate photography to be done during the week of October 12.

We anticipate that mechanicals will be available for review three weeks after the third meeting, ideally the week of October 19. Final approval of all mechanicals will be necessary by October 27.

Phase IV — Printing and Delivery

Printer selection

Savant Associates will ask for bids from three printers and recommend one of the

7

---

three based on a combination of cost and quality factors. Selection will be made by Security Financial Services.

Print Supervision

Savant Associates will oversee printing of the brochure, giving instructions to the printer, supervising color separations and corrections, and checking proofs. However, Security Financial Services will have ultimate responsibility for the accuracy of the brochure as indicated by a signed approval of the final blue line (salt print) proof.

Schedule

Printing and binding of 25,000 four-color, 20-page brochures will take approximately two weeks from the time final, approved mechanicals are turned over to the printer. Assuming that mechanicals are approved by October 27, delivery by November 9 is feasible.

Project Timing

Note: the delivery of this brochure by the required date requires close adherence to the schedule outline above. Delivery cannot be guaranteed unless critical dates are met.

8

416

SAMPLES AND FORMS

Detailed proposal, continued

ESTIMATE OF SAVANT ASSOCIATES' COST

Phases I and II — Information and Idea Development
For three meetings, up to three conceptual approaches, one quarter-size dummy of complete brochure, full-size rendering of cover, and one spread, copy outline, typography sample.

$ 5,600

Phase III — Development and Approval

Copywriting	$ 4,000
Photo supervision and editing	2,800
Design	3,000
Electronic art	3,800
Typography	3,200
Photostats and photo copies	400
	$17,200

Phase IV — Printing and Delivery
Instructions to printer, checking separations, on-press supervision.

$ 2,400

Miscellaneous expenses—our costs +25% markup
Deliveries $ 200

Total of Savant Associates' estimated costs
(Estimated costs do not include taxes.) $ 26,200

9

ESTIMATE OF OTHER COSTS

Photography

4 days @$1,000 day	$ 4,000
Expenses and supplies	750
	$ 4,750

Printing
25,000, 8.5x11," 16-pages plus cover, 4-color process
plus spot varnish on cover, 12 color separations,
saddlewire bind. $19,000

Total of other costs $23,750

Note: this is an estimate for planning purposes only based on our past experience. Actual photography and printing prices will be determined from competitive bids.

All photography and printing will be billed by the vendor directly to Security Financial Services.

Estimates do not include shipping or taxes.

10

WORKING AGREEMENT

Estimates
The costs and expenses cited in this proposal are our best estimates given the information provided. If additional information is forthcoming, the project specifications change, or the scheduling changes, cost and expense estimates may change.
   Cost and expense estimates are appropriate for 30 days from the date of this proposal. Taxes are not included in cost and expense estimates.

Revisions and Alterations
Work not described in this proposal, including but not limited to revisions (AAs), corrections, alterations and additional proofs, will be billed as an additional cost at the hourly labor rate of $125 per hour, or at our cost plus 25% markup.

Terms
Approximately one third of the total estimated costs in advance; approximately one third upon acceptance of the design concept; the balance upon delivery.
   If any phase of the assignment is delayed longer than 60 days, we will bill for work completed to date.

Responsibility
Savant Associates will make every reasonable effort to assure the accuracy of the material produced, but are not responsible for the correctness of copy, illustrations, photographs, trademarks, nor for obtaining clearances or approvals.
   We will take normal measures to safeguard any materials entrusted to us. However, we are not responsible for the loss, damage or unauthorized use of such materials, nor are we responsible for the actions of the vendors and suppliers we utilize.

11

Ownership
All materials used in the production of this assignment—including original artwork and computer generated artwork, formats, and code—remains the property of Savant Associates.
   Unless otherwise agreed upon, all original photographic film (transparencies and negatives) will remain the property of the photographer selected.
   Unless otherwise agreed upon, all printing materials (primarily films, plates, and electronic files) remain the property of the printer selected.
   Ideas which are not accepted remain the property of Savant Associates and may be used in the future in the course of other assignments.

Purchase Order
If this proposal is acceptable, a Security purchase order in the amount of $27,000 should be initiated. All invoices submitted against the purchase order will be net, payable within 30 days of receipt. Interest may be charged on past due invoices.
   We shall be pleased to begin work upon receipt of your purchase order.

Submitted by:

Sarah S. Smart
Principal
Savant Associates

Approved by:

Sally Client
Director of Marketing Support
Security Financial Services

12

Detailed proposal, continued

EXAMPLE OF SAVANT FINANCIAL EXPERIENCE

(Illustration here)

The symbol of South Florida Savings and Loan is one of the most recognizable in the state. Because it is so strongly identified with the organization, any change is risky. Yet an organization's visual identity must also be strong and contemporary, or its market position can suffer.

Updating South Florida's symbol while also protecting it and building upon its equity was the challenge faced by Savant Associates.

The result of our efforts is a symbol with a much friendlier, more contemporary feeling. Equally important, along with it we developed a comprehensive corporate identity manual. It informs employees about the invaluable asset the symbol represents, and provides guidelines for its use on media ranging from calling cards, to ads, to company vehicles, to signage.

13

EXAMPLE OF SAVANT FINANCIAL EXPERIENCE

(Illustration here)

For Retirement Funds Investments we were asked to audit their communications programs to employees, shareholders, and customers. What we found were sporadic efforts that were expensive in terms of confusion, redundancies, and missed marketing opportunities.

Our challenge was to create an economical, effective, and coordinated program.

The result is a redesigned "RIF Weekly," the newsletter for employees, quarterly and annual reports that further reinforce the company's market positioning, and a new quarterly house organ, "The Sentinel," sent to all customers.

14

Detailed web proposal

(letterhead)

July 21, 0000

Ms Sally Client
Director of Marketing
The Wagging Tail Dog Care Centres, Inc.
88 Fido Circle
Any City, XX, 12345

Dear Sally:

It was a pleasure meeting again with you and your staff last Thursday.

Ever since our presentation last Spring, I have been waiting to hear the good news that The Wagging Tail has secured venture funding. Congratulations!

We are excited about the opportunity JustDoit Design can play in making The Wagging Tail a local success initially, and a national franchising success ultimately.

In the Thursday meeting we discussed your need to have a Web site up and running a week before the first location opens. This will be approximately a month after the first lease is signed, which you indicated could be as early as next week. As you will see on page 3 of the attached proposal, it will take us approximately six weeks to build your site, so this should be no problem. In fact, most of the work in Phase 1 and 2 of site development can be started before your locations are known. So we can start at your earliest convenience.

The first page of the following proposal summarizes the information we received at the meeting regarding The Wagging Tail's market niche (Project Background), Target Market Individuals, and Web Site Objectives. Please review this material carefully for our accuracy in interpretation as it is the basis for the way we will approach developing your site.

After the meeting, our staff met to rough out a preliminary approach. Our initial thoughts are presented on page 2 in the proposal sections Site Style and Appearance, Site Features, and Site References. Here, too, check to make sure that we are on the right track at this early stage.

JustDoit's Development Process on page 3 will provide a rough guide to various project functions and stages. It also provides cost estimates based on the information provided so far. The range reflects the fact that some site features have yet to be determined. Other factors that can effect the final cost are explained in Estimate Options and Additions on page 4.

More > > > >

Although I have tried to anticipate most factors that will affect cost, a final estimate can only be given after the site direction and design has been finalized.

Lastly, please familiarize yourself with the Working Agreement text on pages on pages 5 and 6. These are our regular procedures, which also closely follow standard industry practices.

I'll call you early next week to answer any questions that the proposal might raise, and to discuss a schedule for moving forward.

Again, thanks for the confidence you have shown in JustDoit Design. My staff and myself are excited about the opportunity. We look forward to starting what will be a rewarding project for our team and for yours

Sincerely,

Justin Doit
Principal
JustDoit Design

Web Site Proposal For
The Wagging Tail Dog Care Centres

Project Background

The number of dogs in urban areas continues to grow, especially among young professionals. While these individuals desire the love and companionship of man's best friend, they often lack the time or accessibility to space required to provide proper exercise, care, and grooming. Many dogs spend all day sleeping and get only an inadequate walk on city streets in the evening.

The Wagging Tail Dog Care Centres, Inc. (TWT) is a new corporation founded to provide owners with attractive and affordable short-term daycare, including occasional boarding when their owners travel. It will offer the dog equivalent of child daycare for urban professionals—a safe, healthy, educational, and socializing atmosphere in which dogs can spend the day.

Three initial company-owned locations are planned in the metropolitan area—MetroNorth, MetroSouth, and MetroCentral.

Locations in other markets will be considered on a franchise basis later.

Target Market Individuals (from meeting of July 14th)

• Single or married males, 25 to 40 without children (primary).
• Single or married females 25 to 40 without children (secondary).
• Care as much about their dogs as parents do about their children.
• Often feel guilty, conflicted between career and pet needs.
• Reside in multi-unit buildings in densely populated areas.
• Cost is not a major factor, but must not appear excessive.
• Convenience, including pickup, is crucial factor in appealing to them.

Web Site Objectives (from meeting of July 14th)

• Promote that TWT is a new concept focused around customer ease and convenience.
• Show loving care, happy pets, appreciative owners.
• Create awareness in the "non-kennel" home-like atmosphere.
• Indicate availability of veterinarian care when needed.
• Show each of the three locations and facilities and list its staff biographies.
• Provide employment information for each location.
• Solicit interest among possible franchisees.
• Make sure the creative approach is also applicable to later printed material.

-1-

Site Style and Appearance

• Warm, friendly, and comfortable—like one dog owner talking to another.
• Urban male style/color palette but with recognition that many viewers will be female.
• Inviting, non-serious, humorous—quip of day, cartoons, and animation are all appropriate.
• Easy accessibility—fast, well organized, navigation ease, no need for special plug ins.
• Must also appear professional, trustworthy, stable.

Site Features

• 15 to 20 pages as appropriate.
• To be built using up to five different, original page templates.
• One quarter of pages (25%) devoted to each of the three locations' facilities and staff.
• On-line registration to accommodate complete owner and dog data, including services requested.
• Registration data to be automatically entered into TWT FileMaker Pro database. (Automatic updating by customers will not be available initially, but may later.)
• E-commerce gateway to allow charging registration fees to MasterCard, VISA, American Express, or Discover. (Back-end arrangements to be handled by TWT)
• Routine maintenance possible by TWT in-house staff using GoLive.
• JustDoit Design will be available to help with non-routine maintenance.
• Site hosting to be determined by TWT prior to first location opening.

Site References

It is helpful when developing a new site to look at what competitors and others have done. Although there are no direct competitors, and the site we develop will be stylistically and operationally unique, the following have some of the features and style we believe should be in the TWT site.

www.xxxxx.com—has the humorous, yet professional approach we feel is suitable.
www.yyyyyy.com—has the ease of navigation and use we feel works particularly well.

Other sites we like, and the reasons why are:

www.zzzzz.com—has online registration for services similar TWT's needs.
www.uuuuu.com—its treatment of facilities and staff biographies is very informative.
www.ttttt.com—it is a professional services site that uses a novel approach to humor.
www.sssss.com—it shows franchise potential and opportunities well.

-2-

Detailed web proposal, continued

JustDoit's Development Process

Phase 1—Orientation and development of strategic concept (approximately two weeks).
- Confirm and refine objectives with TWT marketing staff.
- Confirm and refine target market with TWT marketing staff.
- Establish success criteria with TWT marketing staff.
- Establish preliminary site and page hierarchy.
- Develop three strategies/concepts.
- Develop one or more graphic options for each strategy/concept.
- Present options for evaluation (color prints & electronic files) to Sally Client.

Estimate $13,000

Phase 2—Concept approval and initial development (approximately two weeks).
- Sally Client to select concept for refinement.
- Incorporation of feedback and revisions.
- Create site breakdown—site map, layout, style sheets, color palette, navigation, and copy, illustration and photography needs.
- Review site in light of programming expectations and limitations.
- Develop site artwork.
- Present artwork for approval to Sally Client.

Estimate $4,500/$6,500

Phase 3—Revisions, final development and programming (approximately two weeks).
- Incorporate artwork feedbacks and revisions.
- Finalize illustration, photography, and animation.
- Program a 15-20 page editable site including: template based for global editing, cascading style sheets (CSS), multi-platform Mac and Windows testing on several browsers, key words and meta tags for page indexing.
- Off line preview to Sally Client.
- Revise site as necessary.
- Installation and testing on designated server.
- Go live (date to be determined).

Estimate $11,000/$13,000

Estimate total $28,500/$32,500

Please see the following page for estimate options and additions

-3-

Estimate Options and Additions

Copy strategy is included in Phase 1. Copy development is not included in Phase 2. Copy can be provided by TWT or JustDoit Design will provide it at an estimated cost of $6,000 to $8,000.

Miscellaneous expenses, such as deliveries, prints, messengers, and travel are not included, and will be billed at cost. We estimate them to be between $250 and $500.

Royalty-free stock photography and illustration will be used where appropriate. These costs will be estimated at the end of Phase 1. Original photography, and any original illustration or animation will also be estimated at that time. Original photography is $2,500 to $3,000 a day plus expenses, models, and location fees. Usage for original photography or illustration beyond the Web site might be additional. (See Ownership on page 6.) Photo art direction is $1,200 per day plus expenses. Photoshop retouching, if necessary, is extra and is billed at $150 per hour. Illustrations are $400 to $1,800 depending on complexity. Animation costs are $500 to $2,000 depending on complexity. As proposed the site does not require complex Flash programming. If it is later required, it is available at $150 per hour.

-4-

Working Agreement

Estimates

The costs and expenses cited in this proposal are our best estimates given the information provided. They include meetings, consultation time, design, programming, and production time, and a reasonable amount of revisions. If additional estimate is forthcoming, project specifications change, or the scheduling changes, cost and expense estimates may also change.

The effect of major changes, additional services, and delays cannot be determined until a final design direction has been established. If requirements arise for additional work or scheduling changes not reflected in this estimate, we will provide an updated estimate when the final design direction has been approved.

Cost and expense estimates are appropriate for 30 days from the date of this proposal. Taxes are not included in cost and expense estimates.

Revisions & Alterations

Work not described in this proposal, including but not limited to revisions (AAs), corrections, alterations and additional proofs, will be billed as an additional cost at the hourly labor rate of $150 per hour, or at our cost plus 25% markup.

Terms

Unless otherwise arranged in advance, a retainer fee of 50% of the design, production, and expense estimates is required upon initiation of each project phase. The remainder of the costs for each phase will be invoiced upon its completion. Invoice terms are net 30 days. Invoices remaining unpaid after 30 days will be assessed interest at 1.5% per month (18% annually). If any phase of this project is delayed longer than 60 days, we will bill for work completed to date.

Should TWT elect to terminate this project, JustDoit Design will invoice 50% of the lowest total estimate figure, or for actual work performed, which is greater, plus expenses.

Should JustDoit Design find it necessary to refer past due accounts to an attorney for collection, then TWT shall reimburse JustDoit Design for all attorney's fees and collection costs incurred. Any such fees incurred in the collection process will be added to the amount due, and the account shall not be considered paid in full until the entire debt has been settled.

Responsibility

JustDoit Design will make every reasonable effort to ensure the accuracy of what is produced, but is not responsible for the correctness of copy, illustrations, photographs, nor for obtaining clearances or approvals.

TWT shall assume full responsibility for any accepted graphic recommendations from JustDoit Design including, but not limited to trademark and patent searches, registrations, feasibility

-5-

---

testing, and legal compliance responsibilities. TWT shall indemnify JustDoit Design and hold it harmless from any damages, costs, or losses that might arise as the result of any action against either party regarding products and/or services performed with regards to this project.

JustDoit Design will take normal measures to safeguard any materials entrusted to us. However, we are not responsible for the loss, damage or unauthorized use of such materials, nor are we responsible for the actions of the vendors and suppliers we utilize.

Ownership

This proposal is for the development and implementation of one strategic idea or concept. All preliminary concepts, ideas, approaches, plans, reports, recommendations, designs, artwork, and electronic files remain the sole property of JustDoit Design, and may be used in the future at their discretion.

All materials used in the production of this assignment—including original artwork and computer generated artwork, formats, and electronic code—remains the property of JustDoit Design.

Unless otherwise agreed upon, all original photography and illustration are for the sole purpose of the Web site and may not be used in other applications. If TWT wishes to purchase unlimited rights to the use of original photography or illustration (ownership of copyright), please inform JustDoit Design and this will be a consideration in the selection of and negotiation with photographers or illustrators.

Copyright to the Web site design will be considered transferred and reproduction rights granted upon receipt of payment in full.

Purchase Order

If this proposal is acceptable, please sign as indicated below and initiate a purchase order in the amount of $28,500.

We shall be pleased to begin work on the schedule you determine after receipt of the TWT purchase order.

Submitted by: _____ Date:_____
      Justin Doit
      Principal
      JustDoit Design

Approved by: _____ Date:_____
      Sally Client
      Director of Marketing
      The Wagging Tail Dog Care Centres

-6-

Index

bookkeeping
  accounting and, 46, 56
  hiring employee for, 325–27
  record keeping for, 56
  start-up preparations for, 56–57
  time allocation for, 377
brainstorming, 339–42
branded services, 216–17
breakfast, meeting client for, 276
Business and Legal Forms for Illustrators, 209
business brokers/intermediaries, 375
business cards, 93, 279, 383, 385
business interruption insurance, 73
business operations
  accounting services for, 41–46
  billable and nonbillable hours in, 100–101
  bookkeeping for, 56–57
  creativity and, 356
  credit checks on clients, 186–87
  daily record keeping of, 56
  financial norms, 96, 190, 368–71
  financial priorities of, 143–44
  insurance services for, 47–48
  location for, 34–36
  maintaining professional standards in,
    82–83
  managing accounts receivable in, 169–70
  permits for, 55–56
  preparations for establishing, 49–53, 95
  principal's style and, 356
  record keeping to monitor quality of,
    168–69
  retaining legal counsel for, 48–49
  selecting a name for, 38–41
  selecting a start date for, 57
  selection of structure for, 54–55, 381–97
  standards and procedures for, 337–38
  start-up costs for, 26–27, 96
  strategies for reducing tax burden in,
    152–54
  tax-deductible expenses in, 145–50, 167
  trouble-prone situations, 170–73, 189
  see also business plan; managing a
    business; office
business plan
  basic internal, 53, 398
  choosing structural models for
    management, 289–95
  determinants of effectiveness of, 287–88
  formal, 53, 286–88
  goal setting for, 288
  information needs for, 288–89
  need for, 53, 285–86
  personnel structuring in, 289

  sample, 398–400
  size of firm in, 295–96

cancellation of projects before completion,
  135
capital business expenses, 146
capital requirements for freelancers, 26–28,
  163–64
capital reserve fund, 103–4, 163–64
cash flow, 365–67, 376
C corporations, 45, 153–54, 370, 395
certified management accountants, 42–43
certified public accountants, 42
chain-of-command business model, 289–90
Chapter 7 bankruptcy filing, 187, 188
Chapter 11 bankruptcy filing, 187, 188
Chapter 13 bankruptcy filing, 187
Chapter 20 bankruptcy filing, 187
checking accounts, 56–57
civil court proceedings, 182–85
classified ads, 234–35
clients
  background information on, 408
  bankruptcy filings by, 187–88
  best and worst, by type, 199–204
  business perspective toward creative
    services, 265
  buying responsibility, by type of, 224–26
  characteristics of main types of, 194–99
  consistency in pricing to, 105–6, 118
  contact with, prior to establishing
    business, 49–50, 51
  credit checks on, 186–87
  determinants of contracting decisions by,
    99–100
  disagreements with, 165
  dormant, 209
  educating, about creative services, 37–38
  excessive demands on time by, 127
  excessive revisions to concepts by, 86
  expectations of, 86–88
  getting new business from established,
    274–76
  good mix of, 81, 275, 368
  ideas solicited by, without contract,
    85–86, 121
  invoice processing system of, 136
  local market analysis of, 215–18
  maintaining professional standards in
    relations with, 29, 82–83
  need for face-to-face interaction with, 216
  need for signed agreements with, 141, 173
  not-for-profit, 106
  on online freelance job sites, 237–38

of in-house production *versus* outside
    contracting, 262
insurance total, 96
job production, record keeping of, 359
labor, 102–3
of leased office space, 64, 299–300
legal counsel, 49
life insurance, 71
of mail lists, 234
marketing expenditures, 231, 377
overhead, 18, 60, 103, 117, 377
payroll, 377
of preparing job estimates, 119–20, 132
of rented office space, 63–64, 296, 298
umbrella liability insurance, 73
valuable papers insurance, 73–74
court
    civil, 182–85
    small claims, 176–77
Creative Business, 88, 114, 128, 132, 151, 231,
    238, 262, 285, 349, 355, 369, 370, 371
creative director, 362
creative services
    business perspective on, 265
    client expectations for, 86–88
    commoditization of, 216–18
    copyright issues, 106–8
    educating clients about, 37–38
    financial norms, 190, 368–71
    in niche economy, 14
    organized business operations and, 356
    survival rate of firms in, 284, 285
    use-based pricing, 110
    value of established business in, 371–75
creative standards, 82
credit checks, 186–87
critiques
    of employee's work, 342–44
    of your work by client, 249–50

deadlines, 78–79, 87
delegation of responsibility, 331, 334–37
dental insurance, 69
depreciation, 149
design and illustration work
    client sources of, 194–205
    contract cancellation fees for, 135
    copyright ownership of, 106–8, 110
    job quotes for, 104
    preparation and presentation of
        concepts, 270
    pricing guidelines for, 128–29
    using talent rep to contact clients for, 207
design studios, 202. *see also* agencies
development fee, 120

direct mail promotions, 232–34, 281
direct marketing industry, 203–4
disability insurance, 69
donated work, 126–27
drop-off of samples and work, 127, 244–45
dummy ledger, 366–67
Dun & Bradstreet, 179, 186–87

e-mail promotions, 236–37
    response rate, 281
employee allowance certificate, 328
Employee Retirement Income Security Act,
    158
employees
    in associate business model, 292–95
    benefit packages for, 153, 319–21
    billable income produced by, 318, 355
    in chain-of-command business model,
        289–90
    in coaching business model, 290–92,
        332–34
    critiquing work of, 342–44
    employer tax and bookkeeping
        requirements for, 328–29
    family members as, 152–53
    firing, 331–32, 350–52, 354, 376
    giving raises to, 348–49
    income per, 368
    income related to number of, 369–70
    income tax withholding for, 159
    laying off, 352–54, 376
    marketing effort for, 213
    need for sales rep, 213, 281
    noncompete agreements, 329–30
    pay, 318
    performance reviews, 311, 344–50, 351
    personnel policies, 310–12
    productivity measurement, 359–60, 369
    retirement plans for, 157–58
    size of creative services firms, 295–96
    social security tax withholdings of, 160
    staff structuring, 289
    tax definition of, 305–6
    temporary, 307
    time management, 364–65
    time sheets, 359
    turnover, 369
    see also hiring employees; managing a
        business; staffing
Employee Stock Ownership Plan, 158
employer identification number, 56, 328
employment agencies, 307, 312
employment eligibility verification, 328
enrolled agents, 43
entertainment expenses, 150, 276–77

Keogh plans, 156, 158
keyword advertising, 238
kickbacks, 276
kill fee, 135

labor costs, 102–3
Landor Associates, 295
larger firms
    competitive advantages and
        disadvantages of, 260–61
    job estimate preparation in, 118
laying off employees, 352–54, 376, 377
leasing
    equipment, 146–47
    office space, 64, 298–301
legal issues
    attaching assets for nonpayment of debt,
        180–82
    civil court proceedings, 182–85
    copyright ownership, 106–8, 165–66,
        170–71
    employee noncompete agreements,
        329–30
    in firing employees, 351
    harassment for overdue payment, 175
    in laying off employees, 352–53
    maintaining self-employed tax status,
        92–94
    need for contracts, 133
    in partnerships, 384–85
    permits, 55–56
    project cancellation fees, 135
    retaining counsel for, 48–49
    in running incorporated businesses,
        395–96
    in selecting business name, 39, 40–41
    in selection of business structure,
        54–55
    in separating from employer, 59–60
    sources of contracts, 132–33
    strategies for collecting unpaid debt,
        176–85
    strength of contracts, 131, 133
    in use of home for business, 63
letter of agreement, 133, 134
liability insurance, 72
life insurance, 70–71
lighting, office, 66–67
limited liability companies, 45, 54, 147,
    396–97
line of credit, 27–28
LinkedIn, 222, 238
liquidity, 367
location for freelance business, 34–38, 58,
    60–65

logos, 225
lunch, treating client to, 276–77

mail lists, 233, 234
    for e-mail, 236–37
managing a business
    challenges of, 331
    creative direction responsibilities, 362
    decentralized project management, 362
    delegating as part of, 331, 334–37
    employee performance evaluations in,
        344–50
    establishing shop standards and
        procedures, 337–38, 355
    financial indicators for, 367–68
    financial management, 365–67
    interactive decentralization model, 13–14
    keeping normal work hours, 338
    meetings, 365
    paperwork, 363
    personnel decisions and, 331
    project management, 361
    shop management responsibilities, 362
    staff meetings, 362
    staff relations in, 332–34
    stimulating creative productivity, 339–42
    structural models for, 289–95, 361
    time management in, 363–65
    tracking time in, 355–56
    trend calculator, 411
    see also business operations; employees;
        hiring employees; record keeping;
        staffing
market conditions
    adapting to, in rural areas, 36–37
    analysis of, for sales strategy, 215–18
    trends favoring freelance businesses,
        11–14, 95
marketing communications
    media commissions for ads, 109
    recent evolution of, 12
    trends favoring freelance businesses, 12
marketing of services
    contacting clients for, 206
    during downtime, 79, 162
    hiring a sales rep for, 213, 281, 321–25
    identifying potential types of clients,
        193–94
    importance of, 29, 81, 192, 280, 364
    need for ongoing effort at, 162, 163, 213
    norms, 281
    to other creative services firms, 233
    purpose of, 81
    in rural areas, 37
    selection of business name and, 38–41